What's Trending in Canadian Politics?

COMMUNICATION, STRATEGY, AND POLITICS
Thierry Giasson and Alex Marland, Series Editors

Communication, Strategy, and Politics is a groundbreaking new series from UBC Press that examines elite decision making and political communication in today's hyper-mediated and highly competitive environment. Publications in this series look at the intricate relations among marketing strategy, the media, and political actors and explain how they affect Canadian democracy. They also investigate such interconnected themes as strategic communication, mediatization, opinion research, electioneering, political management, public policy, and e-politics in a Canadian context and in comparison to other countries. Designed as a coherent and consolidated space for diffusion of research about Canadian political communication, the series promotes an interdisciplinary, multi-method, and theoretically pluralistic approach.

Other volumes in the series are

Political Marketing in Canada, edited by Alex Marland, Thierry Giasson, and Jennifer Lees-Marshment
Political Communication in Canada: Meet the Press and Tweet the Rest, edited by Alex Marland, Thierry Giasson, and Tamara A. Small
Framed: Media and the Coverage of Race in Canadian Politics, by Erin Tolley
Brand Command: Canadian Politics and Democracy in the Age of Message Control, by Alex Marland
Permanent Campaigning in Canada, edited by Alex Marland, Thierry Giasson, and Anna Lennox Esselment
Breaking News? Politics, Journalism, and Infotainment on Quebec Television, by Frédérick Bastien
Political Elites in Canada: Power and Influence in Instantaneous Times, edited by Alex Marland, Thierry Giasson, and Andrea Lawlor
Opening the Government of Canada: The Federal Bureaucracy in the Digital Age, by Amanda Clarke
The New NDP: Moderation, Modernization, and Political Marketing, by David McGrane

See also:

Canadian Election Analysis 2015: Communication, Strategy, and Democracy, edited by Alex Marland and Thierry Giasson. Open access compilation available at http://www.ubcpress.ca/canadianelectionanalysis2015.

What's Trending in Canadian Politics?

UNDERSTANDING TRANSFORMATIONS IN POWER, MEDIA, AND THE PUBLIC SPHERE

EDITED BY
MIREILLE LALANCETTE, VINCENT RAYNAULD,
AND
ERIN CRANDALL

UBCPress · Vancouver · Toronto

© UBC Press 2019

All rights reserved. No part of this publication may be reproduced, stored in a retrieval system, or transmitted, in any form or by any means, without prior written permission of the publisher, or, in Canada, in the case of photocopying or other reprographic copying, a licence from Access Copyright, www.accesscopyright.ca.

28 27 26 25 24 23 22 21 20 19   5 4 3 2 1

Printed in Canada on FSC-certified ancient-forest-free paper (100% post-consumer recycled) that is processed chlorine- and acid-free.

Library and Archives Canada Cataloguing in Publication

Title: What's trending in Canadian politics? : understanding transformations in power, media, and the public sphere / edited by Mireille Lalancette, Vincent Raynauld, and Erin Crandall.

Other titles: What is trending in Canadian politics?

Names: Lalancette, Mireille, 1974- editor. | Raynauld, Vincent, 1982- editor. | Crandall, Erin, 1983- editor.

Description: Includes bibliographical references and index.

Identifiers: Canadiana (print) 20190094117 | Canadiana (ebook) 20190094176 | ISBN 9780774861151 (hardcover) | ISBN 9780774861175 (PDF) | ISBN 9780774861182 (EPUB) | ISBN 9780774861199 (Kindle)

Subjects: LCSH: Communication in politics – Canada.

Classification: LCC JA85.2.C3 W53 2019 | DDC 320.01/40971–dc23

Canadä

UBC Press gratefully acknowledges the financial support for our publishing program of the Government of Canada (through the Canada Book Fund), the Canada Council for the Arts, and the British Columbia Arts Council.

This book has been published with the help of a grant from the Canadian Federation for the Humanities and Social Sciences, through the Awards to Scholarly Publications Program, using funds provided by the Social Sciences and Humanities Research Council of Canada, and with the help of the University of British Columbia through the K.D. Srivastava Fund.

Printed and bound in Canada by Friesens
Set in Univers Condensed, Sero, and Minion by Artegraphica Design Co. Ltd.
Copy editor: Dallas Harrison
Proofreader: Lana Okerlund
Indexer: Noeline Bridge
Cover designer: Will Brown

UBC Press
The University of British Columbia
2029 West Mall
Vancouver, BC V6T 1Z2
www.ubcpress.ca

Contents

List of Figures and Tables / vii

Foreword | Politics in a Revolutionary Time: Trending in Canada / ix
KENNETH M. COSGROVE

Acknowledgments / xv

List of Abbreviations / xvii

Introduction: Identifying and Studying Trends in Canadian Politics / 3
VINCENT RAYNAULD, MIREILLE LALANCETTE, AND ERIN CRANDALL

PART 1: TRENDS IN POLITICAL ENGAGEMENT AND DEMOCRATIC PRACTICE

1 Social Uses of the Web by Environmental Activists: A Look at Digital Engagement / 25
GHADA TOUIR, FLORENCE MILLERAND, AND GUILLAUME LATZKO-TOTH

2 Rethinking Digital Activism as It Unfolds: Ambient Political Engagement on Twitter during the 2012 Quebec Student Strike / 44
VINCENT RAYNAULD, MIREILLE LALANCETTE, AND SOFIA TOURIGNY-KONÉ

3 Bytes and Bitumen: A Case Study of Mediated Discourse on, and Digital Advocacy for, TransCanada's Proposed Energy East Pipeline / 63
PATRICK McCURDY AND JACOB GROSHEK

4 Transforming the Disengaged: Social Media and Youth in Canada / 86
SHELLEY BOULIANNE

5 Trolling Stephen Harper: Internet Memes as Online Activism / 106
MIREILLE LALANCETTE, TAMARA A. SMALL, AND MAXIME PRONOVOST

6 From Spheres to Trajectories of Publicness: Exploring How the 2010 Toronto G20 Protests Were Communicated through Social Media / 127
THOMAS POELL

PART 2: POLITICAL ACTORS TRENDING, INTERACTING, AND REACHING THEIR AUDIENCES

7 Of Walls and Whispers: The Use of Facebook during the 2012 Quebec Election / 149
YANNICK DUFRESNE, THIERRY GIASSON, AND MICKAEL TEMPORÃO

8 Cabinet Solidarity in an Age of Social Media: A Case Study of Twitter Use by MP Carolyn Bennett / 170
J.P. LEWIS, MIREILLE LALANCETTE, AND VINCENT RAYNAULD

9 Does the Difference Compute? Data-Driven Campaigning in Canada / 194
FENWICK McKELVEY AND JILL PIEBIAK

10 Beyond Market Intelligence: New Dimensions in Public Opinion Research / 216
ANDRÉ TURCOTTE

PART 3: ENGAGING, CONSULTING, AND FRAMING: TRENDING PRACTICES IN INSTITUTIONS AND THE GOVERNMENT

11 Covering the Court: How News Media Frame Social Science Evidence and Supreme Court Decisions on Physician-Assisted Dying / 237
ERIN CRANDALL, KATE PUDDISTER, AND MARK DAKU

12 The Notion of Social Acceptability: Lay Citizens as a New Political Force / 257
STÉPHANIE YATES WITH MYRIAM ARBOUR

Conclusion: Unpacking Trending Practices in Canadian Politics / 276
MIREILLE LALANCETTE, ERIN CRANDALL, AND VINCENT RAYNAULD

Contributors / 297

Index / 303

Figures and Tables

FIGURES

2.1 Trends in #ggi tweeting on fifteen days between April 22 and July 31, 2012 / 53
3.1 Volume of Energy East social media posts over time from June 1, 2013, through June 1, 2016 / 72
3.2 Cluster graph of most prominent keywords within the Energy East corpus in relation to one another / 74
5.1 Generic image macromeme / 110
5.2 Example of a governance meme related to Harper as an authoritarian / 114
5.3 Example of a governance meme related to Harper's censorship and lack of media transparency / 114
5.4 Example of a society-focused political meme / 115
5.5 Example of a policy-focused political meme / 117
5.6 Example of a society-focused meme / 117
5.7 Example of a policy-focused political meme / 118
5.8 Example of a policy-focused political meme / 118
5.9 Example of a personality meme / 119
5.10 Example of a personality meme / 119
5.11 Example of a Justin Trudeau meme / 123
7.1 Activities on parties' Facebook walls / 156
7.2 Partisan or issue oriented? Topics of Facebook messages / 158
7.3 Positive or negative? Tones of Facebook messages / 160
7.4 Media components in parties' posts / 161
8.1 Grand categories of tweets by Carolyn Bennett as backbencher and cabinet member / 179
8.2 Broadcast tweets by Carolyn Bennett as backbencher and cabinet member / 180

8.3 Social tweets by Carolyn Bennett as backbencher and cabinet member / 182
8.4 Attack tweets by Carolyn Bennett as backbencher and cabinet member / 184
8.5 Personal tweets by Carolyn Bennett as backbencher and cabinet member / 185
11.1 Overall media coverage of doctor-assisted death / 246
11.2 Media coverage of doctor-assisted death, before and after Supreme Court decisions / 247
11.3 Media coverage by newspapers / 250

TABLES

1.1 Detailed list and description of the five groups studied / 30
2.1 Six phases of digital grassroots protest / 49
2.2 Fifteen key dates related to the 2012 Quebec student strike / 51
3.1 Top Twitter users who used #EnergyEast ranked by number of posts / 77
4.1 Literature results related to mobilization and reinforcement/virtuous circle / 91
4.2 Descriptive statistics on social media use and engagement / 93
4.3 Partial correlation matrix / 97
4.4 Summary of findings / 100
5.1 Categories of denunciation in political internet memes about Prime Minister Stephen Harper / 113
5.2 Images used in Stephen Harper memes / 114
8.1 Types of tweets / 178
9.1 Political technology use by federal parties in 2014 and 2017 / 199
9.2 List of interviewees (names disclosed with consent) / 200
9.3 Political technology use by provincial parties in 2014 / 203
10.1 Difference between traditional polling and market intelligence / 222
10.2 Looking ahead at market surveillance / 231
11.1 Summary statistics by case / 246
11.2 Summary statistics by status of case / 247
12.1 Questions and challenges associated with participatory processes / 260
12.2 Degree of exchange between participants on the online platform / 265

FOREWORD

Politics in a Revolutionary Time
Trending in Canada

KENNETH M. COSGROVE

We as a global community have lived through a series of huge transformations in a short period of time. One can argue that the transformation that we are living through is bigger than the invention of the printing press and the industrial revolution combined because this period features new means of communication, production, social engagement, and political behaviour that have emerged simultaneously. In this revolution, as in the time of the development of the printing press, a new technology undermined a literal priesthood of information. As Zito and Todd (2018) point out, something like the death of deference and expertise has occurred because of the Web 2.0 revolution, thus giving citizens the opportunity to make up their own minds and curate their own news products. The ramifications for political marketing are obvious. Just as in the Protestant Reformation driven by the printing press, so too the new political world unleashed by technology lets citizens read and interpret political affairs on their own. Just as many Protestant sects evolved to encourage a personal rather than a mediated relationship with sacred texts and the Bible, so too the new web and mobile technology allow citizens to build personal relationships with politicians and make up their own minds about public affairs in unmediated ways. Just as in the rise of Protestantism, so too this ability has undermined the power and legitimacy of extant institutions. Parties and the media might complain about a given candidate or leader (as in Canada when the partisan press has complained about either Stephen Harper or Justin Trudeau depending on the alignment of the news outlet), but complaining about candidates or leaders or pointing out factual mistakes made by them might have a lot less impact than it once did because of the declining reach and a much larger number of market competitors than once was the case.

Our politics and indeed our world now are much different from the industrial world in which many of us were raised, but that world represented a transformation itself away from a rural, agrarian model toward an urban model. A little over a century ago, most people lived on farms or worked in factories. Even compared with thirty years ago, our world is much different from how it used to be. Now the bulk of the population lives in urban areas, and many people work for a living with their heads, not their hands, and much of this work is global in nature, meaning that it is not attached to a physical location as once was the case. This is not to say that there are not places such as Hamilton, Ontario, or Fort McMurray, Alberta, in which many people perform difficult physical labour. But even in such places we see the same technological changes that have caused other cities and industries to boom, and cities such as Toronto and Vancouver influence their work and all other aspects of their lives, including their political lives.

In this environment of technological revolution, it is no surprise that dramatic changes have taken place in politics and political marketing. The impacts of advertising and marketing for politics became obvious only during the second part of their first century of existence, and only now are we really beginning to understand Web 2.0 and social media–heavy politics, and this volume will enhance that understanding. *Trending in Canada* is an important volume because it examines the impacts of these transformations on political life. This volume is about Canada, but it is also an in-depth look by experts at how the dramatic transformation around us is playing out in politics. The biggest advantage of the volume is that the authors represented in it come from a variety of areas of interest and take a variety of methodological approaches. Such diversity is ideal for increasing our understanding of the complex and rapidly changing politics in Canada and beyond. The chapters show that change has taken place at every level of government and altered how political marketers and voter consumers interact; they also show that public sector entities have taken up the tools of political communication in order to reach the public themselves. The volume demonstrates that political marketing is still all about promoting products, identifying customers, creating brands, and building lasting relationships between producer and consumer.

The technical revolution has led to the development of huge databases and given political marketers the ability to understand much more about their consumers than was once possible. It has especially made it more possible to segment the electorate using a variety of metrics, including demographics, geography, and psychographics. Thus, it is possible to build a tight relationship with an audience and present it with a coherent brand narrative without the scrutiny of the media or opposition voices.

The technological revolution has lowered the barriers to entry into politics for social movements and nontraditional candidates. *Trending in Canada* presents the cases of the Maple Spring and the Energy East Pipelines. In both cases, citizens were able to mobilize and shape the terms of policy debates in ways that they might not have had a chance to do in an earlier time. Canada is not alone; these technologies have been used all over the world to facilitate democratic participation. From Iran to Ukraine to the Arab Spring to the overthrow of a dictator in The Gambia, these tools have allowed people to stand up for themselves in ways that have had more dramatic results than blocking a pipeline or reducing university fees. The technical revolution has empowered more people to make their voices heard in public affairs, and as a mature democracy Canada points the way toward what could eventually happen globally.

The technological revolution has brought us closer to the people and the causes that we support, but it has also allowed us to isolate ourselves from the parties and the politicians that we find disagreeable. Joseph Turow's (1998) point that in a segmented society people are more likely to talk within their own segments than across them is the case in the United States and beyond. We have seen how politicians – including prime ministers of Canada and presidents of the United States – have been deified by their supporters and demonized by their opponents, who demonize each other at the same time. The same mentality has recently emerged in battles over the continuation of trade agreements such as NAFTA and affiliation agreements such as that between the United Kingdom and the European Union. Although opponents of NAFTA and British participation in the European Union have existed since the talks first began, these new technologies have allowed more voices to enter the debates, but they have also created either leaders or referendum results that support the undoing of extant political arrangements, and this in turn generates vehement if siloed opposition from supporters of the status quo. Thus, one has to question the extent to which there can be vibrant debate in the public square when these technologies allow us to retreat into our own gated communities of the like-minded. Furthermore, these technologies can build strong emotive ties between the political marketer and the political consumer. Many politicians, notably Donald Trump and Justin Trudeau, understand this. They use social media as a way to re-emphasize their brands and to show delivery in an effort to strengthen the emotive ties that their brands have with voters. Thus, they have a continual social media presence that leaks into other media platforms and means that we are never far away from hearing from our elected leaders whether we want to or not.

It is also possible for opponents to communicate their enmity in ways that they never could before. Although comedians have always made jokes at the expense of politics and politicians, the difference now involves the use of stylized images called "memes" on social media to do so. This literally puts individual voters in charge of creating and sharing the content. Enough sharing of a similar message can be very damaging to a politician's brand or proposals. Consider how Trump's "Crooked Hillary" meme took off and how individuals were able to customize it themselves. Memes can be part of the activism that these new tools make possible at the same time that their use resembles the anticorporate campaigns that Manheim (2000) wrote about because multiple producers aim at a single target. The meme is a version of the anticorporate messaging, but it is integrated with the kinds of crowdsourcing about which Tapscott and Williams (2008) wrote. Because these new technologies allow a meme to spread quickly like a virus (hence the term "going viral"), it is not clear what a political marketer can do in response other than be fast and be able to shift the subject: two things that Trump has mastered in the United States. One thing that online activism and social media–driven news coverage ask us to consider is does the idea of a news cycle really exist anymore, and what or who are the media? Are Rick Mercer and Trevor Noah part of the media, or do they just make jokes on TV? Is there anything like a news cycle anymore, or do we live in a constant tit-for-tat battle of memes and ever-shorter soundbites intended more to either attract or repel than to inform or build the strength of democratic institutions?

Trending in Canada asks us to consider how the technological revolution has affected mediating institutions. The volume looks at how these new technologies are used for politics and examines who organizes and tries to benefit from these new forms of participation. At a minimum, it is likely that these technologies have allowed more people to have their voices heard if they so desire, but it is also possible that the voices being heard are loud but not representative of the public as a whole. Such activism can also be unevenly distributed generationally and demographically. Some people literally are better equipped than others to engage in such participation or because they believe that their positions are socially unacceptable, which Zito and Todd (2018) argue happened with specific categories of Trump voters leading up to voting day. The idea that people adjust their public personas to the surrounding environments is in keeping with the findings of Noelle-Neumann (1993) about an earlier generation in Germany. The line of inquiry about some folks being more empowered than others by technology is in keeping with what American political scientist E.E. Schattschneider (1975) wrote about in the twentieth century, in which the pluralist heaven was populated with the upper class; the promise of these technologies has been that more people can participate, but *Trending in Canada* shows that this might be true only some of the time. At other times, the technical revolution has made politics into a data-driven activity aimed at generating participation from the desired audience but nobody else. Such targeting can produce narrow electoral wins but not necessarily broad social appeal, meaning that a president or prime minister can end up more as the leader of segments than of the country. One interesting question that this book asks and answers affirmatively is do politicians change their uses of social media based on their positions in the government? Knowing this is important because it shows us that institutions still matter and can shape the behaviour of political actors. One question that this raises is the extent to which politicians who change their social media personas run the risk of undermining their authenticity. In branded politics, authenticity is everything. The one great thing that can be said about Trump and Trudeau from a marketing sense is that they have been largely true to their brand promises, though it is not clear that this is always a good thing for governance.

Trending in Canada is a worthy study of how the technological revolution is playing out in the political life of a mature democracy. How politics play out now are very different from the days when American presidential candidates had voters come to them during a campaign or when Wilfrid Laurier made stump speech after stump speech while riding the rails across Canada during the 1911 election campaign (which Dutil and MacKenzie present in depth in their 2011 book). The technological revolution has occurred quickly, and it has altered the political and social worlds in which we live utterly. A volume that takes on such a huge topic by breaking it into smaller elements is a welcome contribution to how this revolution is changing our world on the ground.

REFERENCES

Dutil, Patrick, and David MacKenzie. 2011. *Canada 1911: The Decisive Election that Shaped the Century.* Toronto: Dundurn.

Manheim, Joseph. 2000. *The Death of a Thousand Cuts: Corporate Campaigns and the Attack on the Corporation.* New York: Routledge.

Noelle-Neumann, Elizabeth. 1993. *The Spiral of Silence: Public Opinion Our Second Skin.* Chicago: University of Chicago Press.

Schattschneider, Elmer E. 1975. *The Semi-Sovereign People: A Realist's View of American Democracy.* Boston: Cengage Learning.

Tapscott, Donald, and Anthony D. Williams. 2008. *Wikinomics: How Mass Collaboration Changes Everything.* New York: Portfolio.

Turow, Joseph. 1998. *Breaking Up America: Advertisers and the New Media World.* Chicago: University of Chicago Press.

Zito, Salena, and Brad Todd. 2018. *The Great Revolt: Inside the Populist Coalition Reshaping American Politics.* New York: Crown Forum.

Acknowledgments

The production of a book identifying, characterizing, and analyzing trends in political communication and behaviour in Canada would have been impossible without the innovative and thoughtful research of dedicated scholars from a wide range of disciplines, including political science, political management, communication, sociology, and journalism. The editors would first like to thank all of the contributors to this book not only for sharing their work but also for exploring emerging areas of research likely to foster fascinating studies over the next decade. We would also like to acknowledge the support of federal and provincial funding agencies, including the Fonds de recherche société et culture and the Social Sciences and Humanities Research Council, as well as numerous universities for making this research possible. In particular, we would like to thank the Département de lettres et communication sociale as well as the Décanat de la recherche et de la création of the Université du Québec à Trois-Rivières and its dean, Sébastien Charles, for their financial support for production of the book. Our thanks are also extended to the Department of Communication Studies of Emerson College and Acadia University for their institutional and, in many instances, personal support.

We gratefully acknowledge the unparalleled assistance and support provided by the editors of the book series Communication, Strategy, and Politics with UBC Press, Alex Marland from Memorial University and Thierry Giasson from Université Laval. By guiding our work and providing helpful feedback, this book is undoubtedly better because of them, and it complements previous works published in the series. The guidance and encouragement of UBC Press editors Emily Andrew and Randy Schmidt were also instrumental in the production of this volume. Heather Bastedo was an enthusiastic supporter of this project in its early stages and helped to bring us together as an editorial team. Thank you, Heather. We would also like to thank the Canadian Political Science Association for enabling us to host a workshop that gave contributors the opportunity to present their work and interact with their peers.

Finally, we would like to recognize and thank Nishtha Yadav, at Emerson College, and Cisco Watson, at Acadia University, for their copy-editing work. Despite a tight schedule and their own studies, these two master's students worked together to help ensure the production of a high-quality book.

Abbreviations

BSD	Blue State Digital
CAQ	Coalition avenir Québec
CATI	computer-assisted telephone interviewing
DMP	data management platform
EI	Employment Insurance
INM	Institut du Nouveau Monde
MP	member of Parliament
NDP	New Democratic Party
ON	Option nationale
PLQ	Parti libéral du Québec
PQ	Parti québécois
PVQ	Parti vert du Québec
QS	Québec solidaire
SPSS	Statistical Package for the Social Sciences
TCMN	Toronto Community Mobilization Network

What's Trending in Canadian Politics?

Introduction
Identifying and Studying Trends in Canadian Politics

VINCENT RAYNAULD, MIREILLE LALANCETTE, AND ERIN CRANDALL

THE NEED TO STAY AWARE AND AHEAD OF THE CURVE

Politics is multifaceted and dynamic. Although the distinct nature of this area of research and practice means that it can be studied through a variety of lenses, one approach to understanding the dynamics of politics is to look at how new media and methods for acquiring and sharing information can affect political norms and practices. Social media serve as an important example. With the rise of mobile devices such as smartphones, tablets, and wearable technologies, social media have emerged as key features of Canadians' daily lives. User-generated communication channels – including Twitter, Facebook, Instagram, and Snapchat – are increasingly used by members of the public to engage in a large number of personal and professional activities. These activities include mass-broadcasting updates about personal life, interacting with friends and colleagues, and sharing opinions on wide-ranging issues and events with peers and members of the public. These communication platforms can also change how people understand and participate in politics. For example, activities such as documenting police misconduct in real time, participating in social-acceptability consultations and open-government projects, or simply accessing political information can be done more easily with these tools. Scholars and practitioners in the fields of political science, journalism, sociology, and political communication have made significant efforts in recent years to identify trending phenomena and to understand better how new digital media channels and approaches to information and participation have transformed modes of communication and redefined, to some degree, political behaviour.

Such trends have manifested in the Canadian political and social spheres over the past few years, from the election of Justin Trudeau in October 2015, to the Indigenous-led Idle No More protest movement, to the Quebec student strike in 2012 – all of which saw their key players using new media technologies to further their goals. They have also manifested on a global level through galvanizing political moments, including Barack Obama's election in 2008 and re-election in 2012, Donald Trump's electoral success in 2016, the transnational Occupy movement, and the Arab Spring uprisings. These events brought emerging practices and modified expectations about political campaigning, protesting, policy making, political engagement, and political expression to public consciousness.

The adoption and shaping of trends in the worlds of political communication and behaviour have been fuelled by both established and emerging political players with varying interests and objectives. The emergence, rapid adoption, and constant evolution of internet-based media tools with varying structural and functional properties have also played important roles in this dynamic. This introductory chapter examines what is fuelling and shaping these changes – phenomena that we refer to here as "trends" – in the Canadian context. Our objective is first to examine the concept of trends and then to make the case for the value of identifying and analyzing their impacts on the Canadian political landscape. As we argue here, trends are expected to have lasting transformative effects on different facets of research and practice related to political communication and behaviour in Canada and will ultimately pave the way to further changes.

Over the past few decades, political communication both in Canada and abroad has undergone a series of developments. At the same time, there has been a re-evaluation of patterns of political behaviour, namely how individuals and organizations conceive and take part in different forms of political and civic action, whether through formal or informal channels of engagement. These transformations, which have manifested at municipal, provincial, and federal levels, can be partly attributed to a host of social, political, cultural, economic, and technological trends that have affected and will continue to affect all dimensions of the political landscape. These trends include the use and effect of mass media on the acquisition, cultivation, distribution, exercise, and manifestation of political power; on acquiring, archiving, and dispersing information; and on detecting patterns of mobilization, persuasion, and organization. From a broader perspective, these changes are contributing to the reconfiguration of the structure and composition of the public sphere.

These trends have affected how two categories of actors contribute to formal and informal political processes. On the one hand, they have led established political elites – or political insiders – to rethink and, in many cases, retool their politicking strategies and practices in the context of intensifying nonstop, or permanent, campaigning in and out of elections (Marland 2016; Marland, Giasson, and Esselment 2017). For example, these trends have affected how political parties and candidates engage in voter identification, outreach, and mobilization when building and cultivating support ahead of and during elections. They have also led elected officials, public servants, and government agencies to alter how they circulate information and, to a lesser extent, connect and interact with citizens as well as their approaches to decision making. On the other hand, they have redefined how members of civil society – more likely to be on the periphery of the formal political arena (e.g., citizen organizations, interest groups, grassroots movements, individual citizens) – interact with media, policy, and established political elites. Once viewed as political outsiders, these actors share information, attract public attention to their causes, raise money, mobilize support, and generate political action in ways that are challenging traditional understandings of their influence on politicking. From a broader perspective, these trends have been leading to the reconfiguration of democratic life in Canada.

IDENTIFYING, CHARACTERIZING, AND UNDERSTANDING TRENDS

This volume takes a deep dive into these issues through chapters that identify and explore how these trends are affecting political communication and behaviour in Canada. Contributors take a look at the ripple effects of these trends on political and civic life. They leverage interdisciplinary theoretical and methodological approaches, as well as more applied perspectives, to examine trending phenomena through case studies. This book is especially relevant for students who want to explore questions related to the evolution of contemporary political communication and behaviour both in Canada and in comparable national contexts. Practitioners seeking insights into emerging dynamics of politicking in and out of peak moments of political communication and mobilization, such as elections and intense policy debates, should also find this book helpful.

The concept of trends – the anchoring theme of this volume – has become a staple feature of the social media environment. Social media services, including Facebook, Twitter, and YouTube, often provide users with one or multiple lists of topics for discussion or digital material deemed to be "trending." These trending news items have fast-growing traction among internet users over a short period of time, a phenomenon referred to by some authors as "virality" (Klinger and Svensson 2014; Nahon et al. 2011).[1] Trending lists can be customized independently by users or tailored based on algorithms taking into account users' personal profiles, including their ideological dispositions, interests, and current geographical locations. Additionally, the hashtag #trending is frequently embedded in posts by users to highlight digital material (e.g., text, video, and picture) expected to gain in importance or popularity. According to Poell and van Dijck (2015, 534), virality is one of the core components of "social media's DNA" alongside "personalization" and "real-timeness." In the world of marketing, trends refer to directions in which consumers' general attitudes, values, and preferences evolve and, by extension, affect how consumers perceive, evaluate, and consume brands, goods, and services. These trends matter because they can alter cognitive and social processes through which one decides on making purchases.

In the context of this volume, the concept of trends is used to pinpoint emerging areas of both scholarly research and practice – at the intersection of political science, communication, sociology, political management, and journalism – likely to gain prominence and, to some degree, influence different spheres within Canadian politics over the next decades. More importantly, some of these trends could have reshaping effects on the conceptualization, categorization, and understanding of these contemporary academic disciplines. They have the potential to alter how research is thought out, planned, and executed, ultimately fostering more research outside well-established traditional scholarly silos or disciplines. Such work on interdisciplinary areas or objects of study can yield increased levels of academic innovation and, to some degree, lead to further scholarly research. From a broader perspective, trends can be viewed as themes of varying specificity that can foster new, or affect existing, conversations on political communication and behaviour among diverse publics, including students, politicians, scholars, and practitioners.

The theoretical, methodological, and more applied dimensions of trends in the field of political communication and behaviour have received some academic attention internationally over the past decade. Although the ensuing work has been the source of valuable insights, research tackling trends has been mostly dispersed, fragmented, and highly eclectic. Of interest are works by Anika Gauja (2015), who examines patterns of individualization of party politics in Australia and the United Kingdom; James Sloam (2014), who looks at youth political engagement in Europe; Loni Hagen and colleagues (2015), who explore the adoption of e-participation around the world; and Peter Van Aelst and colleagues (2017, 4), who explore how specific trends affect the structure and composition of contemporary political information environments and reshape the functioning of democracy. In Canada, scholars have looked at trends in political communication, mobilization, and organization. The notion of trends has implicitly been introduced and studied in edited volumes focusing on political marketing (Marland, Giasson, and Lees-Marshment 2012) and political communication (Marland, Giasson, and Small 2014) published in the Communication, Strategy, and Politics series by UBC Press in recent years. The edited volume, *Canadian Democracy from the Ground Up: Perceptions and Performance*, a comprehensive look at the dynamics of political and civic engagement that can affect democratic participation in Canada, also offers some perspectives on trends in political communication and behaviour (Gidengil and Bastedo 2014). However, trends in Canadian politics – especially those with a strong social media component – have never been the object of a stand-alone volume. The chapters presented here attempt to fill this gap by addressing these issues. This volume is a one-stop shop for a cohesive, interdisciplinary analysis of phenomena anticipated to have transformational effects on dynamics of political and civic life in the Canadian context as well as the international context.

To explore these trends, this volume takes a decisively – and unapologetically – multifaceted approach. Some chapters identify and investigate causal factors that have led to the emergence and evolution of trends as well as their effects on the Canadian political environment. From a more technologically deterministic – or "technocentric" (Monterde and Postill 2014, 430) – perspective, the development and growing adoption of communication technologies (internet or Bluetooth-enabled mobile devices such as smartphones, tablets, and wearable gadgets) coupled with the rise of digital media channels (social networking services and microcommunication sites) have helped to foster change in the realm of political communication and behaviour (Forum Research 2015). On the one hand, their distinct capabilities and low costs have led to the decentralization, fragmentation, acceleration, and in some cases renationalization of flows of information and social interactions of a political nature. To some degree, they have rendered political processes more inclusive, diverse, and competitive. By enabling individuals and organizations that previously stood on the sidelines of formal politics to have their voices heard and potentially to have impacts on the political process, these technologies have transformative implications. On the other hand, their flexible technical and structural properties, sometimes significantly different from those of offline-based media channels, have enabled individuals and organizations to contribute to political processes on their own terms. In other words, they have contributed to the hybridization of existing repertoires of political action and the emergence of new ways of being involved in and influencing politics. The role played by mobile communication devices as tools for political and civic participation has been largely overlooked or occasionally ignored in studies of digital electioneering and e-activism. As noted by Arnau Monterde and John Postill (2014, 429), significant academic attention has been given to the "purported role of social media platforms such as Facebook and Twitter, but the mobile aspects of this usage have remained largely implicit." More research on this dynamic is needed.

From a more socially deterministic perspective, new generations of citizens with different social, political, and ideological inclinations and objectives are contributing to the advent and the strengthening of trends affecting political communication and behaviour in Canada. Some commentators and academics have adhered to a more "pessimistic disaffected citizen" perspective (Cammaerts et al. 2013) and claimed that younger adults are increasingly apathetic toward politics in its more traditional sense (Farthing 2010; Henn, Weinstein, and Forrest 2005; Henn, Weinstein, and Hodgkinson 2007). However, others have argued that youth are increasingly active politically through more unconventional – or informal – paths of engagement not necessarily recognized by established political elites (e.g., Loader, Vromen, and Xenos 2014; Quaranta 2016; Vromen, Xenos, and Loader 2015). In other words, their distinct sociopolitical profile is fostering the emergence of trends likely to affect political and civic action from a bottom-up perspective. This situation is also likely to lead scholars to review and, if warranted, rethink and adapt existing definitions of more conventional norms and practices of political communication and engagement. As noted by M. Kent Jennings and Richard G. Niemi (2014), there has been both a microlevel and a macrolevel generational transition when it comes to perception of, and participation in, politics. This transition has been fuelled by an array of factors, including declining levels of confidence in political authorities, institutions, and individual politicians; reshaping of the contemporary mass media environment with the rise of Web 1.0 and social media; and growth of political empowerment and influence among social, political, economic, and cultural minorities (Jennings and Niemi 2014). A number of the chapters in this volume address this question.

TRENDING IN THE CANADIAN POLITICAL CONTEXT

Although the repercussions of these changes are many and complex, this volume isolates and explores transformations in key areas of communication and political behaviour in the Canadian context. These complementary areas include

- the rise of social media as dominant tools of communication, mobilization, and organization
- the growing traction of a new breed of grassroots-driven political protest phenomena
- technological advances and other interconnected sociopolitical factors affecting day-to-day politics
- the recalibration of relationships among members of civil society and political institutions

- the emergence of tools (e.g., surveys, advanced audience research, big data analytics, social science evidence) for predicting the public's behaviour as well as for deliberation and governance.

Interestingly, these areas of interest overlap with the three main challenges facing political communication researchers, according to Bruce Bimber (2015, 215), a leading US scholar in the fields of digital media, political organization, and collective action:

1 the conceptualizing of digital media, especially the extent to which research focus[es] on technology itself as opposed to the content of communication
2 the challenges and opportunities associated with "Big Data"
3 the need to revisit old problems of causation and linearity.

First, social media have become vital components of the Canadian political mediascape. The 2006 federal election saw a growing number of individuals and organizations use blogs for electioneering purposes (Small 2008). Web 2.0 media channels (e.g., Facebook, Twitter, Snapchat, and Instagram) have since grown in popularity among all segments of the public and, as of 2019, affect nearly all dimensions of political communication, mobilization, persuasion, and organization in Canada. For example, political parties, elected officials, candidates during elections, and other formal political players at all levels of government are sharing mixed-media information with mass audiences to mobilize and cultivate support; reach out to potential supporters; launch, promote, and coordinate mobilization initiatives; raise funds; and, to a much lesser extent, interact with members of the public. Conversely, social media are providing an outlet for members of civil society to express themselves in largely unfiltered fashions and to be politically active in often decentralized and highly specific ways outside the realms of political and media establishments. Several social scientists – several of whom are contributors to this volume – have taken an under-the-hood look at these dynamics in the Canadian context over the past decade (see Elmer, Langlois, and McKelvey 2012; Lalancette and Raynauld 2017; Raynauld and Greenberg 2014; Small 2011, 2012, 2016; and Small et al. 2014).

Building on the findings and conclusions of existing research, contributors to this volume tackle trending dimensions in uses of social media by formal and informal political actors for outreach and engagement. In Chapter 7, Yannick Dufresne, Thierry Giasson, and Mickael Temporão discuss how six provincial political parties and their leaders turned to Facebook for voter outreach during the 2012 election in Quebec. They do so through an analysis of the format, tone, and interactive nature of Facebook posts during the campaign. In Chapter 8, J.P. Lewis, Mireille Lalancette, and Vincent Raynauld compare the tweeting practices of Carolyn Bennett – MP for the riding of Toronto–St. Paul's – as an opposition backbencher and as the minister of Indigenous and Northern Affairs in Justin Trudeau's Liberal government in order to consider how parliamentary conventions, such as cabinet solidarity, hold up in an age of social media. In Chapter 4, Shelley Boulianne examines social media's effects on youths' levels of engagement in civic and political life. She takes a deep dive into the uses of Web 2.0 platforms to understand better interactions with and connections to political issues.

Second, recent years have seen the development and popularization of new grassroots-driven political protest phenomena that have shaped politics in Canada and abroad. In some cases, such activities have challenged the modus operandi of established political elites, not necessarily equipped to deal with the political, economic, and social repercussions of their actions. To some degree, this situation has shown the presence of a clear – and potentially deepening – disconnect between two political forces (grassroots and political elites) that often have vastly different visions and understandings of politics and operate in very different ways. Whereas some protest initiatives have emerged in a more conventional manner, all have distinguished themselves from more traditional political mobilization phenomena in the following ways: they have appealed to and mobilized younger segments of the public who tend to be largely disenchanted with and disengaged from formal political life; they have energized individuals and organizations with frequently narrow political interests, preferences, and objectives; their supporters' actions have often been outside established paths of political and civic engagement; and their supporters have used social media and other digital media channels extensively for political engagement (Raynauld, Lalancette, and Tourigny-Koné 2016;

Valenzuela, Arriagada, and Scherman 2012). The growing traction of these political mobilization initiatives in recent years can be attributed to different elements, including, among the public, rising levels of cynicism about and estrangement from governments, institutionalized political processes, and legacy media, especially with the 2008 worldwide economic downturn, the austerity measures implemented by governments to mitigate its effects, as well as the perceived degradation of democratic institutions by some segments of the public (Della Porta 2015).

Although some researchers have explored contemporary political protest in Canada (e.g., Dufour and Savoie 2014; Poell 2014; Raynauld et al. 2016), much work remains. Chapters in this book explore aspects of these trends and complement existing academic literature. In Chapter 2, Vincent Raynauld, Mireille Lalancette, and Sofia Tourigny-Koné examine the factors that shaped the Quebec student strike in 2012 in the Twitterverse. In Chapter 6, Thomas Poell looks at social media–based activist communication in the context of the G20 summit in Toronto in 2010. He does so through an analysis of the hyperlink network that allowed flows of protest communication between various actors and localities as well as the contents of their exchanges. He also develops a typology of connections and vistas enacted through the various social media channels.

Third, technological advances and other interconnected sociopolitical innovations have played prominent roles in rearticulating, expanding, and occasionally enhancing offline modes of day-to-day political and civic engagement, especially when it comes to younger adults who tend to be more digitally savvy. As noted already, they have affected how political elites, as well as individuals and organizations on the periphery of the traditional political arena, interact with each other, and by extension they have redefined the dividends coming out of these interactions (Jensen and Anduiza 2012; Yamamoto, Kushin, and Dalisay 2015). From a broader perspective, these changes have played a key role in redefining repertoires of political action. These repertoires can be defined as the actions taken by members of civil society to influence institutionalized decision-making processes, whether through traditional or more unconventional – or in some cases illegal – channels of political and civic action (Dalton 2008). Several scholars (Bennett and Segerberg 2016; Theocharis et al. 2015) have noted that this process has been marked by subprocesses, including the personalization, individualization, and privatization of political participation. This area of research has received some attention in the Canadian context; however, important questions remain.

Contributors to this volume take on this field of research through a number of case studies. Chapter 3, by Patrick McCurdy and Jacob Groshek, provides an account of digital campaigning tactics developed and deployed by corporate stakeholders to address issues related to TransCanada's proposed 4,600-kilometre Energy East Pipeline, which generated significant public protest. They do so through a two-step process, including a critical case study of TransCanada's proposed digital-advocacy tactics and an analysis of the structure of social media networks and discourses pertaining to Energy East online. Ghada Touir, Florence Millerand, and Guillaume Latzko-Toth explore environmental activists' political engagement in Chapter 1. To do so, they offer an empirical assessment of Quebec's online engagement through the consideration of environmental issues and pay close attention to its gendered dimension. In Chapter 5, Mireille Lalancette, Tamara Small, and Maxime Pronovost look at political memes and, by extension, the redefinition of the grammar of digital activism. They examine how some internet users employed memes extensively to express their opposition to the actions and decisions of then Canadian prime minister Stephen Harper.

Fourth, these transformations in political communication and behaviour in Canada have recalibrated the relationship between members of civil society and long-established political and media institutions. For example, institutionalized political players (e.g., elected officials, government branches, agencies, and political parties) have been adapting specific organizational processes (e.g., leadership and decision making), as well as communication, mobilization, and organizing practices, in order to meet the evolving expectations of a public that increasingly seeks personalization, institutional adaptability and responsiveness, flexibility, openness, and transparency (Bimber, Flanagin, and Stohl 2012; Ellison and Hardey 2014). In Canada, scholars have studied these dynamics. However, more work is required because these areas of political activity are in a state of perpetual evolution.

In Chapter 12, Stéphanie Yates and Myriam Arbour define the concept of social acceptability, and how it affects governance in Canada, by establishing that citizen consultations on major public infrastructure projects are now expected to be part of the process of social responsibility. They argue that its achievement is a prerequisite for a project to move forward, comparable to environmental certifications or financial warranties. In Chapter 11, Erin Crandall, Kate Puddister, and Mark Daku set their sights on a different branch of government, the courts, and consider the increasing importance of social science evidence in the Supreme Court's decision making. As that chapter highlights, the prominence of social science evidence has important implications for citizens and groups who seek to use the courts to change laws and public policies through constitutional litigation. By taking an in-depth look at legacy news media organizations' coverage of the court's decisions on physician-assisted death, the authors shed light on its framing effects and how they can affect the public's understanding of both the nature and the implications of Supreme Court decisions.

Fifth, there has been growing interest among academics in the uses of survey designs and functionalities, advanced audience research, algorithmic politics, big data analytics, and software-based campaign management for understanding and, in some cases, forecasting the behaviour of the public during elections and day-to-day governing. Although these areas of research have received some attention in the United States and globally (Dalton 2016; Kreiss 2016; Woolley 2016), they remain largely underexplored in Canada (McKelvey 2014; Redden 2015). André Turcotte, as well as Fenwick McKelvey and Jill Piebiak, fill part of this gap in the Canadian scholarly literature. In Chapter 10, Turcotte makes the case that new developments in data analytics and digital research are affecting political polling. He argues that data management platforms, digital tagging, audience insights, and segmentation are converging with increased modelling capacities to allow political actors not only to know but also to track citizen behaviour at a high level of granularity. In Chapter 9, McKelvey and Piebiak look at the state of data-driven political campaigning in Canada. Building on in-depth interviews with key stakeholders, they examine how both technologies and the interests and objectives of practitioners are shaping data-driven politicking and the ways in which these elements are affecting the dynamics of permanent campaigning.

WHAT DOES ALL OF THIS MEAN FOR CANADIAN DEMOCRACY?

On top of investigating transformations related to trends in five key areas of political communication and behaviour, the contributors to this volume address indirectly the broader implications of this dynamic for the structures and inner workings of Canadian democracy. Although several conceptions of democracy (e.g., representation, expertise, and participation) have been identified and analyzed in both the recent scholarly literature (e.g., Almond and Verba 2015; Bengtsson and Christensen 2016; Skocpol and Fiorina 2004) and older studies (e.g., Dahl 1989, 1994), scholars generally consider political and civic communication, as well as engagement in patterns of formal and informal politicking, to be cornerstones of the functioning and, by extension, the relevance of democracy (Norris 2002; Oser and Hooghe 2016). From a more traditional perspective, Dahl (1994, 25) defines democracy through the consideration of three "great transformations" that have led to the emergence and evolution of institutionalized norms and practices of varying depth and scope guiding how people and organizations function. To use the terminology of this volume, one can say that Dahl (1994) identified early trending phenomena that shaped the evolution of democracy. This volume builds on Dahl's work and further unpacks the effects of trending phenomena on democracy.

The growing traction of trends in different realms of politicking in Canada has contributed to the remodelling of ways that individuals and organizations envision and, more importantly, take part in and contribute to democratic mechanisms (Bengtsson and Christensen 2016; Oser and Hooghe 2016). As Oser and Hooghe (2016) observe, citizens' attitudes toward democracy are tied to the ways in which and the extent to which they are active both politically and civically. Several researchers and organizations have focused on the state of Canadian democracy in recent years but have done so through a generally holistic – or macro – analytical perspective (e.g., Howe, Blais, and Johnston 2005; Hilderman, Anderson, and Loat 2015). This volume makes a unique contribution because it approaches this question in an interdisciplinary and compartmentalized – or micro – way.

By examining how social, technological, political, cultural, and economic trends are reshaping specific dimensions of Canadian politics, including electioneering, sociopolitical protest, and constituent communication, the contributors to this volume collectively make the case that these transformations have a multitude of ramifications for Canadian democracy, whether from the top down or from the bottom up. However, questions remain regarding their effects on several dimensions of the Canadian democratic model, including social and political cohesion, inclusivity, and accessibility. For example, significant work is required to assess in a more granular fashion whether trends are strengthening or weakening democratic processes and values within Canadian society.

Several chapters in this volume explore, both qualitatively and quantitatively, how trends are affecting political insiders' communication, mobilization, and organization in and out of elections. Other chapters provide insights into how grassroots stakeholders try to influence public political discourses as well as decision-making processes otherwise under the control of political insiders. Although this volume sheds some light on these questions, it stops short of determining whether trends are intensifying, enhancing, or to some extent bettering relations between formal and informal political actors or whether they are contributing to further fragmentation of Canadian society. In other words, a key question remains. Has there been a progressive hyperfragmentation of the political environment, which could lead to the rise and strengthening of a disconnect between different segments of the Canadian public? If so, then this disconnect could be fostering a sociopolitical environment detrimental to a shared consciousness among Canadians and, by extension, could be weakening Canadian democracy. Although not answering this question explicitly, the chapters in this volume make an important contribution as they break theoretical and methodological grounds for future research.

STRUCTURE OF THE CHAPTERS

This volume fills significant gaps in the academic literature by examining dynamics of political communication, mobilization, and organization that we anticipate will have transformational impacts on Canadian political and civic landscapes. It features work by scholars from different fields who draw from various theoretical backgrounds and methodological perspectives to explore trending patterns of political communication, mobilization, and engagement through case studies. By exploring trends in five key areas of communication and political behaviour in the Canadian context, they provide answers to three lines of questioning:

1 What is the nature of recent changes in media practices and political behaviour and communication?
2 How are these changes transforming political engagement and political action repertoires? To what extent do these trends transform the relationships between political actors and institutions and democracy in general?
3 What are the consequences for the practice and study of Canadian politics?

Readers of this volume will have a more in-depth, interdisciplinary understanding of key trends affecting the tools used and of the impacts of citizens, media institutions, political elites, and grassroots organizations on the Canadian political environment. From a broader perspective, they will gain a better appreciation of the implications of these trends for the Canadian political system as a whole. Finally, they will be more in tune with emerging fields of study and practice at the intersection of communication, political science, sociology, polling, political management, and journalism. The emerging use of social media for politicking can be seen as the tip of the iceberg when it comes to new elite-led and grassroots-driven conceptions and practices of political communication and behaviour in the Canadian context. This volume provides readers with much-needed context for these transformations and their effects on the evolution of the Canadian political landscape.

NOTE

1 This concept is defined as "the process which gives any information item the maximum exposure, relative to the potential audience, over a short duration, distributed by many nodes" (Nahon et al. 2011, 1).

REFERENCES

Almond, Gabriel Abraham, and Sidney Verba. 2015. *The Civic Culture: Political Attitudes and Democracy in Five Nations.* Princeton, NJ: Princeton University Press.

Bengtsson, Åsa, and Henrik Christensen. 2016. "Ideals and Actions: Do Citizens' Patterns of Political Participation Correspond to Their Conceptions of Democracy?" *Government and Opposition* 51, 2: 234–60.

Bennett, W. Lance, and Alexandra Segerberg. 2016. "The Logic of Connective Action: Digital Media and the Personalization of Contentious Politics." In *Civic Media: Technology, Design, Practice,* edited by Eric Gordon and Paul Mihailidis, 77–106. Cambridge, MA: MIT Press.

Bimber, Bruce. 2015. "What's Next? Three Challenges for the Future of Political Communication Research." In *New Technologies and Civic Engagement: New Agendas in Communication,* edited by H. Gil de Zúñiga, 215–33. New York: Routledge.

Bimber, Bruce, Andrew Flanagin, and Cynthia Stohl. 2012. *Collective Action in Organizations: Interaction and Engagement in an Era of Technological Change.* Cambridge, UK: Cambridge University Press.

Cammaerts, Bart, Michael Bruter, Shakuntala Banaji, Sarah Harrison, and Nick Anstead. 2013. "The Myth of Youth Apathy: Young Europeans' Critical Attitudes toward Democratic Life." *American Behavioral Scientist* 58, 5: 645–64.

Dahl, Robert A. 1989. *Democracy and Its Critics.* New Haven, CT: Yale University Press.

–. 1994. "A Democratic Dilemma: System Effectiveness versus Citizen Participation." *Political Science Quarterly* 109, 1: 23–34.

Dalton, Russell J. 2008. "Citizenship Norms and the Expansion of Political Participation." *Political Studies* 56, 1: 76–98.

–. 2016. "The Potential of Big Data for the Cross-National Study of Political Behavior." *International Journal of Sociology* 46, 1: 8–20.

Della Porta, Donatella. 2015. *Social Movements in Times of Austerity: Bringing Capitalism Back into Protest Analysis.* Malden, MA: Polity Press.

Dufour, Pascale, and Louis-Philippe Savoie. 2014. "Quand les mouvements sociaux changent le politique: Le cas du mouvement étudiant de 2012 au Québec." *Canadian Journal of Political Science* 47, 3: 475–502.

Ellison, Nick, and Michael Hardey. 2014. "Social Media and Local Government: Citizenship, Consumption, and Democracy." *Local Government Studies* 40, 1: 21–40.

Elmer, Greg, Ganaele Langlois, and Fenwick McKelvey. 2012. *The Permanent Campaign: New Media, New Politics.* New York: Peter Lang.

Farthing, Rys. 2010. "The Politics of Youthful Antipolitics: Representing the 'Issue' of Youth Participation in Politics." *Journal of Youth Studies* 13, 2: 181–95.

Forum Research. 2015. "Instagram Tops in User Satisfaction." *Forum Research.* http://poll.forumresearch.com/post/213/facebook-leads-in-penetration-linkedin-shows-most-growth/.

Gauja, Anika. 2015. "The Individualisation of Party Politics: The Impact of Changing Internal Decision-Making Processes on Policy Development and Citizen Engagement." *British Journal of Politics and International Relations* 17, 1: 89–105.

Gidengil, Elisabeth, and Heather Bastedo, eds. 2014. *Canadian Democracy from the Ground Up: Perceptions and Performance*. Vancouver: UBC Press.

Hagen, Loni, Jess Kropczynski, Catherine Dumas, Jisue Lee, Fatima Espinoza Vasquez, and Abebe Rorissa. 2015. "Emerging Trends in the Use and Adoption of E-Participation around the World." *Proceedings of the Association for Information Science and Technology* 52, 1: 1–4.

Henn, Matt, Mark Weinstein, and Sarah Forrest. 2005. "Uninterested Youth? Young People's Attitudes towards Party Politics in Britain." *Political Studies* 53, 3: 556–78.

Henn, Matt, Mark Weinstein, and Sarah Hodgkinson. 2007. "Social Capital and Political Participation: Understanding the Dynamics of Young People's Political Disengagement in Contemporary Britain." *Social Policy and Society* 6, 4: 467–79.

Hilderman, Jane, Kendall Anderson, and Alison Loat. 2015. "A Report Card on How Canadians Communicate, Participate, and Lead in Politics." *Samara Canada*. https://www.samaracanada.com/docs/default-source/triorio-dropbox/democracy 360_story_digital_final.pdf?sfvrsn=2.

Howe, Paul, André Blais, and Richard Johnston. 2005. *Strengthening Canadian Democracy*. Montreal: IRPP.

Jennings, M. Kent, and Richard G. Niemi. 2014. *Generations and Politics: A Panel Study of Young Adults and Their Parents*. Princeton, NJ: Princeton University Press.

Jensen, Michael J., and Eva Anduiza. 2012. "Online Political Participation in the United States and Spain." In *Digital Media and Political Engagement Worldwide: A Comparative Study*, edited by Eva Anduiza, Michael J. Jensen, and Laia Jorba, 80–101. Cambridge, UK: Cambridge University Press.

Klinger, Ulrike, and Jakob Svensson. 2014. "The Emergence of Network Media Logic in Political Communication: A Theoretical Approach." *New Media and Society* 17, 8: 1241–57.

Kreiss, Daniel. 2016. *Prototype Politics: Technology-Intensive Campaigning and the Data of Democracy*. New York: Oxford University Press.

Lalancette, Mireille, and Vincent Raynauld. 2017. "The Power of Political Image: Justin Trudeau, Instagram, and Celebrity Politics." *American Behavioral Scientist, OnlineFirst*, November 30. https://doi.org/10.1177/0002764217744838.

Loader, Brian D., Ariadne Vromen, and Michael A. Xenos. 2014. "The Networked Young Citizen: Social Media, Political Participation, and Civic Engagement." *Information, Communication, and Society* 17, 2: 143–50.

Marland, Alex. 2016. "Justin Trudeau's Sunny Grip of Control." *Inroads Journal* 39. http://inroadsjournal.ca/justin-trudeaus-sunny-grip-control/.

Marland, Alex, Thierry Giasson, and Anna Esselment, eds. 2017. *Permanent Campaigning in Canada*. Vancouver: UBC Press.

Marland, Alex, Thierry Giasson, and Jennifer Lees-Marshment, eds. 2012. *Political Marketing in Canada*. Vancouver: UBC Press.

Marland, Alex, Thierry Giasson, and Tamara A. Small, eds. 2014. *Political Communication in Canada: Meet the Press and Tweet the Rest*. Vancouver: UBC Press.

McKelvey, Fenwick. 2014. "Algorithmic Media Need Democratic Methods: Why Publics Matter." *Canadian Journal of Communication* 39, 4: 597–613.

Monterde, Arnau, and John Postill. 2014. "Mobile Ensembles: The Uses of Mobile Phones for Social Protest by Spain's Indignados." In *Routledge Companion to Mobile Media*, edited by G. Goggin and L. Hjorth, 429–38. Abingdon, UK: Taylor and Francis.

Nahon, Karine, Jeff Hemsley, Shawn Walker, and Muzammil Hussain. 2011. "Fifteen Minutes of Fame: The Power of Blogs in the Lifecycle of Viral Political Informtion." *Policy and Internet* 3, 1: 1–28.

Norris, Pippa. 2002. *Democratic Phoenix: Reinventing Political Activism*. Cambridge, UK: Cambridge University Press.

Oser, Jenny, and Marc Hooghe. 2016. "The Effect of Democratic Ideals on Political Participation: The Role of Political and Social Conceptualizations of Democracy." Paper presented at the Midwestern Political Science Association Annual Conference, Chicago, April 7–10.

Poell, Thomas. 2014. "Social Media and the Transformation of Activist Communication: Exploring the Social Media Ecology of the 2010 Toronto G20 Protests." *Information, Communication, and Society* 17, 6: 716–31.

Poell, Thomas, and José van Dijck. 2015. "Social Media and Activist Communication." In *The Routledge Companion to Alternative and Community Media*, edited by C. Atton, 527–37. London: Routledge.

Quaranta, Mario. 2016. "An Apathetic Generation? Cohorts' Patterns of Political Participation in Italy." *Social Indicators Research* 125, 3: 793–812.

Raynauld, Vincent, and Josh Greenberg. 2014. "Tweet, Click, Vote: Twitter and the 2010 Ottawa Municipal Election." *Journal of Information Technology and Politics* 11, 4: 412–34.

Raynauld, Vincent, Mireille Lalancette, and Sofia Tourigny-Koné. 2016. "Political Protest 2.0: Social Media and the 2012 Student Strike in the Province of Quebec, Canada." *French Politics* 14, 1: 1–29.

Redden, Joanna. 2015. "Big Data as System of Knowledge: Investigating Canadian Governance." In *Compromised Data: from Social Media to Big Data*, edited by G. Elmer, G. Langlois, and J. Redden, 17–39. New York: Bloomsbury Academic.

Skocpol, Theda, and Morris P. Fiorina, eds. 2004. *Civic Engagement in American Democracy*. Washington, DC: Brookings Institution Press.

Sloam, James. 2014. "The Outraged Young: Young Europeans, Civic Engagement, and the New Media in a Time of Crisis." *Information, Communication, and Society* 17, 2: 217–31.

Small, Tamara A. 2008. "The Facebook Effect? On-Line Campaigning in the 2008 Canadian and US Elections." *Policy Options* 14, 1: 85–87.

–. 2011. "What the Hashtag? A Content Analysis of Canadian Politics on Twitter." *Information, Communication, and Society* 14, 6: 872–95.

–. 2012. "E-Government in the Age of Social Media: An Analysis of the Canadian Government's Use of Twitter." *Policy and Internet* 4, 3–4: 91–111.

–. 2016. "Parties, Leaders, and Online Personalization: Twitter in Canadian Electoral Politics." In *Twitter and Elections around the World: Campaigning in 140 Characters or Less*, edited by R. Davis, C. Holtz Bacha, and M.R. Just, 173–89. New York: Routledge.

Small, Tamara A., Harold Jansen, Frédérick Bastien, Thierry Giasson, and Royce Koop. 2014. "Online Political Activity in Canada: The Hype and the Facts." *Canadian Parliamentary Review* 37, 4: 9–16.

Theocharis, Yannis, Will Lowe, Jan W. van Deth, and Gema García-Albacete. 2015. "Using Twitter to Mobilize Protest Action: Online Mobilization Patterns and Action Repertoires in the Occupy Wall Street, Indignados, and Aganaktismenoi Movements." *Information, Communication, and Society* 18, 2: 202–20.

Valenzuela, Sebastián, Arturo Arriagada, and Andrés Scherman. 2012. "The Social Media Basis of Youth Protest Behavior: The Case of Chile." *Journal of Communication* 62, 2: 299–314.

Van Aelst, Peter, et al. 2017. "Political Communication in a High-Choice Media Environment: A Challenge for Democracy?" *Annals of the International Communication Association* 41, 1: 3–27.

Vromen, Ariadne, Michael A. Xenos, and Brian D. Loader. 2015. "Young People, Social Media, and Connective Action: From Organisational Maintenance to Everyday Political Talk." *Journal of Youth Studies* 18, 1: 80–100.

Woolley, Samuel C. 2016. "Automating Power: Social Bot Interference in Global Politics." *First Monday* 21, 4. https://doi.org/10.5210/fm.v21i4.6161.

Yamamoto, Masahiro, Matthew J. Kushin, and Francis Dalisay. 2015. "Social Media and Mobiles as Political Mobilization Forces for Young Adults: Examining the Moderating Role of Online Political Expression in Political Participation." *New Media and Society* 17, 6: 880–98.

PART 1

Trends in Political Engagement and Democratic Practice

1

Social Uses of the Web by Environmental Activists
A Look at Digital Engagement

GHADA TOUIR, FLORENCE MILLERAND,
AND GUILLAUME LATZKO-TOTH

Recent developments in the online media environment have led to many changes in the communication practices of civil society actors. These changes become particularly visible when we look at social media, which bring together hundreds of millions of users. The unprecedented networking and sharing opportunities brought about by these media channels have contributed to the emergence of new forms of citizen engagement made possible through "networks of indignation," social movements, and political uprisings (e.g., the Arab Spring, Occupy Wall Street, and the Indignados) (Castells 2015). This trend is especially prevalent when we look at ecocitizenship movements. Beyond respect for the environment, this form of citizenship "is characterized by ... its ability to create social ties and include them within the framework of a living environment" (Sauvé 2015, 284). The emergence of new "online social micro-ties" (Galibert 2012) is said to form the basis of a "distanced engagement" (Ion 1997).

Ecocitizenship initiatives have emerged online with the goals of educating citizens, influencing public policy that encourages the resolution of social-ecological problems, and protecting and preserving the environment (Douay 2014). Among them are Coule pas chez nous, opposed to oil transportation in Quebec; Pipe-Up Against Enbridge, which mobilized citizens and Indigenous peoples in British Columbia against oil pipelines; and Zéro déchet or Zero Waste, an initiative (located across major Canadian cities) dedicated to the public dissemination of knowledge and environmental expertise.

Various forms of ecocitizenship can be seen on video- and photo-sharing platforms (Fotolia, Flickr, Dailymotion, YouTube). They can also be seen in personal or collective self-publishing platforms that support the posting of comments, such as Facebook, LinkedIn, and MySpace (Coutant and Stenger 2009). These spaces, emblematic of the modern internet, facilitate exchanges between citizens and promote the creation of grassroots movements on issues related to the environment. Faced with considerable diversity and apparent fragmentation of social web uses (Millerand, Proulx, and Rueff 2010), several researchers have begun to study emerging citizen participation practices and to identify significant trends in social and political engagement (Denouël, Granjon, and Aubert 2014), particularly within the environmental sector (Ackland and O'Neil 2011). One of these trends is linked to the concept of connective action, namely "action based on personalized content sharing across media networks" (Bennett and Segerberg 2012, 739).

This stands in contrast to the logic of traditional collective action mediated by major organizational structures (e.g., unions, associations). By working inside a collective action framework, connective action logic encourages participation through the circulation of political messages within networks of mutual trust. Social media play a critical role as organizing and coordinating mechanisms. Within these new forms of connective action, two models dominate: 1) the self-organizing network model, which excludes any form of support from existing organizations that rely exclusively on the internet as an organizing agent; 2) the network models "enabled" by organizations ("organizationally enabled networks") that provide support and, most often, political leadership (Bennett and Segerberg 2012). It is the former model that we focus on in this chapter.

The various forms of ecological activism that have developed on social media allow us to observe different types of engagement (e.g., online petitions, reports, videos, photo sharing, tweeting, blogging, Facebook pages or groups) (Segerberg and Bennett 2011). They reveal the emergence of a new culture of engagement among "ordinary citizens," who seem to be abandoning more "traditional" engagements with structured social groups, associations, and even political parties. This new engagement culture comes with the emergence of what has been referred to as "ecological citizenship" or "ecocitizenship." It can be defined as a relation to environmental protection "characterized not by rights but by the self-imposed duties of the citizen" regarding environmental responsibility (Connelly 2006, 63). It goes beyond citizenship as ordinarily understood because it is "global" instead of "territorial." It also relies on an extended range of "forms of political engagement in different parts of the public and private spheres" (65).

For example, Facebook has become a mobilization tool for young Chileans (aged eighteen to twenty-nine) on environmental public policy issues, such as the construction of power plants in Patagonia and other protected areas (Scherman, Arriagada, and Valenzuela 2015). Salas (2010) emphasizes the importance of strategic uses of the web for sociopolitical engagement, including personal blogging, as a key part of the antitrust movements against the Free Trade Agreement with Central America and the Dominican Republic (CAFTA). Similarly, debates in the form of online comment chains on activist videos posted on YouTube, like those focused on the 15th Copenhagen Conference (COP15) of the Parties to the United Nations Framework Convention on Climate Change (UNFCCC), have contributed to a new culture of civic engagement (Rodriguez 2016) and public policy influence (Uldam and Askanius 2013). This new type of engagement counterbalances frequent use of negative labels such as "slacktivism" (Christensen 2011; Morozov 2013) and "political consumerism" (Stolle and Micheletti 2013) to describe online engagement on these digital platforms.

In the Canadian context, certain studies have focused on the uses of social media by political parties in Quebec (Giasson et al. 2013) and Canada (Small 2010, 2011), by pressure groups (Obar 2014), and by public institutions or agencies in their daily activities and services to citizens (Yates and Arbour 2013). Other studies have looked at Indigenous peoples (Myloneaux et al. 2014) or online citizen movements involved in the struggle for the visibility of francophone minorities in Canada (Millette 2015). Few studies have focused on environmental issues and uses of digital media, including social media.

As is the case with American grassroots movements, we have seen an increase in bottom-up ecocitizenship participation and collective action in recent years.[1] Such actions grow out of an associative framework outside institutions or other organizations that have a top-down hierarchical structure. They are spontaneous movements emerging from ordinary citizen initiatives "without expert, professional or institutional titles other than being inhabitants of a common space" (Chanez and Lebrun-Paré 2015, 145). These engagements and activities are all the more interesting to observe because they seem to be emerging specifically from and within a digital context (Théviot and Mabi 2014).[2]

To understand further digital engagement phenomena concerning environmental issues, we present an exploratory empirical study of trends in environmental engagement in the province of Quebec. The central question guiding our research is to what extent are we witnessing the emergence of new forms of citizen engagement on the internet, particularly concerning environmental issues?

CASE STUDY
Methods

To answer this question, we use an exploratory approach to analyze the changes in citizens' social and political engagement in environmental matters. Specifically, we focus on social media engagement outside the framework of structured associative groups. Our research uses a mixed-methods approach that is predominantly qualitative but includes some quantitative data analysis. The advantage of such an approach is that it facilitates the triangulation of data from multiple sources.

Because of the unavailability of an online citizen environmental group register, we identified these groups through a three-step approach. First, we created a directory of online citizen groups related to environmental protection, with the aim of identifying a diverse range of groups. Through keyword searches related to environmental issues in Quebec (e.g., "citizen movements," "environment," "pipeline," "tar sands," etc.) and suggestions from Google and Facebook's internal search engine (in March 2015), we identified 130 Quebec-based groups working on environmental causes and issues.

Second, we selected 39 of the 130 groups identified and observed them in further detail. We selected these groups based on relevant criteria

(Pires 1997): the environmental cause or issue (to ensure a certain level of diversity), the level of activity of the group (a group had to show daily activity such as posts or comments), and the ease of access and contact (for interviewing purposes). We conducted observations of these groups within a virtual ethnographic perspective (or framework) (Hine 2013) between July 2015 and January 2016.[3]

Third, we selected five of these thirty-nine groups for in-depth analysis. These choices were based on the same selection criteria used in the second stage, to which we added the criterion of the willingness of the group and its representative to collaborate on the research. Specifically, we selected five groups after attempts at contact were made with the thirty-nine groups initially identified. These contacts were made via emails, private messages on Facebook, phone calls, or on-site trips and face-to-face meetings. The five final groups are listed in Table 1.1.

The online citizen advocacy groups considered in this chapter are focused on ecological, environmental, and sustainable development issues (e.g., waste management and recycling, opposition to oil sands, oil pipelines) and various forms of action (e.g., producing information, networking, mobilizing). The observations of the thirty-nine preliminary groups explored new trends and forms of citizen engagement on the environment. The detailed analysis of the five final groups focused on an in-depth study of these new forms of engagement. We used two data collection techniques when studying the five chosen groups: an analysis of the statistical data provided by the platforms (Facebook, Google, WordPress) and semi-structured interviews with the individuals responsible for the creation of these groups.

Findings

Our directory of online citizen advocacy groups revealed that Facebook by far is the platform with the highest number of citizen-based groups in the field of environmental issues. These advocacy groups can take diverse forms: 1) open (public) or closed (private, requiring authentication) groups (e.g., Mouvement Stop Oléoduc); 2) pages (e.g., Ensemble contre les sables bitumineux or Together against Oil Sands); 3) personal accounts (e.g., Marc Anticosti). Another element that distinguishes these groups is their

TABLE 1.1
Detailed list and description of the five groups studied

Group	Description	Digital platforms used
Ensemble contre les sables bitumineux	A citizen advocacy group created in 2010 (the first francophone one) opposed to oil sands.	Its Facebook page currently has more than 18,000 members, the vast majority of whom come from Quebec.[a] Video clips are available on YouTube.
Les citoyens au courant	A citizen advocacy group established in February 2013 opposed to the Enbridge 9B Pipeline. It is made up primarily of residents from the villages of Très-Saint-Rédempteur, Sainte-Justine-de-Newton, Rigaud, and Pointe-Fortune.	Its Facebook page has 466 members (primarily residents of the villages mentioned).[b] It joined Twitter in March 2015 and as of August 2016 had more than 2,600 tweets. As part of its activities, it has also produced video clips on YouTube.
Bric à bacs	A blog aimed at allowing citizens to "become informed on, demystify and think about waste" under the URL https://bricabacs.com/.	It has a Facebook page (https://fr-ca.facebook.com/bricabacs/) with 871 members and is present on Twitter.
Citoyen du monde J.D.	A blog for citizens in the Outaouais region established in 2010, against urban sprawl and "developments that hamper improvements in the quality of life."[c]	Although the blog has been inactive since the end of 2015, the administrator is active on Facebook through his homepage and has a public profile that has more than 3,000 friends.
Dans ma cour + Martinoutaouais	A blog dedicated to the protection of nature and bird conservation (http://dansmacour.quebec/) and a public Facebook group (https://www.facebook.com/groups/Martinoutaouais/) dedicated to the chimney swift in the Outaouais region.	The Facebook page has forty-one members. The same person created both collectives. Video clips are available on YouTube.

Notes: Data were collected in February 2016. Group members might vary significantly since then, as might group names (e.g., Ensemble contre les sables bitumineux became Ensemble accélérons la transition énergétique and had almost doubled its membership by the time this chapter was completed).
a https://fr-ca.facebook.com/Ensemble-contre-les-sables-bitumineux--132842486751654/.
b https://fr-fr.facebook.com/Les-Citoyens-au-Courant-529200363768200/.
c https://www.blogger.com/profile/06762795301340140153.

purpose. We can differentiate between 1) groups created in a specific context, such as in reaction to an event (e.g., Coule pas chez nous), and 2) groups created to promote and defend broader environmental causes (e.g., Pour une moratoire sur le gaz de schiste or For a Moratorium against Shale Gas).

For the most part, the thirty-nine observed groups were very active online. Several significant environment-related events took place during the period of observation (July 2015–January 2016) that sparked renewed activities within the groups. Among them was the waste water discharge from Montreal into the St. Lawrence River, the World March for Climate, COP21,[4] the Canadian federal election, and the TransCanada and Energy East Pipeline crisis. Under different circumstances, the same groups undoubtedly would have been less active.

Online observation of groups, content analysis of self-presentation (the "about" section), and interviews with their founders revealed that most leaders of ecocitizen groups had long-standing experience in environmental activism (fifteen years or more in the subset of the five selected groups). However, though some have had prior involvement as members (or donors) in official environmental organizations, most are ordinary citizens dedicated to protecting the environment. In fact, the motivations leading to the creation of these citizen groups are diverse. For some, it is a desire to solve a specific issue. For others, it is to get their voices heard as environmental activists. Some want to do things differently, especially because they think that formal organizations are either too busy or too "politicized" to talk about causes in a "proper" way. For some, participation in an online ecocitizen group provides an outlet for their passion for and commitment to the environment. For others, it renews past forms of activism.

Moreover, the technical characteristics and constraints of the platforms have structuring effects on these groups. For example, the number of members that a Facebook group can have is currently limited to 5,000, whereas for a page the number is unlimited. Also, on a page, only publications by its administrators are highlighted. Unlike other platforms, such as Twitter and Google+, Facebook provides detailed statistics on its pages (under the "Overview" or "Statistics" tab), therefore providing the founders of these groups with tools to track their activities and members.

Following these general observations, how does environmental engagement manifest itself in these online groups? Our analysis has identified several trends that we have categorized into four types of activities.

First, news sharing and information watching are important parts of the activities carried out by citizen groups online. The goal is to select, relay, and comment on news media information (e.g., press, television, radio, online platforms) as well as content from other sources, including other online groups. This type of activity seems to be consistent with the concept of "citizen informant" or, to some extent, "citizen reporter," who collects, analyzes, and disseminates information. In fact, these concepts are relatively similar to the concept of "Internet activist user" (Granjon 2014). Some moderators take their role seriously and carry out thorough information monitoring and formatting activities:

> I look at any page in Quebec that is interested in the cause and what they publish ... I'll either take some of what they've published[, or] I will choose a different angle ... Or if they've placed a link, I'll add a picture ... Sometimes if I see, all right, that their publication is really successful, well, then I'll go look for something else because I am looking for information complements.[5] (Normand)

Second, digital platforms provide social interactive opportunities, including criticizing, discussing, and commenting. These interactions can be viewed as opportunities for networking and social capital building that can facilitate interpersonal relations (Touir 2015). An exchange between two members of one of our sampled groups illustrates this trend. One member expressed her lack of understanding of the dangers of pipelines for human health. Another member provided clear explanations in plain language. From that day forward, the respondent's name was regularly tagged or quoted when participants asked about environmental issues. In an example of teamwork, one of the group administrators interviewed mentioned that an active member of his group, whom he had not known before, offered to take care of the Facebook page during his two-week vacation. Although social and collaborative behaviour has been present from the beginning of the internet, it can be seen as a driver of the development of the modern web (Lefebvre 2005).

Third, among the most visible online activities, two are at the heart of engagement: mobilization and action. Social media's unique responsiveness – giving users the ability to react very fast – and ability to reach a wider audience (Ellison and Boyd 2013) are used by advocacy groups to mobilize their members around specific events or actions. For example, during the Global Climate March in Ottawa on November 29, 2015, the mobilization of online groups supporting various causes played a crucial role in the circulation of information and the coordination of thousands of people (approximately 25,000) who came to demonstrate on Parliament Hill.[6] The same phenomenon was observed in the case of the petition addressed to the Quebec government in June 2016 protesting against oil and hydrocarbon projects in the province.

Fourth, our observation of interactions and comments on digital platforms has allowed us to see the importance of sharing practical know-how and expertise regarding recycling, composting, or zero waste, whether it is from an ecological, economic, or social perspective. Sharing this type of knowledge is a mobilizing, appreciated, and emancipatory activity among online citizen groups and evidenced by the intensity of the activity surrounding such publications (e.g., the publication of instructions to create an eco-friendly cleaning product or to make reusable bags). Aligned with educational strategies for environmental issues (Sauvé 2000), the dissemination of practical know-how and expertise seems to chronicle the development of an "active" and a "can-do" attitude sought by group members.

In practice, these four types of online activities (news monitoring, networking, mobilizing-acting, and sharing) are interrelated. For example, comments on current events can be accompanied by editorial and policy viewpoints, or by calls to action, as illustrated by a comment from a member of an online group on an article published in *Le Devoir*.[7] In her comment denouncing the Energy East plan to build a pipeline through eastern Canada, the member stressed the links among the company, the federal authorities, and English-speaking Canadians while openly expressing her ideological proximity to the sovereignist movement in Quebec. She saw

Energy East's choice to distribute its publications exclusively in English as a form of discrimination against Canada's francophone population (concentrated in Quebec) (see Patrick McCurdy and Jacob Groshek's chapter on the Energy East project in this volume). This citizen linked the issue of environmental protection in Quebec to political sovereignty and invited Quebec to mimic the position of British Columbia on the TransCanada pipeline in what can be interpreted as a pan-Canadian ecological front.

A strong trend observed throughout this exploratory study was participants' clear preference for online forms of engagement instead of traditional offline avenues. The following excerpt is exemplary of this trend: "I felt [better] able behind my keyboard [laughs] to do things, to talk about the cause, to aggregate the news ... and to inspire people. But engagement on the ground, no" (Normand). Sometimes the reasons for this online engagement have more to do with personal preferences. Normand thought that he can better mobilize people from behind a keyboard. Distance and anonymity enable him to "reach people" even without knowing them personally. Also, he does not see himself as an on-the-ground activist who can inspire crowds and lead a demonstration, even if he sometimes participates in such events. Other reasons mentioned related to time constraints. Indeed, online engagement can become extremely time consuming and, in some cases, even be like a full-time job.

That online participation is more significant than offline participation for the people managing an online group is understandable. However, this form of exclusive online engagement also seems to exist among other citizen members. Observations made by the founders of the groups, as well as our observations of citizen environmental movements, lead us to think that online engagement is a full and self-sufficient commitment that does not need to rely on the work or support of a formal organization. In this regard, the hypothesis of slacktivism appears to be overly simplistic.

Furthermore, observation of participation and discursive exchanges within the thirty-nine groups allowed us to discern that slightly more women mobilize around environmental issues than men, particularly those affecting Quebec. On the page for Ensemble contre les sables bitumineux, women account for 57 percent of the online activity versus 42 percent for men.[8] Within Les citoyens au courant, women make up

50 percent of the membership, compared with 47 percent for men, and they are very much engaged, representing 56 percent of the overall activity on the site. On the Bric à bacs blog, women make up the vast majority of the members (67 percent compared with 30 percent for men) and are responsible for most of the activity (77 percent compared with 27 percent for men). The fact that the author of the blog is a woman might explain, in part, this strong female presence. These initial findings support a tentative hypothesis that there is an online engagement differentiation based on gender, particularly with regard to environmental issues.

TRENDING IN CANADA

The findings of our research on the emergence of new forms of environmental engagement in the context of present-day uses of the internet allow us to identify several trends.

Online groups are opening up new spaces for engagement with and expression of support for environmental causes. A large number of the online citizen-based advocacy groups considered here support the hypothesis that the internet, and social media in particular, are facilitating citizen engagement. They illustrate new ways through which ordinary citizens can have their voices heard. Although they are not members of associations or political parties, they express themselves, take positions, exchange opinions, and participate in discussions. We appear to be witnessing an opening up of citizen speech that takes new online forms and consequently helps to shape contemporary political behaviour.

The internet plays a critical role by offering various platforms that enable social interaction, information sharing, and the development of relationships. A platform such as Facebook, initially designed for private use and social contacts among friends and relatives, has become a catalyst and an aggregator for social participation and engagement (Le Caroff 2015). Participation in these groups is anchored in social media spaces. The structure of the platform plays a key part in the possible uses of these spaces. Just clicking on a link can be a form of (albeit rudimentary) commitment (Badouard 2013, 105). It is an important step to infer from this simple action social and political commitment. Indeed, some have dismissed outright the risk of "slacktivism," a fashionable and well-known derogatory term that refers to lazy and soft commitment (Morozov 2013). Yet slacktivism can also be used in a positive sense, "such as the wearing of political messages of various forms on your body or vehicle, joining Facebook groups, or taking part in short-term boycotts such as Buy Nothing Day or Earth Hour" (Christensen 2011). That said, social media have become essential spaces in which to exchange information and learn about and possibly commit to a cause. They cannot be understood exclusively as spaces for slacktivism.

The nature of the activities around which online advocacy groups are organized (monitoring, networking, mobilizing, and sharing) is not much different from the nature of activist movements (Touir 2015). However, some uses are specific to the digital environment and show an evolution in practices. Alongside traditional activist practices (petitions, marches, protests, etc.), great importance is attached to the flow and sharing of information by online groups; publishing information is itself proof of engagement. The internet allows for an expanded spectrum of engagement, enabling citizens to become active in particular causes (e.g., by contributing diligently to the activities of the group) or allowing them to keep their distance and follow information from afar.

What seems to be new is the form of commitment that takes place exclusively online and is not accompanied by offline activism. Members of the groups considered here show high ecological and environmental awareness, though it is weakly associated with a practical, on-the-ground approach. As suggested by one of our participants, "we let associations take care of on-the-ground activities." For some, online engagement seems to be sufficient and meaningful. Most of the activities take place in front of a screen and behind a keyboard. This form of engagement reflects the notion of "distanced engagement" proposed by Ion (1997), highlighting the "flexible and non-binding" character of new activist practices. Importantly, this distanced attitude is not necessarily related to a decrease in intensity. Again, online engagement, in some cases, can take as much time as a full-time job.

Our findings also suggest a possible emerging trend: online environmental engagement led by women. Could it be because of a broader trend in which online engagement is a gendered practice? Several authors have already noted higher daily web use by women, especially on social networking sites (Clipson, Wilson, and DuFrene 2012; Le Caroff 2015; Vollman, Abraham, and Mörn 2010). Moreover, national Canadian surveys, as well as studies on female engagement (Murphy 2010; Quéniart and Lamoureux 2002), including a study by Lalanne and Lapeyre (2009) on "daily ecological commitment," support the idea that women are more engaged than men on issues related to the environment. Although the limits of our case study mean that we cannot confirm the existence of an online engagement dominated by women, it appears to be a compelling hypothesis. Women are heavy users of social media, and online engagement seems to be well suited to their lifestyles because of its flexible nature.

Online groups seem to reach people who would otherwise not necessarily become engaged, for example, through associations. This hypothesis stems from our observations of the thirty-nine online groups studied. We note that, throughout the discussion threads, participants showed little interest in engaging on the ground or with formal organizations. So, though some groups do have links with associations, most stem from spontaneous and autonomous civic initiatives. Moreover, how groups are organized online resembles the self-organizing network model described by Bennett and Segerberg (2012). They can be viewed as independent of organizations or institutions. They also rely mainly on the internet as an organizing element and operate through a flexible method of coordination (with a more or less active moderator). Finally, they favour an individual action framework.

The particularity of online engagement seems to lie within the framework of individual action. The internet plays a strategic role by supporting this form of engagement built on social networks. Sociological work on activist engagement has noted a link between the emergence of engagement practices on the internet, which were developed relatively autonomously, and the network structure of the movements that supported them (Granjon 2001). These online networks seem to promote the consolidation of dispersed and heterogeneous interests, based on flexible modes of coordination that favour consensus building rather than pre-existing ideological commitments. In the words of Bennett and Segerberg (2012), the methods of online mobilization reveal the importance of "individualized orientations [that] result in engagement with politics as an expression of personal hopes, lifestyles, and grievances" (743). They also allow for greater personalization of methods of action: "The ideas and mechanisms for organizing action become more personalized than in cases where the action is organized by social group identity, membership, or ideology" (744).

To what extent do these trends have a more profound impact on the relationships among policy, political actors and institutions, and democracy in general? What lessons can be drawn from them for the study of political practices in Canada? The magnitude of these ongoing changes is difficult to assess. More extensive empirical studies are needed. However, it is important to note that online engagement appears to contribute to the development of a feeling of greater proximity between citizens and their representatives and political institutions. Additionally, it contributes to a greater sense of agency and capacity for action, though we should point out that our conclusions are based on interviews with leaders, among the most active members of these groups. The resonance effects of actions against shale gas and preservation of the natural environment for belugas from hydrocarbons or the Enbridge 9B Pipeline (the latter echoed the televised leaders' debate during the previous federal election) are part of this increase in the sense of empowerment felt by members of these collectives. Online advocacy groups act like laboratories of social experimentation. They are places where different ways of "doing" politics are being elaborated, which will possibly shape the policy-making practices of tomorrow. As such, they deserve the full attention of researchers.

Contrary to studies on organizations and actors known to be inherently political, our study looked at online engagement spaces not identified a priori as being significant areas of political debate and action. Likewise, it would be worthwhile to explore further the issue of differentiated online engagements between men and women, including in other national contexts. It is essential to understand better the properties of the movements emerging on the internet and to examine the range of commitments stemming from them while taking into account the accelerated pace of change in software-based communication devices. It is likely that the collective movements observed in our study will migrate to other platforms and experience changes in the coming years.

Finally, the value that citizens place on their online environmental engagement invites us to refine our theoretical and methodological frameworks for this new culture of engagement. The question of what role digital technologies, and social media in particular, play in protests set up by ordinary citizens is a thought-provoking and important one. We suggest that the reflective discourses of ordinary ecocitizens can contribute significantly to this understanding. Consideration should also be given to the possibility that this new culture, which in some cases entails abandoning actions on the ground, bears the risk of limited engagement or even early disengagement as a result of power struggles within the online movement.

NOTES

1 See, for example, Lummis et al. (2017); and Zeng, Sweet, and Cheng (2016).
2 The notion of "engagement" should be clarified since it is increasingly confused with a simple expression of interest, including by online platform designers that, like Facebook, classify it as any interaction with their technical devices. In our view, engagement is linked to Becker's (1960) concept of "commitment," defined as consisting of a coherent line of action that is persistent over time and has consequences for other aspects of the life of the individual committed, in addition to the cause to which he or she is committed. Similarly, like other authors (Amato and Boutin 2012; Bernard 2014), we consider engagement to be a form of spontaneous, voluntary, and convinced individual action aimed at producing social change within a certain period of time.
3 These observations were made on a daily or weekly basis according to the group's activity level. The newsfeed displayed in the directory of environmental collectives in Quebec, which Touir had created on Facebook, gave her information on the activity taking place on the page or among the group, without having to "like" the page. Observational notes were recorded in a logbook dated with comments, following repeated proofreading.
4 Short for the 21st Conference of the Parties held in Paris from November 30 to December 12, 2015.
5 Because interviews were conducted in French, all quotations from them in this chapter have been translated into English.
6 As reported by the administrators of online collectives whom we interviewed and who participated in the march.

7 A. Shields, "TransCanada présente la version finale de son projet de pipeline," *Le Devoir*, December 17, 2015, A1.
8 The percentages do not add up to 100 percent because some users did not specify any gender in their personal profiles.

REFERENCES

Ackland, Robert, and Mathieu O'Neil. 2011. "Online Collective Identity: The Case of the Environmental Movement." *Social Networks* 33, 3: 177–90.

Amato, Stéphane, and Eric Boutin. 2012. "Engagement online et expérimentation en milieu naturel: Retours d'expériences." In *Actes de la Journée de recherche, L'engagement, de la société aux organisations*, 1–14.

Badouard, Romain. 2013. "Les mobilisations de clavier." *Réseaux* 5: 87–117.

Becker, Howard S. 1960. "Notes on the Concept of Commitment." *American Journal of Sociology* 66, 1: 32–40.

Bennett, W. Lance, and Alexandra Segerberg. 2012. "The Logic of Connective Action: Digital Media and the Personalization of Contentious Politics." *Information, Communication, and Society* 15, 5: 739–68.

Bernard, Françoise. 2014. "Imaginaire, participation, engagement, et empowerment: Des notions pour penser la relation entre risques et changements." *Communication et organisation* 45: 87–98.

Castells, Manuel. 2015. *Networks of Outrage and Hope: Social Movements in the Internet Age.* Cambridge, UK: Polity.

Chanez, Amélie, and Félix Lebrun-Paré. 2015. "Villeray en transition: Initiatives citoyennes d'appropriation de l'espace habité?" *Cahiers de recherche sociologique* 58: 139–63.

Christensen, Henrik S. 2011. "Political Activities on the Internet: Slacktivism or Political Participation by Other Means?" *First Monday* 16, 2. http://firstmonday.org/ojs/index.php/fm/article/viewArticle/3336.

Clipson, Timothy W., S. Ann Wilson, and Debbie D. DuFrene. 2012. "The Social Networking Arena Battle of the Sexes." *Business Communication Quarterly* 75, 1: 64–67.

Connelly, James. 2006. "The Virtues of Environmental Citizenship." In *Environmental Citizenship*, edited by A. Dobson and D. Bell, 49–74. Cambridge, MA: MIT Press.

Coutant, Alexandre, and Thomas Stenger. 2009. "Les configurations sociotechniques sur le web et leurs usages: Le cas des réseaux sociaux numériques." In *7ème Colloque du chapitre français de l'ISKO, Intelligence collective et organisation des connaissances*, Lyon, 27–34.

Denouël, Julie, Fabien Granjon, and Aurélie Aubert. 2014. *Médias numériques et participation: Entre engagement citoyen et production de soi.* Paris: Mare et Martin.

Douay, Nicolas. 2014. "Mouvements sociaux numériques et aménagement de l'espace." *Informations sociales* 5: 123–30.

Ellison, Nicole B., and Danah Boyd. 2013. "Sociality through Social Network Sites." In *The Oxford Handbook of Internet Studies*, edited by W.H. Dutton, 151–72. Oxford: Oxford University Press.

Galibert, Olivier. 2012. "Engagement éco-citoyen et participation en ligne: Entre agir communicationnel et agir stratégique." In *Actes du colloque "Organisations, performativité, et engagement" 80e congrès international ACFAS*, edited by D. Cordelier and G. Gramaccia, 138–49. Ottawa: Bibliothèques et Archives Canada.

Giasson, Thierry, Gildas Le Bars, Frédérick Bastien, and Mélanie Verville. 2013. "#QC2012: L'utilisation de Twitter par les partis." In *Les Québécois aux urnes: Les partis, les médias, et les citoyens en campagne*, edited by F. Bastien, É. Bélanger, and F. Gélineau, 135–48. Montréal: Presses de l'Université de Montréal.

Granjon, Fabien. 2001. *L'internet militant: Mouvement social et usage des réseaux télématiques*. Rennes: Apogée.

—. 2014. "Introduction." In *Médias numériques et participation: Entre engagement citoyen et production de soi*, edited by J. Denouël, F. Granjon, and A. Aubert, 7–19. Paris: Mare and Martin.

Hine, Christine. 2013. *Virtual Research Methods*. London: Sage.

Ion, Jacques. 1997. *La fin des militants?* Paris: L'Atelier.

Lalanne, Michèle, and Nathalie Lapeyre. 2009. "L'engagement écologique au quotidien a-t-il un genre?" *Recherches féministes* 22, 1: 47-68.

Le Caroff, Coralie. 2015. "Le genre et la prise de parole politique sur Facebook." *Participations* 2: 109-37.

Lefebvre, Alain. 2005. *Les réseaux sociaux: Pivot de l'internet 2.0*. Paris: MM2 Éditions.

Lummis, Geoffrey W., Julia E. Morris, Graeme Lock, and Judith Odgaard. 2017. "The Influence of Ecological Citizenship and Political Solidarity on Western Australian Student Teachers' Perceptions of Sustainability Issues." *International Research in Geographical and Environmental Education* 26, 2: 135–49.

Millerand, Florence, Serge Proulx, and Julien Rueff, eds. 2010. *Web social: Mutation de la communication*. Québec: Presses de l'Université du Québec.

Millette, Mélanie. 2015. *L'usage des médias sociaux dans les luttes pour la visibilité: Le cas des minorités francophones au Canada anglais*. Montréal: Université du Québec à Montréal.

Morozov, Evgeny. 2013. *To Save Everything, Click Here: Technology, Solutionism, and the Urge to Fix Problems that Don't Exist*. New York: Penguin.

Murphy, Kate. 2010. "Feminism and Political History." *Australian Journal of Politics and History* 56, 1: 21–37.

Myloneaux, Heather, Susan O'Donnell, Crystal Kakekaspan, Brian Walmark, Philipp Budka, and Kerri Gibson. 2014. "Social Media in Remote First Nation Communities." *Canadian Journal of Communication* 39, 2: 275–88.

Obar, Jonathan A. 2014. "Canadian Advocacy 2.0: An Analysis of Social Media Adoption and Perceived Affordances by Advocacy Groups Looking to Advance Activism in Canada." *Canadian Journal of Communication* 39, 2: 211–33.

Pires, Alvaro. 1997. "Échantillonnage et recherche qualitative: Essai théorique et méthodologique." In *La recherche qualitative: Enjeux épistémologiques et méthodologiques*, edited by J. Poupart, L.-H. Groulx, J.-P. Deslauriers, A. Laperrière, R. Mayer, and A. Pires, 113–69. Montréal: Gaëtan Morin.

Quéniart, Anne, and Jocelyne Lamoureux. 2002. "Femmes et engagement." *Cahiers de recherche sociologique* 37: 5–18.

Rodriguez, Sandra. 2016. "J'aimerais être une antenne: Pratiques et sens de l'engagement à l'ère des cultures en réseaux." *Agora débats/jeunesses* 73, 2: 61–76.

Salas, M. 2010. "Internet, Power, and Politics: Gender and ICTs in the Movement against CAFTA." *Journal of Community Informatics* 6, 1. http://ci-journal.net/index.php/ciej/article/view/530/468.

Sauvé, Lucie. 2000. "L'éducation relative à l'environnement – Entre modernité et post-modernité: Les propositions du développement durable et de l'avenir viable." In *The Future of Environmental Education in a Postmodern World*, edited by A. Jarnet, B. Jickling, L. Sauvé, A. Wals, and P. Clarkin, 57–70. Whitehorse: Yukon College.

–. 2015. "L'écocitoyenneté: Apprendre ensemble au cœur des débats." In *Sortir le Québec du pétrole*, edited by Y. Marcil, 283–89. Montréal: Somme Toute.

Scherman, Andrés, Arturo Arriagada, and Sebastián Valenzuela. 2015. "Student and Environmental Protests in Chile: The Role of Social Media." *Politics* 35, 2: 151–71.

Segerberg, Alexandra, and W. Lance Bennett. 2011. "Social Media and the Organization of Collective Action: Using Twitter to Explore the Ecologies of Two Climate Change Protests." *Communication Review* 14, 3: 197–215.

Small, Tamara A. 2010. "La politique canadienne en 140 caractères: La vie des partis dans l'univers Twitter." *Revue parlementaire canadienne* 33, 3: 41–48.

–. 2011. "What the Hashtag? A Content Analysis of Canadian Politics on Twitter." *Information, Communication, and Society* 14, 6: 872–95.

Stolle, Dietlind, and Michele Micheletti. 2013. *Political Consumerism: Global Responsibility in Action*. Cambridge, UK: Cambridge University Press.

Théviot, Anaïs, and Clément Mabi. 2014. "Revue politiques de communication (3 – Politiques de s'engager sur internet. Mobilisations et pratiques politiques). Théviot Anaïs and Mabi Clément (coord.)." https://halshs.archives-ouvertes.fr/halshs-01119060/.

Touir, Ghada. 2015. "S'approprier les technologies numériques: Étude des dynamiques, des pratiques, et des usages du web de quatre associations environnementales québécoises." PhD diss., Department of Information and Communication, Université Laval.

Uldam, Julie, and Tina Askanius. 2013. "Online Civic Cultures? Debating Climate Change Activism on YouTube." *International Journal of Communication* 7: 1185–1204.

Vollman, Andrea, Linda Abraham, and Marie Pauline Mörn. 2010. "Women on the Web: How Women Are Shaping the Internet." *Comscore Inc.* https://www.comscore.com/Insights/Presentations-and-Whitepapers/2010/Women-on-the-Web-How-Women-are-Shaping-the-Internet.

Yates, Stéphanie, and Myriam Arbour. 2013. "L'usage des médias socionumériques par les organismes publics: Le cas du Québec." *Communiquer: Revue de communication sociale et publique* 9: 55–76.

Zeng, Chen, William Sweet, and Qian Cheng. 2016. "Ecological Citizenship and Green Burial in China." *Journal of Agricultural and Environmental Ethics* 29, 6: 985–1001.

2

Rethinking Digital Activism as It Unfolds
Ambient Political Engagement on Twitter during the 2012 Quebec Student Strike

VINCENT RAYNAULD, MIREILLE LALANCETTE, AND SOFIA TOURIGNY-KONÉ

In the past decade, social media have become critical tools for individuals and organizations at the periphery of the formal political arena to challenge and, to some extent, question the legitimacy of established elites and power structures (see Freelon, McIlwain, and Clark 2016; Hussain and Howard 2013; White, Castleden, and Gruzd 2015). The structural and functional properties of these user-generated media channels have given their users the ability to act outside institutionalized and centralized paths of political and civic engagement in order to reach their objectives on their own terms (Poell 2014). Here we dive into this dynamic by unpacking a grassroots-driven protest that emerged as a powerful force in the Quebec political ecosystem in 2012: the student strike against higher university tuition fees, also known as the "Maple Spring."

Dufour and Savoie (2014, 475) argue that this student protest movement affected the Quebec political landscape in many ways, including the temporary suspension of norms and practices guiding relations between individual and collective political players in the context of governing. However, this movement emerged and gained traction like most offline-based movements of contestation. In early 2012, university and CEGEP (Collège d'enseignement général et professionnel[1]) student unions and student leaders took the lead in mass-circulating information, building and cultivating support, as well as organizing and coordinating mobilization initiatives of various sizes in a mostly top-down fashion (Bégin-Caouette and Jones 2014; Sorochan 2012). The strike evolved quickly over the weeks that followed. Maple Spring supporters and opponents turned heavily to social media to self-organize and engage in wide-ranging protest activities (e.g., Jochems, Millette, and Millette 2013; Raynauld, Lalancette, and Tourigny-Koné 2016). As observed by Jordan and colleagues (2015, 183), "Quebec students used online social media to organize and promote participation in what some activists have called the largest act of civil disobedience in Canadian history." Between February 12 and June 4, 2012, a time period considered to be the height of the student strike, 194,594 Maple Spring–related tweets appeared on Twitter's public timeline (Marcoux and Lusseau 2014). We use the 2012 Quebec student strike against higher university tuition fees as a case study to identify, characterize, and analyze trends shaping dynamics of grassroots-intensive activism in the Canadian social mediascape. This field of study has garnered some academic attention in recent years. Poell (2014, 717) took an interest in political engagement through social media during the G20 protest in Toronto in 2010. He explored how "intersecting techno-cultural and political economic relations" influenced how these tools were used for political action (see also his chapter in this volume). White and colleagues (2015) studied activists' motivations for using Twitter for information sharing and discussion regarding two environmental issues: the Alberta oil sands and the Northern Gateway Pipelines in British Columbia. They found that Twitter helped to establish a partial "green virtual sphere" by enhancing the access of public members to information as well as providing them with a digital arena for open debate (see also McCurdy and Groshek's chapter in this volume). When examining patterns of tweeting related to the Indigenous-led Idle No More movement in late 2012 and early 2013, Callison and Hermida (2015, 713) found that hashtags led to the emergence of "a crowdsourced elite" comprising a "greater proportion of indigenous and alternative voices" (see also Raynauld, Richez, and Boudreau Morris 2018).

These studies, alongside others conducted internationally, have generated valuable insights into social media–intensive grassroots protests. Many of them, in fact, have helped to develop in-depth knowledge of student-driven protest in the Web 2.0 environment (e.g., Hensby 2017; Scherman, Arriagada, and Valenzuela 2015). However, this scholarly work has relied for the most part on relatively similar theoretical and methodological frameworks. Specifically, most authors have considered public protest phenomena as a whole or focused on uses of specific media channels for protest based on specific geographical considerations or during specific time periods (e.g., Della Porta and Mattoni 2014; Gottlieb 2015). Following the work of Khazraee and Losey (2016), it can be argued that they have taken a predominantly holistic approach to the study of social media activism. As a result, little light has been shed on how this type of grassroots-intensive protest evolves over time as it emerges, gains traction, and, in many cases, winds down.

Here we take a different approach and fill part of an important and long-standing gap in the academic literature. We examine the evolution of dynamics of contention on social media over time in the context of a specific protest movement. We do so through the consideration of cycles of political protest online as well as by introducing the concept of digital ambient political engagement. This concept provides a much-needed explanatory framework for understanding the highly reactive, decentralized, and personalized nature of social media–intensive dynamics of political protest. In other words, we treat social media–fuelled protest phenomena as evolving processes, not as singular events. This can be seen as an important contribution to the academic literature. Furthermore, because a large portion of existing scholarly work on social media and dissent in Canada has been quantitative in nature, we complement it by offering a qualitative look at protest tweets' contents and purposes as well as their impact on political and civic engagement.

Although many aspects of bottom-up political contention on social media have been investigated, the concept of protest repertoire has received the lion's share of attention. Building on many scholars' work (Bennett 2012; Della Porta and Mattoni 2014; Theocharis et al. 2015; Van Laer and Van Aelst 2010), we define digital protest repertoire as an ensemble of noninstitutionalized, decentralized, and highly fragmented modes of internet-based political and civic action geared to contesting or, in other cases, defending and promoting the existence, influences, purposes, decisions, or actions of established media, government, and political entities. This repertoire is twofold (Van Laer and Van Aelst 2010). It consists of offline-inspired modes of protest action tailored to exploit digital media's distinct opportunities (e.g., temporality and directionality of information flow, content, and social interactivity). It also includes newer forms of digital contention, such as hashtag activism (Bastos, Mercea, and

Charpentier 2015) and "Twitter storms" (LeFebvre and Armstrong 2018), which make use of social media's distinct properties. Several factors have contributed to the rise of these more recent modes of e-protest. They include social media's structural and functional opportunities as well as the changing norms of citizenship of a growing number of societal players whose involvement in political and civic life is driven increasingly by "post-material, lifestyle politics" (Bimber 2012, 121; Turcotte and Raynauld 2014). Over the past ten years, Canadians have turned to Twitter in increasing numbers for wide-ranging activities, such as political information acquisition, self-expression, and engagement. In 2012, close to 22 percent of Canadian adults reported having at least one Twitter account (Forum Research 2015), up from 4.35 percent in 2010 (Sysomos 2010).[2]

In Quebec, a CEFRIO (Centre facilitant la recherche et l'innovation dans les organisations) survey (2012) revealed that 10 percent of Quebec adults were active on Twitter in 2012, spending an average of five hours per week on this social media site.[3] Twitter is particularly popular among students. A March 2012 survey conducted among 526 students enrolled in English-language Canadian universities revealed that 30 percent of them had at least one profile on Twitter, compared with 92 percent who reported having a profile page on Facebook (Vissers and Stolle 2014).

Information dispersion and social interactions on Twitter have been studied by researchers across many academic disciplines. Of particular interest are works tackling issues in journalism (e.g., Hermida 2012; Vis 2013). They point out that this microcommunication service provides its users with the capacity to share on a large scale short-form digital material (e.g., text, pictures, videos) that can be newsworthy. Also, it allows them to take part independently and on their own timelines in all facets of news reporting. This can include contributions in real time, in an informal tone, and from a personal vantage point to the coverage of issues or events, especially during breaking news situations (e.g., Hermida 2012; Vis 2013).

As Hermida (2012) notes, this reconfiguration of patterns of information acquisition, verification, and dissemination has led to the rise of "ambient journalism." It can be defined as an individually specific "awareness system where multi-faceted, real-time digital networks enable the flow of news and information in the periphery of a user's awareness" (660). In other words, the contemporary journalistic paradigm is "being refashioned by the architectures of distributed, networked digital technologies" (662), coupled with the evolution of the sociopolitical profiles of a growing number of individuals and organizations taking part in different facets of the journalistic process through social media. This state of awareness can affect users' perceptions and understandings of issues and events. In other words, because users are constantly exposed to streams of information and updates in their social media feeds, how they see their immediate environments is reshaped, whether voluntarily or involuntarily. This reshaping can also inform and influence their behaviour. Users' awareness is constantly affected by a myriad of ever-evolving factors, including the structure and composition of their social network or their level and timing of use of Twitter.

This state of ambient awareness can affect political and civic action. Building on Clark's research (2016, 236), we argue that social media allow for uncontrolled and fragmented flows of user-generated digital "artefacts of political engagement," defined as "photos, memes, quotes, sayings, and original or curated commentary [embedded in streams of information dispersion and social interaction] that evince ... people's emotional investment and participation in unfolding events" (see also Lalancette, Small, and Pronovost's chapter on political memes in this volume). In this sense, they can shape political and civic behaviour, especially during peak moments of political communication or engagement characterized by heightened levels of public political awareness, mobilization, and responsiveness. This situation can lead to heightened levels of ambient political engagement.

This dynamic must be understood in the broader context of cycles of digital grassroots protest that can lead, in some cases, to political change. As shown in Table 2.1, Hussain and Howard (2013) identify six phases of political protest in the digital media environment that have specific yet complementary characteristics.

CASE STUDY

The growing traction of the Maple Spring movement among the Quebec public can be attributed to a series of events. On March 17, 2011, the Quebec government, led by the Liberal Party of Jean Charest, released a document on higher education funding. The plan put forth measures that

TABLE 2.1
Six phases of digital grassroots protest

Phase of political protest	Characteristic(s)
Preparation	Identification of grievances and goals Protest network building
Ignition	Moment or event galvanizing the public
Protest	Manifestation of contention
External buy-in	Growth of awareness Mass circulation of information Mobilization among people or other social entities external to the original protest movement
Climax	Response of established political elites and power structures to protesters' actions and demands
Follow-on information warfare	Efforts deployed by formal and informal players to share "the future of civil society and information infrastructure" (Hussain and Howard 2013, 50)

Note: The table is based on work by Hussain and Howard (2013). These stages of protest can lead to "rapid diffusion of collective action, innovation in the forms of contention employed, new or transformed collective action frames, the coexistence of organized and unorganized participation, and information flow between challengers and authorities" (Gottlieb 2015, 236).

would affect students financially, including an increase in annual university tuition fees amounting to a 75 percent increase over a five-year period ($1,625 between 2012 and 2017 or $325 per year) (Bégin-Caouette and Jones 2014). A significant gap existed between the position of the provincial government and that of many students. Government officials argued that this raise would bring yearly university tuition fees in Quebec to a level comparable to those in other Canadian provinces. Student unions pointed out that this raise would make education less financially accessible to many Quebecers and considered it to be a departure from principles that had emerged during the 1960s when the Quiet Revolution had led to education as a core value of Quebec society (Spiegel 2015, 771).

The Quebec student strike began on February 13, 2012, when Université du Québec à Montréal and Université Laval students voted in favour of the strike and walked out of classes (Sorochan 2012). Over the following weeks, this protest initiative expanded, diversified, and gained momentum across all segments of Quebec society. It energized individuals and organizations with preferences, interests, and goals not necessarily linked to those of students, including social and ethnic minorities, labour unions, and activist groups (Fortin 2014). As mentioned previously, social media became a key component of this protest initiative, with Maple Spring supporters and opponents using them extensively to be active politically. The student strike ended on August 17, 2012, with CEGEP and university students returning to classes and completing the spring 2012 semester (Simard 2013).

Methods
To identify, characterize, and analyze the factors that shaped the evolution of the Maple Spring in the Twitterverse, we conducted a hybrid quantitative and qualitative content analysis of mostly French-language tweets. The tweets considered for this study had at least one ggi hashtag and appeared on Twitter's public timeline between April 22 and July 31, 2012 (Sorochan 2012).[4] Hashtag-based sampling has been used frequently by scholars studying Twitter-based dynamics of elite-led or grassroots political communication, mobilization, and organization (e.g., Bastos et al. 2015; Raynauld and Greenberg 2014). Although various hashtags referring to often highly specific dimensions of the Maple Spring were used by tweeters throughout the strike (e.g., #manifencours, #non1625, #casseroles), #ggi by far had the most traction in the Twitterverse (Marcoux and Lusseau 2014; Ménard 2012). It was also used by politicians, police departments, and legacy media active on Twitter during the strike.

The data set was built through a three-step sampling process. Initially, all 66,282 tweets comprising at least one #ggi hashtag that appeared on Twitter's public timeline between April 22 and July 31, 2012, were collected and archived with Tweet Archivist. This data mining and archiving platform, used by other researchers (e.g., Croeser and Highfield 2014; Raynauld and Greenberg 2014), allowed for the acquisition of all aspects of #ggi tweets, including their contents (e.g., text, hashtags, hyperlinks), times of publication, and details about their authors when available.

We narrowed down this data set by keeping 17,406 #ggi tweets shared on the fifteen days identified by academics and commentators as key Maple Spring moments. These days were marked by phenomena that affected in important ways the course of the student strike, including real-world demonstrations, meetings between student leaders and government officials, and clashes between protesters and police forces (see Table 2.2) (Bonenfant 2013; Nadeau-Dubois 2013; Simard 2013).[5] They were spread out across the broader time period considered for this study. Finally, we further trimmed down the data set by limiting our analysis to the first 100 #ggi tweets shared on Twitter's public timeline on these fifteen days for a total of 1,500 tweets. The nonrandomized nature of the third step of the sampling strategy allowed for the capture of potential social interactions between #ggi tweeters through Twitter-specific functionalities.

This sampling approach could have led to selection biases. Specifically, #ggi tweeting during the time period considered for our study could have been affected by different variables, including news media coverage, patterns of grassroots student activism, and tweeting practices specific to

TABLE 2.2
Fifteen key dates related to the 2012 Quebec student strike

Date (2012)	Event description	Phases of protest
April 22	Major demonstration marking Earth Day in the streets of Montreal.	Preparation Ignition
April 23	185,000 university and CEGEP students announce strike.	Protest
April 24	Minister of Education Line Beauchamp requests a pause in the strike ahead of the start of the negotiations between government officials and student leaders. First night of the demonstration.	
May 3	Parti Québécois leader Pauline Marois announces that if her political party, the official opposition, wins the next provincial election she will raise the tuition fees only according to the indexation of living costs.	
May 5	Following twenty-two hours of negotiations, a tentative agreement is reached and signed between provincial government officials and student leaders.	
May 6 and 7	Negotiations between provincial government officials and student leaders.	
May 15	The provincial police force Sûreté du Québec conducts an operation at Collège Lionel-Groulx to evict protesters blocking access to a building. Gabriel Nadeau-Dubois – spokesperson for the student association CLASSE – is indicted for contempt of court.[a]	

▶

Date (2012)	Event description	Phases of protest
May 17	Introduction of Bill 78 by the Liberal government, which introduces legislative measures specifically designed to end the student strike.	International buy-in
May 19	In reaction to Bill 78, people demonstrate in the streets of major cities, including Montreal.	Climax
May 21	The student association CLASSE announces that it will not respect the special law.	
May 31	Negotiations between provincial government officials and student leaders are terminated.	
June 8	Laurent Proulx, who had successfully obtained an injunction to force his professor to teach, drops his anthropology course.	
June 22	Between 3,000 and 5,000 people take part in a demonstration in Quebec City, while thousands of people join a demonstration in Montreal.	
July 13	The student association CLASSE releases its manifesto titled "Nous sommes avenir" ("We Are the Future") and launches a province-wide tour to explain its positions to the public.	Follow-on information warfare

Note: The preparation stage was ongoing before these dates as student unions prepared for the strike.
a CLASSE stands for Coalition large de l'association pour une solidarité syndicale étudiante (Large Coalition of the Association for Student Unions' Solidarity).

certain time periods (e.g., topic of tweets, frequency of publication) (see Table 2.2). However, we are confident that the three-step sampling procedure developed for this project limited selection biases. Tweets were collected during the same time periods on fifteen key days marked by known events, thus reducing the likelihood of a biased data set.

Findings

As shown in Figure 2.1, #ggi tweeters engaged in four main modes of protest in the Twitterverse (for a more detailed look at these dynamics of protest, see Raynauld et al. 2016). First, the mass circulation of strike-related information constituted by far the most frequent form of #ggi tweeting on all days considered for our study. Second, the most popular form of protest was sharing opinions, some of which were in support of the strike, whereas others were in opposition to it. Third, Twitter's

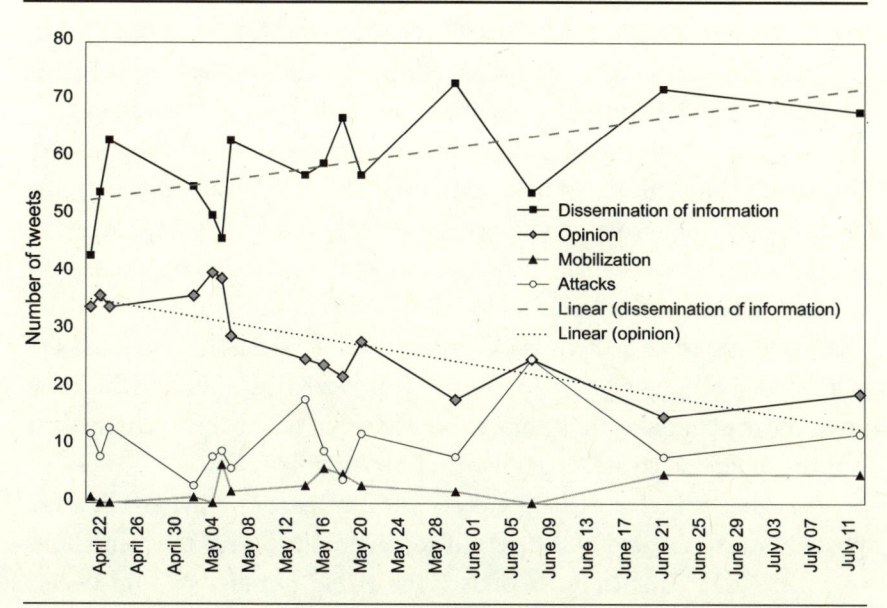

FIGURE 2.1
Trends in #ggi tweeting on fifteen days between April 22 and July 11, 2012

functionalities were leveraged by #ggi tweeters to launch, organize, promote, or coordinate, often in real time, mobilization efforts. In some cases, it could have generated and cultivated support among their followers and, to some degree, casual observers. Fourth, #ggi activists turned to Twitter to attack political opponents and journalists, for example by criticizing their actions or positions.

A closer look at the #ggi data set provides insights into the evolution of Twitter-based protest as the Maple Spring unfolded. It shows that larger volumes of #ggi tweets serving a mass information dissemination function were posted on days toward the end of the period considered for our study. Conversely, more #ggi posts featuring opinion or commentary were shared toward the beginning of the period considered (see the trend lines in Figure 2.1). This is consistent with Hussain and Howard's (2013) work on cycles of digital grassroots protest. The first two phases (preparation and ignition) are generally centred on the framing of problems and demands, establishment or reinforcement of protest networks, and building public awareness of the cause. These activities are more likely to generate opinions and commentary and less likely to be centred on information dispersion.

As the Maple Spring unfolded, levels of opinion-based #ggi tweeting declined as tweeters had a more reactionary approach to the strike. Conversely, levels of news or fact-based tweeting increased over time. Specifically, #ggi tweets featured updates on different facets of the Maple Spring, including negotiations between government officials and student leaders, introduction of bills, demonstrations, and mass arrests. In other words, they offered an information-heavy discourse, reframing and in some cases countering legacy media's strike coverage, generally supportive of the government and police forces. For example, the following post highlighting the reaction of CLASSE to Bill 78 was published on May 21, 2012: "Fin du pt de presse de la classe: C'est pas une loi spéciale qui va nous faire plier. Grève génér – #ggi live on http://t.co/h9crKvQo" ("End of the press conference of la classe: It is not a special law that will make us change our position. General strike – #ggi live on http://t.co/h9crKvQo").

A higher number of #ggi tweets with at least one hyperlink were posted toward the end of the period considered here (see the trend lines in Figure 2.1). This trend is tied to the rising number of #ggi tweets serving information dissemination purposes shared toward the end of the period studied. These tweets were far more likely to include at least one hyperlink, often pointing to legacy media's digital resources, than tweets serving opinion sharing, mobilizing, or attacking. Specifically, #ggi tweeters shared links pointing to news media content discussing different aspects of the strike, such as the work of police forces, negotiations between the government and student unions, or celebrities' views on the Maple Spring debate (120 links embedded in #ggi tweets), as well as providing opinion and commentary through editorials, readers' letters, or cartoons (82 links embedded in #ggi tweets) (for more details, see Raynauld et al. 2016). This can be viewed as consistent with the climax phase of digital contention. Protesters reacted in response to established political and media elites' framing of student unions' demands and actions (Hussain and Howard 2013).

Legacy media's coverage of the Maple Spring, which tended for the most part to be unfavourable to students and their supporters (Giroux and Charlton 2014a, 2014b), played a central role in shaping the dynamics of political protest in the Twitterverse. #ggi tweets often recalibrated the public discourse by contrasting legacy media's generally negative coverage of the strike with a more positive vision of the Maple Spring. For example, the following post criticizing journalists' work was shared on June 22, 2012: "@vergas22 La manipulation des masses par les mass-médias. Consentement fabriqué, #ggi" ("@vergas22 The manipulation of masses by mass media. Fabricated consent, #ggi").

Another tweet raising concerns about news media coverage of the student strike was retweeted several times that day: "J'aime toujours pas ce que j'entends aux médias, je trouve que leur contenu est très dangereux pour la santé mental!! #ggi" ("I still don't like what I hear from the media, I think their content is very dangerous for our mental health!! #ggi").

A large number of tweets comprising at least one hyperlink providing information contextualizing the Maple Spring were shared on days when major strike-related announcements were made by the government or student unions (May 17 and May 31, 2012). This type of tweeting, which offered a positive outlook on the strike and student demands, is consistent with the protest and international buy-in phases (Hussain and Howard 2013). For example, the following tweet, posted on May 31, 2012 (toward the end of the period considered here), offered details on international support for the student strike: "Solidarity Forever: Occupy Throws Support Behind Struggles in Quebec, Mexico http://t.co/TdOWEmyK #1u #p2 #labor #ows #occupy #ggi."

The review of #ggi data also demonstrated that strike-related news or events that happened on days considered in our study (see Table 2.2) affected patterns of #ggi-related information dispersion, mobilization, and organization. Clear spikes in the volume of #ggi tweets serving mobilization functions were observed on days marked by strike-related announcements by Quebec officials or student unions or updates about negotiations between student leaders and government officials. This is consistent with the ambient political engagement hypothesis. In response to the introduction of Bill 78 by the Liberal government, the following post, which comprised a hyperlink pointing to a Facebook page with strike-related calls for demonstrations in front of the Quebec National Assembly, was retweeted on several occasions on May 17, 2012: "Ce soir à 20h, encore une fois, devant l' #assnat, Dénonçons ce projet de loi spéciale!

#nonàlaloispéciale #GGI http://t.co/g5CTys61" ("RT @Sapaq23: Tonight at 8pm, again, in front of l' #assnat, let's denounce this special bill! #nonàlaloispeciale #GGI http://t.co/g5CTys61").

As shown in Figure 2.1, higher volumes of #ggi tweets serving an attack function were observed on days marked by news of verbal or physical confrontations between student leaders or activists and individuals or organizations associated with the more traditional political sphere. For example, several tweets featured attacks against journalist Claude Poirier after he criticized the student protest. A qualitative review of the posts by #ggi tweeters showed that they tended to have a reactionary approach to confrontational moments during the strike and shared tweets that were more aggressive and, to some extent, emotional. As the strike unfolded, more hashtags serving a self-expression function (e.g., emotion and commentary), such as #corruption, #collusion, and #repression, were embedded in #ggi tweets. These hashtags were used for sharing commentaries and emotions rather than for joining a specific conversation or for tagging content related to the student strike. Hashtags embedded in #ggi tweets became increasingly hostile as negotiations between government representatives and student leaders grew more tense and difficult as the strike continued. For example, the following hashtags were embedded in #ggi posts: #OffreDeMarde (#ShittyOffer), #CharestDémissionne (CharestResign), and #LibérauxCorrompus (#CorruptedLiberals).

Finally, there was an evolution of the issues discussed in #ggi tweets as the Maple Spring unfolded. Whereas #ggi tweeters focused on police forces, violence, and ongoing negotiations in the early days of the student strike, they shared more posts discussing matters related to the legacy media's coverage of the Maple Spring in its later stages.

TRENDING IN CANADA

In this chapter, we have identified, characterized, and analyzed trends in protest action in the Twitterverse in the context of the Quebec student-led strike in 2012 against higher tuition fees. We have unpacked how different endogenous and exogenous factors shaped dynamics of strike-related political and civic engagement in the Twitterverse as the strike emerged, gained traction, and wound down by late summer 2012. We have also explored the evolution of the Maple Spring by considering cycles of political protest online following the work of Hussain and Howard (2013) and the digital ambient political engagement hypothesis. In doing so, we have filled theoretical and methodological gaps in the current academic literature. The overwhelming majority of scholarly works on social media and political protest, both in Canada and in other countries, have taken a predominantly holistic approach and explored grassroots political protest phenomena as a whole or uses of specific Web 2.0 media channels for contestation. In other words, they have treated social media–fuelled protests as stand-alone phenomena instead of constantly evolving processes. We have brought to light how patterns of Maple Spring–related political contention in the Twitterverse evolved over fifteen key days across a time period considered to be the height of the 2012 Quebec student strike.

The in-depth analysis of #ggi data reveals significant transformations in dynamics of strike-related activist communication and engagement in the Twitterverse as the Maple Spring unfolded. The analysis shows that #ggi-related political engagement followed the course of the six-phase cycle of digital grassroots protest. More importantly, it identifies clear signs of rapid-fire ambient digital political engagement – which can affect the direction, intensity, and nature of modes of political action – fuelled and shaped by usually short-term contextual factors often specific to individual #ggi tweeters. Patterns of #ggi tweeting morphed progressively over the strike as tweets focused on the overall strike, specific events, and its protagonists that offset and, in some cases, countered the mass media coverage of the Maple Spring (see Giroux and Charlton 2014a, 2014b). Although there were higher volumes of opinion- and commentary-driven tweets in the early days of the protest movement than toward the end, the data show the opposite dynamic when it comes to information-sharing tweets.

Twitter was used by a variety of actors with often highly specific interests and objectives to take part in #ggi-related political engagement, including elected officials, police departments, labour and student unions, legacy media, and ordinary citizens. It allowed for the circulation of tweets on a diverse range of issues and events, some of which did not relate to the Quebec student strike. Twitter provided an alternative to formal political and media elites' discourses, for the most part unfavourable to student protesters, their allies, and their cause. In this sense, it fostered an open discursive environment mostly outside the purview of established power structures.

Although the Maple Spring did not lead to the emergence of transformative Twitter-based modes of political engagement different from offline-based patterns of political action (Van Laer and Van Aelst 2010), it did lead to the morphing of political action over time as students' interests and objectives shifted in response to the natural unfolding of the strike coupled with short- and medium-term contextual factors. These factors included decisions and announcements by the Quebec government, dynamics of negotiations between student leaders and government officials, and clashes between police forces and protesters during demonstrations in the streets of major Quebec cities. Again this supports the ambient digital political engagement hypothesis introduced in this chapter. It suggests that #ggi tweeters' political engagement on Twitter was deeply influenced by their exposure to and understanding of public information flows and decentralized political action, both online and offline, related to the strike, whether it was voluntary or involuntary. Building on this observation, we argue that social media are contributing to the ever-evolving state of ambient digital political engagement, constantly reshaping all facets of protest movements as they unfold. This can affect levels of mobilization, awareness, and understanding of political issues and events as well as modes of social media–based and, by extension, offline political engagement.

Although Twitter was still in its infancy as a tool for grassroots politicking in Quebec in 2012 (CEFRIO 2012), its structural and functional properties made political engagement more spontaneous, informed, and ambient. It enabled Maple Springers and their opponents to be active politically on their own terms. More importantly, it allowed them to take part in a larger debate, mobilizing formal and informal political players with different preferences, interests, and objectives. As a system of awareness fostering greater connectivity to the immediate political environment, Twitter enabled its users to be engaged in all facets of the Maple Spring that were of interest and made sense to them at the moment. It allowed them to keep track of and, in some cases, take part in strike-related debates, discourses, and protest initiatives, both online and offline. These conditions appear to be conducive to connective leadership, which can be understood as decentralized, highly fragmented, and constantly evolving patterns of "inviting, connecting, steering, and stimulating, rather than directing, commanding, and proclaiming" (Poell et al. 2016, 1009). This type of leadership can reshape how political protests materialize and evolve. More work to explore this hypothesis is required. Our conclusions address theoretical and methodological gaps in the academic literature related to social media and protest in liberal democracies such as Canada. Further research could help to unpack the evolution of the manifestation of political protest in the social mediascape as well as its evolution in different types of democracies.

NOTES

1 This French expression can be translated into English as "general and vocational college." CEGEPs can be defined as "publicly funded or private postsecondary educational institutions providing students with pre-university education as well as more skill-based programs for students intending to join the workforce without going to university."
2 As of January 2015, 25 percent of all Canadians reported using Twitter an average of five hours per week or less than one hour every day (Forum Research 2015).
3 As of July 2015, 10 percent of Quebec adults had at least one Twitter account (CEFRIO 2015).
4 The expression ggi stands for *grève générale illimitée* ("unlimited general strike").
5 Approximately 26.3 percent of all #ggi tweets collected during the first step of the sampling process were shared on these fifteen days.

REFERENCES

Bastos, Marcos T., Dan Mercea, and Arthur Charpentier. 2015. "Tents, Tweets, and Events: The Interplay between Ongoing Protests and Social Media." *Journal of Communication* 65, 2: 320–50.

Bégin-Caouette, Olivier, and Glen A. Jones. 2014. "Student Organizations in Canada and Quebec's 'Maple Spring.'" *Studies in Higher Education* 39, 3: 412–25.

Bennett, Lance W. 2012. "The Personalization of Politics: Political Identity, Social Media, and Changing Patterns of Participation." *The ANNALS of the American Academy of Political and Social Science* 644, 1: 20–39.

Bimber, Bruce. 2012. "Digital Media and Citizenship." In *The SAGE Handbook of Political Communication*, edited by H.A. Semetko and M. Scammell, 115–26. Thousand Oaks, CA: Sage.

Bonenfant, Maude. 2013. *Le printemps québécois: Une anthologie*. Montréal: Écosociété.

Callison, Candis, and Alfred Hermida. 2015. "Dissent and Resonance: #IdleNoMore as an Emergent Middle Ground." *Canadian Journal of Communication* 40, 4: 695–716.

CEFRIO. 2012. "Netendances 2012: Les médias sociaux ancrés dans les habitudes des Québécois." *CEFRIO.* http://www.cefrio.qc.ca/media/uploader/NETendances1-reseauxsociauxLR.pdf.

–. 2015. "Les médias sociaux: Plus présents dans le processus d'achat des Québécois." *CEFRIO.* http://www.cefrio.qc.ca/netendances/les-medias-sociaux-plus-presents-dans-le-processus-d-achat-des-quebecois/plateformes-sociales-utilisees-par-les-adultes-quebecois/#facebook-et-youtube-au-dessus-de-la-melee.

Clark, Lynn Schofield. 2016. "Participants on the Margins: # BlackLivesMatter and the Role that Shared Artifacts of Engagement Played among Minoritized Political Newcomers on Snapchat, Facebook, and Twitter." *International Journal of Communication* 10, 26: 235–53.

Croeser, Sky, and Tim Highfield. 2014. "Occupy Oakland and #oo: Uses of Twitter within the Occupy Movement." *First Monday* 19, 3. http://firstmonday.org/ojs/index.php/fm/article/view/4827.

Della Porta, Donatella, and Alice Mattoni. 2014. *Spreading Protest: Social Movements in Times of Crisis.* Colchester, UK: ECPR Press.

Dufour, Pascale, and Louis-Philippe Savoie. 2014. "Quand les mouvements sociaux changent le politique: Le cas du mouvement étudiant de 2012 au Québec." *Canadian Journal of Political Science* 47, 3: 475–502.

Fortin, Claude. 2014. "The Maple Spring as the Background for the Flourishing of the Fifth Estate in Québec." *Stream: Culture/Politics/Technology* 6, 1: 23–52.

Forum Research. 2015. "Instagram Tops in User Satisfaction." *Forum Research.* http://poll.forumresearch.com/post/213/facebook-leads-in-penetration-linkedin-shows-most-growth/.

Freelon, Deen G., Charlton D. McIlwain, and Meredith D. Clark. 2016. "Beyond the Hashtags: #Ferguson, #Blacklivesmatter, and the Online Struggle for Offline Justice." *Center for Media and Social Impact.* http://archive.cmsimpact.org/sites/default/files/beyond_the_hashtags_2016.pdf.

Giroux, Daniel, and Sebastien Charlton. 2014a. "Les médias et la crise étudiante: Traitement du conflit par la presse quotidienne montréalaise." Centre d'études sur les médias, Université Laval.

–. 2014b. "Les médias et la crise étudiante: Traitement du conflit par les réseaux de télévision." Centre d'études sur les médias, Université Laval.

Gottlieb, Julian. 2015. "Protest News Framing Cycle: How the *New York Times* Covered Occupy Wall Street." *International Journal of Communication* 9: 231–53.

Hensby, Alexander. 2017. "Open Networks and Secret Facebook Groups: Exploring Cycle Effects on Activists' Social Media Use in the 2010/11 UK Student Protests." *Social Movement Studies* 16, 4: 466–78.

Hermida, Alfred. 2012. "Tweets and Truth: Journalism as a Discipline of Collaborative Verification." *Journalism Practice* 6, 5–6: 659–68.

Hussain, Muzammil M., and Philip N. Howard. 2013. "What Best Explains Successful Protest Cascades? ICTs and the Fuzzy Causes of the Arab Spring." *International Studies Review* 15, 1: 48–66.

Jochems, Sylvie, Mélanie Millette, and Josiane Millette. 2013. "Hybridization of Engagement Practices: Use of Communications Technology during the Quebec Red Square Movement." *Networking Knowledge: Journal of the MeCCSA Postgraduate Network* 6, 3: 38–56.

Jordan, Gerard, Megan Pope, Patrick Wallis, and Srividya Iyer. 2015. "The Relationship between Openness to Experience and Willingness to Engage in Online Political Participation Is Influenced by News Consumption." *Social Science Computer Review* 33, 2: 181–97.

Khazraee, Emad, and James Losey. 2016. "Evolving Repertoires: Digital Media Use in Contentious Politics." *Communication and the Public* 1, 1: 39–55.

LeFebvre, Rebecca K., and Crystal Armstrong. 2018. "Grievance-Based Social Movement Mobilization in the #Ferguson Twitter Storm." *New Media and Society* 20, 1: 8–28.

Marcoux, Marianne, and David Lusseau. 2014. "The Influence of Repressive Legislation on the Structure of a Social Media Network." *EPL (Europhysics Letters)* 104, 5: 1–4.

Ménard, Marc-Antoine. 2012. "Conflit étudiant: La 'twittosphère' passée au crible." *Radio-Canada*, July 4. http://ici.radio-canada.ca/nouvelles/societe/2012/07/04/002-analyse-tweets-conflit-etudiant-beauchesne.shtml.

Nadeau-Dubois, Gabriel. 2013. *Tenir tête*. Montréal: Lux.

Poell, Thomas. 2014. "Social Media and the Transformation of Activist Communication: Exploring the Social Media Ecology of the 2010 Toronto G20 Protests." *Information, Communication, and Society* 17, 6: 716–31.

Poell, Thomas, Rasha Abdulla, Bernhard Rieder, Robbert Woltering, and Zack Liesbeth. 2016. "Protest Leadership in the Age of Social Media." *Information, Communication, and Society* 19, 7: 994–1014.

Raynauld, Vincent, and Josh Greenberg. 2014. "Tweet, Click, Vote: Twitter and the 2010 Ottawa Municipal Election." *Journal of Information Technology and Politics* 11, 4: 412–34.

Raynauld, Vincent, Mireille Lalancette, and Sofia Tourigny-Koné. 2016. "Political Protest 2.0: Social Media and the 2012 Student Strike in the Province of Quebec, Canada." *French Politics* 14, 1: 1–29.

Raynauld, Vincent, Emmanuelle Richez, and Katie Boudreau Morris. 2018. "Canada Is #IdleNoMore: Exploring Dynamics of Indigenous Political and Civic Protest in the Twitterverse." *Information, Communication, and Society* 21, 4: 626–42.

Scherman, André, Arturo Arriagada, and Sebastian Valenzuela. 2015. "Student and Environmental Protests in Chile: The Role of Social Media." *Politics* 35, 2: 151–71.

Simard, Marc. 2013. *Histoire du mouvement étudiant québécois 1956–2013: Des trois braves aux carrés rouges*. Québec: Presses de l'Université Laval.

Sorochan, Cayley. 2012. "The Québec Student Strike: A Chronology." *Theory and Event* 15, 3. muse.jhu.edu/article/484441.

Spiegel, Jennifer B. 2015. "Rêve Général Illimité? The Role of Creative Protest in Transforming the Dynamics of Space and Time during the 2012 Quebec Student Strike." *Antipode* 47, 3: 770–91.

Sysomos. 2010. "Worldwide Twitter Data: Number of Twitter Users by Country." *Sysomos*. http://sysomos.com/inside-twitter/number-twitter-users-country.

Theocharis, Yannis, Will Lowe, Jan W. van Deth, and Gema M. García-Albacete. 2015. "Using Twitter to Mobilize Protest Action: Online Mobilization Patterns and Action Repertoires in the Occupy Wall Street, Indignados, and Aganaktismenoi Movements." *Information, Communication, and Society* 18, 2: 202–20.

Turcotte, André, and Vincent Raynauld. 2014. "Boutique Populism: The Emergence of the Tea Party Movement in the Age of Digital Politics." In *Political Marketing in the U.S.*, edited by J. Lees-Marshment, B. Conley, and K. Cosgrove, 161–84. New York: Routledge.

Van Laer, Jeroen, and Peter Van Aelst. 2010. "Internet and Social Movement Action Repertoires: Opportunities and Limitations." *Information, Communication, and Society* 13, 8: 1146–71.

Vis, Farida. 2013. "Twitter as a Reporting Tool for Breaking News: Journalists Tweeting the 2011 UK Riots." *Digital Journalism* 1, 1: 27–47.

Vissers, Sara, and Dietlind Stolle. 2014. "Spill-Over Effects between Facebook and On/Offline Political Participation? Evidence from a Two-Wave Panel Study." *Journal of Information Technology and Politics* 11, 3: 259–75.

White, Britany, Heather Castleden, and Anatoliy Gruzd. 2015. "Talking to Twitter Users: Motivations behind Twitter Use on the Alberta Oil Sands and the Northern Gateway Pipeline." *First Monday* 20, 1. http://www.ojphi.org/ojs/index.php/fm/article/view/5404/4196.

3

Bytes and Bitumen
A Case Study of Mediated Discourse on, and Digital Advocacy for, TransCanada's Proposed Energy East Pipeline

PATRICK McCURDY AND JACOB GROSHEK

The Energy East project is dead. On October 5, 2017, TransCanada publicly announced that, after four years of pushing to make the project happen, it was no longer pursuing the $15.7-billion pipeline project. Environmental activists celebrated the announcement, framing it as yet another victory for the "keep it in the ground" and fossil fuel–free movement. Noted campaigner Bill McKibben (2017) tweeted "another one bites the dust – TransCanada terminates Energy East Pipeline project from the tarsands." Meanwhile, oil sands supporters saw the move as a travesty. Then premier of Saskatchewan Brad Wall (2017) tweeted "#EnergyEast dead. 1000s new jobs lost. Cda to keep importing foreign oil. West can't get oil to tidewater. Mtl mayor calls it 'major victory.'" If built, this 4,600-kilometre pipeline proposed by TransCanada would have transported approximately 1.1 million barrels of crude oil and bitumen (a black viscous mixture of hydrocarbons, a residue of petroleum distillation) per day from Alberta to the port city of Saint John, New Brunswick (TransCanada 2016a).

Although oil sands supporters were quick to point the finger at environmentalists for killing Energy East and, indeed, environmentalists were quick to accept responsibility, the reality had more to do with economics. Energy East was proposed in 2013, and since then the price of oil crashed, and the cost of oil sands projects increased, but with the 2016 election of Donald Trump as president of the United States new life was breathed into TransCanada's other project, Keystone XL. However, as of publication, Keystone XL continues to face legal challenges and activist opposition, putting its future in doubt. Killing Energy East, as a University of Alberta economist wrote in the *Globe and Mail,* was a business decision (Leach 2017). Nonetheless, the fate of Energy East, and that of the oil sands more generally, have been the subject of a relentless mediated struggle among industry, politicians, and civil society, all of which are actively trying to shape public perception of the costs and benefits of oil sands development. Indeed, in October 2018, Canadian Conservatives marked the one-year anniversary of Energy East's death with a lament for an unrealized nation-building project and a promise of pipeline resurrection should they seize federal power.

While politicians continue to espouse Energy East pipedreams, in this chapter we explore digital debates on Energy East that took place from June 2013 to June 2016. Our interest in the debate over Energy East is grounded in a view of the digital mediascape as a site and source of political struggle. We take a broader look at mediated discourse on Energy East through an analysis of social media content, Twitter in particular, posted between June 1, 2013, and June 1, 2016, and the users who posted this content. In particular, our analyses examine trends related to the status of influential users online and offline, their stances on Energy East, geolocation, and engagement patterns among users, as well as networked relationships of content and how this discourse developed and changed over time. We argue that, though social media platforms can create spaces for public discourse, the quality of that discourse is questionable. We suggest that, instead of fostering a measured debate on Energy East, social media were used primarily as a tool to connect with and mobilize an already sympathetic and bifurcated public. Extending from this, our conclusion reiterates the dangers of reifying social media platforms as digital public spheres.

Our argument is based on the premise that the mediated representations of social and political issues are both sites and sources of political contention (Castells 2009; Couldry 2013). In the broadest sense, media create representational arenas in which actors with competing ideas and resources actively engage in "symbolic contests," with each party deliberately packaging and framing issues to best represent its stance and stake in the matter at hand (Gamson and Wolfsfeld 1993).

Social media comprise one such arena in which contemporary debates take place. To be clear, we share Chadwick's (2013, 4) characterization of the media environment as a "hybrid media system" that is "built upon interactions among older and newer media logics – where logics are defined as technologies, genres, norms, behaviours and organizational forms – in the reflexively connected fields of media and politics." Moreover, we view the realm and logic of social media as entangled with, and doubly articulated within, the material reality of everyday life. That is, social media inform and influence our material realities while our material realities simultaneously underwrite and influence our social media practices.

As a means to untangle conceptually the material from the digital, Van Laer and Van Aelst (2010) suggest differentiating between two types of internet-enabled collective action. First are "real" actions whereby technology is used to support activities in a material reality, such as demonstrations or protest camps, and second are "virtual" actions that are "internet based, such as email bombs, websites, and online petitions" (1149) (see also the chapter by Raynauld, Lalancette, and Tourigny-Koné in this volume). Debate on the utility of such "internet-based political action has grown and continues to be a source of contention" (e.g., Morozov 2009). Nonetheless, Van Laer and Van Aelst's distinction is helpful in trying to understand trends on Twitter and linking them back to the political realities of social actors.

A large and growing body of academic scholarship on the social media platform Twitter as a site of political engagement already exists (see Weller et al. 2014). Of note is Poell and Borra's (2012) study of how social media were used as platforms for alternative journalism reporting on the G20 protests in Toronto during 2010 (also see Poell's chapter in this volume). Although the authors acknowledge the merits of social media, their conclusion questions and problematizes the democratic worth of "alternative journalism" via social media, reasserted by Poell and van Dijck (2015). Further attention has also been given to dynamics of the management of social media accounts (Gerbaudo 2016), shifts in campaign practices (Gibson 2015; Karlsen and Enjolras 2016), and collective action (Gerbaudo and Treré 2015).

Within this rich framework of academic activity, we advance here an analysis of digital discourse and campaigning related to the oil sands as a divisive but distinctly Canadian issue. Proponents of Energy East often highlighted the potential economic benefits (Sweeny 2010) and political virtues of developing "ethical oil" (Levant 2010). Meanwhile, critics warned of the environmental costs (Gailus 2012; Marsden 2008) as well as the economic myopia of an economy based on fossil fuels (Nikiforuk 2010). While advocates and activists continue to debate the merits of developing (or not) the vast bitumen deposits in northern Alberta, fewer scholars have examined how oil sands have been framed either in the news media or by interested stakeholders. Of that relevant work, scholars have often focused on journalists or news media output (Gunster and Saurette 2014; Paskey, Steward, and Williams 2013; Perron 2013; Way 2011).

Although such scholarship is both insightful and valuable, there remains a palpable gap in studies examining online campaigning and discourse related to the oil sands. Our study is a contribution toward filling this gap. Hestres (2014) analyzed the "climate advocacy ecosystem" of climate change advocates using the proposed Keystone XL Pipeline as his case study. Based on qualitative interviews with key eNGO stakeholders, Hestres captured the extent to which social media have become a key tool for mobilizing unconcerned publics. White, Castleden, and Gruzd (2015) also conducted qualitative interviews but focused on Twitter users who employed the #tarsands. These scholars wanted to see whether the #tarsands amounted to a "green virtual sphere" by providing a digital arena in which to access and debate environmental issues of concern. Their findings were mixed because interviewees were conscious of social media monitoring, but the authors concluded that Twitter could eventually be used for environmental consultation.

Although the merits of using Twitter for this purpose can be debated, the platform remains a site of political discussion regarding the fate of Canada's tar/oil sands. Consequently, our research offers a modest contribution to analyses of the features and contents of political debate on social media, and Twitter in particular, as they evolve, unfold, and trend. Moreover, our mixed-methods approach, which combines big data with qualitative interpretive analysis, offers an avenue for additional scholarship interested in critically examining the online realm of political actors and social media users, their dynamics, reach, and impact. Through our analysis of social media discussions pertaining to one of Canada's largest proposed energy projects, we advance understanding of trending topics and public discourse. Moreover, the data offer insights into the political players – both at the centre and at the periphery – of these discussions and align key moments with social media discourse on Energy East to the material reality of energy politics in Canada.

CASE STUDY

The Alberta oil sands, also referred to as bitumen sands or tar sands, are a vast deposit (142,200 square kilometres) of sand, clay sand, and heavy oil known as bitumen. Alberta's bitumen sands are the third largest proven resource of oil in the world at 166 billion barrels of oil (Government of Alberta 2016). Currently, the oil sands produce 2.4 million barrels of oil per day (BPD), which account for 55 percent of crude production in Canada (CAPP 2015a; Government of Alberta 2016). Bitumen production is anticipated to grow, with the Canadian Association of Petroleum Producers (CAPP) projecting 3.08 million BPD by 2020 and 4 million BPD by 2030 (CAPP 2015b, ii). Unlike conventional light crude oil, bitumen is incredibly difficult to refine. Recovering and producing oil from bitumen require massive and extremely costly infrastructure (Council of Canadians 2015; Greenpeace Canada 2015), though industry reports indicate that such costs and inefficiencies are declining (CAPP 2015a). Greenhouse gas emissions also remain a visible concern (Dyer, Grant, and Angen 2013).

With these concerns in mind, environmental and climate change campaigners have concentrated on the projected increases in oil sands production and emission as a political, symbolic, and discursive opportunity to discuss climate change and tie the issue of oil sands production to unsustainable carbon-based lifestyles. Early campaigning against Alberta's bitumen sands involved "image events" (DeLuca 2005) such as banner drops at open-pit bitumen mines and symbolic protests in front of or even inside oil-related political events and conferences (McCurdy 2017, 2018). However, more recently, oil sands opponents have targeted pipelines as the primary means used to deliver the oil sands to tidewater.

Specifically, activists have reacted to moves to expand and improve Canada's capacity to pump diluted bitumen out of landlocked Alberta by protesting projects such as the proposed Keystone XL, Trans Mountain, and Northern Gateway Pipelines at events within and outside Canada's national borders. These projects have also faced political and legal difficulties. The south-running Keystone XL Pipeline was initially rejected by President Barack Obama in November 2015 but resurrected and approved by the Trump administration in May 2017 but faces ongoing legal challenges. In addition, the western-running Northern Gateway Pipelines had their approval revoked by the Federal Court of Appeal in June 2016 for failing to consult sufficiently with affected First Nations communities living along the route of the pipeline (Proctor 2016). In January 2017, Enbridge formally withdrew Northern Gateway from British Columbia's environmental assessment, thereby ending the proposed project (Hoekstra 2017). Meanwhile, despite ongoing opposition from Indigenous groups, environmentalists, and local and provincial politicians, Kinder Morgan's Trans Mountain Pipeline expansion project plows ahead. In May 2016, the Trudeau Liberal government approved Trans Mountain subject to 156 National Energy Board conditions (Shaw 2016). In May 2017, following a provincial election in British Columbia, the NDP and Green Party formed a coalition government unified in its opposition to the Trans Mountain Pipeline. One year later, in May 2018, against the backdrop of rising interprovincial tensions between British Columbia's anti-pipeline stance and Alberta's pro-pipeline position, the federal Liberals announced their intention to purchase the Trans Mountain Pipeline from Kinder Morgan for $4.5 billion (Canadian Press 2018). The political struggles over Trans Mountain continue, and pipeline politics will no doubt remain an ongoing issue of contention.

Returning to Energy East, it was against the backdrop of rising political contention over Canada's fossil fuel use that vested political and financial capital mobilized and sought to build the now cancelled pipeline. With a projected cost of over $15 billion Canadian, Energy East would have begun in Hardisty, Alberta, and travelled 4,600 kilometres to Saint John, New Brunswick (TransCanada 2016a). If completed, the pipeline would have had the capacity to transport up to 1.1 million BPD of several types of crude oil (TransCanada 2016a). Energy East was selected specifically for our research because it was a major national pipeline announced when McCurdy (2019) was already conducting a research project on oil sands campaigning (see www.mediatoil.ca). So there was the opportunity to analyze public discourse from the initial announcement of the project.

Most attention from both TransCanada and critics, however, was on its transport of diluted bitumen (e.g., Council of Canadians 2014; Harden-Donahue 2016; TransCanada 2013b, 2016a, 2016b). As a "heavy oil," bitumen is incredibly viscous. To be transported, it must be diluted with a "lighter" petroleum product to form dilbit (TransCanada 2015a). Dilbit cannot be transformed into synthetic crude by a conventional refinery but must be handled by a specialized upgrader in Canada or abroad – by tanker – where the costs of refining are cheaper. The precise volume of oil sands dilbit that Energy East would transport remained to be seen. However, critics were quick to label Energy East as an "export" pipeline that would hasten bitumen development and thus framed Energy East as a "tar sands" pipeline (Harden-Donahue 2016).

In addition to the climate change–related concerns, critics expressed environmental concerns framing Energy East as a threat to the environment and water sources (Council of Canadians 2014). In contrast, TransCanada presented Energy East as a nation-building project and means for eastern provinces to reduce their reliance on foreign oil (TransCanada 2015b). The potential risks and rewards of Energy East were the focus of active industry and eNGO campaigning both online and offline, with its fate actively reported in the news and discussed on social media.

Methods
We began our study by collecting social media textual content that included the keywords "Energy East" via complete historical access provided by the data analytics vendor Crimson Hexagon. More specifically, we collected all posts that mentioned Energy East (with or without a hashtag) on Twitter, Facebook, Tumblr, and all major blog platforms, including WordPress, as well as chat forums and comment areas where users share opinions and exchange ideas publicly (Crimson Hexagon 2012a, 2012b). This analysis is unique in that the data collected here over this three-year time period

can be considered a full census of all publicly available social media users and content that engaged these keywords.

Although it is possible, of course, that there would be relevant posts that did not use these keywords, we maximized their explanatory capacity by using the key term that is also the official Twitter handle of TransCanada's Energy East Pipeline (@EnergyEast) as well as that which represents an accessible topical public sphere across social media platforms where all users can participate in a decentralized, nonhierarchical manner.

As a data provider, Crimson Hexagon has been similarly used for other research studies (Ampofo et al. 2015; Breese 2016), and its built-in capabilities of cluster analysis, geolocation, and machine learning have proven to be industry leading. Further details on specific algorithms can be found on the Crimson Hexagon website (see Hopkins and King 2010), but for the most part we relied on top-level analyses only to identify the most prominent users and content by frequency and/or measure of influence, such as Klout (Bode and Epstein 2015) and keyword clusters (Hopke and Simis 2017a, 2017b). Additional analyses provided here otherwise employ more qualitative and thematic approaches based on the analysis of specific user posts or content identified with the Crimson Hexagon interface. This combination of big and small data has been effectively applied in previous studies (Groshek and Al-Rawi 2013, 2015; Groshek and Engelbert 2012) and is often called on as a necessary complement in big data inquiries, which can otherwise lack context.

Findings

To begin, 121,279 posts across all social media platforms considered here – namely Twitter, Facebook, Tumblr, blogs, forums, and comment areas – were considered. Interestingly, 99 percent of all Energy East posts were from Twitter, with the other platforms combined constituting less than 1 percent of posts. In terms of time, discourse on Energy East was virtually nonexistent before June 1, 2013, with just sixty posts before that time and no public awareness easily observable on social media.

The first notable amount of activity was on June 7, 2013, with 269 posts that day, which can be attributed to premier of Alberta Alison Redford's visit to New Brunswick to lobby for the pipeline project and to deliver a speech to the provincial legislature (Bissett 2013). The issue of Energy East next peaked on social media starting August 1 and 2, 2013, with 494 and 209 posts, respectively, because TransCanada formally announced its plans to go ahead with Energy East (TransCanada 2013a).

Discussion on social media channels was relatively dormant until October 30, 2014, when there were 1,533 posts sparked by TransCanada's application to the National Energy Board (NEB) for Energy East approval (CBC 2014). On November 18, 2014, Greenpeace Canada published a leaked copy of a proposed astroturf campaign for the Energy East Pipeline authored by public relations firm Edelman.[1] This leak was significant because it revealed the extent to which public relations companies are willing to use digital resources to run and manage "grassroots" digital campaigns for corporate clients. Although Edelman's twenty-four-page document for TransCanada was just a "draft" dated May 14, 2014, many parallels can be seen with the current Energy East campaign, including email blasts, social media, online ads, a "grassroots website" to activate motivated publics, and suggestions for specific prompts and actions (e.g., commenting on social media, writing letters, and starting petitions). In essence, the campaign co-opted the tried-and-tested analogue and digital tactics of civil society for corporate ends.

In addition, when public figures speak out, social media posts are more frequent. For example, the day that Liberal prime minister Justin Trudeau announced his support for premier of Alberta Rachel Notley's Energy East Pipeline push (January 22, 2016) had the most social media content posted (2,822 posts) (Taber, McCarthy, and Fife 2016). That week then Mayor of Montreal Denis Coderre went public with his concerns about Energy East, which culminated in a meeting and press conference with Trudeau on January 26, 2016 (Feith 2016). It is also worth noting that Canadian satirist Rick Mercer (2016) released one of his trademark "Rick's Rants" criticizing Coderre and arguing that Energy East is in Canada's national interest.

The overall volume of social media posts across the three-year time frame of our study is presented in Figure 3.1. It shows a clear relation between "real" political events (Van Laer and Van Aelst 2010) and social media activity.

FIGURE 3.1
Volume of Energy East social media posts over time from June 1, 2013, through June 1, 2016

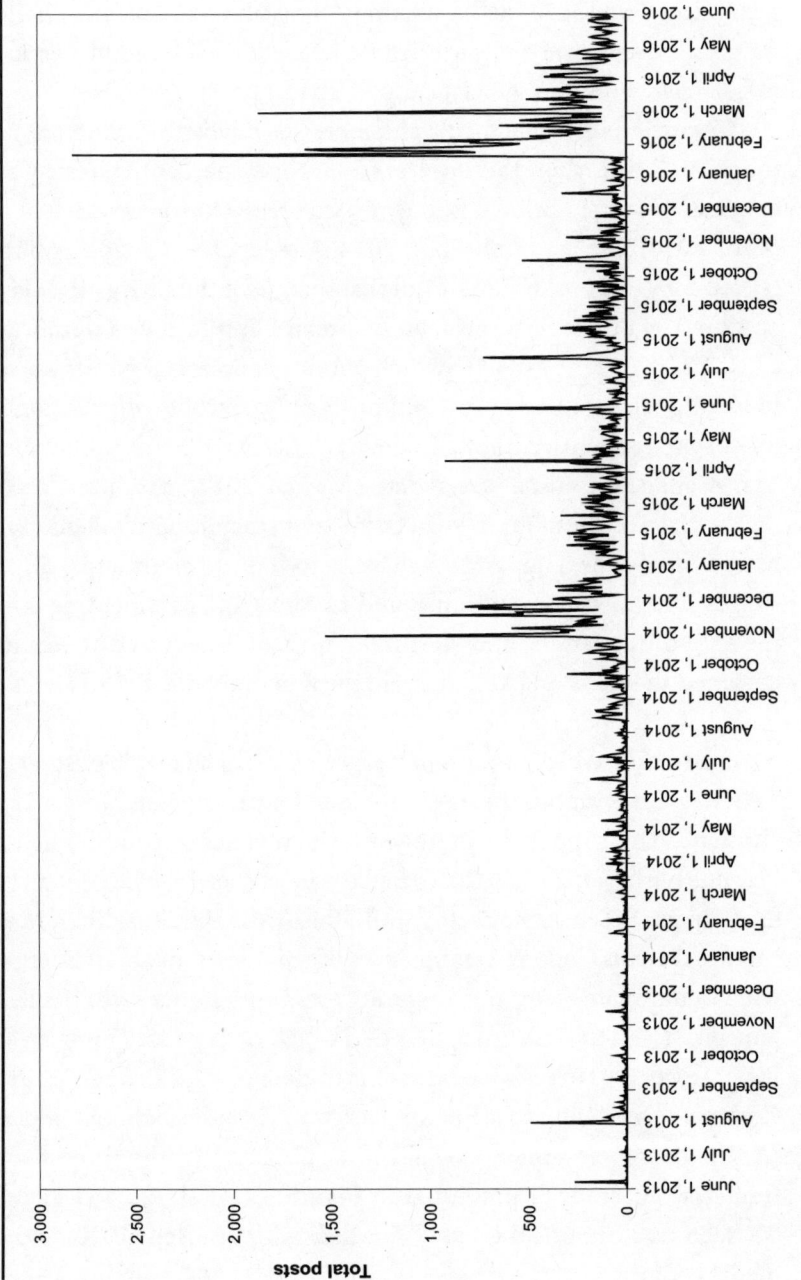

When we looked at tweets using Energy East by keyword clustering (Hopke and Simis 2017a), certain topics rose to prominence, and they connected to other topics in an overall network of distribution. Moreover, the topics and patterns discussed on Twitter map neatly to events and discussions in mainstream media and unfolding political events related to the Energy East Pipeline. A cluster graph of the most prominent keywords within the Energy East corpus in relation to one another is presented in Figure 3.2. Three vital thematic groupings or clusterings are evident in this graph and guide further study.

The most prominent word during the period studied was "pipeline," which occurred 30,649 times as a simple descriptor. The word "TransCanada," the corporation proposing to build Energy East, was next with 17,506 posts. As prominent as the term "pipelines" in Figure 3.2 is the term "Cdnpoli," an abbreviation of "Canadian Politics" and the most popular hashtag on Twitter for discussing and tagging matters related to Canadian national politics (Blevis 2013). Additional, though less prominent, political hashtags are also visible. Among them are #onpoli, used to discuss Ontario politics, and #ableg and #abpoli, both used to discuss Alberta politics. The linking of Energy East with hashtags used to discuss provincial and national politics establishes Energy East as a political issue.

The prominence of the term "tar sands" within this cluster and thus within online political discussion is also important to consider. The politically loaded term was used by campaigners who opposed bitumen extraction and the Energy East project. The association of "tar sands" with "transcanada" and "pipeline" suggests that those who opposed Energy East actively sought to situate it within the established tar sands frame. The prominence of this key term is also associated with two NGOs within a tar sands framing of Energy East. Specifically, the Twitter handles of both Environmental Defence (@envirodefence) and the Council of Canadians (@councilofcdns) are situated in this cluster, and both organizations purposefully refer to the bitumen sands as tar sands. Moreover, use of the #tarsands can be read as a means to link Energy East discussion with larger issues, such as climate change or other pipelines.

Also prominent in this first cluster is Mike Hudema (@mikehudema), an active and well-networked anti–tar sands Greenpeace campaigner.

FIGURE 3.2

Cluster graph of most prominent keywords within the Energy East corpus in relation to one another

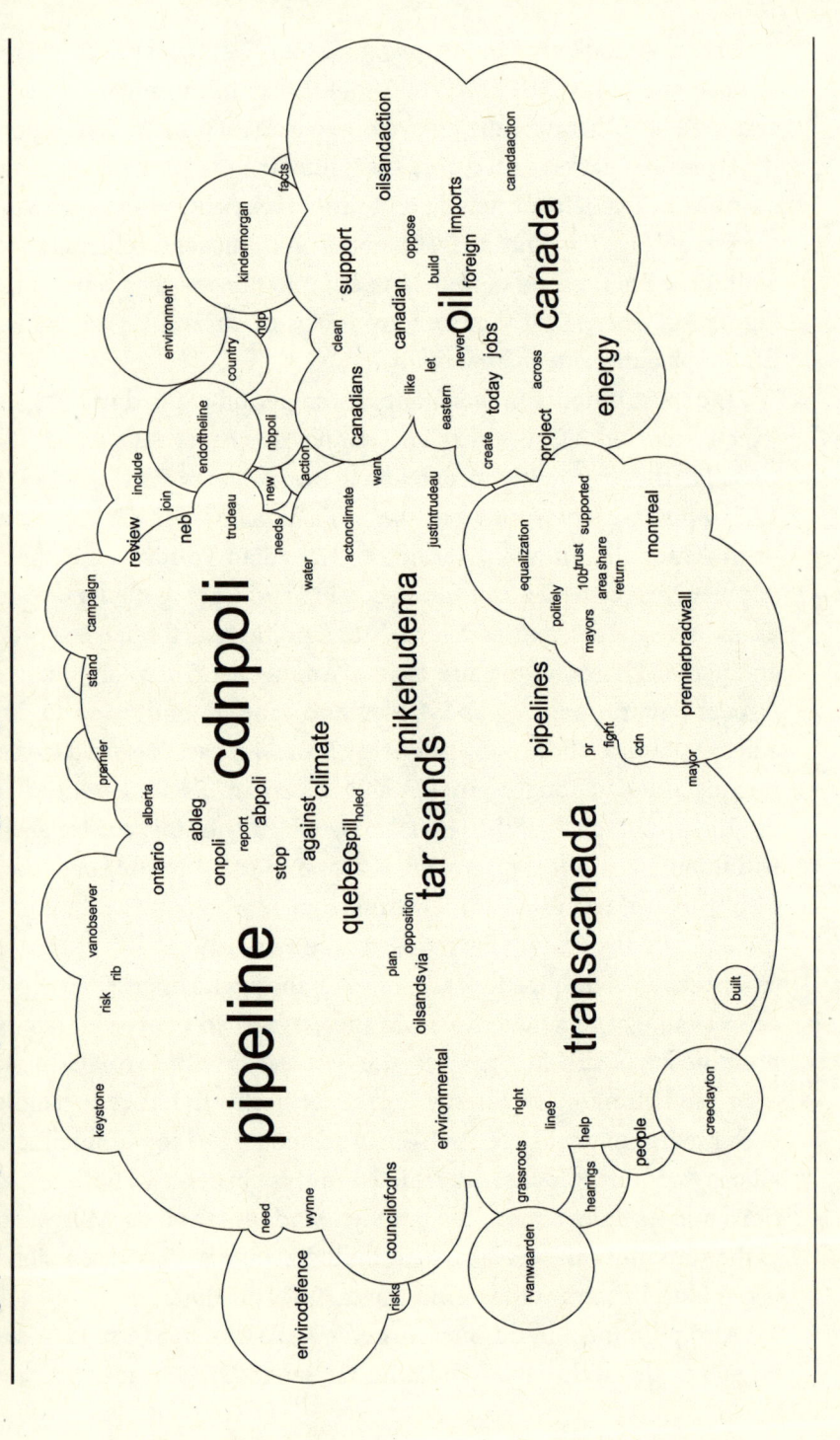

Although he was not a top tweeter by volume on Energy East (with 236 tweets in the sample), he was prominent in online discussions through retweets (RTs) and responses to his Energy East tweets. Crimson Hexagon data estimate that Hudema's tweets had over 6.4 million total potential impressions. His tweets were the most active in #EnergyEast (230+) and #cdnpoli (170+), which placed Hudema as a campaigner who took an active role in message promotion.

A second cluster of prominent keywords in Figure 3.2 is visible on the right of the graphic with the word "oil" at its centre. Within this cluster, the handles of two prominent pro–oil sands Twitter accounts are visible: @OilsandsAction and @canadaaction. These accounts are run by Canada Action, which describes itself as an "entirely volunteer-led grassroots movement encouraging Canadians to take action and work together in support of our vital natural resources sector" (Canada Action 2016). Words in this cluster are consistent with Canada Action's campaigning about Energy East and the oil sands more generally, which centres on nationalism, the economy, job creation, and reducing Canada's reliance on foreign oil imports. These key messages also parallel and complement TransCanada's own messages on Energy East (see TransCanada 2015b, 2016a, 2016b). In addition, the Twitter account @OilsandsAction produced four of the ten most retweeted tweets related to Energy East using a nationalist timbre.

A third cluster, situated in the network graph between the other two primary clusters already discussed, features "premierbradwall" and "montreal." Brad Wall (@PremierBradWall), the former premier of Saskatchewan, spoke publicly in support of Energy East. The keywords in this cluster can be linked directly to a tweet sent on January 21, 2016, by @PremierBradWall stating that "I trust Montreal area mayors will politely return their share of $10B in equalization supported by west #EnergyEast." This item was the most retweeted tweet in the data set, accruing 1,597 RTs and 1,372 likes. In fact, @PremierBradWall had three tweets in the top ten most retweeted related to Energy East. Moreover, nine of the top ten most retweeted tweets in this entire data set were supportive of Energy East, which also consisted of four tweets from pro–oil sands group @OilsandsAction and two from Alberta politician Brian Jean, leader of the Wildrose Party of

Alberta and MLA for Fort McMurray. These top RTs all came from prominent users. The sole anti–Energy East tweet among the top ten was from user @education5288 (account since suspended), referencing the leaked TransCanada public relations plan. The cluster graph used to guide accounts and topics of interest is summarized in Figure 3.2.

Although an analysis of keyword clustering provides insight into the content of messaging, which users were especially central to furthering discussion about Energy East on social media? Of course, some users have a more demonstrable "influence" that extends from their social and political roles, along with their particular audience of followers and engagement on social media, and these users are summarized to some extent by their Klout scores, outlined by Bode and Epstein (2015) and used by Crimson Hexagon to identify and rank influential users. Yet, because of the weighting given to numbers of followers, Klout scores tend to favour institutions and actors with an already established power base, such as news organizations, celebrities, and politicians. This finding holds to some extent in this instance, in which the *Globe and Mail, Toronto Star,* Greenpeace, hacktivist collective Anonymous, sci-fi author William Gibson, Environment Canada, speaker and activist Naomi Klein, CBC Radio, former premier of Alberta Alison Redford, and musician David Crosby round out the top ten highly ranked #EnergyEast users by Klout score.

Alternatively, when examining users in terms of the frequency of their posts, the ten most prolific #EnergyEast users in terms of volume are presented in Table 3.1.

The most active #EnergyEast account, @BhiveD321, was actually created by the Canadian social media marketing company BHIVE to test its ability to curate content and target specific industries and audiences. This account began posting material on January 18, 2016, and was suspended by Twitter on February 19, 2016.[2] The second most active Twitter user was @CamFenton, an anti–tar sands activist with the prominent environmental group 350.org. Meanwhile, TransCanada's own official Twitter account (@EnergyEast) had the third most tweets. Of the top ten accounts tweeting about Energy East, two can be seen as neutral, four were actively tweeting in opposition to Energy East, and four were actively tweeting in support of Energy East. This mix of users in terms of official and unofficial actors

TABLE 3.1
Top Twitter users who used #EnergyEast ranked by number of posts

Rank by volume	Twitter user handle	Number of tweets	Stance on Energy East
1	@BhiveD321	1,166	Neutral
2	@CamFenton	1,078	Anti-Energy East
3	@EnergyEast	1,030	Pro-Energy East
4	@RecruiterHouTX	874	Pro-Energy East
5	@envirodefence	569	Anti-Energy East
6	@TarSandsSolns	531	Anti-Energy East
7	@RelaxInCanada	476	Neutral
8	@rvanwaarden	352	Anti-Energy East
9	@BigBoss861988	352	Pro-Energy East
10	@littleshasta	335	Pro-Energy East

and the range of viewpoints suggest that the orientation of the discursive space on Energy East was open, at least in terms of frequency if not necessarily influence on the debate.

Concerning geographical location, 85,744 (71 percent) of all posts had identifiable locations. Of those posts, 63,920 were from Canada, followed by 17,244 from the United States and 1,177 from the United Kingdom. All other countries had less than 0.5 percent of the posts. Indeed, there have been active oil sands campaigns in Europe, including the United Kingdom, on the EU Fuel Quality Directive, which proposed labelling oil sands as a high-polluting form of oil. The proposal was eventually dropped by the European Commission after much lobbying by the Canadian government under Stephen Harper. Meanwhile, American eNGOs and campaigners set their sights on campaigning against both Keystone XL and the oil sands more generally, including Energy East as another proposed tar sands pipeline (see McCurdy 2017). So, though Energy East was framed by TransCanada as a national project, it was a topic with international reach and interest.

Perhaps unsurprisingly, Energy East was discussed the most within Canada. It is worth noting that the distribution of posts across Canada's major cities was relatively even, with Calgary having the most posts (6,124), followed by Toronto (5,496), Ottawa (4,345), Montreal (3,927), Vancouver (3,708), Edmonton (3,092), Winnipeg (1,173), Saint John (1,063), Halifax (993), and Fredericton (966). Other Canadian cities accounted for less than 2 percent of all Canadian posts with identifiable geographical information. This finding indicates that the majority of users in Canada who discussed Energy East did so from urban centres. Interestingly, though the Energy East Pipeline would have run from Hardisty, Alberta, to Saint John, New Brunswick, very few users appear to have discussed the issue from Canada's east coast.

TRENDING IN CANADIAN POLITICS

Putting these analyses in a broader context suggests certain shifts and trends in the nature of communication and political behaviour in Canada. First and foremost, though social media have clearly opened the potential for a range of stakeholders to engage and participate in political and policy debates, the social media playing field is not necessarily level, with only some platforms – in this case Twitter – meaningfully engaged with by citizens to effect change. Much like traditional political engagement strategies that rely on highly mobilized and involved activists, social media campaigning is still reliant on the same sorts of activist users who can reach a much broader audience. In fact, Crimson Hexagon data show that over the three years examined here the audience was over 3 million people. This reach, however, might or might not stimulate mobilization or lead to greater consensus among the public.

In sum, social media engagement, in the context of this study, can be conceptualized as a constraint or, to a lesser extent, an obstacle that policy makers and power holders must consider but whose impact and reach are questionable. We see evidence of that in this study, in which some of the most influential and prolific users were aligned with pre-existing power blocks, and these actors sought to leverage their existing influence in the social media sphere. Thus, though social media space might be somewhat new, the influence and presence of traditional power structures remain.

Grassroots campaigning, even that which can be more effectively facilitated through social media engagement, still faces an uphill challenge to overcome limited participation and political engagement by the public. This assertion is reflected in the fact that people in a wide geographical area of Canada who would likely be directly affected by the Energy East Pipeline were silent on social media. Indeed, of Canada's estimated 35.1 million residents, just 5.9 million (Statista 2016) were reported to be on Twitter in 2014 – just 16 percent of the entire country – and concentrated in urban areas. Those who discuss social media in terms of transforming democratic and political engagement must keep this figure in mind and acknowledge that the majority of Canadians are not directly active politically on these platforms.

Despite the relatively low numbers, it could be argued that the Twittersphere in Canada is robust and active. Indeed, as our data show, Twitter is a medium used by both those in favour of and those opposed to Energy East. However, though social media can form an arena for public discourse, especially with the hashtag functionality used to link conversations, the quality of that discourse is highly questionable. As opposed to engaging in Habermasian debate, Energy East stakeholders used the platform to mobilize and to push messages to an already sympathetic and bifurcated audience. In fact, the analysis offered in Figure 3.2 suggests that competing and polarized publics were fractured along the already established lines of the oil sands debate, trapped in the false dichotomy of environment versus economy. So there is no convincing evidence that either side "won" the social media debate or even that it won over other citizens or built in compromises to the policy itself. Consequently, though we are sympathetic to White et al.'s (2015) hope that Twitter could evolve into a public sphere for debating environmental issues, or other issues relevant to the Canadian public, we are highly skeptical of its ability to do so given the quality of discourse and polarized publics. Moreover, recent trends in energy discourse see further efforts to polarize public discourse using a populist approach to social media that is primed by affect, rooted in emotion, bifurcated, and inward looking (McCurdy 2019).

That said, previous work by both Chadwick (2013) and Groshek (2012) has pointed to transformational changes in the relationships among political actors, institutions, and democracy writ broadly. Specifically, because the perceived impact of social media on citizen mobilization has been credited with contributing to the rise of grassroots movements that allow for the rise of "counter-power" (Castells 2009), it has likewise activated a response among politicians to diffuse such potentialities by being noticeably active in the same social media spaces. The social media history of Energy East, both online and offline, makes explicit the corporate shift online in an effort to win social licence. Leaked internal documents pertaining to TransCanada's proposed media and communication strategy for Energy East reveal the resources and depths of corporate campaigning (see Greenpeace Canada 2014). These leaks and tactics demand further academic scholarship and critical reflection, which also raise the importance of mapping and understanding the corporate repertoire of digital astroturfing. Thus, the rise of targeted and digitally intrusive campaigning meant to sway public discourse combined with the algorithms of corporate social media platforms designed to influence which messages are visible or invisible to users are strong signals to researchers that, though social media platforms offer a space in which politics can be discussed, it is not a public sphere but another media battlefield.

The mixed-methods analyses reported here demonstrate how big data approaches can be combined with interpretive and more qualitative work to add insights into contested political spaces online to reveal more carefully constructed interplays of political actors and social media users. What is clear from our analysis is that discussions online correlate with events offline and that often these events spurred activities; when projects or political milestones related to Energy East transpired, online discussions also picked up, so it is especially important to draw explicit connections between material and mediated arenas.

Here contemporary politics is mediated politics. Yet there is equally a danger of reifying social media platforms of connectors, such as hashtags within them, as public spheres. They are not. Although social media have become integrated into present-day political practice, scholars must view such platforms and their use by political actors skeptically. Moreover, social media are part of a hybrid media environment situated within temporal social, political, environmental, and economic contexts. In sum, with greater opportunity for increased political engagement among citizens, political action repertoires, both among activist groups and industry or government agencies, have clearly evolved. The case study reported here crucially identifies not only bottom-up connective activity but also the management of such efforts by agents, organizations, and institutions that maintain real-world political clout.

ACKNOWLEDGMENTS

This research has been funded in part by an Insight Development Grant from the Social Sciences and Humanities Research Council of Canada. Patrick McCurdy would also like to acknowledge his time as a fellow at the Centre for Media, Communication, and Information Research (ZeMKI), University of Bremen, Germany, which afforded him the time and space to revise this chapter.

NOTES

1 An astroturf campaign is a paid advocacy plan designed to look like a grassroots campaign.
2 Personal communication with the director of BHIVE. The text of the account read "BhiveD321. Sharing the latest in #oil & #gas news for our growing @bhivec2 community."

REFERENCES

Ampofo, Lawrence, Simon Collister, Ben O'Loughlin, and Andrew Chadwick. 2015. "Text Mining and Social Media: When Quantitative Meets Qualitative and Software Meets People." In *Innovations in Digital Research Methods*, edited by P. Halfpenny and R. Procter, 161–91. London: SAGE.

Bissett, Kevin. 2013. "Alberta Premier Touts West-East Pipeline Project in New Brunswick." *CTV News*, June 13. http://atlantic.ctvnews.ca/alberta-premier-touts-west-east-pipeline-project-in-new-brunswick-1.1315319.

Blevis, Mark. 2013. "Anatomy of a Hashtag: Who Tweets about Canadian Politics?" *Globe and Mail*, February 6. http://www.theglobeandmail.com/news/politics/anatomy-of-a-hashtag-who-tweets-about-canadian-politics/article8292353/.

Bode, Leticia, and Ben Epstein. 2015. "Campaign Klout: Measuring Online Influence during the 2012 Election." *Journal of Information Technology and Politics* 12, 2: 133–48.

Breese, Elizabeth Butler. 2016. "When Marketers and Academics Share a Research Platform: The Story of Crimson Hexagon." *Journal of Applied Social Science* 10, 1: 3–7.

Canada Action. 2016. "About." *Canada Action*. http://www.canadaaction.ca/about.

Canadian Press. 2018. "Timeline: Key Dates in the History of the Trans Mountain Pipeline." *Financial Post*, August 30. https://business.financialpost.com/pmn/business-pmn/timeline-key-dates-in-the-history-of-the-trans-mountain-pipeline-4.

CAPP (Canadian Association of Petroleum Producers). 2015a. "Basic Statistics." *CAPP*. http://www.capp.ca/publications-and-statistics/statistics/basic-statistics.

–. 2015b. "Pipelines." *CAPP*. http://www.capp.ca/canadian-oil-and-natural-gas/infrastructure-and-transportation/pipelines.

Castells, Manuel. 2009. *Communication Power*. New York: Oxford University Press.

CBC. 2014. "TransCanada's Energy East Pipeline Project Goes to NEB for Approval." *CBC News*, October 31. http://www.cbc.ca/news/business/transcanada-formally-applies-to-neb-for-energy-east-pipeline-approval-1.

Chadwick, Andrew. 2013. *The Hybrid Media System: Politics and Power*. New York: Oxford University Press.
Couldry, Nick. 2013. *Media, Society, World: Social Theory and Digital Media Practice*. Cambridge, UK: Polity Press.
Council of Canadians. 2014. "Countering Energy East Pipeline Spin: Talking Points." *Council of Canadians*. http://canadians.org/sites/default/files/publications/energyeast-spin-talking-points.pdf.
–. 2015. "Tar Sands." *Council of Canadians*. http://canadians.org/tarsands.
Crimson Hexagon. 2012a. "Technical Specifications." *Crimson Hexagon*. http://www.crimsonhexagon.com/technical-specifications/.
–. 2012b. "Our Quantitative Analysis Methods." *Crimson Hexagon*. http://www.crimsonhexagon.com/quantitative-analysis/.
DeLuca, Kevin Michael. 2005. *Image Politics: The New Rhetoric of Environmental Activism*. New York: Routledge.
Dyer, Simon, Jennifer Grant, and Eli Angen. 2013. "Forecasting the Impacts of Oilsands Expansion." *Pembina Institute*. http://www.pembina.org/pub/forecasting-impacts-of-oilsands-expansion.
Feith, Jesse. 2016. "Justin Trudeau, Denis Coderre Meet against Backdrop of Energy East Tuesday." *Gazette* [Montreal], January 26. http://montrealgazette.com/business/energy/justin-trudeau-denis-coderre-meet-against-backdrop-of-energy-east-tuesday.
Gailus, Jeff. 2012. *Little Black Lies: Corporate and Political Spin in the Global War for Oil*. Calgary: Rocky Mountain Books.
Gamson, William A., and Gadi Wolfsfeld. 1993. "Movements and Media as Interacting Systems." *Annals of the American Academy of Political and Social Science* 528, 1: 114–25.
Gerbaudo, Paolo. 2016. "Social Media Teams as Digital Vanguards: The Question of Leadership in the Management of Key Facebook and Twitter Accounts of Occupy Wall Street, Indignados, and UK Uncut." *Information, Communication, and Society* 20, 2: 1–18.
Gerbaudo, Paolo, and Emiliano Treré. 2015. "In Search of the 'We' of Social Media Activism: Introduction to the Special Issue on *Social Media and Protest Identities*." *Information, Communication, and Society* 18, 8: 865–71.
Gibson, Rachel K. 2015. "Party Change, Social Media, and the Rise of 'Citizen-Initiated' Campaigning." *Party Politics* 21, 2: 183–97.
Government of Alberta. Energy Alberta. 2016. *Facts and Statistics*. https://www.energy.alberta.ca/OS/Pages/default.aspx.
Greenpeace Canada. 2014. "Leaked Documents Show TransCanada Planning 'Dirty Tricks' Campaign to Support Energy East Pipeline." *Greenpeace*, November 18. http://www.greenpeace.org/canada/en/recent/Leaked-documents-show-TransCanada-planning-dirty-tricks-campaign-to-support-Energy-East-pipeline/.
–. 2015. "Tar Sands." *Greenpeace*. http://www.greenpeace.org/canada/en/campaigns/Energy/tarsands/.

Groshek, Jacob. 2012. "Forecasting and Observing: A Cross-Methodological Consideration of Internet and Mobile Phone Diffusion in the Egyptian Revolt." *International Communication Gazette* 74, 8: 750–68.

Groshek, Jacob, and Ahmed Al-Rawi. 2013. "Public Sentiment and Critical Framing in Social Media Content during the 2012 US Presidential Campaign." *Social Science Computer Review* 31, 5: 563–76.

–. 2015. "Anti-Austerity in the Euro Crisis: Modeling Protest with Online-Mobile-Social Media Usage, Users, and Content." *International Journal of Communication* 9: 3280–3303.

Groshek, Jacob, and Jiska Engelbert. 2012. "Double Differentiation in a Cross-National Comparison of Populist Political Movements and Online Media Uses in the United States and the Netherlands." *New Media and Society* 15, 2: 183–202.

Gunster, Shane, and Paul Saurette. 2014. "Storylines in the Sands: News, Narrative, and Ideology in the *Calgary Herald.*" *Canadian Journal of Communication* 39, 3: 333–59.

Harden-Donahue, Andrea. 2016. "Myth Busting: Energy East Is Canadian Oil for Canadians." *Council of Canadians,* January 15. http://canadians.org/blog/myth-busting-energy-east-canadian-oil-canadians.

Hestres, Luis E. 2014. "Preaching to the Choir: Internet-Mediated Advocacy, Issue Public Mobilization, and Climate Change." *New Media and Society* 16, 2: 323–39.

Hoekstra, Gordon. 2017. "Enbridge Removes Already-Dead Northern Gateway from B.C. Environmental Assessment." *Vancouver Sun,* January 25. https://vancouversun.com/business/energy/enbridge-removes-already-dead-northern-gateway-from-b-c-environmental-assessment.

Hopke, Jill E., and Molly Simis. 2017a. "Discourse over a Contested Technology on Twitter: A Case Study of Hydraulic Fracturing." *Public Understanding of Science* 26, 1: 105–20.

–. 2017b. "Response to 'Word Choice as Political Speech': Hydraulic Fracturing Is a Partisan Issue." *Public Understanding of Science* 26, 1: 124–26.

Hopkins, Daniel J., and Gary King. 2010. "A Method of Automated Nonparametric Content Analysis for Social Science." *American Journal of Political Science* 54, 1: 229–47.

Karlsen, Rune, and Bernard Enjolras. 2016. "Styles of Social Media Campaigning and Influence in a Hybrid Political Communication System Linking Candidate Survey Data with Twitter Data." *International Journal of Press/Politics* 21, 3: 338–57.

Leach, Andrew. 2017. "How Donald Trump Killed the Energy East Pipeline." *Globe and Mail,* October 9. https://beta.theglobeandmail.com/report-on-business/rob-commentary/how-donald-trump-killed-the-energy-east-pipeline/article36527153/.

Levant, Ezra. 2010. *Ethical Oil: The Case for Canada's Oil Sands.* Toronto: McClelland and Stewart.

Marsden, William. 2008. *Stupid to the Last Drop: How Alberta Is Bringing Environmental Armageddon to Canada (and Doesn't Seem to Care)*. Toronto: Vintage Canada.

McCurdy, Patrick. 2017. "Image Events, Disaster Events, and the Struggle over Canada's Oil/Tar Sands." In *Carbon Capitalism and Communication: Confronting Climate Crisis*, edited by B. Brevini and G. Murdock, 131–46. Basingstoke, UK: Palgrave Macmillan.

–. 2018. "From the Natural to the Manmade Environment: The Shifting Advertising Practices of Canada's Oil Sands Industry." *Canadian Journal of Communication* 43, 1: 33–52.

McCurdy, P. 2019. "Fanning Flames of Discontent: A Case Study of Social Media, Populism,and Campaigning." In *Political Leadership and Social Media*, edited by D. Taras and R. Davis. London and New York: Routledge.

McKibben, Bill. 2017. "Another one bites the dust – Transcanada terminates Energy East pipeline project from the tarsands" [tweet]. https://twitter.com/billmckibben/status/915926564512178176.

Mercer, Rick. 2016. "Rick's Rant – Energy East Pipeline." *The Mercer Report*. CBC Televison, January 26. http://www.cbc.ca/mercerreport/videos/clips/ricks-rant-energy-east-pipeline.

Morozov, Evgeny. 2009. "From Slacktivism to Activism." *Foreign Policy* 5. https://foreignpolicy.com/2009/09/05/from-slacktivism-to-activism/.

Nikiforuk, Andrew. 2010. *Tar Sands: Dirty Oil and the Future of a Continent*. Vancouver: Greystone Books.

Paskey, Janice, Gillian Steward, and Amanda Williams. 2013. "The Alberta Oil Sands Then and Now: An Investigation of the Economic, Environmental, and Social Discourses across Four Decades." *Oils Sands Research and Information Network*. https://era.library.ualberta.ca/items/e2e74e71-9160-4a5d-92c9-d06b00d0844.

Perron, Dominique. 2013. *L'Alberta autophage: Identités, mythes, et discours du pétrole dans l'ouest canadien*. Calgary: University of Calgary Press.

Poell, Thomas, and Erik Borra. 2012. "Twitter, YouTube, and Flickr as Platforms of Alternative Journalism: The Social Media Account of the 2010 Toronto G20 Protests." *Journalism* 13, 6: 695–713.

Poell, Thomas, and José van Dijck. 2015. "Social Media and Activist Communication." In *The Routledge Companion to Alternative and Community Media*, edited by C. Atton, 527–37. London: Routledge.

Proctor, Jason. 2016. "Northern Gateway Pipeline Approval Overturned." *CBC News*, June 30. http://www.cbc.ca/news/canada/british-columbia/northern-gateway-pipeline-federal-court-of-appeal-1.3659561.

Shaw, Rob. 2016. "Province of B.C. Formally Opposes Kinder Morgan Expansion." *Vancouver Sun*, November 1. http://www.vancouversun.com/technology/province+formally+opposes+kinder+morgan+expansion/11642943/story.html.

Statista. 2016. "Number of Twitter Users in Canada from 2012 to 2018 (in Millions)." *Statista*. http://www.statista.com/statistics/303875/number-of-twitter-users-canada/.

Sweeny, Alastair. 2010. *Black Bonanza: Canada's Oil Sands and the Race to Secure North America's Energy Future*. Mississauga, ON: John Wiley and Sons.

Taber, Jane, Shawn McCarthy, and Robert Fife. 2016. "Trudeau Supports Notley on Energy East Pipeline." *Globe and Mail*, January 22. http://www.theglobeandmail.com/news/politics/montreal-area-mayors-energy-east-criticisms-short-sighted-notley-says/article28339330/.

TransCanada. 2013a. "TransCanada to Proceed with 1.1 Million Barrel/Day Energy East Pipeline Project to Saint John." *TransCanada Corporation*. http://www.transcanada.com/announcements-article.html.

–. 2013b. "Inside the Pipeline: Crude Oil Facts." Fact Sheet, July 2013. *TransCanada Corporation*. http://www.energyeastpipeline.com/wp-content/uploads/2013/07/Energy-East-Pipeline-Inside-The-Pipeline-Crude-Oil-Facts.pdf.

–. 2015a. "5 Oil Myths that Don't Hold Up." *TransCanada Corporation*. http://www.energyeastpipeline.com/the-truth-about-diluted-bitumen/.

–. 2015b. "Oil Imports: The Truth behind Canada's Oil." *TransCanada Corporation*. http://www.energyeastpipeline.com/canadian-energy-independence-is-a-pipeline-away/.

–. 2016a. "Energy East 101: Questions on Energy East." *TransCanada Corporation*. http://www.energyeastpipeline.com/facts/oil-and-pipelines-101-2/.

–. 2016b. "Dispelling Myths." *TransCanada Corporation*. http://www.energyeastpipeline.com/facts/dispelling-myths/.

–. 2017. "TransCanada Announces Termination of Energy East Pipeline and Eastern Mainline Projects." *TransCanada Corporation*. https://www.transcanada.com/en/announcements/2017-10-05-transcanada-anounces-termination-of-energy-east-pipeline-and-eastern-mainline-projects/.

Van Laer, Jeroen, and Peter Van Aelst. 2010. "Internet and Social Movement Action Repertoires: Opportunities and Limitations." *Information, Communication, and Society* 13, 8: 1146–71.

Wall, Brad. 2017. "#EnergyEast dead. 1000s new jobs lost. Cda to keep importing foreign oil. West can't get oil to tidewater. Mtl mayor calls it 'major victory'" [tweet]. https://twitter.com/PremierBradWall/status/915975743280050176.

Way, Laura. 2011. "An Energy Superpower or a Super Sales Pitch? Building the Case through an Examination of Canadian Newspapers Coverage of Oil Sands." *Canadian Political Science Review* 5, 1: 74–98.

Weller, Katrin, Axel Bruns, Jean E. Burgess, Merja Mahrt, and Cornelius Puschmann. 2014. *Twitter and Society: An Introduction*. Vol. 89. New York: Peter Lang.

White, Brittany, Heather Castleden, and Anatoliy Gruzd. 2015. "Talking to Twitter Users: Motivations behind Twitter Use on the Alberta Oil Sands and the Northern Gateway Pipeline." *First Monday* 20, 1–5. https://firstmonday.org/ojs/index.php/fm/article/view/5404/4196.

4

Transforming the Disengaged
Social Media and Youth in Canada

SHELLEY BOULIANNE

Social networking sites are extremely popular, with three-quarters of Americans and Canadians using them (Pew Research Center 2016; Statistics Canada 2014). Approximately 61 percent of Canadians have engaged in at least one form of online political discussion, such as posting political information on social media, blogging, emailing about politics, or participating in an online group (Hilderman, Anderson, and Loat 2015). However, the implications of social media for democratic participation remain unclear. There is an abundance of research, as shown in these meta-analyses (Boulianne 2015a, 2017). However, most of this research has a built-in assumption that social media are producing more engaged and politically interested citizens. The assumption has implications for digital infrastructure investments for social movement organizations, interest groups, and political campaigns (e.g., Stromer-Galley 2014). Is this infrastructure supporting the process of transforming citizens into *being* politically interested and engaged? Or is it limited to supporting citizens who are already politically interested and engaged: that is, the usual suspects? If the latter is occurring, then digital media, including social media, might be reinforcing or expanding inequalities in political participation rather than addressing them. The findings in this chapter should appease concerns about expanding participatory inequality among youth. However, there are some concerns about inequality related to protesting and connecting with candidates, officials, and political parties on social media.

Here I examine how social media use is transforming political engagement and the consequences for Canadian politics. Much of the research on social media use focuses on political elites (Boulianne 2016b), particularly in Canada. Highlighting ordinary citizens addresses a clear gap in existing research on social media in the Canadian context. Internationally, most of the research on citizens' use of social media and political participation is based on cross-sectional surveys (Boulianne 2015a). Cross-sectional designs are weak for assessing causal processes, such as whether social media are an outcome or a predictor of political engagement. The answer to this question will determine whether social media will replicate, expand, or diminish inequalities in participation.

Finally, this research is distinctive in highlighting social media use for a population that tends to be disengaged from formal political life but is active outside institutional channels (Boulianne 2015a, 2016a; see the chapter by Raynauld, Lalancette, and Tourigny-Koné in this volume). The 2015 federal election (Elections Canada n.d.) might have been an exception to these patterns, but the effect of social media on voting is unclear. Given youth's greater use of social networking sites (Pew Research Center 2016; Statistics Canada 2014), the effects of social media on political attitudes and behaviours are expected to be larger than they are for older citizens. Social media have reshaped day-to-day life for younger citizens (see the chapter by Raynauld, Lalancette, and Tourigny-Koné in this volume). Indeed, a recent meta-analysis of social media and political participation suggests that the effects of social media are strongest among young people (Boulianne 2015a). Here I examine whether social media use is limited to youth already interested and engaged in politics, or can social media use transform its young users into being interested and engaged in politics? The question is important for addressing the role of social media in replicating, expanding, or diminishing gaps in participation that undermine democratic representation.

The effects of media depend on the nature of media use. The use of social media tends to be divided into information or news gathering, network building, and political expression (Boulianne 2017), but the three uses flow seamlessly together. On social networking sites, users can acquire political information or news by following or "friending" political candidates and news organizations. In 2016, approximately 62 percent of adult Americans acquired their news from social networking sites (Gottfried and Shearer 2016). These sites can be attractive to those who seek more interaction with, rather than mere exposure to, political content (Bode 2012). This interaction could involve posting content, reposting or retweeting content, forwarding, liking, or "favouriting" content (Bode et al. 2014; Yamamoto, Kushin, and Dalisay 2015). Social networking sites are important venues for connecting with friends who are also interested in politics and want to discuss political issues. Social networking sites provide alternative spaces in which to discuss a broad range of issues that might not be on the government's or media's agenda (Boulianne 2011, 2015b). Social networking sites are also important for creating connections between citizens and political officials. These connections provide opportunities for individuals to discuss political issues with their elected representatives and for elected representatives to solicit citizens' votes and opinions (Gainous and Wagner 2014; Kruikemeier 2014). These processes and features are probably most appealing to those already interested and engaged in the political process. Social networking sites merely ease the effort to become informed, to interact on political issues, as well as to connect with other politically interested and engaged friends and political officials. Social media are a *tool* for reinforcing participation among a select group of citizens. This process has been labelled the reinforcement or normalization hypothesis (Norris 2000; Theocharis and Quintelier 2016; Vissers and Stolle 2014). Social media effects are limited to those who are already part of the political process; if social media expand their engagement, then the gap between the engaged and the disengaged will expand.

Yet social networking sites can help to generate political interest and expand participation to a broader set of citizens. Indeed, these sites offer many opportunities for those who are not politically interested to be exposed to political content by monitoring their friends' activities (Dimitrova et al. 2014; Tang and Lee 2013; Xenos, Vromen, and Loader 2014). Vaccari, Chadwick, and O'Loughlin (2015) suggest that this type of accidental exposure favours more community-oriented and discursive forms of engagement (e.g., political talk) rather than campaign-focused activities. Users can track their friends' activities to find out what their friends think about various political issues (Valenzuela, Park, and Kee 2009). Users can trust this information because it is circulated by friends (Bode 2012). Social networking sites present opportunities to make connections with political candidates and political parties without making long-term commitments to them. Such sites eliminate the mediator (e.g., news media) and connect voters directly to political candidates. For those with limited financial resources, limited appetites for news media, or busy work-family schedules, these online networking opportunities can be critical to enabling their engagement. In these ways, social media can provide opportunities for a new set of political actors to emerge and reduce inequalities in participation. These media enable a transformative process, turning users into interested and engaged citizens. This process has been labelled the mobilization hypothesis (Norris 2000; Theocharis and Quintelier 2016; Vissers and Stolle 2014).

Cross-sectional research cannot determine whether the correlation among variables is explained by a process of self-selection: that is, whether those who are more engaged select social networking sites or whether the use of these sites causes them to become more politically engaged (Bode 2012; Tang and Lee 2013; Valenzuela et al. 2009; Xenos et al. 2014). This nuance is important in addressing the question of whether social media will ameliorate inequalities in participation or whether they will reinforce or expand inequalities in participation by enabling a select group of people to engage in civic and political life.

The framing of reinforcement versus mobilization is a bit problematic because both processes can occur simultaneously but with clear differences for participation. The difference in outcome depends on the characteristics of the group affected by digital media use. For example, a select group of citizens already engaged could be further mobilized by social media, expanding their participation advantage and consequently increase participation inequality. Norris (2000) describes this process as a virtuous circle – media use enables further participation among those already engaged. This process would be evident in a series of positive and significant effects between prior levels of engagement and interest (moving forward prior engagement and interest will be designated as time 1) and social media use as well as between social media use and current or future political interest and engagement (moving forward current or future engagement and interest will be designated as time 2).

Another possibility is that this process would lead to transformative effects that reduce participation inequality by engaging a broader set of citizens in the political process. This process would be evident if there is no significant relationship between prior levels of engagement and interest (time 1) on social media use and if there is a positive and significant relationship between social media use and current or future political interest and engagement (time 2). This process would be indicative of a transformational effect – transforming disengaged and uninterested citizens into engaged and interested citizens.

A handful of studies have collected longitudinal data to examine the effects of social media on political engagement (Bode et al. 2014; Dimitrova et al. 2014; Ekström, Olsson, and Shehata 2014; Holt et al. 2013; Towner 2013). However, these studies have a built-in assumption about mobilization/transformation and rarely find statistically significant effects (Boulianne 2015a). These studies consistently model social media use as a predictor of engagement and do not assess how prior engagement predicts social media use. As such, these studies do not examine reinforcement effects. This study is a key contribution to the literature because of its focus on reinforcement effects. It also explores the virtuous circle, a theory that remains untested in social media research. Two studies are distinct in this field of longitudinal research because they examine mobilization versus reinforcement effects: Vissers and Stolle (2014) and Theocharis and Quintelier (2016).

Vissers and Stolle (2014) offer a variety of findings exploring reinforcement versus mobilization effects using a sample of university students in Quebec. Their findings demonstrate that the relationship depends on the type of social media use and the type of engagement (Table 4.1). For example, when political activity is measured as signing petitions, social media use for political expression is not a significant predictor or outcome of engagement. Political expression on Facebook is a positive outcome and predictor of protest participation, such as participating in demonstrations or marches. The findings suggest a pattern of reinforcement, particularly a virtuous circle, that would reinforce inequalities in participation.

Theocharis and Quintelier (2016) also find that the type of social media use matters in whether the effects are significant and positive using a sample of fifteen- and sixteen-year-olds from Belgium (Table 4.1). When social media use is measured simply as having a Facebook account, social media are not a significant predictor or outcome of civic participation, such as membership in an association. When Facebook use is measured as the

TABLE 4.1
Literature results related to mobilization and reinforcement/virtuous circle

	Social media use	Engagement	Conclusion
Vissers and Stolle (2014)	Index	Index	No relationship
	Political expression	Signing petitions	No relationship
	Political expression	Contacting officials	Reinforcement
	Political expression	Protesting	Reinforcement/ virtuous circle
	Joining Facebook group	Protesting	Mobilization
Theocharis and Quintelier (2016)	Facebook account	Group memberships	Reinforcement
	Number of Facebook friends	Group memberships	Reinforcement
	Time spent on Facebook	Group memberships	Reinforcement

number of friends on Facebook, social media use (time 1) is not a significant predictor of civic participation (time 2), but civic participation (time 1) does predict the number of friends on Facebook (time 2). Finally, they examine the time spent on social networking sites. This measure of use (time 1) does not have a significant effect on civic participation (time 2), but civic participation (time 1) has a positive effect on this measure of use (time 2). Both findings suggest a clear and consistent pattern of reinforcement.

Neither study highlights the important role of political interest in this process. Political interest is a key attitude driving political behaviour. Indeed, political interest is a necessary precondition for political participation, so changes in interest are necessary for changes in behaviour (Boulianne 2011). However, in the two studies, political interest is used as a statistical control and given little attention (Theocharis and Quintelier 2016; Vissers and Stolle 2014). Studies are inconsistent in controlling for political interest. When studies do control for it, they tend to be cross-sectional in design (e.g., Scherman, Arriagada, and Valenzuela 2015). Treating political interest as a secondary variable is not appropriate since many longitudinal studies document the critical importance of political interest and its reciprocal relationship with media use and engagement (Boulianne 2011, 2015b; Holt et al. 2013; Kruikemeier and Shehata 2016). Here I highlight the role of political interest in the process of reinforcement and mobilization.

CASE STUDY

I looked at whether social media are a significant, positive predictor and outcome of civic and political engagement among youth. The question is relevant for understanding the transformative effects of social media on engagement. My research builds on studies by Vissers and Stolle (2014) and Theocharis and Quintelier (2016). I examined multiple forms of social media use as well as different forms of political engagement; however, unlike other studies, my study highlights the role of political interest in this relationship. Given the precedents set by other studies, the key question is whether social media are reinforcing engagement among a select group of users and whether the reinforcement effect can further be described as a virtuous circle (Norris 2000). In a virtuous circle, social media use is both a positive predictor and an outcome of engagement. Social media mobilize citizens, but this mobilization is limited to those already interested and engaged in politics. This process would have dire consequences for inequalities in participation.

Methods

The data source that I used to conduct this work was a two-wave panel survey of a random sample of students and former students of MacEwan University (Edmonton). The first wave of the survey was completed in 2010, 2011, or 2013 ($n = 875$) while the students were enrolled part time or full time, following much of the research in this field (see Boulianne 2015a, 2017). Each year a list of current students was acquired from the Registrar's Office and stratified by gender, and then a random sample of students was chosen to contact to participate. All participants were resurveyed in January–May 2014. Approximately 37 percent of the respondent pool were no longer students at this institution (see Boulianne 2016a), creating a pool of youth living across Canada. The response rate to the second wave of the survey was 60 percent ($n = 495$).

Findings

Descriptive statistics on political engagement and social media use demonstrate that this sample is comparable to other student or youth surveys in this field of research. The descriptive statistics are comparable to those

TABLE 4.2
Descriptive statistics on social media use and engagement

	Vissers and Stolle (2014) (dates: 2011, 2012)	Theocharis and Quintelier (2016) (dates: 2012, 2013)	Current study (dates: 2010, 2011, 2013, and 2014)
Signed petition	39%, 39%	NA	37%, 28%
Marched/demonstrated	23%, 22%	NA	6%, 8%
Contacted official	14%, 11%	NA	10%, 13%
Group membership	NA	Averages: 1.68, 1.63	Averages: 1.50, 1.65
Political interest	Average: 2.28	Average: 2.01	Averages: 2.37, 2.62
Facebook account	92%	90%, 94%	100%
Frequency of use of social networking sites	NA	71% daily	82% daily
Post thoughts on social networking sites	52%, 64%	NA	51%
Friend/like official on Facebook	22%, 20%	NA	18.5%

of Theocharis and Quintelier (2016) and Vissers and Stolle (2014) except in relation to the rate for protests and the portion of youth with Facebook accounts (Table 4.2). As mentioned, Vissers and Stolle used a survey of Quebec university students conducted in 2011 and 2012, whereas Theocharis and Quintelier used a survey of Belgian fifteen- and sixteen-year-olds conducted in 2012 and 2013. Approximately 37 percent of the sample at time 1 had signed a petition in the previous year, similar to Vissers and Stolle's estimate of 39 percent based on the past six months (for both of their waves). The time periods for their surveys and the first wave of the current survey are similar; the similarity in frequencies is assurance of representativeness. In the current survey, at time 2 (2014), 28 percent of the sample had signed a petition.

Approximately 6–8 percent of the sample (depending on the wave) had engaged in protests (i.e., participated in marches or demonstrations during the past year), whereas the sample of Vissers and Stolle (2014) had a higher rate of this behaviour (22–23 percent depending on the time) based on the past six months. However, the spring of 2012 was an unusual period for Quebec university students as they took to the streets to protest tuition changes (see the chapter by Raynauld, Lalancette, and Tourigny-Koné in this volume). Other international surveys have set the incident rates at 7–8 percent of youth (Cohen et al. 2012; Holt et al. 2013), similar to the rates in my study.

Approximately 10–13 percent of the sample (depending on the wave) had contacted a public official in the past year, identical to the estimates of Vissers and Stolle (2014), providing assurance of representativeness. These estimates are similar to each other, and both surveys use Canadian data, but in a Swedish survey of eighteen- to thirty-three-year-olds 6 percent had contacted an official (Holt et al. 2013). Canadian youth might be distinctive in their more frequent engagement in this behaviour.

As for civic participation, Theocharis and Quintelier (2016) asked fifteen- and sixteen-year-olds to indicate "yes" or "no" for membership in fifteen different groups, then added up the number of group memberships. The mean was 1.68 in wave 1 and 1.63 in wave 2 (range 0–9). In my survey, participants were provided with a list of different groups (similar to those of Theocharis and Quintelier) and asked about the number of group memberships across these different types (range 0–5 or more). The average at time 1 was 1.50 ($SD = 1.22$), and the average at time 2 was 1.65 ($SD = 1.32$). The estimates are similar despite the differing data collection periods, age groups, national contexts, and questions.

Political interest is measured on a four-point scale in Theocharis and Quintelier (2016; average 2.01) and in Vissers and Stolle (2014; average 2.28). Political interest is measured as a five-point scale in my study with an average of 2.37 ($SD = .96$) at time 1 and 2.62 ($SD = .98$) at time 2. Despite the different number of response options, the averages are similar.

Theocharis and Quintelier (2016), as well as Vissers and Stolle (2014), ask about social media at both waves (time 1 and time 2), whereas I asked only about social media use at time 2 (collected in 2014). Because of this design, I can address questions about reinforcement and a virtuous circle, an underexamined hypothesis in the literature. The mobilization hypothesis has been well tested in the existing literature (Boulianne 2015a). Theocharis and Quintelier asked about having a Facebook account (90 percent had an account at wave 1 and 94 percent at wave 2). For Vissers and Stolle, 92 percent of the sample reported having a Facebook account. This line of questioning was repeated in my survey. The entire sample had Facebook accounts, reflecting the state of social media use among youth in 2014.

Participants were asked about the frequency of using social media in the past week, whereas Theocharis and Quintelier (2016) asked about the frequency of use over one month, but they found that 71 percent of the sample used social networking sites daily. In my study, 82 percent of the sample used these sites at least once per day. Again the difference reflects the growing use of social media in 2014 compared with 2012–13.

Theocharis and Quintelier (2016) asked about the number of friends using a 200-person interval, for example 0–199 and a top category of 1,000 friends, whereas I used a 100-person interval with a top category of 500 friends or more. Their average was 345 friends at time 1 and 425 friends at time 2. Vissers and Stolle (2014) used a 100-friend interval and found the averages to be 300 and 399. The comparable statistic in my study is 200 friends ($SD = 200$).

Borrowing from Rainie et al. (2012), I also asked about the use of social networking sites to post one's thoughts or comments on a political issue. The question was similar to that of Vissers and Stolle (2014). The questions tapped into interaction on social media about political issues. Based on a 2011 survey using this question, the Pew Research Center reports that 42 percent of American youth posted their thoughts or comments about an issue on a social networking site (Rainie et al. 2012). I found that 51 percent of youth engaged in this activity in 2014. In Vissers and Stolle's sample, approximately 52 percent of students had engaged in this activity at time 1 (2011) and 64 percent at time 2 (2012, a period of intense engagement for Quebec students).

Many studies have examined the use of social media to like, friend, or link to political candidates or parties (Cohen et al. 2012; Holt et al. 2013; Rainie et al. 2012; Tang and Lee 2013; Towner 2013). In the original survey, these two groups were asked separately, but to offer comparability to Vissers and Stolle (2014) the variable was transformed into having a connection to either a political party or a political official or candidate. Approximately 18.5 percent of the sample had this type of connection, similar to Vissers and Stolle's incident rate (20–22 percent).

For the final multivariate analysis, I examined the relationships among political engagement and interest prior to and after social media use, controlling for age (four groups defined by three-year intervals), gender, and mother's education. Whereas the gender control is standard in this area of research, inclusion of the mother's education was an effort to replicate Vissers and Stolle's (2014) model, and the inclusion of age was a necessity because this group contained a wider range of youth than that in Vissers and Stolle or Theocharis and Quintelier (2016). Statistical Package for the Social Sciences (SPSS) was used to create a partial correlation matrix of the variables, controlling for demographic variables (similar to Theocharis 2011). Table 4.3 presents the partial correlation matrix. For simplicity, the table does not include the correlations among social media measures. In addition, it does not include the correlations among engagement variables. However, as one would expect, the different measures of social media use (and the different measures of engagement) are highly correlated with each other.

As a collective set of findings, there are twenty tests of whether prior engagement or political interest predicts social media use (reinforcement). Almost all of these coefficients are positive, but only seven of these relationships are statistically significant. This collection of findings appeases concerns about a reinforcement (or virtuous circle) process among youth. For the most part, prior levels of engagement and interest do not determine social media use among youth. However, there are some clear exceptions.

As noted by Vissers and Stolle (2014), protesting (participating in marches and demonstrations) is a distinctive political activity in its relationship to social media. Unlike in Vissers and Stolle, the use of social media to post opinions or the overall frequency of use neither predicts nor is a significant outcome of protesting. Prior protesting (time 1) positively and significantly predicts the number of friends on social media (time 2) (.128, $p = 0.034$) and the use of social media to like or follow a candidate or party (time 2) (.300, $p < .001$). Both social media measures represent social network building or social connections. The number of friends on social media (.183, $p < .001$) and connecting to a candidate or party on social media (.134, $p = 0.021$) positively and significantly relate to current protesting (time 2). In sum, the use of social media for social connections

TABLE 4.3
Partial correlation matrix

		How many such groups do you belong to?		Contacted a politician or elected government official		Signed a petition online or on paper		Participated in a demonstration or march (protest)		How interested are you in local community politics and local community affairs?	
		Time 1	Time 2	Time 1	Time 2	Time 1	Time 2	Time 1	Time 2	Time 1	Time 2
In a typical week, how often do you use social networking sites?	Coefficient	0.021	0.087	-0.032	-0.032	0.083	0.155	0.017	-0.014	0.012	0.001
	p value	.688	.091	.603	.551	.168	.003	.776	.796	.811	.987
Thinking only about your Facebook profile, how many friends do you have?	Coefficient	0.095	0.195	0.061	-0.012	0.075	0.106	0.128	0.183	-0.009	0.038
	p value	.072	.000	.317	.829	.214	.044	.034	.000	.864	.468
Have you ever used Facebook to friend or like elected officials, candidates for office, or other political figures OR a political party?	Coefficient	0.173	0.183	0.246	0.207	0.183	0.193	0.300	0.134	0.300	0.313
	p value	.003	.001	.000	.000	.003	.001	.000	.021	.000	.000
Do you ever use social networking sites to ... post your own thoughts or comments on an issue?	Coefficient	0.073	0.109	0.073	0.201	0.077	0.190	0.023	0.094	0.150	0.151
	p value	.180	.044	.228	.000	.204	.000	.700	.084	.005	.005

Note: Pairwise n = 266–372, controls for age group, gender, mother's schooling.

(two measures) predicts and is an outcome of protesting. These findings on protesting suggest a pattern of reinforcement, highlighting a virtuous circle, when it comes to social connections. As further evidence of reinforcement, the sizes of the coefficients for the reinforcement process are larger than the sizes of the effects of mobilization/transformation for protesting (.300 versus .134). The combination of social media use for liking a candidate, official, or party and a focus on protesting provides the strongest support for reinforcement, particularly a virtuous circle.

Connecting to a political candidate, official, or party is a distinctive form of social media use. Prior levels of engagement (all four measures) and political interest significantly affect liking or following a political candidate, official, or party (time 1) (coefficients are .173, $p = .003$; .246, $p < .001$; .183, $p = .003$; .300, $p < .001$, and as mentioned .300, $p < .001$ for prior protesting). This social media activity also significantly relates to engagement (time 2) (coefficients are .183, $p = .001$; .207, $p < .001$; .193, $p = .001$; .313, $p < .001$; and as mentioned .134, $p = .021$ for protesting). Those most interested and engaged use social media for this purpose, and this use leads to further engagement. For this type of use, there is clearly a pattern of reinforcement, highlighting a virtuous circle.

Signing petitions is also distinctive in that every type of social media use predicts this behaviour. Using social media frequently (.155, $p = .003$), having many friends on social media (.106, $p = .044$), connecting to a candidate or party (as mentioned, .193, $p = .001$), and posting opinions on social media (.190, $p < .001$) positively and significantly relate to signing petitions. This activity is also unique because having signed petitions in the past does not affect three of the four types of social media use (liking candidates, officials, or parties is the exception, as mentioned). In terms of signing petitions, there is strong evidence of a process of mobilization/transformation.

The use of social media for posting opinions is an outcome and predictor of political interest. Prior political interest affects the use of social media to express opinions (.150, $p = .005$), and this particular use correlates with current political interest (.151, $p = .005$). Although this pattern supports a process of reinforcement, for other types of social media use it was not evident. Political interest does not affect the frequency of social media use or the number of friends on social media, nor is political interest an outcome of these two types of social media use. In terms of political interest, the findings are mixed.

The number of group memberships, or civic participation as Theocharis and Quintelier (2016) label it, at time 1 does not predict three of the four social media use measures at time 2 (the exception, as mentioned above, is connecting to a candidate, official, or party). In contrast, for three of the four social media use measures (the exception is frequency of social media use), use correlates with the number of group memberships (coefficients are .195, $p < .001$; .109, $p = .044$; and as mentioned .183, $p = .001$ for connecting to a candidate or party). Again this is evidence in favour of a process of mobilization/transformation.

The findings, as a collection, challenge the conclusion of a process of reinforcement (Table 4.4). Of the twenty relationships testing reinforcement, only seven of the coefficients are significant. The exceptions are largely explained by social connections, especially connections to parties, officials, and candidates and to a smaller extent the number of friends.

The number of friends on social media reinforces protest behaviour. Although the measure is not considered by Vissers and Stolle (2014), it is consistent with their findings suggesting that social media use benefits those already engaged in protests. As mentioned, they find a positive, reciprocal relationship between political expression on Facebook and protesting. My study did not replicate this finding for political expression, but it did find this pattern for connecting to parties and candidates. These findings align with the reinforcement hypothesis.

Vissers and Stolle (2014) find that social media use does not predict and is not an outcome of signing petitions. In contrast, I found that all four types of social media use predict signing petitions. In other words, they do not find any relationship between signing petitions and social media use, whereas my study suggests an effect of transformation/mobilization. The two studies are consistent in finding minimal effects of prior behaviour regarding petitions on social media use (the exception is liking candidates or officials). Again the findings align with an effect of transformation/mobilization rather than reinforcement when it comes to signing petitions.

Both activities are examples of participation (attractive to youth) outside existing institutional channels (see the chapter by Raynauld, Lalancette,

TABLE 4.4
Summary of findings

	How many such groups do you belong to?	Contacted a politician or elected government official	Signed a petition online or on paper	Participated in a demonstration or march (protest)	How interested are you in local community politics and local community affairs?
In a typical week, how often do you use social networking sites?	No relationship	No relationship	Mobilization/ Transformation	No relationship	No relationship
Thinking only about your Facebook profile, how many friends do you have?	Mobilization/ transformation	No relationship	Mobilization/ Transformation	Reinforcement/ virtuous circle	No relationship
Have you ever used Facebook to friend or like elected officials, candidates for office, or other political figures OR a political party?	Reinforcement/ virtuous circle	Reinforcement/ virtuous circle	Reinforcement/ virtuous circle	Reinforcement/ virtuous circle	Reinforcement/ virtuous circle
Do you ever use social networking sites to ... post your own thoughts or comments on an issue?	Mobilization/ transformation	Mobilization/ transformation	Mobilization/ Transformation	No relationship	Reinforcement/ virtuous circle

and Tourigny-Koné in this volume). As such, the distinct patterns of signing petitions versus protesting are surprising. One possible explanation of these different findings is that protest behaviour occurs offline, whereas signing petitions can occur online or offline but tends to be online. Another explanation is the different level of effort required to engage in these activities. Signing petitions is a low-effort activity compared with showing up to offline protests. One cannot decipher from the data whether there are distinct patterns in these activities or whether they represent an online versus offline divide in terms of mobilization versus reinforcement.

In terms of group membership, the findings are opposite to those of Theocharis and Quintelier (2016). They find that, for two of three social media uses, prior group membership predicts social media use (reinforcement). In my study, prior group membership only affects connecting to a candidate, official, or party. Specifically, the findings suggest that prior group membership has little impact on frequency of social media use and number of friends, the two social media use measures used by Theocharis and Quintelier. My study suggests an effect of mobilization/transformation.

TRENDING IN CANADA

The focus on ordinary citizens addresses a clear gap in existing research on social media in the Canadian context (see the chapter by Raynauld, Lalancette, and Tourigny-Koné in this volume). This research is distinctive in documenting the effects of social media use for a group that tends to be disengaged from formal political life but is active outside institutional channels (see chapter by Raynauld, Lalancette, and Tourigny-Koné in this volume). The different measures of social media use and engagement offer a multitude of tests on reinforcement/virtuous circle and mobilization/transformation processes. The findings offer some clear implications for social movement organizations, interest groups, and political campaigns. However, the implications are different for these different organizations. For protest-oriented groups, social media use among young people activates a virtuous circle. Social media comprise an effective tool for engaging young supporters already involved in protests and other activities. Social media can be used to mobilize their future protest behaviour as well.

For petition-oriented groups, social media effects have a different set of implications. Social media use predicts, rather than is an outcome of, signing petitions. This is the strongest evidence of a distinctively transformative effect in which diverse sets of youth engage in politics, specifically signing petitions, because of social media use. The findings suggest that such use can expand the number of youth engaged in politics by offering low-effort forms of engagement such as signing petitions.

Social media are an effective tool for expanding group ties and thus can be used to expand the membership bases of social movements and interest groups. Social media serve to engage a new set of young political actors. Other than the generic measure of frequency of social media use, all other measures of their use point to increases in group memberships. In sum, the results affirm an effect of mobilization/transformation in terms of civic participation. Social media enable new relationships with civic and political groups.

For political campaigns, the results suggest a virtuous circle – social media mobilize a select group of citizens to engage further in the political process. These patterns are strongest when we examine social media use to follow candidates, officials, and parties. Those who engage in such use are not a representative set of citizens. They are distinctive in being highly engaged and very interested in the political process. Social media might not transform apathetic citizens into voters. Election campaigners who hope to tap into these likely voters can scan their own and their opponents' lists of followers/friends to try to solicit voters. This group is already well connected to the political process, so campaigners need not worry about the barriers of apathy.

In terms of posting opinions online, the people who engage in this form of social media use are highly interested in politics but do not have well-established histories of participation. This pattern is consistent with existing literature (see Vaccari, Chadwick, and O'Loughlin 2015). This group of people could represent a key demographic for social movement organizations, interest groups, and election campaigns in terms of mobilizing or transforming participation. This group is not apathetic but not fully engaged either. Its members are waiting for an invitation to participate, particularly in discursive ways, such as deliberative events or public consultations on political issues (Vaccari et al. 2015). Social media use not only transforms political engagement but also enables new, more discursive political action repertoires.

REFERENCES

Bode, Leticia. 2012. "Facebooking It to the Polls: A Study in Online Social Networking and Political Behavior." *Journal of Information Technology and Politics* 9, 4: 352–69.

Bode, Leticia, Emily Vraga, Porismita Borah, and Dhavan Shah. 2014. "A New Space for Political Behavior: Political Social Networking and Its Democratic Consequences." *Journal of Computer-Mediated Communication* 19, 3: 414–29.

Boulianne, Shelley. 2011. "Stimulating or Reinforcing Political Interest: Using Panel Data to Examine Reciprocal Effects between News Media and Political Interest." *Political Communication* 28, 2: 147–62.

–. 2015a. "Social Media Use and Participation: A Meta-Analysis of Current Research." *Information, Communication, and Society* 18, 5: 524–38.

–. 2015b. "Generating Political Interest with Online News." In *Communication and Information Technologies Annual*, vol. 9 of *Studies in Media and Communications*, edited by L. Robinson, S.R. Cotten, and J. Schulz, 53–76. Bingley, UK: Emerald Group.

–. 2016a. "Online News, Civic Awareness, and Engagement in Civic and Political Life." *New Media and Society* 18, 9: 1840–56.

–. 2016b. "Campaigns and Conflict on Social Media: A Literature Snapshot." *Online Information Review* 40, 5: 566–79.

–. 2017. "Revolution in the Making? Social Media Effects across the Globe." *Information, Communication, and Society*: Online First, 1–16. https://doi.org/10.1080/1369118X.2017.1353641.

Cohen, Cathy, Joseph Kahne, Benjamin Bowyer, Ellen Middaugh, and Joel Rogowski. 2012. *Participatory Politics: New Media and Youth Political Action*. Oakland: YPP Research Network. https://ypp.dmlcentral.net/sites/all/files/publications/YPP_Survey_Report_FULL.pdf.

Dimitrova, Daniela, Adam Shehata, Jesper Strömbäck, and Lars Nord. 2014. "The Effects of Digital Media on Political Knowledge and Participation in Election Campaigns: Evidence from Panel Data." *Communication Research* 41, 1: 95–118.

Ekström, Mats, Tobias Olsson, and Adam Shehata. 2014. "Spaces for Public Orientation? Longitudinal Effects of Internet Use in Adolescence." *Information, Communication, and Society* 17, 2: 168–83.

Elections Canada. n.d. "Voter Turnout by Age Group." http://www.elections.ca/content.aspx?section=res&dir=rec/part/estim/42ge&document=p1&lang=e.

Gainous, Jason, and Kevin Wagner. 2014. *Tweeting to Power: The Social Media Revolution in American Politics*. New York: Oxford University Press.

Gottfried, Jeffrey, and Elisa Shearer. 2016. "News Use across Social Media Platforms." *Pew Research Center*. http://www.journalism.org/2016/05/26/news-use-across-social-media-platforms-2016/.

Hilderman, Jane, Kendall Anderson, and Alison Loat. 2015. "Samara's Democracy 360: The Numbers." *Samara Canada*. http://www.samaracanada.com/docs/default-source/trioro-dropbox/democracy360_numbers_digital_final.pdf?sfvrsn=2.

Holt, Kristoffer, Adam Shehata, Jesper Strömbäck, and Elisabet Ljungberg. 2013. "Age and the Effects of News Media Attention and Social Media Use on Political Interest and Participation: Do Social Media Function as Leveller?" *European Journal of Communication* 28, 1: 19–34.

Kruikemeier, Sanne. 2014. "How Political Candidates Use Twitter and the Impact on Votes." *Computers in Human Behavior* 34: 131–39.

Kruikemeier, Sanne, and Adam Shehata. 2016. "News Media Use and Political Engagement among Adolescents: An Analysis of Virtuous Circles Using Panel Data." *Political Communication* 33, 4: 1–22.

Norris, Pippa. 2000. *A Virtuous Circle: Political Communications in Postindustrial Societies.* New York: Cambridge University Press.

Pew Research Center. 2016. "Social Networking Use." *Pew Research Center.* http://www.pewresearch.org/data-trend/media-and-technology/social-networking-use/.

Rainie, Lee, Aaron Smith, Kay Lehman Scholzman, Henry Brady, and Sidney Verba. 2012. "Social Media and Political Engagement." *Pew Internet and American Life Project.* http://pewinternet.org/Reports/2012/Political-engagement.aspx.

Scherman, Andrés, Arturo Arriagada, and Sebastián Valenzuela. 2015. "Student and Environmental Protests in Chile: The Role of Social Media." *Politics* 35, 2: 151–71.

Statistics Canada. 2014. "General Social Survey: Social Identity, 2013." *The Daily,* December 23. http://www.statcan.gc.ca/daily-quotidien/141223/dq141223b-eng.pdf.

Stromer-Galley, Jennifer. 2014. *Presidential Campaigning in the Internet Age.* New York: Oxford University Press.

Tang, Gary, and Francis L.F. Lee. 2013. "Facebook Use and Political Participation: The Impact of Exposure to Shared Political Information, Connections with Public Political Actors, and Network Structural Heterogeneity." *Social Science Computer Review* 31, 6: 763–73.

Theocharis, Yannis. 2011. "Young People, Political Participation, and Online Postmaterialism in Greece." *New Media and Society* 13, 2: 203–23.

Theocharis, Yannis, and Ellen Quintelier. 2016. "Stimulating Citizenship or Expanding Entertainment? The Effect of Facebook on Adolescent Participation." *New Media and Society* 18, 5: 817–36.

Towner, Terri. 2013. "All Political Participation Is Socially Networked? New Media and the 2012 Election." *Social Science Computer Review* 31, 5: 527–41.

Vaccari, Cristian, Andrew Chadwick, and Ben O'Loughlin. 2015. "Dual Screening the Political: Media Events, Social Media, and Citizen Engagement." *Journal of Communication* 65, 6: 1041–61.

Valenzuela, Sebastián, Namsu Park, and Kerk Kee. 2009. "Is There Social Capital in a Social Network Site? Facebook Use and College Students' Life Satisfaction, Trust, and Participation." *Journal of Computer-Mediated Communication* 14, 4: 875–901.

Vissers, Sara, and Dietlind Stolle. 2014. "Spill-Over Effects between Facebook and On/Offline Political Participation? Evidence from a Two-Wave Panel Study." *Journal of Information Technology and Politics* 11, 3: 259–75.

Xenos, Michael, Ariadne Vromen, and Brian Loader. 2014. "The Great Equalizer? Patterns of Social Media Use and Youth Political Engagement in Three Advanced Democracies." *Information, Communication, and Society* 17, 2: 151–67.

Yamamoto, Masahiro, Matthew Kushin, and Francis Dalisay. 2015. "Social Media and Mobiles as Political Mobilization Forces for Young Adults: Examining the Moderating Role of Online Political Expression in Political Participation." *New Media and Society* 17, 6: 880–98.

5

Trolling Stephen Harper
Internet Memes as Online Activism

MIREILLE LALANCETTE, TAMARA A. SMALL,
AND MAXIME PRONOVOST

Digital media can facilitate online activism, offering possibilities to spread political messages and mobilize protesters almost instantly. They can support online demonstrations as well as traditional forms of dissent (e.g., protests) by allowing for easy organizing and coverage by traditional media. They can be seen as a tool for helping social movements and individuals to expand and complement their repertoires of collective action (Bennett and Segerberg 2013). In this chapter, we document a specific form of online activism: political internet memes.

In scholarly research, the term "meme" refers to information diffused between individuals. It is derived "from the Greek *mimema,* signifying 'something which is imitated'" (Shifman 2013a, 363). In 1976, biologist Richard Dawkins coined the term in his book *The Selfish Gene* as part of his larger effort to apply evolutionary theory to cultural change. Dawkins defined memes "as small cultural units of transmission, analogous to genes, which are spread from person to person by copying or imitation" (Shifman 2013a, 363). Examples of memes in his pioneering text include specific signifiers such as melodies, catchphrases, and clothing fashions. Accordingly, internet memes are "a piece of digital content that spreads quickly around the web in various iterations and becomes a shared cultural experience" (Shifman 2013b, 18). Memes can take the form of texts, images, videos, and songs shared through social media, and they can be subsequently retransmitted on different online platforms. They can be distributed in their original forms or in derivative variations. Once a meme has been created, it evolves and can take many shapes. Following the genetic metaphor, memes, like genes, can self-replicate and mutate, carrying along information and cultural ideas. Along the line of the theory of evolution, only the "best" memes have long lives, and the weak ones disappear (Harlow 2013, 63). Some memes are relevant for short periods of time, and their meanings are often deeply tied to specific political, social, or cultural contexts. Some newly created memes go "viral" in a couple of clicks as they are reposted and reshared by multiple internet users across a wide range of platforms. In this sense, "going viral" is an important component of memes because they can be shared by many users.

The political meme is just one subtype of the broader memes that exist. Political memes can be seen as a form of participation in debates about governance and about actors in power. Shifman (2013b, 122–23) suggests that internet-based political memes fulfill three interwoven functions: 1) memes as forms of persuasion or political advocacy; 2) memes as grassroots actions (following the logic of "connective action" of Bennett and Segerberg 2013); and 3) memes as modes of expression and public discussion. When used in different contexts, such as during protests or when politicians are the objects of criticism, memes can play roles in public discourse and collaborative action (Huntington 2015, 79). They are shared by citizens of participatory digital culture in order to converse. In this sense, they have "discursive purposes" and can be seen as a "genre ... not a medium of online communication" (Wiggins and Bowers 2015, 1892, 1896).

Political internet memes also have argumentative significance (Sci and Dewberry 2015) since they can serve the rhetoric of political movements (Shifman 2013b, 129). In this sense, they are part discourse, part political action. They are about making points and, at the same time, participating in normative debates (Shifman 2013b, 120). Because memes can be used for political denunciation, as well as for endorsement, they can be useful for highlighting which controversies are fuelling citizens' attention and involvement and which values citizens are mobilizing when discussing them. In this line of thought, *"memes serve as pivotal links between the personal and the political. Since they are based on shared frameworks that call for variation, memes allow citizens to participate in public, collective* actions, while maintaining their sense of individuality" (Shifman 2013b, 129; emphasis added). In accordance with Sci and Dewberry (2015), memes can be seen as artifacts that allow for the study of their relationships to politics.

Political memes are similar to editorial cartoons since they present issues of the moment using a humorous tone to convey a message (Kligler-Vilenchik and Thorson 2015). Humour serves as a "unique key for the understanding of social and cultural processes" (Shifman 2007, 187). The appeal of memes resides in their intertextuality as they "take images from dominant media structures, juxtaposing and remixing them to create new layers of meaning" (Huntington 2015, 78). Both memes and cartoons refer to popular culture and news events within a humorous context. For some scholars (e.g., Jenkins, Ford, and Green 2013), memes are part of the new participatory culture that includes practices of culture jamming, in which pastiche and subversion are used to criticize and denunciate.[1] For example, at the beginning of 2000, some activists used memes to condemn Nike's sweatshops (Lievrouw 2011). In this case, memes were not just a form of entertainment but also a new form of online participation and political engagement.

Since memes are a relatively new political form of online activism, very little has been written about how and to what extent they are used in the Canadian political context. A few studies have been conducted in the United States and elsewhere in which scholars have analyzed memes in order to understand citizens' reactions to political events. For example, Sci and Dewberry (2015) explored memes from a rhetorical perspective as part of a larger discussion of citizens' assessment of Joe Biden's performance during a vice-presidential debate in 2012. Milner (2013) studied the Occupy Wall Street–related memes as a form of political discourse. He showed that creating memes, sharing them via participatory media such as Reddit and Tumblr, and using images and references from popular culture allow for positive relationships among users while creating conversations and news modalities of expression and engagement. Milner used the expression "pop polyvocality" to explain the richness of these memes, which discussed, among other things, citizenship, police brutality, and capitalism. Clark (2016) studied the production of memes by young people at the margins of traditional politics following the protests in Ferguson and the emergence of #BlackLivesMatter. She viewed memes as "artifacts of engagement" in line with Bennett and Segerberg's (2013) connective action theory. In this context, memes allow for citizens to express themselves in an unfettered manner and offer an alternative vision of events. Huntington (2015) adopts a rhetorical view of memes in order to understand the discourse of social movements. Based on the case of the "Pepper Spray Cop" meme shared during the Occupy Wall Street demonstrations, she shows that protesters used images and discourses to make specific claims about politics.[2] Popular ideas related to the myth of the American Dream (e.g., liberty, fairness, power to the people) were used to critique how the American system works.

Elsewhere in the world, Gerbaudo (2015) turned his attention to the use of memes as a way to identify with protest movements. For example, during the different protest waves in 2011 in Egypt, Spain, and the United States, citizens changed their WhatsApp and Facebook personal profile pictures to protest avatars as ways to identify themselves with the issues and claims of various social movements. Protest avatars constitute, for Gerbaudo, "memetic signifiers" (918) since they often have symbolic references, from images of famous protesters such as Khaled Said to the fist representing the revolution to various reproductions of the Anonymous mask placed on an Egyptian mummy, on Che Guevara's face, or on Shepard Fairey's Obama Hope poster. These memes spread rapidly and were part of the collective identification of digital activists. Some images were quickly printed on T-shirts, stickers, flags, and buttons. They became parts of the activists' communication strategies. Kligler-Vilenchik and Thorson (2015) analyzed the memetic reactions to the highly popular *Kony 2012* video and social change campaign. In 2012, a group called "Invisible Children" created a video to

> spread awareness of atrocities committed by Ugandan warlord Joseph Kony to create pressure toward the goal of tracking Kony down and bringing him to justice. In the background of images of people using YouTube, Facebook, Skype, and Twitter, the film promises that the connection of people forged through social media "is changing the way the world works." ... The movie advocated for the power of the "networked citizen." (Kliger-Vilenchik and Thorson 2015, 2)

The authors analyzed the memes created after the diffusion of *Kony 2012* to theorize the tensions among different conceptions of good citizenship put forward in the images and discourses. Memes were used to criticize what was seen as "slacktivism" since sharing content was not considered "real" political activism. In this sense, memes were normative artifacts allowing Kligler-Vilenchik and Thorson to identify citizens' definitions of "good citizenship."

CASE STUDY

Methods

This research focuses on one specific form of meme: the image macro. These memes comprise an image that remains fairly constant and text that is usually two phrases (see Figure 5.1): the expression at the top of the image sets up or contextualizes the message, and the bottom expression is the witty message, catchphrase, or punchline. The text is generally written in capital letters, and the font is usually Impact (a font now closely associated with memes) (Brideau and Berret 2014). Memes circulate in an open, adaptable, and collaborative environment. An image macro can be created through various sites such as memegenerator.net or quickmeme. com (Milner 2012, 12).

To explore this practice, we analyzed internet memes featuring former Prime Minister Stephen Harper and the Conservative Party (2006–15). The Harper memes were collected continuously from Facebook pages,

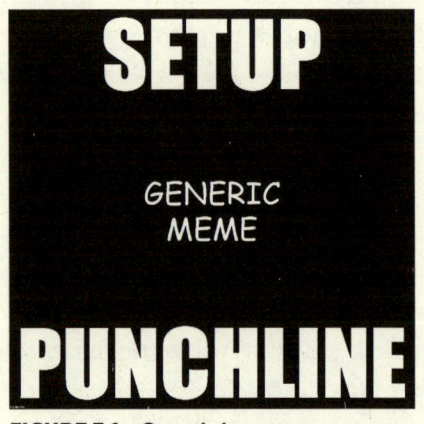

FIGURE 5.1 Generic image macromeme

websites, blogs, and archiving platforms (e.g., 4chan, 9gag, Imgur, Know Your Meme, Quickmeme, and Theharpergov).[3] The following keywords were used in Google.ca and Google Images between November 1, 2014, and January 15, 2015, to find the memes in the resources noted above: "Stephen Harper meme," "Harper meme," "Canada Conservative Party meme," "Conservative Harper meme," "Canada meme," and "Canadian meme." We originally collected 300 memes. After duplicates were removed, our final corpus included 250 memes. Although this extensive way of collecting data allowed us to locate a wide range of Harper memes, we do not claim that the corpus was a representative sample of Harper memes at the time of the study.

Political memes are understudied in the academic literature dealing with digital politics. As is the case with understudied objects of research, the first studies are generally exploratory and offer analytical snapshots of what is occurring. We offer descriptive statistics and further conceptualize the uses of memes in the last part of the chapter. Our research furthers the understanding of political memes in a number of ways. To our knowledge, there are no published studies that focus on political memes in Canada. However, our study differs from international scholarship, which generally focuses on memes within the context of a political event, such as a protest. Here we focus on memes related to political leadership. This is not to say that our conclusions differ vastly from those of previous studies. Yet it is important to recognize that political memes can be of many types, and scholarship should take note of this. Finally, we make an important methodological contribution since few studies have focused on memes' content or, in this case, macro-images.

Findings

We focused on the rhetorical content of memes. What was the purpose of Stephen Harper memes? What were the topics and approaches taken by meme creators when focusing on Harper? We randomly selected fifty memes and let categories emerge until saturation using an iterative approach to create a coding grid. This first round of analysis showed that memes generally denounced or "trolled" Harper and his party/government. The term "troll" is internet slang for a person who makes a deliberately offensive, inflammatory, or provocative statement online (Underwood and Welser 2011). In fact, no meme examined lauded Harper or the Conservatives. The memes portrayed him as both a bad politician and a bad human being. However, we see these meme creators not simply as trolls but also as internet activists. As in Clark (2016), these memes allowed citizens to express political dissatisfaction through their lack of support for Harper. The denunciations of him occurred in two broad categories: governance and personality. Governance memes focused on political actions and decisions by Harper and the Conservative Party, whereas personality memes criticized Harper himself.

After these two broad categories were formalized in the first round of analysis, we created and defined metacategories, categories, and subcategories (see Table 5.1). The coding grid was tested with multiple coders (intercoder reliability of 93.3 percent). Each meme was coded by searching for the presence/absence of the dominant category. The dominant denunciation was coded because categories were mutually exclusive and because memes often discussed one subject.

Before analyzing the memes' rhetorical contents, it is worth discussing briefly the images used. Table 5.2 shows that different images were used in the trolling of Harper. By far, the most popular was the bust of Harper against a blue background (see Figure 5.2). Three-quarters of the memes featured this image. The next most common image was a variation of Harper standing in front of the Canadian flag. Although the other images were used less frequently, they were used with intention. That is, the picture was related to the punchline of the meme. For instance, the beer cheers image features a picture of Harper with a pint of beer taken during a campaign stop at a pub during the 2011 federal election. In the meme, he appears to be toasting the punchline. The thumbs-up image is similar. This is an image of Harper giving two thumbs up – again the representation tends to be related to the punchline. Meme creators occasionally mash up popular (nonpolitical) meme stock characters, such as Scumbag Steve or the Success Kid with Harper.[4] The Success Kid meme is of a baby clenching his fist while having a determined look on his face. It is used to designate either success or frustration. Finally, Hipster Harper is an image of a younger Harper with long hair wearing a plaid shirt. These memes centre on how a cooler, younger Harper would act in contrast to his older self.

TABLE 5.1
Categories of denunciation in political internet memes about Prime Minister Stephen Harper

Meta-categories	(%)	Categories	(%)	Subcategories	(%)
Governance (N = 196)	78.4	Government (N = 119)	47.6	Authoritarian figure	8.8
				Election malpractice	8.4
				Censorship and lack of transparency	8.0
				Lying	6.4
				Negative attack ads	3.6
				Disrespect of electoral promises	3.2
				Judiciarization of political processes	3.2
				Corruption	2.8
				Militarization of the Canadian army	1.6
				Adoption of a Republican agenda	1.6
		Policy (N = 31)	12.4	Ideological management of the state	7.6
				Capitalist and neoliberal practices	4.8
		Society (N = 46)	18.4	Antagonistic relationship with the scientific community	6.0
				Racism and xenophobia	4.8
				Sexism	3.2
				Discrimination against the artistic community	2.0
				Homophobia	1.6
				Ageism	0.8
Personality (N = 41)	15.2			Incompetence	6.8
				Inhumane character	4.4
				Disregard	2.0
				Narrow-mindedness	2.0

The simplicity and repetitiveness of the memes allow, according to Shifman (2012, 196–97), for easy imitation and encourage involvement and memorability. These images, like the protest avatars studied by Gerbaudo (2015), can be seen as emblems fuelling the collective identification of the memes' producers and consumers and helping engagement and contestation.

Turning to the rhetorical contents of memes, Table 5.1 shows that the vast majority of them focused on the governance of Harper and the Conservatives. Fewer than one in five memes focused on his personality. A small number of memes could not be categorized into either of these metacategories, and no dominant denunciation could be determined. The

TABLE 5.2
Images used in Stephen Harper memes

	Political practice (%) (N = 196)	Personality (%) (N = 41)	Other (%) (N = 13)	Total (%) (N = 250)
Harper bust	75.0	78.0	69.2	75.5
Harper with flag	11.7	7.3	7.7	10.8
Beer cheers	2.0	7.3	23.1	4.0
Stock character	3.1	2.4	0.0	2.4
Hipster Harper	1.5	2.4	0.05	1.6
Thumbs up	2.0	0.0	0.0	1.6
Other	4.6	2.4	0.0	4.0

dominance of governance memes is interesting because it demonstrates that political meme creators use memes to criticize the actions and behaviours of a leader/party/government and suggests higher political engagement and knowledge among the creators. Moreover, like Clark's (2016) analysis of memes about Ferguson, the discussion on Harper's actions can be seen as creating counterpublics committed to offering different discourses on his actions. Although dominant forms of denunciation (governance and personality) are probably applicable to any political leader, we found that memes were specific to particular actions, policies, and behaviours of Harper and the Conservatives.

The first category of memes is composed of denunciations of actions and decisions of Harper and the Conservative Party. The meme creators expressed political dissent by presenting him as a bad politician. Within this category, three subcategories emerged related to the themes of government, policy, and society. Government memes include those criticizing the Harper Conservatives by highlighting their disrespect for democratic norms and rules. These memes also denounce both secretly and publicly acknowledged manoeuvres intended to benefit the Conservative Party. Policy memes are denunciations of the Harper government's policies, including those related to the economy and health care. Finally, society memes criticize Harper and the Conservative Party's treatment of different segments of Canadian society. These memes present Harper as someone unable or unwilling to do a good job. They also present him as a blindly ideological leader who does not care for Canadians and pursues power for his own partisan ends.

As Table 5.1 shows, almost 50 percent of governance memes were focused on the government. A popular subcategory was composed of memes referring to Harper as an authoritarian figure (Figure 5.3 and 5.4). As we can see in Figure 5.2, the message put forward was that Canada was "Harperland." This likely referred to Lawrence Martin's *Harperland: The Politics of Control.* Published in 2010, the book discusses Harper's first two terms as prime minister, from 2006 to 2011, and the transformations in the way that Canada worked and was perceived under his leadership.

Facing page:

FIGURE 5.2 Example of a governance meme related to Harper as an authoritarian

FIGURE 5.3 Example of a governance meme related to Harper's censorship and lack of media transparency

Right:

FIGURE 5.4 Example of society-focused political meme

Martin examines different practices, including silencing public servants and diplomats, using prorogation in order to stymie the work of Parliament, and bypassing journalists and the media. The evidence suggests that meme creators are politically knowledgeable.

Pierre Elliott Trudeau is referenced in the second meme in Figure 5.3. Many scholars consider him to have been the first prime minister to centralize the government (Savoie 1999). The quotation marks around the term "totally" give this meme an ironic tone, for many believed that Harper took centralization to a whole new level (Martin 2010). This meme emerged in June 2013 following Brent Rathgeber's resignation from the Conservative caucus. His stated reasons for leaving were the "government's lack of commitment to transparency and open government" (Rathgeber 2013). The nod to Trudeau shows political knowledge among meme creators since the notion of increased centralization under the former Liberal prime minister is likely not common knowledge. As Milner (2013) showed in the case of Occupy Wall Street, citizens customize information to construct their discourses. In the case of the Harper meme, they used a past politician's actions in order to prove their point.

Another common focus of Harper memes was election malpractice and disrespect of electoral promises. For instance, a meme said "Increase popular vote share by 2% ... /Win 24 more seats and a majority government." This meme demonstrates the creator's knowledge of electoral results and the tendency of the first-past-the-post electoral system to manufacture majorities. The Harper government's censorship and lack of media transparency were also popular topics of discussion in memes. Figure 5.4, for instance, refers to a Conservative policy in 2011 that limited journalists to five questions per day (Kaplan 2016). The focus on Harper and the press is perhaps not surprising given their tumultuous relationship (see Paré and Delacourt 2014). Soon after Harper was elected in 2006, the Prime Minister's Office instituted policies limiting the media's access to him and cabinet ministers, including asking reporters to put their names on a list so that they could pick which ones could ask questions. These types of memes speak to specific events in Canadian politics and, again, to higher than normal levels of political knowledge among meme-makers. It is also worth noting that this meme refers to Harper as a machine or robot, and he was often portrayed in memes as lacking human characteristics.

FIGURE 5.5 Example of a policy-focused political meme

FIGURE 5.6 Example of a society-focused meme

Almost 20 percent of governance memes criticized the Conservatives' and Harper's treatment of different groups in Canadian society, including the muzzling of scientists, racism and xenophobia, sexism, discrimination against artists, homophobia, and ageism. The antagonistic relationship between Harper and the scientific community is questioned in Figure 5.5. Earlier we noted that a small number of memes in our corpus incorporate popular meme stock characters to denounce the Conservatives. An example is the "anti-joke chicken." The "anti-joke chicken meme features an image of a hen accompanied by a top line of text that sounds like the introduction of a joke (e.g., Why did the chicken cross the road), but the bottom line provides an unexpected anticlimax."[5] The meme creator is clear in the belief that Harper would have nothing to say to Stephen Hawking, one of the most famous scientific figures in the world. Figure 5.6 provides another example of a society meme. This meme criticizes gender parity in the Conservative cabinet. In Harper's first cabinet (2006), six of twenty-six ministers were women. In his final cabinet, 30 percent of ministers were women (Warzecha 2015).

Finally, we also found memes that criticized Conservative policy on issues such as health care, child care, corporate taxes, Employment Insurance (EI), and foreign relations (Figure 5.7 and 5.8). The two final

FIGURES 5.7 AND 5.8 Examples of policy-focused political memes

memes are particularly noteworthy. Following the original publication of the EI meme, it was used to criticize other political practices of the prime minister. The criticism of the Conservatives' relationship with China features another popular meme image of celebrity chef Gordon Ramsay. Ramsay is famous for his brash talk, and his photo is used in memes criticizing how things are done.

Our second broad category of memes focuses on Harper's personality. As noted, this category is far smaller than the governance category, with fewer than one in five memes focused on personality issues (15.2 percent). This is an interesting finding because it seems to demonstrate that political meme creators were not interested in cheap or lowbrow humour. That is, most memes do not attempt to make a joke at Harper's expense. Although some meme creators did seek to make fun of Harper, most engaged in what can be better understood as a form of online political dissent. In this sense, they had relationships to politics organized around the actions of the politician and not his personality, as also observed by Sci and Dewberry (2015). As demonstrated earlier, most memes are denunciations of Harper's political approach and actions. Nevertheless, memes in this category questioned his competence and his perceived inhuman character, disregard for others, religious beliefs, and narrow-mindedness. Overall, memes in this category questioned whether Harper cared about others.

For example, his seeming inability to understand simple concepts was raised with a question: "Peace? ... /I don't eat them." Here Harper is presented as being unable to understand the difference between the

FIGURES 5.9 AND 5.10 Examples of personality memes

words "peace" and "peas." Moreover, the meme suggests that he was not interested in peace. His seemingly inhuman character is also raised in some of the memes analyzed, in which he is presented as a zombie, a Romulan, an alien, or a robot, as seen in Figure 5.9.

The caricature of Harper as lacking human characteristics has been ever present in popular culture. For instance, CBC Television's *Royal Canadian Air Farce* had a recurring skit in which the actor impersonating Harper has robotic movements and speech patterns (using terms such as "affirmative" or calling his wife by her first and last names) and refers to having "heat visions."[6] There was also a Tumblr account called "Stephen Harper Isn't a Killer Robot" and one called "Things Harper Does to Seem Human."[7] Posts were presented as attempts by Harper to convince people that he was not a robot.[8] Finally, Harper's perceived lack of care can be seen in Figure 5.10. This meme uses another popular meme picture known as "Grumpy Cat," the nickname of a cat named Tardar Sauce that became an internet sensation after several pictures of her annoyed facial expressions appeared on Reddit in 2012.

TRENDING IN CANADA

Although we considered only memes related to a single politician, we can draw many conclusions from our assessment of political memes that can be applicable beyond our analysis. First, political memes are foremost about politics rather than personality. Memes are not only about making fun of a politician but also about challenging a politician's politics and policies. Although the memes *generally* use Harper's image, they do so merely to show that the meme is about him and his policies. Moreover, the various denunciations analyzed here can be seen as a struggle over the framing of the ideal politician or what makes a good politician.

Second, evidence suggests that meme creators are knowledgeable about politics. The examples that we considered show that meme creators were aware of Harper's and the Conservative Party's style of governing, their policy choices, and their relationships with different groups in society. Memes tended to be not vague generalizations but specific denunciations of Harper's and the Conservative Party's actions and behaviours. In that sense, we suspect that many of these memes were also timely, appearing shortly after the events occurred. This would also be consistent with our early research findings on memes focused on Justin Trudeau in which events such as "elbowgate" and the announcement of the first gender-balanced federal cabinet were quickly followed by related memes. We find that the use of Harper's image in memes is consistent with the personalization of politics in Canada. Meme creators use popular images in order to formulate their critiques of governance and politicians' actions and personalities.

Third, we see that some meme creators are steeped in broader meme culture, as seen through the use of popular, nonpolitical memes such as Scumbag Steve, the anti-joke chicken, and Grumpy Cat. Yet, as noted in Table 5.2, we found that images of Harper are the most common. In light of these observations, the memes studied here can be seen as a form of political advocacy (Shifman 2013b). They are also part of larger grassroots actions characterized by the possibility of spreading messages using various platforms. This offers citizens the possibility of communicating in their own terms (Bennett and Segerberg 2013, 37–38). As such, political meme-making could lead to a renewed relationship between politics and democratic practices.

Fourth, this brings us to consider how we can understand the Harper memes within a broader conversation about the evolution of communication and political behaviour. As noted earlier, we see political memes as a new form of political action and self-expression for individuals in Canada. The Harper memes express political dissent over the actions and policies of Harper and the Conservative government. The portrait offered by our research shares similarities with the good citizen debates studied by Kligler-Vilenchik and Thorson (2015). Following their line of thought, we can see the debate about Prime Minister Harper as normative and entailing "judgments about what kind of behaviors are valued and which are not" (15). The denunciation of authoritarian practices, lies, and electoral malpractices are pleas for democratic leadership, honesty, and ethical political behaviour.

Moreover, political memes such as those examined here are what Van Laer and Van Aelst (2010) describe as an internet-based political action repertoire: that is, a form of activism made possible largely because of the internet. Whereas signing a petition on the internet is merely a digital way to do something that exists offline, political image macromemes have no corollaries. It is difficult to imagine what the offline versions of such macromemes (political or otherwise) would look like. Indeed, even though memes existed long before the internet, online memes encapsulate the participatory culture of Web 2.0 (Shifman 2013b). The participatory web allows individuals not only to create but also to share memes. Harper meme creators used the internet as a tool to criticize and mock the political leader and used social media platforms, such as Facebook, to share their critiques with others. Such creating and sharing are important political activities that allow memes to become viral and give them new dimensions and magnitudes.

One might suggest that the offline corollary of a political meme is the editorial cartoon. On one level, we agree. Political memes share similarities with editorial cartoons. For instance, Tay (2015) notes that political memes, like editorial cartoons, tend to be created in response to current events or news. For memes and cartoons to be successful, the political context must be recognizable to the audience. We saw this in the vast majority of Harper memes, which were topical and directly tied to current political events, including the muzzling of scientists and journalists or financial issues. According to Trimble, Way, and Sampert (2010), editorial cartoons use humour, irony, pop culture, and satire as visual and rhetorical strategies. We saw such features in the various Harper memes examined here. However, though political memes belong to the family of political humour (see Tay 2015), we still argue that they are a unique form of political activity. This uniqueness comes from the fact that they are made not by elites but by amateurs. Editorial cartoonists are professional artists employed by major media organizations. Political humour programs such as *The Daily Show* or *The Rick Mercer Report* feature professional comedians working on major television networks. The creators of the Harper memes were likely not professionals paid to engage in political humour but individual Canadians engaged in political activism. This fact makes them part of an evolution of communication and political behaviour. The critical difference is that the tools to create and share memes tear down traditional barriers, thus opening up this form of political action to non-elites. Sites and tools online allow citizens to create memes fairly easily and automatically (e.g., memegenerator.net), thus aiding amateurs to create such content. With a few clicks, lay citizens can express themselves about political issues and post their creations on their Instagram and Twitter accounts or on their Facebook pages.

One accusation that could be levelled at meme creators, such as those who created the Harper memes, is that of slacktivism. "Slacktivism" is a pejorative term related to some online actions that have little or no effect on offline political outcomes (Christensen 2011). The online activity does not serve any social purpose other than increasing "the feel-good factor of the participants" (Christensen 2011). Many political uses of social media are accused of slacktivism, such as changing one's Facebook pictures to French flag colours in support of Paris after a terrorist attack or hashtag activism such as #bringbackourgirls. It is easy to see how the creator of a political meme can fit into this conceptualization of online political activism. The type of research that we conducted does not allow us to measure influence and diffusion patterns of the Harper memes (see Spitzberg 2014). Unlike editorial cartoons, viewed by millions daily, it is difficult to know how many people saw these memes and what, if any, impact they had. Graeff (2016) is not convinced that political memes are a form of slacktivism. As noted earlier, creating and sharing memes are political actions; the sharing does real political work in terms of creating a moment and a networked public with power greater than the sum of its parts. Friends or followers are exposed to the sharer's otherwise unspoken political opinions and given the opportunity to participate by forwarding the meme (Graeff 2016).

Fifth, when it comes to political memes in Canada and elsewhere, much scholarly work remains to be done. Little research has been conducted in Canada, and as the literature review shows research is scant internationally, notably on the subject of memes and public participation. One limitation of our study is that we looked at a single political leader nearing the end of his term in office. It would be instructive to conduct a comparative study of political leaders. In a nonsystematic look at memes about Prime Minister Justin Trudeau, we do not see the level of trolling that Harper received (Figure 5.11). Although the findings presented here focus on denunciations, perhaps studies of different leaders, especially comparative studies, might indicate other purposes for political memes related to leadership. There is also value in exploring the intentions of meme creators. It would be useful to explore through surveys and interviews how individuals create memes and what their intentions are in creating and sharing them. Surveys would also allow us to test our hypothesis that meme creators have higher than normal levels of political knowledge and to assess their overall levels of political behaviour.

FIGURE 5.11 Example of a Justin Trudeau meme

NOTES

1 The word "pastiche" refers to a piece of art (from music to theatre to paintings) that imitates and borrows from other works or styles.
2 Pepper Spray Cop is a meme based on a photograph of a police officer casually pepper-spraying Occupy protesters at the University of California Davis in 2011.
3 All of the memes collected were put into a general database. We did not consider the source of the meme. Hence, we are not able to determine if the source of the meme affects the content of the message.
4 Scumbag Steve is a meme featuring a kid with a sideways cap. The text generally centres on unethical and hedonistic behaviour such as taking drugs and partying. In one meme in our corpus, the meme creator added the Scumbag Steve hat to the prototypical Harper bust image. This meme was about the disabling of comments on Harper's YouTube channel (top text: "Has a YouTube Channel"; bottom text: "Comments Disabled").
5 For more information on and context for this meme and others discussed here, please consult knowyourmeme.com. The website is dedicated to documenting memes, including viral videos, and image macros.
6 Some examples of these *Air Farce* videos can be found on YouTube by searching the terms "Harper robot *Air Farce*."
7 The former account has been disabled and does not exist anymore. For the latter account, see http://thingsharperdoestoseemhuman.tumblr.com.
8 stephenharperisnotakillerrobot.tumblr.com is no longer available online. However, it can be viewed using the Internet Archive Wayback Machine (https://archive.org/web/).

REFERENCES

Bennett, W. Lance, and Alexandra Segerberg. 2013. *The Logic of Connective Action*. Cambridge, UK: Cambridge University Press.

Brideau, Kate, and Charles Berret. 2014. "A Brief Introduction to Impact: 'The Meme Font.'" *Journal of Visual Culture* 13, 3: 307–13.

Christensen, Henrik Serup. 2011. "Political Activities on the Internet: Slacktivism or Political Participation by Other Means?" *First Monday* 16. http://firstmonday.org/article/view/3336/2767.

Clark, Lynn Schofield. 2016. "Constructing Public Spaces| Participants on the Margins: Examining the Role that Shared Artifacts of Engagement in the Ferguson Protests Played among Minoritized Political Newcomers on Snapchat, Facebook, and Twitter." *International Journal of Communication* 10: 235–53.

Gerbaudo, Paolo. 2015. "Protest Avatars as Memetic Signifiers: Political Profile Pictures and the Construction of Collective Identity on Social #Media in the 2011 Protest Wave." *Information, Communication, and Society* 18, 8: 916–29.

Graeff, Erhardt. 2016. "Binders Full of Election Memes: Participatory Culture Invades the 2012 U.S. Election." *Civic Media Project*. http://civicmediaproject.org/works/civic-media-project/binders-full-of-election-memes-participatory-culture-invades-the-2012-us-election.

Harlow, Summer. 2013. "'It Was a Facebook Revolution': Exploring the Meme-Like Spread of Narratives during the Egyptian Protests." *Revista de comunicación* 12: 59–82.

Huntington, Heidi E. 2015. "Pepper Spray Cop and the American Dream: Using Synecdoche and Metaphor to Unlock Internet Memes' Visual Political Rhetoric." *Communication Studies* 67, 1: 77–93.

Jenkins, Henry, Sam Ford, and Joshua Green. 2013. *Spreadable Media: Creating Value and Meaning in a Networked Culture*. New York: New York University Press.

Kaplan, William. 2016. "Stephen Harper's Five-Question Limit." *Globe and Mail*, April 15, 2011. http://www.theglobeandmail.com/opinion/stephen-harpers-five-question-limit/article579733/.

Kligler-Vilenchik, Neta, and Kjerstin Thorson. 2015. "Good Citizenship as a Frame Contest: *Kony 2012*, Memes, and Critiques of the Networked Citizen." *New Media and Society* 18, 9: 1–19.

Lievrouw, Leah A. 2011. *Alternative and Activist New Media*. Cambridge, UK: Polity Press.

Martin, Lawrence. 2010. *Harperland: The Politics of Control*. Toronto: Viking Canada.

Milner, Ryan M. 2012. "The World Made Meme: Discourse and Identity in Participatory Media." PhD diss., Department of Communication Studies, University of Kansas.

–. 2013. "Pop Polyvocality: Internet Memes, Public Participation, and the Occupy Wall Street Movement." *International Journal of Communication* 7: 2357–90.

Paré, Daniel J., and Susan Delacourt. 2014. "The Canadian Parliamentary Press Gallery." In *Political Communication in Canada: Meet the Press and Tweet the Rest*, edited by Alex Marland, Thierry Giasson, and Tamara A. Small, 111–26. Vancouver: UBC Press.

Rathgeber, Brent. 2013. "Tweet 7:22 PM–5 Jun 2013." https://twitter.com/brentrathgeber/status/342466398045478912.

Savoie, Donald J. 1999. *Governing from the Centre: The Concentration of Power in Canadian Politics*. Toronto: University of Toronto Press.

Sci, Susan A., and David R. Dewberry. 2015. "The Laughing Joe Biden Meme as Digital Topoi within Political Argumentation." In *Disturbing Argument: Selected Works from the 18th NCA/AFA Alta Conference on Argumentation*, edited by C.H. Palczewski, 232–37. London: Routledge.

Shifman, Limor. 2007. "Humor in the Age of Digital Reproduction: Continuity and Change in Internet-Based Comic Texts." *International Journal of Communication* 1, 1: 187–209.

–. 2012. "An Anatomy of a YouTube Meme." *New Media and Society* 14, 2: 187–203.

–. 2013a. "Memes in a Digital World: Reconciling with a Conceptual Troublemaker." *Journal of Computer-Mediated Communication* 18, 3: 362–77.

–. 2013b. *Memes in Digital Culture*. Cambridge, MA: MIT Press.

Spitzberg, Brian H. 2014. "Toward a Model of Meme Diffusion." *Communication Theory* 24, 3: 311–39.

Tay, Geniesa. 2015. "Binders Full of LOLitics: Political Humour, Internet Memes, and Play in the 2012 US Presidential Election (and Beyond)." *European Journal of Humour Research* 2, 4: 46–73.

Trimble, Linda, Laura Way, and Shannon Sampert. 2010. "Drawn to the Polls? Representations of Canadian Voters in Editorial Cartoons." *Journal of Canadian Studies* 44, 2: 70–94.

Underwood, Patrick, and Howard T. Welser. 2011. "The Internet Is Here: Emergent Coordination and Innovation of Protest Forms in Digital Culture." Paper presented at iConference 2011, Seattle, February 8–11.

Van Laer, Jeroen, and Peter Van Aelst. 2010. "Internet and Social Movement Action Repertoires: Opportunities and Limitations." *Information, Communication, and Society* 13, 8: 1146–71.

Warzecha, Monika. 2015. "How Justin Trudeau's Cabinet Compares to Stephen Harper's First Team." *National Post*, November 5. http://news.nationalpost.com/news/canada/canadian-politics/how-justin-trudeaus-cabinet-compares-to-stephen-harpers-first-team.

Wiggins, Bradley E., and G. Bret Bowers. 2015. "Memes as Genre: A Structurational Analysis of the Memescape." *New Media and Society* 17, 11: 1886–1906.

6

From Spheres to Trajectories of Publicness
Exploring How the 2010 Toronto G20 Protests Were Communicated through Social Media

THOMAS POELL

In late June 2010, during the Digital Methods Summer School at the University of Amsterdam, a few Canadian participants were feverishly checking their Twitter timelines and Facebook news feeds. As it turned out, at the exact moment that we were experimenting with tools to explore Facebook linking practices, scrape Twitter data, and trace inlinks to YouTube videos, protests against the G20 summit in Toronto were occurring. These ten days of protests were characterized by confrontations between protesters and police, omnipresent in the city, who outnumbered protesters two to one. The confrontations, which frequently turned violent, ultimately led to the temporary arrests of over 1,000 people, making it the largest mass arrest in Canadian history (Renzi and Elmer 2013).

As I observed my Canadian colleagues being thrown between anger and sadness by what they were seeing and reading in their feeds, I became fascinated by the events and started collecting social media data on the protests. When I reviewed this material, its real-time character and its global reach were particularly striking. As I explored the contents, hyperlink networks, user practices, and technologies of the G20 protest stream, it became clear that the topology of contemporary activist communication is particularly complex. Not only does this communication blur the boundaries among the "local," "national," and "global," but also it is characterized by a deep entanglement between social practices and technocommercial architectures. Here I reflect on the changing topology of activist communication which, driven by the development of digital media, has already gone through substantial changes and is bound to evolve further in the coming decade. I take the 2010 Toronto G20 protests as my case study, but I also draw examples from other contemporary protests.

My investigation should be seen against the backdrop of a longer effort to understand how media (re)shape political communication. Since Jürgen Habermas published *Strukturwandel der Öffentlichkeit* in 1962, translated into English in 1989 as *Structural Transformation of the Public Sphere*, public sphere theory has been the main conceptual framework through which this effort has been pursued. Habermas (1989, 25) argued that over the eighteenth century the bourgeois public sphere developed as the "forum in which the private people ... come together to form a public," compelling "public authority to legitimate itself before public opinion." The public employed "publicity," in the form of "rational-critical public debate," as its "principle of control" in opposition to public authority (28). In this constellation, media fulfilled a crucial role, for the emerging periodical press carried the public debate. Habermas subsequently used this historical account as the basis for a critical assessment of the twentieth-century public sphere. According to him, this sphere had effectively collapsed as a result of the development of commercial mass media, which transformed "publicity" into "manufactured publicity" (211). Important to note is that in this theory "public authority" is synonymous with the national state, and media are synonymous with the national media.

Although the original Habermasian conceptualization of the public sphere was extensively criticized in the decades that followed, the national frame of analysis remained largely unquestioned for a long time (Fraser 2007). It remained unquestioned despite the development of a more pluralist conception of the public sphere. Taking issue with the idea that there is a single public sphere, primarily carried by the bourgeois public, critics have argued that there are and should be multiple public spheres (Dahlgren 1995; Fraser 1990; Keane 1991). These critics have demonstrated that over the past centuries different publics, in the words of Nancy Fraser (1990, 67), invented and circulated "counterdiscourses to formulate oppositional interpretations of their identities, interests, and needs." Fraser points out that "subordinated social groups – women, workers, peoples of color, and gays and lesbians – have repeatedly found it advantageous to constitute alternative publics." Corresponding with this observation, a democratic media system ideally should support the articulation of counterdiscourses by such publics to enable their participation in public debates. Evidently, this pluralist perspective undermines the idea of a unitary national sphere and opens up the analysis to the autonomous practices of local and regional, as well as transnational, counterpublics, without having to understand these practices and publics as subordinated to national publics. Nevertheless, even most pluralist public sphere theorists continued, up to the late 1990s, to hold on to the national state, media, and public as comprising the primary framework of analysis.

By the turn of the millennium, however, it became progressively clear that this position could not be maintained. Already in the 1990s, theorists of globalization, most prominently Manuel Castells (1996), showed that the national state is no longer the primary arena in which political and economic processes take shape. The network society, in his terminology, is constituted through global information networks, facilitated by the development of the internet. This transnational perspective has been increasingly adopted by political communication scholars, especially by those working on contentious communication (Arquilla and Ronfeldt 2001; van de Donk et al. 2004). These authors show how many contemporary protests and protest issues are developed through transnational activist networks, which connect local activist groups and organizations from around the globe.

Growing awareness of the impact of globalization on political communication has thoroughly affected public sphere theory, for it is clear that the most pressing political issues of our times, from economic inequality to global warming, can no longer be adequately addressed in national public spheres. Reflecting on this "postnational constellation," Habermas (2001, 103), for one, has argued for the development of a "pan-European political public sphere." He immediately adds, however, that it "presupposes a European civil society complete with interest groups, non-governmental organizations, citizens' movements, and so forth." Fraser (2007, 20), in turn, notes that public sphere theory needs to be fundamentally rethought for a post-Westphalian world. The key for her is to "envision conditions under which current flows of transnational publicity could conceivably become legitimate and efficacious." Ultimately, this means the development of "new transnational public powers, which can be made accountable to new democratic transnational circuits of public opinion." Thus, both Habermas and Fraser are clear that only the development of transnational public powers, accountable to public opinion within a particular region, such as the European Union, can provide the basis for a real transnational public sphere.

Of course, the problem is that we are far removed from such a transnational order and will be for the foreseeable future. Yet it is also clear that transnational activist networks, organizations, and protests constantly address global socio-economic, political, and ecological problems and try to hold local, national, and supranational authorities accountable for these problems (Bennett and Segerberg 2013; Castells 2009; Couldry 2014). Although these authorities tend to remain largely unresponsive to such appeals, transnational protest activity does raise public awareness and does contribute to the articulation of transnational public opinions on key societal issues. The G20 protests and the wave of Occupy protests should be seen in this regard as vital contributions to contemporary democratic discourse.

Yet the question is which kinds of democratic discourse are constituted by online communication on such protest events? Where is this discourse "located" exactly? If both the issues and the actors fundamentally transcend national public spheres, but cannot be understood in terms of transnational public spheres either, then we need to reconsider the concepts employed to locate and evaluate these forms of democratic publicness. This appears to be all the more urgent since various critical theorists have pointed out that the kinds of public interactions and connections that take shape online cannot be adequately understood in terms of public sphere theory. These interactions and connections do not correspond with what public sphere theorists have recognized as democratic forms of political communication.

Studying how the websites of key actors – NGOs, corporations, government agencies – are connected to each other through hyperlinks in controversies over technoscientific issues, Marres and Rogers (2005), for example, are clear that these connections cannot, in the tradition of public sphere theory, be considered as public debates; rather, they should be theorized as "issue networks." Instead of talking to each other, these scholars found, the webpages "in the network were rather defining the issue in question in ways that built from, and countered, issue-definitions presented on other pages in the network" (922). Although these issue networks can be considered as a form of democratic political communication, they do not correspond with the public sphere idea of public debate as the foundation of democratic discourse. In a similar vein, Jodi Dean (2003, 105) has argued that, rather than constituting a public sphere, the web should be seen as "a site of conflict over the meaning, practice, and shape of the global." In this struggle, notions of the "public sphere," "public debate," and "democratic public" function, according to Dean, are ideological constructs employed to legitimize the development of communicative capitalism as it takes shape in the expansion of the infrastructure of the information society.

This critical assessment appears to be all the more relevant today when commercial social media present themselves as platforms of "natural collectivity." This rhetoric, as Couldry (2015, 621) has pointed out, is "intensely motivated by the commercial need to sell the data-based value that derives from assuming that social networking sites are indeed the place where 'we' come together." The hypercommercial nature of social media platforms is important since the business models of these platforms inform the development of technological architectures, which in turn shape how users can connect and interact with each other. Research suggests that the growing use of social media by protesters leads to an acceleration of protest communication while enhancing the personalization and individualization of this type of communication (Fenton and Barassi 2011; Juris 2012; Milan 2015; Poell and van Dijck 2015). Both tendencies appear to conflict with public sphere ideals, for they stand in tension with efforts to draw sustained attention to key political issues as well as to construct alternative publics. Yet these trends also seem to enhance the reach and visibility of protest communication, which brings important strategic advantages to activists.

The development of social media into prominent platforms of protest activity triggers critical questions about the topology of contemporary political communication. Along with the globalization of political-economic relations and related problems, this trend forces us to reconsider the national framework through which we study politics. Social media protest communication fundamentally transcends the framework of national public spheres, but it cannot, in the absence of a supranational public order, be understood in terms of a transnational public sphere. Consequently, it becomes vital to trace and theorize the "where" of social media protest communication. Moreover, contentious social media communication does not conform to what has been considered as democratic discourse from a public sphere perspective. Yet, from other perspectives, the democratic potential of this type of communication, with some major asterisks attached, can be recognized. Thus, we also need to interrogate critically and reconceptualize the "what" of social media protest communication.

CASE STUDY

Methods

I address these questions through a case study of the 2010 Toronto G20 protests. Data collection was effectively facilitated by the Toronto Community Mobilization Network (TCMN), which coordinated many of the protests and carefully orchestrated which social media platforms and tags were employed. The TCMN specifically asked protesters to use Twitter, YouTube, and Flickr, tagging their reports with the #g20report. Furthermore, the TCMN employed the Toronto Media Co-op blog and the Community Solidarity Network Facebook group for communication purposes (Poell 2014; Poell and Borra 2012).

I developed the case study through the following steps. First, all of the reports on the social media advocated by the TCMN were collected for the twelve-day period between June 22 and July 3, 2010. Data were collected starting a few days before the actual G20 summit (June 26–27) because there was already significant protest activity. I collected data until after the summit since several demonstrations protesting the arrests of over 1,000 people took place after the summit. The collected material includes posts on Twitter, YouTube, and Flickr with the #g20report tag as well as posts on the Toronto Media Co-op blog and the Community Solidarity Network Facebook group. The tweets were collected with Google Real-Time Scraper.[1] This produced a set of 11,556 tweets for the twelve-day period. In turn, by searching #g20report on YouTube, 222 videos were harvested with the assistance of TubeKit.[2] And 3,338 Flickr photos were collected manually through Flickr's advanced search interface, which allows one to query for particular tags within a specific date range. The posts on the Media Co-op blog and the Facebook posts were also collected manually. For the latter, specifically the "links" pages of the Facebook group were saved.

Second, to gain insight into the "where" of G20 social media protest communication, I reconstructed the hyperlink network in which this communication was embedded. I did so by collecting the out- and in-links of amassed posts. Outlinks are URLs included in social media posts and refer to other online platforms. Inlinks, in turn, are links received by a particular post, or set of posts, from other platforms. The outlinks were selected from the harvested posts, whereas the inlinks were collected with Yahoo Inlink Scraper.[3] As a result of the particular architecture and the specific linking practices of each platform, there are a number of notable differences in how the inlinks were scraped. For YouTube, the Media Co-op blog, and Flickr, the inlinks for the individual posts were collected. In the case of the Facebook group, the links received by the group as a whole were scraped. And, because it is uncommon to link to individual tweets, I chose to scrape the Twitter search query for #g20report.

Third, to gain insight into "what" was exchanged through social media, I collected the top results from the Twitter, YouTube, and Flickr sets using the native selection principles of these platforms. For Twitter, this meant focusing on the top retweets, which can be seen as the tweets considered to be the most relevant by the users. Given the real-time nature of Twitter, particular accounts could be reconstructed for each of the twelve days under analysis, also making it possible to show how the #g20report account progressed over time. I did this by selecting for each day the top ten most retweeted messages. In addition to these messages, I selected the top ten most tweeted URLs per day. For YouTube and Flickr, determining the results deemed to be the most relevant by the users works somewhat differently. For these platforms, I selected the most relevant results on the basis of numbers of views and numbers of inlinks from other websites. Not surprisingly, these two user-attributed measures of relevance largely overlapped.

Findings

Starting with the "where" of activist social media communication, investigating the collected material reveals a complex, multilayered ecosystem, simultaneously hyperlocal, national, and transnational. Studying the content of the most engaged with tweets, posts, photos, and videos, as well as the hyperlink networks in which this content was embedded, unveils an intricate division of labour.

Most scholarly attention has been devoted to on-the-ground social media protest reporting practices (Earl et al. 2013; Jungherr and Jürgens 2014; Tufekci and Wilson 2012). In the case of the 2010 Toronto G20 protests, several thousand social media users were on the streets with their smartphones documenting what was happening and especially what the police were doing. The combined reports – in the form of tweets, status updates, photos, and videos – provided a highly detailed visual and textual account of the police patrolling the streets, checking IDs, and guarding the three-metre-high security fence around the summit's convention centre. Moreover, it was documented how police illegally searched, detained, and arrested protesters and how they were "beating people," "breaking and stealing," and "firing on the crowd." The focus on police activity became most evident when coding the most viewed and linked #g20report YouTube videos. The weighted share of the police-oriented videos was no less than 89 percent (Poell and Borra 2012, 706). These reports partly served the purpose of showing the larger world what was going on, but they also served the purpose of strategically sharing information with protesters in other parts of the city to coordinate their activities. As Earl and colleagues (2013, 472) have pointed out in their research on the protests against the 2009 G20 summit in Pittsburgh, such use of social media can "reduce information asymmetries between protesters and police." Yet contemporary police and security forces routinely monitor social media communication, giving them detailed insights into protesters' movements and plans (Trottier 2012; Trottier and Lyon 2012).

Depending on the relationship between protesters and security forces, there is substantial variation among different political contexts in how protest reporting takes shape. Even though police and security personnel in Toronto frequently obstructed protesters from filming and taking pictures, there was still a lot of freedom to document unfolding events. This freedom was much more limited during mass protests in Tunisia and Egypt in early 2011 when activists risked their lives by reporting on repressive military and police activities. Since the international press had difficulty gaining access to protest sites on these occasions, these reports were especially important. Because the regimes in these countries tried to prohibit the spread of information about the protests, the activists played a vital role as information brokers (Hänska-Ahy and Shapour 2013; Poell and Darmoni 2012).

Although on-the-ground protest reporting through social media has received most scholarly attention, it is only one layer of a larger ecosystem. A second important layer is constituted by blogs and alternative news sites, already an important online presence before the rise of commercial social media platforms. Blogs and alternative news sites especially have been studied by scholars working on alternative media and journalism (Atton 2015; Atton and Hamilton 2008). The G20 case study suggests, however, that social media protest communication strongly affects the operations of blogs and alternative news sites. During the protests, these outlets drew a lot of material from social media – YouTube videos, photos shared through TwitPic, and links to reports on Twitter – as evidence to reconstruct the confrontations between police and protesters. Many of these blogs and alternative news sites – such as Rabble.ca, Toronto Media Co-op, and Vancouver Media Co-op – were operated locally or nationally. Yet a substantial number of international alternative sites also linked to the social media protest reports, such as Democracy Now!, anarchistnews.org, taz.blogs, Público, Scoop, and Independent Media Centers (Indymedia). Alternative media were connected to social media by drawing material from these platforms, but they were also connected the other way around since social media users frequently shared links to blog posts and alternative news articles. On the Toronto Media Co-op blog, for example, 78 links to other platforms were shared during the period examined, whereas posts on the blog received 120 inlinks. And, of the 1,871 links shared on Twitter through the #g20report tag, 393 (21 percent) referred to blogs and alternative news sites. These practices of circulation, which intensified during the course of the protests, potentially enhance the visibility of posts and articles on alternative media.

In terms of the geography of such protest communication, these linking practices fundamentally defy the distinctions among "local," "national," and "transnational." The bloggers, Twitter and Facebook users, and alternative news sites from the United States, Europe, Southeast Asia, and Australia that shared and discussed on-the-ground social media protest reports were just as much parts of the intricate communication ecosystem that grew around the Toronto protests as local and national Canadian bloggers, alternative journalists, and social media users. Traditional spatial categories – local, national, transnational – made a lot of sense in the era of mass media, when audiences were targeted on the basis of such divisions; in a social media environment, however, these categories have lost much of their meaning since public communication, especially about major protest events, is always simultaneously local, national, and transnational.

Although we are moving from a mass media–dominated system to one in which online platforms increasingly shape the dynamic of public communication, mass media remain key actors in the social media ecosystem. Although less intensely than alternative news sites, mass media also build on material derived from social media platforms. In the case of the Toronto G20 protests, Canadian newspapers, such as the *Toronto Star* and *Globe and Mail,* occasionally referenced YouTube videos and Twitter hashtags. More importantly, social media users frequently shared links to newspaper and television protest reports. However, these links to mass media content constituted a minority (15 percent) of the total number of shared hyperlinks. Most links pointed to audiovisual material on content-sharing platforms such as YouTube, Flickr, and TwitPic. Other studies on social media protest communication show similar linking practices but with some variation in the distribution of links to the different types of media (Raynauld, Lalancette, and Tourigny-Koné 2016; Segerberg and Bennett 2011).

Locating activist social media communication reveals complex divisions of labour and modes of distribution that not only transcend the framework of the national public sphere but also fundamentally blur the boundaries among local, national, and transnational circuits. These connections raise further questions regarding how we need to conceptualize the relationship between media and democratic public discourse. Yet, before I turn to these larger conceptual questions, the "what" of social media protest communication needs to be considered.

Studying the content of the most engaged with G20 protest tweets, posts, photos, and videos, as well as the hyperlink networks in which this content was embedded, it is difficult to find instances of debate or conversation. This material and these links were above all about documenting what was happening in the streets of Toronto. For example, many of the #g20report tweets, 45 percent in total, referred to "media sharing sites" on which new photo and video material on the protest events, and especially on the violent confrontations with police, appeared. This event-oriented focus could even be observed in the hyperlink network in which the posts on the Media Co-op blog were embedded. Although the blogosphere has frequently been understood as a prime instance of online public debate, the hyperlink network of the Media Co-op blog revolved less around conversation than around near-real-time reporting. As in the case of the Twitter linking practices, the blog posts extensively linked to news reports, YouTube videos, and eyewitness blog posts to provide evidence and document the unfolding events in the streets.

A similar event-oriented focus can be observed in social media communication during other major contemporary protests. In our research on Twitter communication during the Tunisian uprising, we observed how this communication was also predominantly concerned with reconstructing unfolding events: activities of protesters, violent reactions by authorities, lack of reporting by national and international news media, and spikes in social media activity. Depending on the language employed, the tweets emphasized one of these aspects (Poell and Darmoni 2012). In turn, an exploration of Twitter activity in the year following the 2012 gang rape incident in New Delhi showed very similar results. The rape of Jyoti Singh Pandey, called "Nirbhaya" or "Damini" before her family agreed to make her name public, sparked mass protests and attracted worldwide media coverage. As in the Tunisian case, the Twitter communication was primarily concerned with the event or crime of the day (Poell and Rajagopalan 2015). Moreover, these Twitter studies did not find much evidence of public debate. In fact, in many instances in which @mentioning, Twitter's primary conversational functionality, was employed, the objective was not to start a discussion but to promote particular content or users as well as to alert users to new events. In the Indian case study, only 35 percent of the @mentioning tweets could be coded as "conversational" (726).

In this regard, activist social media communication mirrors mainstream protest reporting, also characterized by a strong event-oriented perspective.

Already in the 1970s, media scholars pointed out that this perspective tends to centre public attention on the spectacle and violence that accompany many protests (Halloran, Elliott, and Murdock 1970). Although activist social media communication is squarely focused on exposing police and military brutality, rather than the illegal activities of protesters, the resulting accounts still primarily revolve around violence and spectacle. In turn, this suggests that social media protest activity cannot be understood in terms of issue networks either. Rather than moving away, in the words of Dean (2003, 109), from the "drive for spectacle and immediacy that plagues an audience oriented news cycle," the use of social media appears to accelerate activist communication and highlight the visual spectacle that accompanies protest events. The emphasis in activist communication, in this regard, is shifting from the long-term articulation of issues to the rapid exchange of current information through social media ecologies. In the case of the 2010 Toronto G20 protests, the activists' original issues and activities, such as demonstrations for Native land rights, queer liberation, and the environment, were largely lost.

TRENDING IN CANADA

The event-oriented focus of contemporary protest communication has major implications for the formation of communities and publics, which has always been considered a central objective of alternative activist communication and more generally of projects of political emancipation, as understood from the perspective of public sphere theory (Atton 2002; Couldry and Curran 2003; Fraser 1990). The connections established through social media during protest events do not appear to constitute sustainable publics and communities. That is not to say that users who intensely communicate through a particular Twitter hashtag or Facebook page do not experience feelings of solidarity and togetherness. The G20 protest tweets, posts, and videos frequently appealed to a collective we. There were often defiant messages of collectivity, such as "WE WILL NOT BE SILENT," "Today, we march against poverty and displacement, in OUR city," and "They are few! We are many! Ten thousand marching through downtown." Research on other major recent protest events suggests that such appeals are omnipresent in activist social media communication (Gerbaudo and Treré 2015). In their analysis of #egypt, Papacharissi and de Fatima Oliveira (2012, 275) observed, for example, "overwhelming expressions of solidarity" and "camaraderie." And Kavada (2015, 884) notices, in her work on the Occupy movement, that "social media were used to broadcast and amplify the process of 'identization' taking place face-to-face."

Such moments of collectivity and togetherness, however, are highly ephemeral. The moment that a hashtag stops trending, the mass of assembled online users again dissolves. Shortly after the G20 protests ended, use of the #g20report tag quickly dropped on all platforms, which effectively meant that this hashtag stopped organizing publicness. Not surprisingly, many contemporary protests display a similar online dynamic. In our research on the use of Twitter during the Tunisian uprising, the top Twitter users whom we interviewed told us that they almost immediately abandoned #sidibouzid, the main hashtag during the uprising (Poell and Darmoni 2012). Some of these users went on to contribute to the Twitter communication on the following Egyptian revolution (Lotan et al. 2011). Yet they did so in a rather different online configuration, which meant that relations of publicness were also reshuffled. Although more stable communities appear to have been involved in the organization of on-the-ground protests in Toronto, Tunis, and Cairo, the infrastructure of online platforms is fundamentally geared to reshifting relations of publicness continuously.

Reflecting on these trends, it is important to remember that social media are not primarily developed to support activism, or journalism for that matter, but to connect users to targeted advertisements and services. To do so effectively, most platforms personalize the user experience on a number of levels. They push users to create and extend their personal networks by "following" or "friending." They also stimulate users to create their own communication spaces, for example through hashtags or Facebook groups and pages. Finally, social media algorithmically select for each user the content most likely to meet her or his interests, hence serving customized media diets. These different forms of technocommercial personalization drive and shape constantly shifting online activist relations. The ephemerality of online publicness, in this sense, is not simply the result of particular user practices but fundamentally ingrained in the platform architecture (Poell and van Dijck 2015).

Thus, contemporary activist communication through social media does not appear to correspond well with any of the models of the public sphere, which tend to revolve around public debate and the formation of publics and communities. Social media communication, nevertheless, offers important strategic advantages to activists and potentially contributes to the democratic character of public discourse. Activists have evidently become much less dependent on television and mainstream newspapers to influence public communication (Tufekci 2013). Mainstream media are no longer the only available option to reach large audiences. Some of the G20 protest tweets, videos, and photos were widely circulated, reaching large numbers of users. Moreover, given how most people use social media platforms for personal communication, activist social media content also penetrates more deeply into day-to-day communication than could be achieved through alternative media. Finally, the near–real-time and ubiquitous forms of protest communication enabled by platforms far outstretch the reporting capabilities of mass media.

Although the rise of social media has made activists much less dependent on mass media for reaching large audiences, this certainly does not mean that they have more control over the media environments in which they operate. Media power has not been transferred to the public or to activists for that matter; instead, power has partly shifted to the big social media corporations. This means that activists still have to navigate a media landscape dominated by commercial media. The for-profit character of platforms matters, for it informs how these platforms are technologically developed, which in turn steers how activists connect and communicate with each other.

By examining how social media shape contemporary activist communication, it becomes clear that both the content and the geographic distribution of this communication do not correspond with how public sphere theorists have conceived of democratic public discourse. As I have discussed, however, public sphere theory is ill equipped to evaluate the democratic character of online communication. Needed is a more dynamic conception of publicness that can trace the constantly evolving connections among actors, locations, technologies, and issues in a platform ecosystem. Consequently, it appears to be fruitful to shift the focus from "spheres" to "trajectories" of publicness. The notion of "trajectories of publicness" invites us to trace and evaluate precisely the "what" and "where" of activist social media communication.

Reflecting on the 2010 Toronto G20 protests, as well as other examples of contemporary protests discussed, it should be noted that for those "on the ground" it is crucial that unfolding events are documented and that the use and abuse of state violence become visible to the wider world. It is vital for the sustainability of protest movements that state authorities are held accountable for the violence that they inflict on protesters. Omnipresent social media reporting meaningfully contributes to this accountability, especially as documentation of the worst offences tends to circulate widely through the platforms themselves and through alternative and mass media. Given that many more people, including those who do not necessarily have an activist disposition, are confronted with this material makes state violence more publicly visible. The rise of social media, in this regard, has contributed substantially to turning the illegitimate use of state power into a key political issue.

At the same time, from the perspective of activists, mediated publicness should also enable the publicizing and politicizing of a range of other social, cultural, economic, and environmental issues that transcends the protest event itself. As critical work on issue networks has made clear, such processes of publicizing and politicizing do not necessarily need to take the form of public debate. Whatever form these processes take, it is important that public communication is not fully dominated by a drive for immediacy and spectacle and that the larger context and background of socio-economic, cultural, and ecological developments receive ample attention as well. In the current social media ecosystem, it appears to be difficult to find space for long-term trends and larger contexts, especially since alternative and mass media are strongly connected to this ecosystem.

To return to my Canadian colleagues being glued to their social media feeds during the 2010 Toronto G20 protests, they were primarily hooked to see how the violent events and mass arrests were unfolding in their home country. Similarly, for good strategic reasons, the G20 protesters themselves wanted as much public attention as possible on the police violence that they were encountering. Canadian protest communication has been transformed by the rise of social media platforms as much as contentious communication anywhere else. And, to address the central theme of this book, the Canadian public sphere, like national public spheres elsewhere, is dissolving into global streams of social media communication, which not only transcend the boundaries of the "national" but also constitute another type of democratic discourse than conceptualized by public sphere theorists.

In light of this trend, my call to develop a more dynamic and flexible conception of publicness also extends to Canadian political communication and social movement scholars. The aim is to explore and conceptualize contentious publicness as unfolding along specific trajectories rather than taking place in a particular sphere that remains stable over time. Examining contentious publicness as a trajectory, we can trace how different actors, locations, and technologies become entangled in the course of a contentious episode. This should enable a more nuanced understanding of when, where, and how contentious social media communication contributes to democratic discourse. My analysis here suggests that social media platforms fulfill a crucial strategic role but simultaneously put pressure on the articulation of key political issues. From this perspective, it is important that alternative media maintain a particular autonomy and distance vis-à-vis the social media ecosystem to allow for processes of issue formation that transcend the immediacy and spectacle of the event. Given the strength of Canadian alternative media, this appears to be an especially viable option in this country.

NOTES

1 This was a custom scraper built by the Digital Methods Initiative (https://www.digitalmethods.net/) that harvested results from Google Real-Time Search (http://www.google.com/realtime/). The scraper extracted all of the tweets with the #g20report tag and stored them in a database for further analysis. Since then, the Google Real-Time Search service has been discontinued.
2 This is a YouTube crawling and data extraction toolkit (http://www.tubekit.org/) that allows for the collection of up to sixteen different attributes per video.
3 This scraper retrieved all of the inlinks to a webpage, according to Yahoo! (https://tools.issuecrawler.net/beta/yahoo/). Since Yahoo! has discontinued its service, the scraper no longer functions.

REFERENCES

Arquilla, John, and David Ronfeldt. 2001. *Networks and Netwars: The Future of Terror, Crime, and Militancy.* Santa Monica, CA: Rand Corporation.

Atton, Chris. 2002. *Alternative Media.* London: Sage.

–, ed. 2015. *The Routledge Companion to Alternative and Community Media.* London: Routledge.

Atton, Chris, and James F. Hamilton. 2008. *Alternative Journalism.* London: Sage.

Bennett, W. Lance, and Alexandra Segerberg. 2013. *The Logic of Connective Action: Digital Media and the Personalization of Contentious Politics.* Cambridge, UK: Cambridge University Press.

Castells, Manuel. 1996. *The Rise of the Network Society: The Information Age: Economy, Society, and Culture.* Oxford: John Wiley and Sons.

–. 2009. *Communication Power.* Oxford: Oxford University Press.

Couldry, Nick. 2014. "What and Where Is the Transnationalized Public Sphere?" In *Transnationalizing the Public Sphere,* edited by Nancy Fraser, 43–59. Oxford: John Wiley and Sons.

–. 2015. "The Myth of 'Us': Digital Networks, Political Change, and the Production of Collectivity." *Information, Communication, and Society* 18, 6: 608–26.

Couldry, Nick, and James Curran, eds. 2003. *Contesting Media Power: Alternative Media Power in a Networked World.* Lanham, MD: Rowman and Littlefield.

Dahlgren, Peter. 1995. *Television and the Public Sphere: Citizenship, Democracy, and the Media.* London: Sage.

Dean, Jodi. 2003. "Why the Net Is Not a Public Sphere." *Constellations* 10, 1: 95–112.

Earl, Jennifer, Heather McKee Hurwitz, Analicia Mejia Mesinas, Margaret Tolan, and Ashley Arlotti. 2013. "This Protest Will Be Tweeted: Twitter and Protest Policing during the Pittsburgh G20." *Information, Communication, and Society* 16, 4: 459–78.

Fenton, Natalie, and Veronica Barassi. 2011. "Alternative Media and Social Networking Sites: The Politics of Individuation and Political Participation." *Communication Review* 14, 3: 179–96.

Fraser, Nancy. 1990. "Rethinking the Public Sphere: A Contribution to the Critique of Actually Existing Democracy." *Social Text* 25, 26: 56–80.

–. 2007. "Transnational Public Sphere: Transnationalizing the Public Sphere." *Theory, Culture, and Society* 24, 7: 7–30.

Gerbaudo, Paolo, and Emiliano Treré. 2015. "In Search of the 'We' of Social Media Activism: Introduction to the Special Issue on Social Media and Protest Identities." *Information, Communication, and Society* 18, 8: 865–71.

Habermas, Jürgen. (1962) 1989. *The Structural Transformation of the Public Sphere.* Translated by Thomas Burger. Cambridge, MA: MIT Press.

–. 2001. *The Postnational Constellation: Political Essays.* Cambridge, UK: Polity Press.

Halloran, James Dermot, Philip Ross Courtney Elliott, and Graham Murdock. 1970. *Demonstrations and Communication: A Case Study.* London: Penguin Books.

Hänska-Ahy, Maximillian T., and Roxanna Shapour. 2013. "Who's Reporting the Protests? Converging Practices of Citizen Journalists and Two BBC World Service Newsrooms, from Iran's Election Protests to the Arab Uprisings." *Journalism Studies* 14, 1: 29–45.

Jungherr, Andreas, and Pascal Jürgens. 2014. "Through a Glass, Darkly: Tactical Support and Symbolic Association in Twitter Messages Commenting on Stuttgart 21." *Social Science Computer Review* 32, 1: 74–89.

Juris, Jeffrey S. 2012. "Reflections on #Occupy Everywhere: Social Media, Public Space, and Emerging Logics of Aggregation." *American Ethnologist* 39, 2: 259–79.

Kavada, Anastasia. 2015. "Creating the Collective: Social Media, the Occupy Movement, and Its Constitution as a Collective Actor." *Information, Communication, and Society* 18, 8: 872–86.

Keane, John. 1991. *The Media and Democracy*. Cambridge, UK: Polity Press.

Lotan, Gilad, Erhardt Graeff, Mike Ananny, Devin Gaffney, and Ian Pearce. 2011. "The Arab Spring/the Revolutions Were Tweeted: Information Flows during the 2011 Tunisian and Egyptian Revolutions." *International Journal of Communication* 5: 1375–1405.

Marres, Noortje, and Richard Rogers. 2005. "Recipe for Tracing the Fate of Issues and Their Publics on the Web." In *Making Things Public: Atmospheres of Democracy*, edited by B. Latour and P. Weibel, 922–35. Cambridge, MA: MIT Press.

Milan, Stefania. 2015. "When Algorithms Shape Collective Action: Social Media and the Dynamics of Cloud Protesting." *Social Media and Society* 1, 2: 1–10.

Papacharissi, Zizi, and Maria de Fatima Oliveira. 2012. "Affective News and Networked Publics: The Rhythms of News Storytelling on #Egypt." *Journal of Communication* 62, 2: 266–82.

Poell, Thomas. 2014. "Social Media and the Transformation of Activist Communication: Exploring the Social Media Ecology of the 2010 Toronto G20 Protests." *Information, Communication, and Society* 17, 6: 716–31.

Poell, Thomas, and Erik Borra. 2012. "Twitter, YouTube, and Flickr as Platforms of Alternative Journalism: The Social Media Account of the 2010 Toronto G20 Protests." *Journalism* 13, 6: 695–713.

Poell, Thomas, and Kaouthar Darmoni. 2012. "Twitter as a Multilingual Space: The Articulation of the Tunisian Revolution through #sidibouzid." *European Journal of Media Studies* 1, 1: 14–34.

Poell, Thomas, and Sudha Rajagopalan. 2015. "Connecting Activists and Journalists: Twitter Communication in the Aftermath of the 2012 Delhi Rape." *Journalism Studies* 16, 5: 719–33.

Poell, Thomas, and José van Dijck. 2015. "Social Media and Activist Communication." In *The Routledge Companion to Alternative and Community Media*, edited by Chris Atton, 527–37. London: Routledge.

Raynauld, Vincent, Mireille Lalancette, and Sofia Tourigny-Koné. 2016. "Political Protest 2.0: Social Media and the 2012 Student Strike in the Province of Quebec, Canada." *French Politics* 14, 1: 1–29.

Renzi, Alessandra, and Greg Elmer. 2013. "The Biopolitics of Sacrifice: Securing Infrastructure at the G20 Summit." *Theory, Culture, and Society* 30, 5: 45–69.

Segerberg, Alexandra, and W. Lance Bennett. 2011. "Social Media and the Organization of Collective Action: Using Twitter to Explore the Ecologies of Two Climate Change Protests." *Communication Review* 14, 3: 197–215.

Trottier, Daniel. 2012. *Social Media as Surveillance*. Milton Park, UK: Ashgate.

Trottier, Daniel, and David Lyon. 2012. "Key Features of Social Media Surveillance." In *Internet and Surveillance: The Challenges of Web 2.0 and Social Media*, edited by C. Fuchs, K. Boersma, A. Albrechtslund, and M. Sandoval, 89–105. London: Routledge.

Tufekci, Zeynep. 2013. "'Not This One': Social Movements, the Attention Economy, and Microcelebrity Networked Activism." *American Behavioral Scientist* 57, 7: 848–70.

Tufekci, Zeynep, and Christopher Wilson. 2012. "Social Media and the Decision to Participate in Political Protest: Observations from Tahrir Square." *Journal of Communication* 62, 2: 363–79.

van de Donk, Wim, Brian D. Loader, Paul G. Nixon, and Dieter Rucht, eds. 2004. *Cyberprotest: New Media, Citizens, and Social Movements*. London: Routledge.

PART 2

Political Actors Trending, Interacting, and Reaching Their Audiences

7

Of Walls and Whispers
The Use of Facebook during the 2012 Quebec Election

YANNICK DUFRESNE, THIERRY GIASSON, AND MICKAEL TEMPORÃO

In 2016, Facebook was the most popular social networking site and the third most popular website in the world (Digital In 2016). Quebec was no exception: more than 5,000,000 Quebecers – over 65 percent of the population – used the site. It should thus come as no surprise that political parties in Quebec increasingly turn to Facebook to reach voters (see, e.g., Giasson et al. 2014a; Giasson, Greffet, and Chacon 2014). Nevertheless, we know very little about party behaviour on Facebook in Canada. The lacuna is partly explained by the difficulty of collecting and keeping track of the large amounts of information published by political parties on these social media platforms. Moreover, the primacy of the French language in Quebec makes it harder to use analytical tools developed primarily in English to study the large-scale unstructured textual data collected on social media such as Facebook.

With about 1 billion users daily worldwide, Facebook provides political campaigns with access to a broad, heterogeneous audience. Contrary to the highly specialized publics of other social media platforms, such as Twitter, Facebook's user base mirrors more closely sociodemographic variables found in the general population (Sangwon and Cho 2011). The company also provides organizations and businesses with effective analytics to help them reach target audiences through Facebook advertising (Williams and Gulati 2012). However, most research on Facebook political campaigns focuses on the United States. That might not be surprising considering the innovative and influential nature of American-style campaigning (Negrine and Papathanassopoulos 1996; Schulz 2014). It has been shown that American politicians indeed frequently make use of Facebook as a tool for campaigning (Borah 2014; Bronstein 2013; Sweetser and Lariscy 2008).

There are reasons to believe, however, that these findings might not be generalizable to other contexts. For example, differences in levels of party competition and campaign spending can affect the use of Facebook as a tool for campaigning (Williams and Gulati 2012). American parties are atypical when it comes to financial resources at their disposal. Even if social media campaigns can empower smaller political actors (Haynes and Pitts 2009), professional social media campaigns tend to be expensive since they entail paid and targeted advertisements and messages as well as the creation of specific materials such as images and videos. Moreover, the United States has a well-established two-party system in which only the Democratic and Republican Parties undertake large-scale Facebook campaigns. This is significant since contexts with strict party funding rules and multiparty systems might have political parties whose use of Facebook as a campaign tool differs significantly from those in the United States. In fact, even if social media campaigning is often considered cheap compared with more traditional means to reach voters, the increasing use of microtargeted messages and the production of high-quality images and videos in social media posts necessarily raise the costs of such campaigns (Giasson et al. 2014a). It is therefore reasonable to assume that financial limits on political parties can affect the nature of their social media campaigns. Cases such as Canada and the United Kingdom are worth scholarly attention because they allow researchers to study the online campaigns of a wider range of parties and electoral contexts and to test the comparative explanatory value of American findings.

Canadian parties' lagging in the use of social media is well documented (Chen and Smith 2011; Small 2008). In Quebec, Verville (2012) qualifies social media communication strategies by Quebec parties as "embryonic." The 2012 Quebec election was the first campaign in which all six main political parties ran integrated social media campaigns comprising wide ranges of online presence and numerous Facebook pages (Giasson et al. 2014b). This moment clearly consolidated the trend among party organizations to consider social media as an unavoidable component of their campaign strategies. However, little is known about how these pages were actually used. How many parties' posts and users' comments were produced? Which topics were addressed in these messages? Were they more negative or more positive in tone? What proportions of parties' posts included visuals compared with simple text and hyperlinks? This descriptive information is important because it provides the basis to evaluate quantitatively the extent and contour of a party's Facebook campaign. Ultimately, these measures offer opportunities for a more advanced analysis of the determinants of popularity of parties' posts.

The interactivity between parties and voters is the definitional feature of social media (Breindl and Francq 2008). In a nutshell, platforms such as Facebook allow politicians to communicate and potentially engage in dialogues with individual users. However, little of this type of dialogue has been observed in reality (Giasson et al. 2014b; Nielsen and Vaccari 2013; Small 2012). For instance, Sweetser and Lariscy (2008) observe that American politicians' Facebook walls are used to post messages, but little is done to engage in dialogues. Political campaigns use social media as another outlet of communication to broadcast content rather than to engage in truly open dialogues with internet users following and communicating with them. Actually, the most common type of interaction that these authors observe is the deletion of negative comments by candidates.

These findings might disappoint those who see social media as a means to improve the democratic deliberative process (see Anttiroiko 2010). However, from a strict political marketing perspective, dialogues with voters are not necessarily indicators of successful communication campaigns. To reach and to satisfy the needs and wants of segments of potential voters remain the main objectives of most electoral campaigns (Lees-Marshment 2001), and they are not necessarily achieved through close dialogues on social media. However, the digital interactive principle that anchors these communication tools highlights the importance of integrating both parties' and individual users' behaviour when studying social media communication. One cannot look at parties' posts without considering the users' comments that they generate (see Sørensen 2016).

Users' comments are more difficult to study than political parties' posts because of their large number and the use of more informal language

(Caton, Hall, and Weinhardt 2015). However, these messages can greatly enhance our understanding of the dynamics of social media communication. The number, topic, and tone of comments provide hints on parties' ability to connect with these voters. Unfortunately, research frequently focuses only on parties' activities. For instance, Borah (2014) found that in the 2012 US presidential campaign both candidates' Facebook posts tended to be more partisan- than policy-oriented and that there was a clear difference in tone, with incumbent Barack Obama's messages being less negative than those of his challenger, Mitt Romney. In such cases, there is no way to evaluate whether these communication choices are in line or not with voters. Perhaps voters are more attentive to partisan and negative messaging? One way to look at this possibility is to compare the topic and tone of voters' comments to those of parties' posts. Another way is to assess more directly the specific characteristics of parties' posts that trigger the most reactions from voters.

CASE STUDY

Here we explore Quebec political parties' Facebook walls during the 2012 provincial election.[1] This is an interesting case study for two reasons. First, the election represented a historical moment in digital campaigning; it was the first time that all leading parties in Quebec used a combination of integrated web presences, including extensive Facebook use. This was the first "social media" campaign in the province during which online strategists were active members of the parties' war rooms, and the technologies that they harnessed – such as Facebook, Twitter, and YouTube – were fully integrated into campaign strategies (see Giasson et al. 2014a). Because online electoral campaigning has moved toward this integrated and multiplatform format in most Western democracies, we believe that the 2012 online campaign in Quebec represents a strong and generalizable case study. Second, all activities on parties' Facebook walls were monitored during the entire campaign using ASPIRA, textual harvesting software developed by the Groupe de recherche en communication politique.[2] The data collected provide a unique opportunity to observe not only parties' published *posts* on Facebook but also the *comments* that the posts generated.

The context of the 2012 Quebec election was unusual. Premier Jean Charest – leader of the Parti libéral du Québec (PLQ) – dropped the writ in the midst of what was considered by many as a major social crisis in modern Quebec history because of its lasting impact on internal party politics (see Raynauld, Lalancette, and Tourigny-Koné in this volume).[3] The crisis was provoked by the government's proposal to raise post-secondary tuition. For months, the media covered what came to be known as the "Printemps érable" (literally, the Maple Spring, an expression developed by the media to echo the Arab Spring), characterized by massive protests in the streets that often involved violent confrontations with police. The government responded by enacting special measures that expanded the powers of law enforcement officials and limited the rights of protesters.

Meanwhile, the official opposition party – the Parti québécois (PQ) – took the side of the protesters in the hope of rallying public opinion in its favour. Such position taking might have been abetted by the first-past-the-post electoral system that operates in Quebec as in the rest of Canada. Indeed, the other separatist left-wing parties – Québec solidaire (QS) and Option nationale (ON) – took the same stance. The second most important opposition party – Coalition avenir Québec (CAQ) – was the only party to support the government position.

This peculiar context was especially favourable to the development of social media strategies. Student unions used Facebook and Twitter to organize the protests at the same time as enforcement officials used the platforms to inform citizens when some of the protests were declared illegal. Social media became a popular arena in which proponents of each side of the debate met to discuss and argue. For both reasons, traditional media were also increasingly attentive to what was happening on social media, and they often reported some of the information found on them. Given these circumstances, we can think that political parties in Quebec had clear incentives to engage with social media.

In addition to tensions caused by the student crisis, the situation was complicated by persistent allegations of political corruption that eventually forced the government to hold a public inquiry on the issue. In such turbulent times, public opinion was both polarized and highly volatile

(Bastien, Bélanger, and Gélineau 2014). At the beginning of the campaign, the final outcome would have been difficult to predict. In the end, the PQ blocked the PLQ from winning its fourth election in a row but did not gain enough seats to form a majority government.

Methods

We use Facebook data collected with the help of ASPIRA, software developed at Université Laval for the enpolitique.com project. The software makes use of the Facebook Application Programming Interface systematically to monitor and archive all activities appearing on the six main Quebec political parties' Facebook walls. Using the unstructured textual information contained in posts written by party staffers and in users' comments, ASPIRA collects relevant metadata, such as numbers of shares and likes of a post, senders' information, date of publication, and digital content added (e.g., hyperlinks, photos, and videos). This information is stored in data sets suited for analyses that go beyond the mere description of parties' and users' activities.

Automated textual analysis is then used to identify the structure in the raw textual data. This helps us to determine the *topic* and *tone* of 15,715 messages written by political parties and users during the course of the campaign (August 1, 2012, to September 4, 2012). The topics are measured using keyword dictionaries associated with various issues. These dictionaries were originally developed to study the contents of most-important-issue open questions in electoral surveys, and their validity has been assessed in half a dozen elections. These dictionaries help to determine the substance of Facebook messages. For instance, a message that includes words associated with the environment – such as *climate* or *pollution* – is marked as being related to the environmental *issue* topic. In the same way, a Facebook message that mentions leaders' or parties' names is marked as including a *partisan* topic. Note that Facebook messages thus are not classified into mutually exclusive categories. In fact, a Facebook message can be marked as being related to both the environmental issue and partisan elements. The sentiment analyses use Lexicoder, software initially developed in English by Daku, Soroka, and Young (2015) and translated into French by Duval and Pétry (2016). Most messages collected on parties' Facebook walls were written in French (93.5 percent). When possible, analyses were conducted in the language of the messages. Bilingual messages were analyzed in French.

The major challenge of this analysis is the quality of the writing. Although dictionary-based methods are well suited to formal writing, many users' comments include spelling mistakes. It is not rare to see the same word written in different ways. These mistakes or alterations can considerably bias the results of automated content analyses. This is even more problematic when we take into consideration that mistakes are not randomly distributed but often associated with specific sociodemographic factors (e.g., education, income) and, consequently, different types of content. To reduce bias, we automatically checked words for spelling mistakes, and we added stemmed and ad hoc patch words to the dictionaries used for the analyses. We performed validity checks on a random sample of the posts analyzed in this chapter, and these checks indicate that the automated content analysis provides results similar to qualitative content analysis approaches used in other social media studies (see Borah 2014).

Finally, we used a linear model to evaluate the relationship between the characteristics of parties' posts (topic, tone, and media) and the number of Facebook "likes" that the posts generated.[4] The results of this assessment have substantial potential since they can be tested in contexts other than the 2012 Quebec election to evaluate their generalizability.

Findings

The first striking observation regarding the 2012 Quebec Facebook campaign is the imbalance in engagement among political parties. This difference exists both in the usage of social media – measured by the number of posts written by the parties themselves – and in the attention paid to such usage by users – measured by the number of comments generated. Figure 7.1 shows the number of posts and comments associated with each political party's Facebook wall.

The results show that Quebec parties used Facebook often during the 2012 election and that the public reacted to their messages. All parties posted messages, often followed by several hundred user comments each day of the campaign. Posts generated an average of 35 comments ($\sigma = 57.5$). More comparative research is necessary to qualify the significance of these numbers relative to other contexts. Nevertheless, looking merely at a count

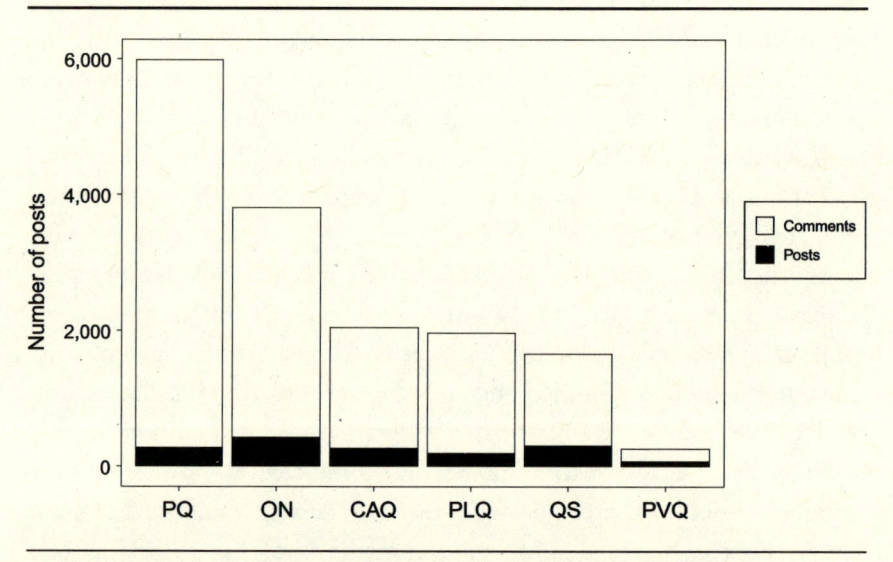

FIGURE 7.1
Activities on parties' Facebook walls

[Bar chart showing Number of posts for PQ (~6,000), ON (~3,800), CAQ (~2,000), PLQ (~2,000), QS (~1,600), PVQ (~400), with Comments and Posts categories]

Note: Data were collected using ASPIRA software developed by political scientists at the Groupe de recherche en communication politique at Laval University.
Source: Facebook, August 1–September 4, 2012 (*N* = 15,715).

of Facebook activities, it appears that Quebec parties engaged more heavily in social media campaigning in 2012 than in previous elections (Giasson et al. 2014b; Verville 2012).

The use of Facebook does not appear to be related to the size of the party.[5] In fact, ON was the most active political party on Facebook among the six main Quebec parties, yet it was founded only a few months before the election and received only 1.89 percent of the popular vote. Moreover, its active social media campaign was not a shout into the abyss, for its Facebook wall generated many user comments. Only the posts on the Facebook wall of the PQ, the party that eventually won the election, generated more comments. This might reflect the fact that the PQ has the largest membership base of all parties in the province. Throughout the campaign, the PQ outnumbered its competitors in terms of Facebook users by a wide margin. On September 13, one week after the election, the PQ's number of supporters stood at 74,790, followed by ON (27,152) and QS (20,672). The outgoing Liberals ended the campaign in fifth place with

7,593 Facebook followers, trailing the newly formed CAQ (8,952) but standing ahead of the Greens (1,754). This incredibly low showing in support for the governing Liberals on Facebook can also be explained by their limited activity on the social media network, with only the Greens – a very minor party in Quebec – producing fewer posts during the campaign.

When it comes to the analysis of topics mentioned on the parties' Facebook walls, our results show that partisan topics are considerably more prominent than policy issues in both posts and comments (see Figure 7.2). This result is in line with what is observed in the United States (Sweetser and Lariscy 2008). But there are exceptions. The three smaller parties – QS, ON, and the Parti vert du Québec (PVQ) – appear to be less prone to write partisan posts and to generate partisan comments. This result might stem from the fact that these smaller opposition parties are shown in previous research to use social media for different strategic goals than larger traditional parties. For instance, Giasson and colleagues (2014a) state that, in addition to having efficiently integrated social media into their 2012 general campaign planning, QS and ON used social media to pursue *political goals* (e.g., mobilizing supporters and promoting ideologies) rather than simply to attain *communication goals* (e.g., personalizing their leaders and teams and attacking their opponents). This pattern might also be attributable to the fact that these smaller opposition parties are more programmatic and ideological than the three bigger parties. Actually, ON and PVQ can even be considered single-issue parties, the former focusing mainly on Quebec independence and the latter on the environment. The clear prominence of the environment among the topics discussed on the Facebook wall of the Greens and social program issues on the Facebook wall of the left-leaning QS is therefore unsurprising. However, ON – a party created principally to promote Quebec independence – focused most of its Facebook posts on ethics and democracy rather than on Quebec's constitutional status. Yet users' comments on ON's Facebook wall included the most mentions of that Quebec issue.

No real difference exists in the topics discussed in parties' posts or in users' comments on those posts. The issues that triggered the most messages during the 2012 Quebec election were those relevant to the peculiarities

FIGURE 7.2
Partisan or issue oriented? Topics of Facebook messages

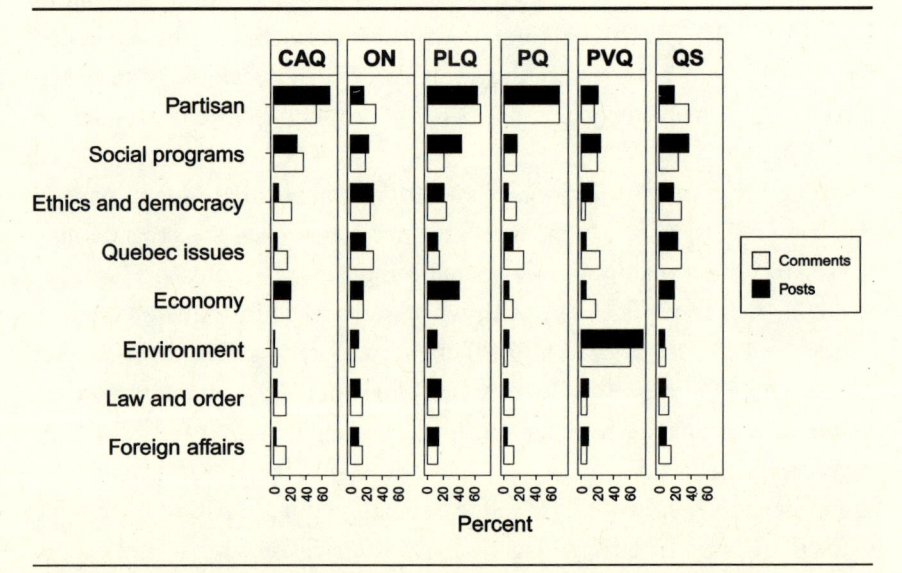

Note: Data were collected using ASPIRA software developed by political scientists at the Groupe de recherche en communication politique at Laval University. The x-axis indicates the percentage of messages on each party's Facebook wall that mentions the topic displayed on the y-axis.
Source: Facebook, August 1–September 4, 2012 (*N* = 15,715).

of that election. In fact, in the midst of unprecedented student protests, it is not surprising that social programs (including education) were the issues most frequently addressed. This finding contrasts sharply with Facebook campaigns in the United States, where the vast majority of posts during midterm and presidential elections tend to be about the economy, a classic valence issue (Borah 2014; Sweetser and Lariscy 2008). Likewise, it seems that the persistent rumours regarding corruption in the government pushed many users to write about political ethics. On more symbolic issues in the province (e.g., independence, identity, language), users were keener than parties to express their thoughts. Perhaps this was because of the polemical and strategic nature of such issues. For instance, the PQ – the largest separatist party – mentioned Quebec issues in only a small fraction of its posts. The party's separatist stance is often mentioned in political commentary as an impediment to its electoral aspirations. This might even explain why the federalist PLQ mentioned Quebec issues more often than the PQ.

Automated content analyses also allow us to evaluate the tone of messages, assessed based on the number of words associated with negative or positive sentiments stored in predefined dictionaries. Such sentiment analyses are increasingly common in social science and other disciplines (see Grimmer and Stewart 2013). Their main advantage is that they offer the opportunity to analyze efficiently large bodies of text. The use of these new analytical tools to study increasingly available big data from social media can greatly improve our understanding of communication dynamics. In fact, recorded digital traces from political parties and average users allow researchers to follow the precise impacts of political messages like never before.

Figure 7.3 summarizes the results of the sentiment analysis of the messages that appeared on the Quebec political parties' Facebook walls during the 2012 electoral campaign. The results show that users' comments generally tended to be more negative than parties' posts. This finding contradicts what Sweetser and Lariscy (2008) observed in the 2006 US midterm election. They found that users' comments on politicians' Facebook walls were overwhelmingly positive in tone. The difference in outcomes might be attributable to the exceptional levels of political cynicism among the Quebec public in 2012 (Bastien et al. 2014), which might have been affected by the social crisis and allegations of government corruption. The tone of messages found on the governing party's (PLQ) Facebook wall seems to support these conjectures. In fact, user comments on the PLQ's wall were the most negative of all the messages that we analyzed. Conversely, the PLQ's posts were the most positive of all parties' posts. This contrast might be explained by the fact that the PLQ was the incumbent at the time. People tend to direct their criticisms toward the government, and in response the government is forced to defend the positive aspects of its decisions. Our data appear to support conclusions on Liberal strategic objectives that Giasson and his collaborators have highlighted elsewhere (Giasson et al. 2014a). Interviews with PLQ strategists revealed that the party followed a cohesive and positive social media campaign aimed primarily at broadcasting messages of the day with limited interactions with internet users. The goal was to remain constantly on message in order to limit possible loss of control on social media (Giasson et al. 2014a, 15–16).

FIGURE 7.3
Positive or negative? Tones of Facebook messages

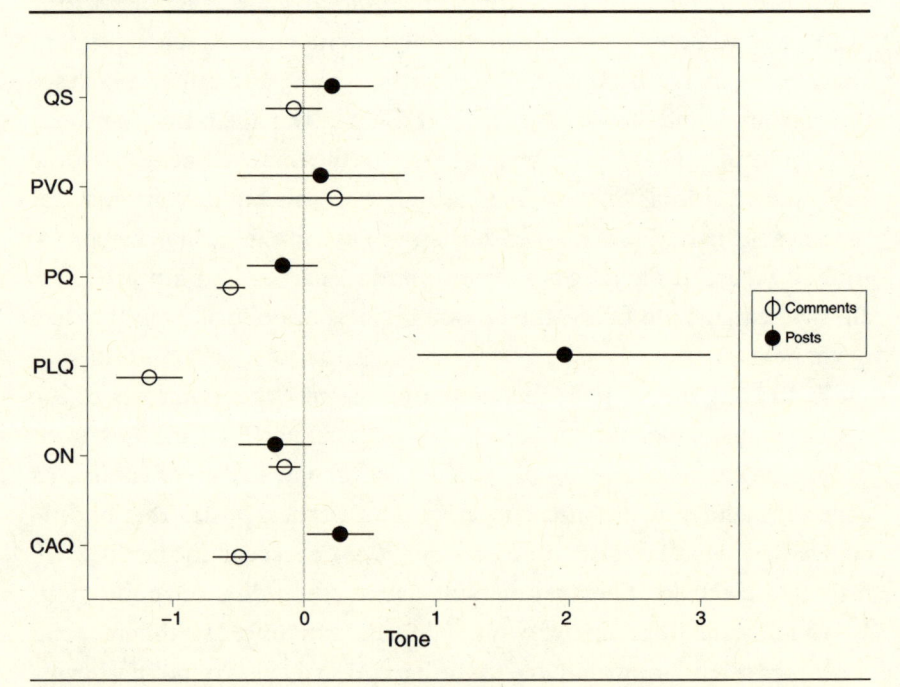

Note: Sentiment analysis (based on the Lexicoder dictionaries). Data were collected using ASPIRA software developed by political scientists at the Groupe de recherche en communication politique at Laval University.
Source: Facebook, August 1–September 4, 2012 (*N* = 15,715).

Facebook posts do not include text only but can include hyperlinks, images, and videos, which cannot be as easily analyzed with automated content analysis tools. These media can offer insights into the social media campaigns run by parties (Borah 2014). Parties can only use Facebook as a means of bringing people to their websites to see advertisements or read press releases. However, parties can also create material suited specifically to a social media campaign such as photos, infographics, memes, and videos. The use of visual media components can be linked to the increased modernization of social media political campaigns (Giasson et al. 2014a). However, these media components are more elaborate and thus more expensive to produce. We should therefore expect more professional and wealthier parties to use more visual media components.

FIGURE 7.4
Media components in parties' posts

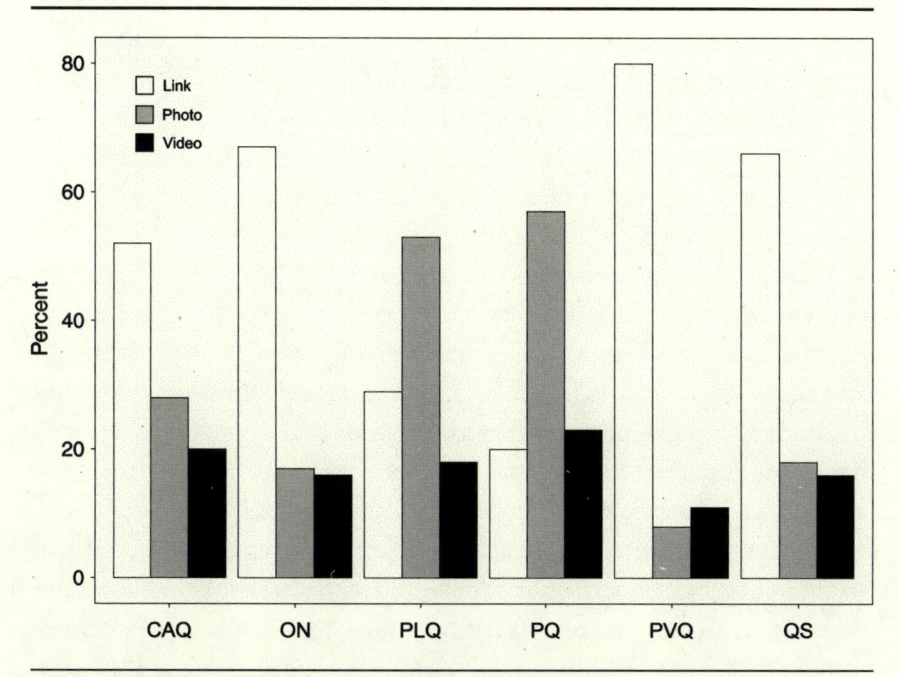

Note: Data were collected using ASPIRA software developed by political scientists at the Groupe de recherche en communication politique at Laval University.
Source: Facebook, August 1–September 4, 2012 (*N* = 15,715).

Figure 7.4 shows the proportion of posts using different media components for each political party. As expected, bigger parties tended to use more visual media components in their Facebook campaigns. More than half of all posts written by the two largest parties – the PLQ and the PQ – included at least one image; this proportion was only 20 percent for the other parties. Smaller parties seemed to use Facebook more as a means of bringing people to their websites.

Hyperlinks were included in a large proportion of the smaller parties' posts, and most of these hyperlinks led to press releases found on parties' websites. The contrast in the use of media components in Facebook posts between large traditional parties and small opposition parties during the 2012 Quebec campaign is clear. Unfortunately, videos and images are difficult to analyze with conventional text analysis methods. The meanings of spoken words and – even more problematically – images cannot be as easily extracted and interpreted as that of written text. If the trend of using visual media components continues, then researchers will have to develop new ways of studying parties' use of Facebook as a campaign tool. Transcriptions of videos and written descriptions of images might be imperfect solutions. One thing is clear, however: researchers cannot simply ignore these meaningful media components.

A defining characteristic of Facebook is the ability that it gives users to interact with party messages by clicking on a "like" button beneath the text or media component. This action not only signifies users' acknowledgment of the message (see Larsson 2015) but also diffuses such liking to friends and is thus an important aspect of viral social media campaigns that aim to reach potential voters. It is therefore important to explore the factors related to users' tendencies to like political parties' Facebook posts. Do partisan posts attract more likes than posts written about substantive issues? What about positive posts compared with negative posts? Does the use of visual media components trigger more likes? To uncover the effects of these factors on the likes of the various Facebook posts, we used an ordinary least squares model assessing the aspects that we studied: topic, tone, and media components. The model estimates the effect of each of these factors net of all other effects.

Topic and positive tone had tiny positive effects on the number of likes that a Facebook post generated during the 2012 Quebec election. However, visual media components had substantial effects. Posts with images generated on average 188 more likes than posts without images, and posts with videos generated 42 more likes. If these last results are generalizable, then we should expect that political parties increasingly create more social media–specific visual content.

TRENDING IN CANADA

Facebook is no longer avoided by political parties. This social media network offers a way for parties to interact with diverse voters at a personal level to an extent not previously possible. The 2012 Quebec election campaign was historical for political communication scholars since it was the first time that all leading political parties had integrated strategies for

Facebook use (Giasson et al. 2014a). In fact, this election clearly set the trend toward considering social media such as Facebook as a pillar of any partisan campaign strategy in Quebec. This type of electioneering can fundamentally transform the relationship between voters and those running for office. However, our analyses show that great discrepancies can exist in the ways that parties use Facebook in their campaigns. During the campaign that we studied, both the substance and the tone of the content differed by party and type of activity (post or comment). The incumbent party also tended to be more positive than its competitors. However, all of the parties were more positive and focused on substantive issues in their posts than were users who commented in reaction to them, comments that also tended to be more clearly centred on partisan rhetoric. Interpretation of these results is complex, though, because the data are unstructured and mostly consist of informal texts – which often contain many spelling mistakes – posted by regular citizens.

However, does the analysis of the 2012 Quebec Facebook campaign teach us anything more general about political communication? Can the patterns identified in this chapter be generalized to other contexts? Of course, only more research can verify the generalizability of our results. However, we believe that some of the findings presented here might be applicable to other contexts. For instance, we can expect that the opposing tones of comments and posts on the incumbents' Facebook wall would generally follow a similar pattern elsewhere. Governing parties have clear incentives to frame their messages in specific ways that present their past actions in a positive light. It is also not surprising to find that the most negatively formulated criticisms were targeted at the party that inevitably had to make difficult decisions at some point while in office.

Another finding that we can expect to observe in other contexts is the difference in the use of Facebook between small opposition parties and large traditional parties. Smaller parties often suffer from a lack of interest among conventional media organizations. Digital communication tools such as Facebook offer opportunities for these small parties to reach voters directly in cheaper and more efficient ways (Giasson et al. 2014a, 2014b). They help to bring new political and partisan voices into the debate and allow citizens to reach and engage with these emergent organizations. In the Quebec context, ON was the most active party on Facebook during the 2012 election. But not all small parties used Facebook so effectively. The Greens' Facebook campaign was next to nonexistent in 2012. There is therefore no automatic correlation between smaller parties and social media activities. However, we tend to interpret this result as simply a missed opportunity for the Greens rather than a substantive pattern. After all, smaller parties are also more prone to lack the resources to run efficient and visually rich social media campaigns. Larger, richer parties can, as we saw in the 2012 Quebec election with the PQ, create elaborate posts that include social media–specific visual media components than can smaller, poorer parties. The use of visual media components might represent a way for larger and more conventional parties to maintain their political communication advantage over their smaller opponents. Our analyses show that this advantage is real. According to our statistical model, images and videos by far have the largest effects on message virality, all else being equal. That said, the use of visual components such as videos and images cannot be considered as contributing to the establishment of a "Web 2.0" type of campaign. After all, videos and images do little to engage voters and parties in dialogues. Communication is still unidirectional in this case or, as Jackson and Lilleker (2009) have stated, somewhat closer to a "Web 1.5" campaign. Therefore, we observe no fundamental transformation yet of the relationship between political parties and voters. That said, the same way that parties do not avoid social media such as Facebook anymore, scholars studying Canadian electoral campaigns cannot ignore candidates' and parties' online strategies.

In 2012, Quebec parties engaged on Facebook with different strategic objectives and tactical approaches. The use of hyperlinks to parties' websites and press releases appears to have been the norm. Substantively, parties' posts tended mainly to be partisan. The data that we used do not allow us to study more precisely political parties' strategic goals and whether messages diffused on social media differed from those advertised in conventional media. However, this does not seem to have been the case during this election. For instance, despite the PQ's emphatic separatist base, remarkably few PQ posts mentioned Quebec separation, an issue known to hurt the party electorally among the general population. Perhaps this was a missed opportunity. After all, Facebook allows political parties to target subgroups of voters with specific sociodemographic characteristics and political interests. It is therefore increasingly possible to develop targeted microcampaigns on positional issues using social media alongside more traditional macrocampaigns focused on valence issues, such as the economy, that target average voters (Marland 2016). This type of social media campaign is already the norm in the United States (McClelland 2012). An analysis of Mitt Romney's social media messaging in 2012 shows that social media posts were used to reach voters directly and to diffuse information regarding specific policy plans and stances (Johnson 2012). Future research will have to find creative ways to monitor, access, and record these multi-channel communication strategies.

We have also highlighted the fact that the study of social media political campaigns will face new and important challenges in the future. One obvious challenge is to find methods that can automatically analyze large quantities of visual media such as videos, photos, and infographics. Automated methods must be developed to allow study of the contents of these visual media. In fact, sole reliance on Facebook posts' textual component represents the main limitation of our study. And, as we have discussed here, such components seem to play important roles in social media political campaigns. Given the growing use of visual media components by political parties, this challenge will become ever more pressing. Finally, more comparative research needs to be conducted on parties' Facebook walls. The peculiarity of the 2012 Quebec election context makes it hard to evaluate the generalizability of the results presented above. However, Facebook remains an important tool for campaign managers in modern political campaigning since it allows political parties to reach specific voters (Štětka et al. 2014). Many scholars even demonstrate how social media activity by political actors can influence voting behaviour, thus affecting electoral outcome (Kovic, Rauchfleisch, and Metag 2017). But many questions remain. For instance, some research has shown how Facebook can unexpectedly bolster the two-way communication between citizens and politicians. Examining the political conversations between Danish politicians and citizens on Facebook, some authors argue that Facebook not only stimulates dialogue between politicians and citizens but also is a key motive for political actors to use that social media tool (Sørensen 2016).

These results add nuance to our findings but mainly contrast with skeptical scholars' comments about "slacktivism" or "clicktivism" to point out an online activism said to have no political impact (Morozov 2009). Do political interest and political participation affect the use of Facebook by political actors during an electoral campaign? After all, Denmark has a high level of trust in politics and in society (Jensen 2011). Hence, differences across Western democratic countries might affect the usefulness and efficiency of Facebook as a tool of electioneering. Different trends regarding the importance of political dialogue for democratic vitality might also help to explain how political conversations on Facebook can be accompanied by hopes for a revitalization of the public sphere. We have provided clear empirical benchmarks on which future research can base comparisons and enhance understanding of social media electioneering.

NOTES

1 Data used in this chapter come from research funded in France by the Agence nationale de la recherche and in Quebec by the Fonds de recherche Québec – Société et culture as part of their interagencies funding strategy. The project – Webinpolitics.com: Strategies, Contents, and Perceptions of Online Political Campaigns. The Case of the French Presidential and Quebec Provincial Elections – was co-directed by Thierry Giasson (Université Laval, Canada) and Fabienne Greffet (Université de Lorraine, France).
2 For more details, see www.grcp.ulaval.ca.
3 The lasting impact of the 2012 Quebec student crisis can be seen in the fact that all three of the student leaders became involved in provincial party politics. One of them, Gabriel Nadeau-Dubois, is now an elected Québec solidaire member of the National Assembly and the party's co-leader. The two others – Martine Desjardins and Léo Bureau-Blouin – ran for the Parti québécois in the 2012 and 2014 elections.
4 The regression model is estimated using all of the Facebook posts written by the political parties during the 2012 Quebec election. The dependent variable is the number of likes, and the independent variables are 1) a "partisan" dummy variable indicating whether the posts included partisan topics; 2) a continuous "tone variable" indicating the negativity (low value) and positivity (high value) of each post; and 3) two dummy variables indicating the visual media components included in the posts (image and video). Controls were included to take into account the party that wrote each post. Detailed results are available on request.
5 The size of the party refers here to the share of votes obtained during the previous elections. Note that, in the Quebec context, vote share is also approximately related to the relative importance of membership and funding.

REFERENCES

Anttiroiko, Ari-Veikko. 2010. "Innovation in Democratic E-Governance: Benefitting from Web 2.0." In *Citizens and E-Government: Evaluating Policy and Management*, edited by C.G. Reddick, 110–30. Hershey, PA: Information Science Reference.

Bastien, Frédérick, Éric Bélanger, and François Gélineau. 2014. "Une élection extraordinaire?" In *Les Québécois aux urnes: Les partis, les médias, et les citoyens en campagne*, edited by Frédérick Bastien, Éric Bélanger, and François Gélineau, 9–21. Montréal: Les Presses de l'Université de Montréal.

Borah, Porismita. 2014. "Facebook Use in the 2012 Presidential Campaign: Obama vs. Romney." In *Social Media in Politics: Case Studies on the Political Power of Social Media*, edited by B. Patrut and M. Patrut, 201–11. Cham, Switzerland: Springer Science+Business Media.

Breindl, Yana, and Pascal Francq. 2008. "Can Web 2.0 Applications Save E-Democracy? A Study of How New Internet Applications May Enhance Citizen Participation in the Political Process Online." *International Journal of Electronic Democracy* 1, 1: 14–31.

Bronstein, Jenny. 2013. "Like Me! Analyzing the 2012 Presidential Candidates' Facebook Pages." *Online Information Review* 37, 2: 173–92.

Caton, Simon, Margeret Hall, and Christof Weinhardt. 2015. "How Do Politicians Use Facebook? An Applied Social Observatory." *Big Data and Society* 2, 2: 1–18.

Chen, Peter J., and Peter J. Smith. 2011. "Digital Media in the 2008 Canadian Election." *Journal of Information Technology and Politics* 8, 4: 399–417.

Daku, Mark, Stuart Soroka, and Lori Young. 2015. *Lexicoder, Version 3.0*. www.lexicoder.com.

Digital In. 2016. "We Are Social (Annual Report)." *We Are Social*. http://www.wearesocial.sg.

Duval, Dominic, and François Pétry. 2016. "L'analyse automatisée du ton médiatique: Construction et utilisation de la version française du Lexicoder." Sentiment dictionary working paper.

Giasson, Thierry, Frédérick Bastien, Mireille Lalancette, and Gildas Le Bars. 2014a. "Is Social Media Transforming Canadian Electioneering? Hybridity and Online Partisan Strategies in the 2012 Quebec Election." Paper presented at the Annual Meeting of the Canadian Political Science Association, Brock University, St. Catharines, ON.

Giasson, Thierry, Gildas Le Bars, Frédérick Bastien, and Mélanie Verville. 2014b. "Qc2012: L'utilisation de Twitter par les partis." In *Les Québécois aux urnes: Les partis, les médias, et les citoyens en champagne*, edited by Frédérick Bastien, Éric Bélanger, and François Gélineau, 135–48. Montréal: Les Presses de l'Université de Montréal.

Giasson, Thierry, Fabienne Greffet, and Geneviève Chacon. 2014. "Digital Campaigning in a Comparative Perspective: Campaign Devices in the 2012 Elections in France and Quebec." Paper presented at the 23rd World Congress of the International Political Science Association, Montreal, July.

Grimmer, Justin, and Brandon M. Stewart. 2013. "Text as Data: The Promise and Pitfalls of Automatic Content Analysis Methods for Political Texts." *Political Analysis* 21, 3: 267–97.

Haynes, Audrey A., and Brian Pitts. 2009. "Making an Impression: New Media in the 2008 Presidential Nomination Campaigns." *PS: Political Science and Politics* 42, 1: 53–58.

Jackson, Nigel, and Darren Lilleker. 2009. "Building and Architecture of Participation? Political Parties and Web 2.0 in Britain." *Journal of Information Technology and Politics* 6, 3–4: 232–50.

Jensen, J. Linaa. 2011. "Citizenship in the Digital Age: The Case of Denmark." *Policy and Internet* 3, 3: 49–70.

Johnson, Janet. 2012. "Twitter Bites and Romney: Examining the Rhetorical Situation of the 2012 Presidential Election in 140 Characters." *Journal of Contemporary Rhetoric* 2, 2–3: 54–64.

Kovic, Marko, Adrian Rauchfleisch, and Julia Metag. 2017. "Brute Force Effects of Mass Media Presence and Social Media Activity on Electoral Outcome." *Journal of Information Technology and Politics* 14, 4: 1–80.

Larsson, Anders O. 2015. "Comparing to Prepare: Suggesting Ways to Study Social Media Today – and Tomorrow." *Social Media + Society* 1, 1: 1–2.

Lees-Marshment, Jennifer. 2001. "The Marriage of Politics and Marketing." *Political Studies* 49, 4: 692–713.

Marland, Alex. 2016. *Brand Command: Canadian Politics and Democracy in the Age of Message Control*. Vancouver: UBC Press.

McClelland, Sara I. 2012. "News Analysis/Blogosphere: Intermedia's Best of the Web." *Intermedia* 40, 5: 16–17.

Morozov, Evgeny. 2009. "Brave New World of Slacktivism." *Foreign Policy*, May. http://www.npr.org/templates/story/story.php?storyId=104302141.

Negrine, Ralph, and Stylianos Papathanassopoulos. 1996. "The 'Americanization' of Political Communication: A Critique." *International Journal of Press/Politics* 1, 2: 45–62.

Nielsen, Rasmus Kleis, and Cristian Vaccari. 2013. "Do People 'Like' Politicians on Facebook? Not Really. Large-Scale Direct Candidate-to-Voter Online Communication as an Outlier Phenomenon." *International Journal of Communication* 7, 1: 2333–56.

Sangwon, Lee, and Moonhee Cho. 2011. "Social Media Use in a Mobile Broadband Environment: Examination of Determinants of Twitter and Facebook Use." *Mobile Marketing Association* 6, 2: 71–87.

Schulz, W. 2014. "Political Communication in Long-Term Perspective." In *Political Communication*, edited by C. Reinemann, 63–86. Berlin: De Gruyter Mouton.

Small, Tamara A. 2008. "The Facebook Effect? On-Line Campaigning in the 2008 Canadian and US Elections." *Policy Options* 14, 1: 51–70.

–. 2012. "Are We Friends Yet? Online Relationship Marketing by Political Parties." In *Political Marketing in Canada*, edited by Alex Marland, Thierry Giasson, and Jennifer Lees-Marshment, 193–208. Vancouver: UBC Press.

Sørensen, Mads P. 2016. "Political Conversations on Facebook: The Participation of Politicians and Citizens." *Media, Culture, and Society* 38, 5: 664–85.

Štětka, Vaclav, Darren Lilleker, Jens Tenscher, and Carlos Jalali. 2014. "Professional Campaigning Online: The Role of New Media as Campaign Platforms." Paper presented at the ECPR general conference, Glasgow.

Sweetser, Kaye D., and Ruthann Weaver Lariscy. 2008. "Candidates Make Good Friends: An Analysis of Candidates' Uses of Facebook." *International Journal of Strategic Communication* 2: 175–98.

Verville, Mélanie. 2012. "Usages politiques des médias sociaux et du Web 2.0: Le cas des partis politiques provinciaux québécois." MA thesis, Department of Information and Communication, Université Laval.

Williams, Christine B., and Girish J. Gulati. 2012. "Social Networks in Political Campaigns: Facebook and the Congressional Elections of 2006 and 2008." *New Media and Society* 15, 1: 52–71.

8

Cabinet Solidarity in an Age of Social Media
A Case Study of Twitter Use by MP Carolyn Bennett

J.P. LEWIS, MIREILLE LALANCETTE, AND VINCENT RAYNAULD

Canadian cabinet government functions through adherence to the principle of cabinet solidarity (White 2005). Traditionally, cabinet solidarity has been demonstrated by voting for government bills and supporting the government on the public record (Aucoin and Turnbull 2003). These demonstrations of support are not optional for cabinet ministers, who must fall in line or leave the cabinet. The discipline of cabinet ministers shapes their roles and, by extension, directly affects their political objectives to 1) support the government, 2) fulfill the mandate, and 3) stay out of trouble. As White (2005, 15) writes, "the doctrine of cabinet solidarity requires ministers to uphold cabinet decisions and government policy regardless of their personal views." However, the emergence of social media as important tools for constituent communication and outreach for members of Parliament (MPs) in Canada (Dickin 2016; Small et al. 2014) has raised questions about this dynamic. Specifically, it has become much easier for ministers to share quickly and to a mass audience personal views on political and policy matters outside more institutionalized – and to some extent controlled – channels of communication. From a broader perspective, social media have enabled them to let their personalities shine through their official constituent communications, possibly testing the doctrine of cabinet solidarity.

Cabinet ministers' extensive adoption of Twitter over the past decade provides researchers with a wealth of publicly shared views. Researchers can examine the strength of cabinet solidarity through how and to what extent ministers act on Twitter in terms of how closely they promote and support government decisions and follow the party line. Recent research has demonstrated how Canadian legislators have adopted social media for politicking in a more conventional rather than transformative way, mostly replicating offline-inspired modes of mass-broadcast politics with little to no interaction with audiences; this behaviour has been found in a variety of political contexts, including electoral campaigns (Francoli 2014; Francoli, Greenberg, and Waddell 2011; Giasson et al. 2013); in polarized, adversarial political communications (Gruzd and Roy 2014; Small 2012); at all levels of government (Hagar 2014); as well as in party politics (Small 2010, 2014). From an international perspective, researchers have studied the tweets of elected officials in order to describe and categorize their behaviour on social media (Conway, Kenski, and Wang 2013; Goldbeck, Grimes, and Rogers 2010; Graham et al. 2013). Yet there is a unique gap in the academic literature on how cabinet ministers behave on Twitter in Canada. The novelty of cabinet ministers on Twitter is that the platform provides them with a potentially quick and easy way to break cabinet solidarity. Few technological developments have created the possibility of such a disruption to how traditional political relationships function in the Westminster system. Ministers do not need to call a press conference or reach out to reporters to complain about the direction of the government. In a matter of seconds, they can tweet their views by simply reaching for their phones and typing 280 or fewer characters.

Furthermore, though predominantly not adopted by politicians in Canada (Small et al. 2014), the dialogic – or social interactive – capabilities of Twitter are antithetical to cabinet solidarity. Ministers must stay on message and support the party line for both the political and the legislative survival of the government (White 2005). Notably, ministers are less likely to tweet like backbench MPs, who – though constrained by party discipline – have more leeway than sworn-in ministers of the crown (Ceron 2017). However easy it is for individuals to break rank at a whim, ministers' behaviour on Twitter is expected to uphold cabinet solidarity, whereas backbenchers can be more likely to cross the party line in their tweets. Here we fill significant gaps in the burgeoning academic literature on social media and constituent communication in Canada by examining the aforementioned phenomenon through an exploratory case study. We unpack how federal Minister of Indigenous and Northern Affairs Carolyn Bennett tweeted as a private Liberal member and then as a Liberal cabinet member a year later following the success of the Liberal Party in the 2015 Canadian federal election.

Cabinet solidarity and collective cabinet responsibility have contributed to shaping communication and message control since Confederation in 1867. However, the past few decades have been marked by increased centralization of power in the government, identified as a problematic development for Canadian democracy by several scholars (Aucoin 2012; Savoie 1999; White 2005). In addition to internal pressures to centralize decision making in the Prime Minister's Office and Privy Council Office since the government of Pierre Elliott Trudeau (1968–79, 1980–84), external developments in digital media – namely the growing traction of social media – and political communications have led to government message control in permanent campaigning, political marketing, and branding (Marland 2016). In an era of nonstop digital media politicking shaped by the speed, interactivity, flexibility, and informal nature of contemporary political communication, individual ministerial communication and government message discipline have the potential to collide.

First heralded as a new medium to mass-broadcast political information similar to the introduction of radio in the 1930s or television in the 1960s, social media were seen by the 2006 Canadian federal election to have greater potential for communication by providing a more inclusive, interactive, and collaborative digital space (Small 2008). Coined the "Web 2.0" mediascape, this online communication arena was defined by user-generated content sharing and social networking services such as Instagram, Snapchat, Facebook, and YouTube. In the case of political insiders in Canada – specifically prime ministers, cabinet ministers, and party leaders – Web 2.0 has provided a way to bypass traditional media and institutional filters in order to deliver messages directly to the public more or less on their own terms. The promise of social media has been framed as participatory democracy with the "broadest opinion formation," but the most recent evidence has pointed to a more legalistic view of democracy, with the web reinforcing more traditional political processes (Van Dijk 2012, 106–8). If these findings carry over to Canadian cabinet government, then we can expect to see ministerial behaviour on social media reinforcing traditional political norms such as cabinet solidarity.

The speed of change in the digital mediascape has made research on its effects an ongoing challenge. Notable gaps in the scholarly literature are found in which trends are forming around the adoption of digital media for political communication. We are interested here in the widespread adoption of Twitter by Canadian federal cabinet ministers to communicate publicly cabinet solidarity and to manage their personal, public, and political images. To explore cabinet ministers' increasingly strategic use of Twitter, we ask the following research questions: How are Canadian federal cabinet ministers appropriating the trend of adopting Twitter as a platform for political communication? Is the use of Twitter challenging the traditional practice of cabinet solidarity? If so, then what implications does Twitter have for the Westminster parliamentary system? These questions are especially important since new trending phenomena in political communication and marketing could transform the role of ministers, increasing their policy influence in cabinet, heightening their public profiles and individual political capital, and having broader impacts on political communication and democracy. The potential impacts could be a reversal or at least a stalling of the centralization of power in the modern Canadian federal cabinet.

Because of when the Conservatives took office (2006), they were the first federal government to have cabinet ministers on Twitter (Curry 2011). Although the Conservative cabinet was routinely accused of being muzzled by Stephen Harper's office (e.g., Campion-Smith 2008), over the years a handful of ministers emerged with notable presences on Twitter. Interestingly, Twitter metrics show quantitatively that ministers were more prominent at times on social media than the prime minister. In 2011, the tracking website Klout.com ranked Minister of Industry Tony Clement's reach and demand (for one's tweets) ahead of those of Prime Minister Stephen Harper (Wherry 2011). Clement was known for a diverse mix of personal and policy-oriented tweets, which sometimes discussed his taste in music, once described his attempts to save a drowning person, but also included debates on serious policy issues such as the government's reversal of a Canadian Radio-Television and Telecommunications Commission decision

(Wherry 2011). Interestingly, social media engagement could also spell the downturn – or end – of Clement's political career. At the time of writing, he lost his role as justice critic and was kicked out of the Conservative caucus over inappropriate interactions with women online (Leblanc and Stone 2018).

Along with Clement, a handful of ministers started using Twitter regularly. Minister of Citizenship and Immigration, and later Defence, Jason Kenney's constant tweeting touched on a range of topics covering both government policy positions and personal political views – from boycotting Chiquita bananas to blaming gun violence on "foreign gangsters" to defending his decision to ban niqabs at citizenship ceremonies. During his time as defence minister, Kenney cemented his role as the "tweeting minister," sometimes in ways not always respecting the party line (Pugliese 2015). He was not alone among cabinet ministers when it came to tweeting beyond the party line. Minister of the Status of Women Rona Ambrose took to Twitter to express her thoughts on sex selection abortion. She responded to criticism that she faced for her support of Conservative MP Stephen Woodworth's motion on abortion (Kirkup 2012). Minister of Foreign Affairs John Baird called a UN choice of judge a sham on Twitter: "UN Human Rights Council continues to be a sham for advancing human rights ... [and does nothing] to promote peace and dignity in Gaza for the Palestinian people" (quoted in Hume 2014). Baird later faced scrutiny from Canada's commissioner of official languages for tweeting unilingually. After receiving complaints, Commissioner Graham Fraser sought to determine whether ministerial tweets fell under official language laws (Ditchburn 2014), demonstrating how ministers are held to different standards on social media than backbenchers.

For the Harper government, Twitter became a go-to platform for important policy announcements and enhanced political communications. By 2013, the Conservative government handled what had long been held as a major media event, the formal announcement of a cabinet shuffle, with a series of tweets, #shuffle13. Critics believed that the use of social media only extended the government's control of traditional media. A *Maclean's* editorial lamented that "reliance on Twitter is entirely consistent with this government's approach to communications: tightly scripted, unmediated contact with the public" (2011, 4).

After the Liberal Party won the federal election in October 2015, a new slate of ministers joined Twitter as members of cabinet. Although having a new roster of political actors is interesting as a case study of political behaviour, newly sworn-in Prime Minister Justin Trudeau brought attention to the role of ministers with his comments at the government swearing-in that "cabinet government is back" (quoted in Leblanc, Chase, and Galloway 2015). The Trudeau government's early emphasis on open and transparent government might also have raised the public's and media's expectations of how ministers should communicate (Leblanc 2015). One minister, the minister of Indigenous and northern affairs, offers an ideal case study as a frequent tweeter during her time both on the opposition party backbenches and on the government cabinet frontbenches.

Research suggests that political actors adapt traditional patterns of dialogue on new platforms, as elite Twitter networks emerge (Ausserhofer and Maireder 2013), and that political elites not only broadcast but also "narrowcast" (Small 2007) to particular groups and use Twitter as a tool of impression management (Frame and Brachotte 2015). Cabinet ministers in Westminster systems, such as in Canada, are ideal case studies for considering changes to political communications because the idea of open, public dialogue conflicts with the traditions of cabinet solidarity and secrecy. In fact, when taking into account traditional cabinet conventions and existing research on politicians who use social media, the most reasonable hypothesis is that a minister's behaviour will change on Twitter as the minister is promoted from the backbenches to the frontbenches. A closer look at the communication patterns of Liberal MP Carolyn Bennett offers insights into how ministerial communications are trending in the Canadian cabinet.

CASE STUDY

We look specifically at Carolyn Bennett's tweeting patterns as a Liberal MP in opposition and then as a Liberal cabinet member a year later following the Liberal Party's success in the 2015 Canadian federal election. A family physician for two decades, Bennett first ran for political office in 1995, losing in the Ontario provincial election. In 1997, she was successful in winning the Toronto-area federal riding of St. Paul. Bennett served in Prime Minister Paul Martin's cabinet as the minister of state for public health from 2003 to 2006 and sat on the opposition backbenches until she was appointed the minister of Indigenous and northern affairs after the Liberal Party formed the government in 2015. An early adopter (for Canadian politicians) of Twitter (May 2009), Bennett is a prolific tweeter, approaching 49,000 tweets (May 2009–December 2016).[1]

The Liberal government had a front-row seat in opposition to the Conservative government's social media approach and strategy. The Liberal government continued with a similar approach to social media while institutionalizing and regulating certain aspects of social media use by ministers. Notably, the government updated the official guide for the conduct of ministers to include social media use.[2] Although the Conservative government's guide noted that ministers' "communications must be timely and clear," there was no mention of social media (Government of Canada 2011, 6). In the 2015 edition of the ministers' guide, the Liberal government included an annex titled "Personal and Partisan Use of Social Media by Ministers and Parliamentary Secretaries." The annex stressed that ministers needed to maintain a "clear distinction" between their official government accounts and their personal or partisan accounts (Government of Canada 2015, 93). Somewhat confusingly, the guide notes that ministers and parliamentary secretaries can choose to use their personal or partisan media accounts to link to, share, or highlight content published on government accounts and websites, where such links are equally available to any outside party. In this context, the creation of official government ministerial social media accounts might not be necessary since messages from these accounts would be largely redundant in relation to any departmental or thematic account content (94). Even if these guidelines provide some rules, the subjectivity inherent in assessing what is redundant means that these instructions are fairly ambiguous. However, the language of "thematic account content" does provide a description of how a cabinet minister, such as Bennett, can use a personal account to stick to government ministerial messaging.

Bennett is ideal for examining the impact of cabinet membership on Twitter use for several reasons. Of interest is her high level of engagement with the social media site Twitter before becoming a minister and the natural evolution of her tweeting habits. Bennett tweeted more than any other MP in 2013, averaging twenty-nine tweets a day (Taras 2015), and in 2014 she averaged twenty-four tweets a day (Tsalamlal 2014; in 2014, the second most frequent MP tweeter was Elizabeth May at fourteen tweets a day). By analyzing two tweet data sets, we can compare how her approach might have differed once she reached the frontbenches and how her messages might have changed under the constraints of cabinet solidarity as her tweeting habits evolved. For this study, we hypothesized that Bennett's behaviour on Twitter changed from her time on the opposition backbenches to her time on the government frontbenches.

Backbench MPs, though constrained by a culture of party discipline, do not follow the convention of cabinet solidarity and have greater freedom than ministers to express their own political views (Godbout and Hoyland 2011). Although both ministers and backbenchers are expected to follow the party line, the extent of this discipline differs between the two groups. We created a data set of Bennett's last six months (February 4–August 4, 2015) as a backbencher in the opposition Liberal Party caucus and the critic for Indigenous and northern affairs and Bennett's first six months (November 6, 2015–May 6, 2016) as a member of the governing Liberal Party and the minister for Indigenous and northern affairs. The period of August 4–November 5, 2015, was left out because it included the election period and the time between the election and the swearing-in of cabinet. This period most likely would have reflected much different behaviour on Twitter as Bennett would have engaged in a high rate of partisan politics during the campaign. The entire number of tweets from these two periods amounts to 902. We selected this data set for two reasons: 1) it provided the most recent substantive (six-month) collection of tweets; 2) a saturation point was reached in the content and type of tweets. The tweets were identified and compiled using Twitter's internal search engine.

Methods

To characterize how a political actor's Twitter behaviour can change as the politician moves from the backbenches to the frontbenches, we coded the data set to identify four types of tweets: broadcast, social, attack, and personal. For each type, we coded every tweet in more detail to identify its content. Table 8.1 presents the codebook that we used.

TABLE 8.1
Types of tweets

Grand categories	Functions of tweets
Broadcast tweets	Party/government events Party/government leader Portfolio Party/government colleagues General at-large issues News events
Social tweets	Informal, casual exchanges Exchanges related to the portfolio Formal exchanges related to government and party business/activities Exchanges with other politicians
Attack tweets	Direct partisan attacks Indirect partisan attacks using media sources
Personal tweets	Relating to the MP's personal life Expressing a feeling Relating to popular culture

The codebook was created following other research on the subject (Evans, Cordova, and Sipole 2014; Graham, Jackson, and Broersma 2018) and to evaluate the potential change in behaviour of an individual on Twitter who moved from the opposition backbench to a government ministry. As an analytical tool, it is an important contribution to the literature. Since Bennett was the opposition critic for Indigenous and northern affairs before she was appointed as the minister, her tweets can be measured based on the proportion of portfolio-related tweets compared with other types of tweets. As Table 8.1 shows, each of the major tweet categories was coded so as to offer a more comprehensive account of her tweeting pattern and to attain a more thorough analysis of the contents of her tweets. Broadcast and social tweets function as either an announcement (broadcast) or a conversation (social); both categories can include political or nonpolitical actors because the focus is on the type of exchange. Attack and personal tweets function to fit certain content or tone. We coded the tweets and then tested for intercoder reliability by a coder with extensive social media and politics research experience with a mixed sample of 181 tweets (an average Cronbach's alpha of .820).[3]

FIGURE 8.1
Grand categories of tweets by Carolyn Bennett as backbencher and cabinet member

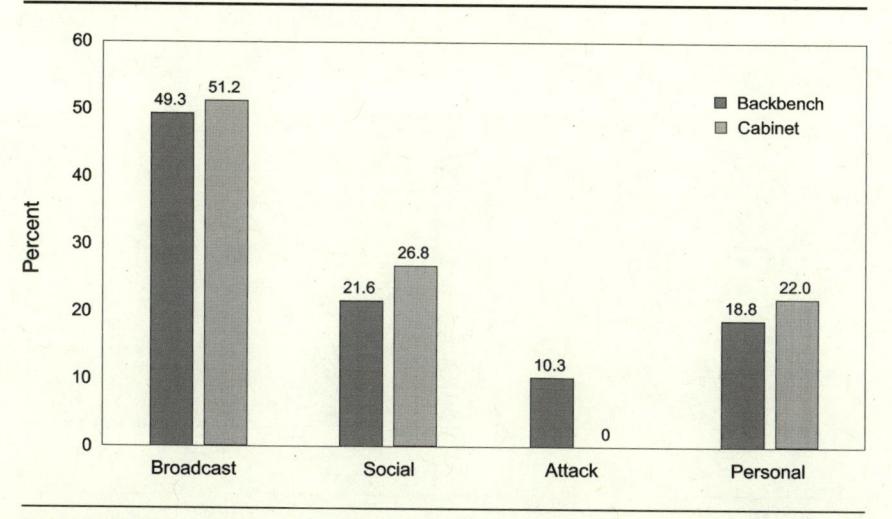

Category	Backbench	Cabinet
Broadcast	49.3	51.2
Social	21.6	26.8
Attack	10.3	0
Personal	18.8	22.0

Note: N = 902.

Findings

The first major difference between the two data sets is the volume of tweets. Bennett tweeted more than twice as much during her six months as a backbencher than during her six months as a cabinet minister. As an opposition MP, she tweeted 611 times in six months; during the first six months after being sworn into cabinet as the minister of Indigenous and northern affairs, she tweeted 291 times, a decrease of 52 percent. The decline is notable considering that the overall pattern was the same. We can hypothesize that Bennett did not need to be as vocal as a minister. As shown in Figure 8.1, in terms of the broad categories of tweets, her uses of Twitter were fairly constant for broadcasting tweets (49.3 percent and 51.2 percent). Bennett was slightly more social (from 21.6 percent to 26.8 percent) as a minister and offered a little more personal information (from 18.8 percent to 22.0 percent). The major difference in content was for attack tweets. Whereas 10.3 percent of her tweets fell into this category while she was an opposition backbencher, as a minister she used zero such tweets.

These are the broad categories. By turning to the subcategories, which offer a more granular look at Bennett's tweeting practices, we can examine

FIGURE 8.2
Broadcast tweets by Carolyn Bennett as backbencher and cabinet member

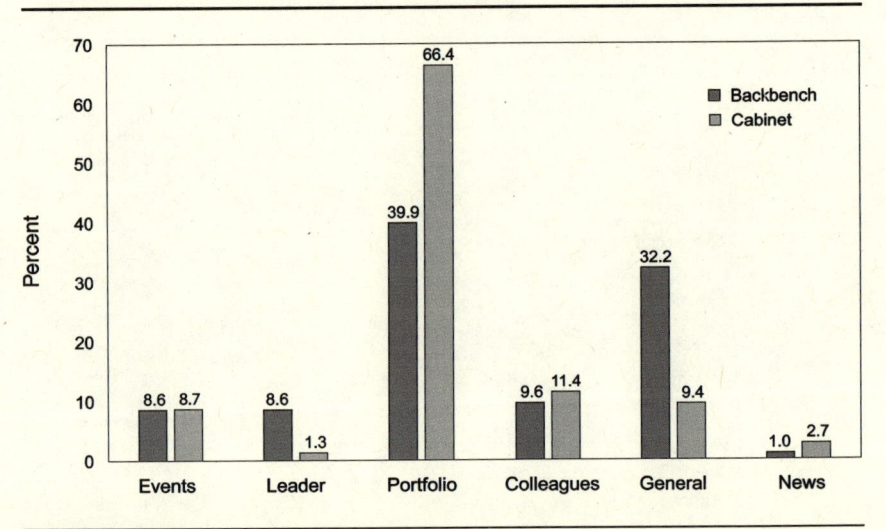

Category	Backbench	Cabinet
Events	8.6	8.7
Leader	8.6	1.3
Portfolio	39.9	66.4
Colleagues	9.6	11.4
General	32.2	9.4
News	1.0	2.7

Note: N = 450.

the subtler but specific quantitative and qualitative changes in her tweeting pattern, which will allow us to assess how cabinet solidarity could have affected it.

The largest collection of tweets (broadcast tweets) is presented in more detail in Figure 8.2. Notably, the percentage of portfolio tweets increased by over 20 percent once Bennett was in cabinet. Also, one-way broadcast tweets on the portfolio are easier to control and thus maintain cabinet solidarity compared with two-way conversational tweets. The other notable change in types of broadcast tweets from backbench to cabinet is found in a 20 percent decrease in tweets on general, at-large policy issues, demonstrating that Bennett as a minister was less inclined to tweet about policy issues outside her portfolio, possibly promoting policy positions that could challenge cabinet solidarity. When she was a backbencher, general issues not related to her portfolio were brought up on her Twitter feed. Bennett discussed subjects such as big data, the Vietnam War, and midwifery. After becoming a minister, she abandoned such issues in favour of portfolio issues. In this sense, she followed the party line and complied with cabinet solidarity rules and message discipline. It is also possible that she had less time as a minister to focus on other issues since the work of a minister is demanding.

For example, here are two of Bennett's broadcast tweets as a backbencher on the topic of her critic portfolio: "Aboriginal women still overrepresented among Canada's missing and murdered women. http://www.cbc.ca/1.3120272 @PnpCBC #MMIW @RCMP #cdnpoli" (June 19, 2015); "Truly important! #CBCNewFire Moments of rebellion & 'red rage' w Lisa Charleyboy @UrbanNativeGirl http://www.cbc.ca/radio/newfire/moments-of-rebellion-and-red-rage-1.3148114 ... #reconciliation" (July 7, 2016). We can see in these tweets that her tone is more direct, and she uses a CBC article as an authoritative source in order to support her claim. In contrast, here are a few examples of Bennett's broadcast tweets as a cabinet minister on the topic of her ministerial portfolio: "The mental health of FN, Inuit and Metis should be a priority for the future of Canada #cdnpoli #BellLets Talk" (January 27, 2016); "We are very grateful to Chief @bruceshisheesh & council-very productive mtg #Attawapiskat @charlieangusndp @justintrudeau @nancyChippNdale" (June 19, 2016); "At the amazing Chippewas of Kettle&StonyPt FN Hillside School-choir singing in OCanada in #Ojibway #reconciliation" (June 14, 2016). In the case of the first tweet, Bennett put forth her leadership as a cabinet minister and discussed the priorities of her government. In the other tweets, she broadcast her interactions with different communities, thus making her actions as a minister visible. These tweets also suggest considerable respect and admiration for the Indigenous communities referenced. We can hypothesize that Bennett was adopting her party's tone of positive messaging and support for reconciliation. Embracing a conciliatory tone, she was staying out of trouble, fulfilling her mandate as a minister, and supporting her government. In a sense, she was more focused on stressing her ministerial commitments and promoting her cabinet agenda.

Using a different analytical approach, Figure 8.3 shows differences in Twitter behaviour from backbench to cabinet. Bennett's informal interactions with citizens grew (34.0 percent to 54.5 percent), her interactions referring to her portfolio went down (39.7 percent to 10.4 percent), Bennett was slightly more formal in her interactions related to official engagements (22.7 percent to 28.6 percent), and her replies to other politicians went up slightly. Since she was more in the spotlight after being appointed

FIGURE 8.3
Social tweets by Carolyn Bennett as backbencher and cabinet member

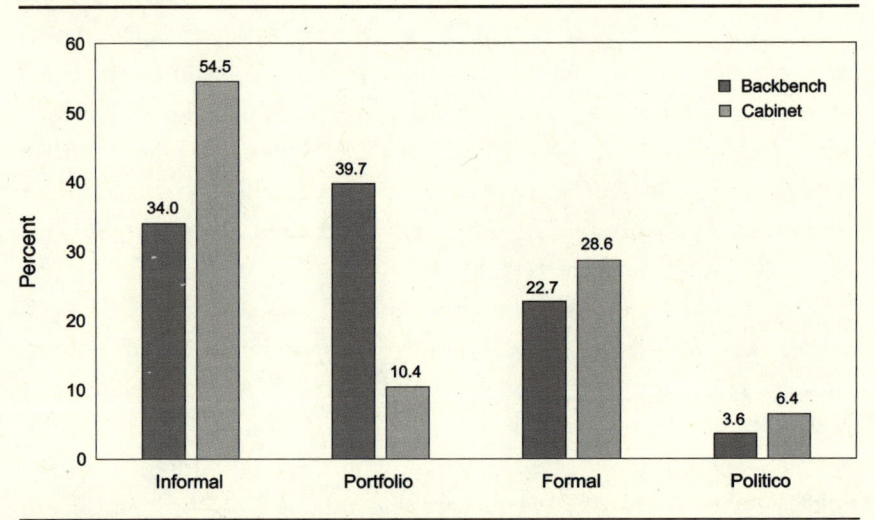

Category	Backbench	Cabinet
Informal	34.0	54.5
Portfolio	39.7	10.4
Formal	22.7	28.6
Politico	3.6	6.4

Note: N = 271.

minister, we suspect that she received more invitations to attend meetings and participate in specific events related to her duties. Bennett might have been contacted by citizens with Twitter accounts and used them to relate to them and thank and congratulate them in various ways. This was in line with her ministerial duties and the idea of building a stronger Canada presented by the Trudeau government. Again, as we can see in this tweet, the positive tone was dominant: "Congrats! @CBCSaskatoon: Saskatoon Cree teacher shortlisted for $1M Global award http://cbc.ca/1.3359107 #yxe #sask" (January 15, 2016).

In the second level of coding for social tweets, differences were observed between backbench and cabinet tweets. Notably, social tweets related to the Indigenous and northern affairs portfolio decreased once Bennett was in cabinet, possibly suggesting that as an opposition critic her behaviour was dictated only by party discipline and not under the control of cabinet solidarity. Her social tweets related to her portfolio decreased by almost 30 percent. Here is an example of a social portfolio tweet that reflects a cautious approach to two-way communication: "Gr8 @NoelineV please email Carolyn.bennett@parl.gc.ca and we'll find a time that works #cdnpoli @CBC_Aboriginal" (January 6, 2016).

As shown in Figure 8.1, attack tweets were found only in the backbencher data set. We found two types of attack tweets: direct partisan attacks on the Conservative and New Democratic Parties or members and indirect partisan attacks with the use of media content through hyperlinks. Here are some examples:

- Reckless Irresponsible Divisive @ThomasMulcair vows to get rid of #ClarityAct @BobHepburn @TorontoStar #cdnpoli (July 5, 2015)
- Harper's refusal to seek residential-schools apology from Pope "deeply disappointing" http://ottawacitizen.com/news/politics/harpers-refusal-to-seek-residential-schools-apology-from-pope-deeply-disappointing/ ... #cdnpoli @trc_en (June 12, 2015)
- The Conservative government continues to show disdain for the #CharterofRights&Freedoms @IrwinCotler http://montrealgazette.com/news/national/opinion-the-conservative-government-continues-to-show-disdain-for-the-charter-of-rights-and-freedoms/ ... #cdnpoli (April 17, 2015).

The set of backbench attack tweets in Figure 8.4 shows that Bennett used media sources in indirect attacks twice as much as direct partisan attacks, a manner of deflecting the attack through an external source and legitimizing the claim with independent validation. Media articles were mostly used in order to make these attacks.

In a way, the fact that Bennett stopped using attack tweets as a minister is telling for cabinet solidarity and, more importantly, supports government protocol and etiquette. On the one hand, stopping attacks means that the positive tone adopted by the Liberals is maintained in her Twitter feed. On the other, since her role changed, there were pressures on her to adapt her tweeting style. Indeed, when sitting in the opposition, one must criticize opponents and highlight how one's own party would do things differently.

As seen in Figure 8.5, of the 178 personal tweets, the notable changes were a decrease from backbench to cabinet in tweets about personal feelings

FIGURE 8.4
Attack tweets by Carolyn Bennett as backbencher and cabinet member

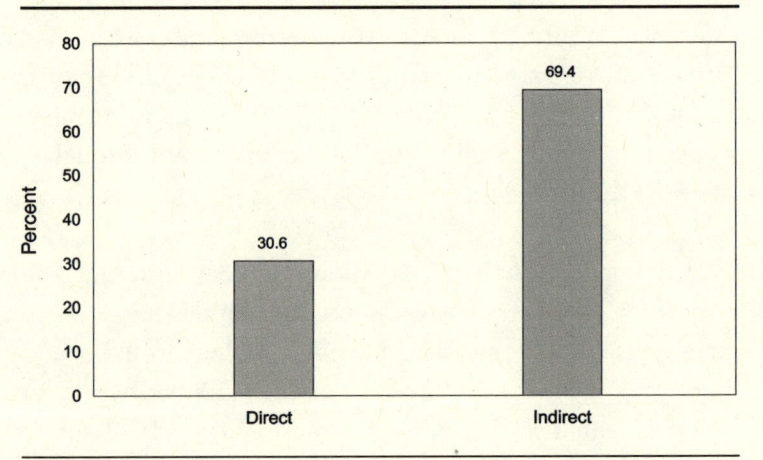

Direct	Indirect
30.6	69.4

Note: N = 62.

and an increase in tweets about pop culture. These tweets reflect both a connection to constituents and a connection to broader Canadian popular culture. For example, Bennett talked about hockey, a sport that can be seen as identity building: "Truly wonderful!! NHL draft lottery: Maple Leafs win 1st-overall pick | CBCSports.ca Mobile http://www.cbc.ca/m/sports/hockey/nhl/nhl-draft-lottery-1st-pick-1.3560960 ... #cdnpoli" (April 30, 2016).

The personal tweets reveal some details of Bennett's personality but are safe enough to reflect a cautious approach. Bennett does not reveal much about her personal life. She expressed her feelings a little more as a backbencher and has shown more restraint as a minister. The feeling put forward is mostly pride in her team as well as acknowledgment of the praise and support of Twitter users. Pride is the sentiment most often used. As we can see in the tweets below, Bennett is supportive of her leader in action – acknowledging, for example, his participation in the Toronto gay pride parade – and of her colleagues: "Fantastic #HopeandHardWork @JustinTrudeau #HappyPride happy happy Liberals!!!! #cdnpoli #onpoli @PrideTO" (June 28, 2016); "Thnx! @tthorntonTO: So proud seeing my MP @Carolyn_Bennett at the UN today representing me, aboriginals,

FIGURE 8.5
Personal tweets by Carolyn Bennett as backbencher and cabinet member

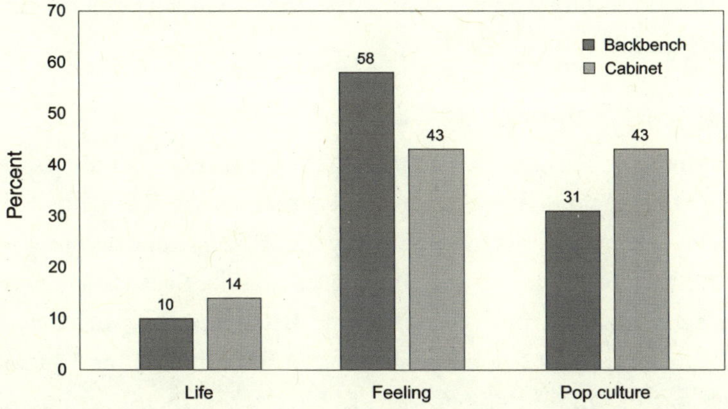

	Life	Feeling	Pop culture
Backbench	10	58	31
Cabinet	14	43	43

Note: N = 178.

women, and Canadians" (March, 16, 2016). Highlighting the team effort and praising their work are ways of showing cabinet solidarity.

In her personal tweets, Bennett tries to understand whom she believes is her audience. One clue is found in her use of hashtags: 82 percent of her tweets include a hashtag, and in over half of them the hashtag is the popular #cdnpoli, denoting a tweet related to the conversation on Canadian politics. However, Bennett also uses #cdnpoli routinely on tweets that have little to do with Canadian politics, suggesting that she sees her involvement as a Canadian politician as enough reason to tag #cdnpoli. This use suggests either a misunderstanding of hashtags or an attempt to gain an audience for nonpolitical tweets with users searching #cdnpoli. Here are a couple of examples of her unorthodox use of #cdnpoli: "Ahhh. Wish i had my tix @NoFlyDawn @MsGladysKnight #BBKing #cdnpoli" (May 15, 2015); "Chag Sameach to all celebrating Passover today! Peter & I extend our best wishes on this day to you & all your family #TorStPauls #cdnpoli" (April 23, 2016).

The change in Bennett's behaviour, as reflected in the two data sets, suggests granular differences that show the impact of cabinet solidarity on her approach to social media communication. Bennett's position as

Indigenous and northern affairs critic before becoming Indigenous and northern affairs minister provides a unique opportunity to study a prolific and authentic tweeter who shows little evidence of talking points or external communication control.

TRENDING IN CANADA

Although the policy challenges that a cabinet minister encounters during his or her tenure are steeped in complexity and learning curves, the political objectives of a minister should be easily identified: support your government, fulfill your mandate, and stay out of trouble. Because social media enhance ministers' ability to communicate instantaneously with the public, staying out of trouble can be more difficult for confident and successful political actors whose political careers have taken them to some of the highest offices in the country. Within this context, we have sought in this chapter to answer the following research questions. How do federal cabinet ministers adopt Twitter as a platform for political communication? Is this adoption challenging the traditional practice of cabinet solidarity? If so, then what implications does Twitter have for the Westminster parliamentary system?

Based on an exploratory case study of Minister Bennett's engagement with Twitter, it appears that politicians can alter their behaviour on social media as they move from the backbenches to the frontbenches, reflecting a cautious approach to the communication platform. The trend of her portfolio tweets increasing by over 20 percent once Bennett was in cabinet, in combination with her social tweets related to her portfolio decreasing by 30 percent from backbench to frontbench, suggests that, though she was active in tweeting about Indigenous and northern affairs both as an opposition critic and as a cabinet minister, the delivery of information changed from a dialogue to a monologue.

As Bennett became a cabinet minister and member of the government, her tweeting activity suggested more political strategy – broadcasting rather than conversing. She appropriated Twitter to communicate in an institutionally conventional and politically safe manner, understood to benefit both a minister's and the government's political brand. As a cabinet minister, Bennett tweeted messages echoing themes of both her portfolio and the government's program while carving space to share individual personality traits. She used Twitter less as a place to attack the opposition, share independent policy positions, or engage with dissenting voices and more as a place to forward the government's agenda and manage its image. Bennett's behaviour did not reflect the type of pitbull engagement exhibited by Conservative ministers Kenney and Clement. Instead, the Liberal government appears to be leaving the hyperpoliticization of its representation and use of Twitter to staff surrogates rather than the prime minister's lieutenants in cabinet (Radwanski 2016). Under the Harper government, senior staff and advisers had little to no presence, whereas under the Liberal government Trudeau's principal secretary and most important adviser, Gerald Butts, quickly became noted as the loudest federal Liberal voice on social media.[4] A *Maclean's* writer described Butts as "both Trudeau's top adviser and the loudest Liberal in the catty online mini-world of Canadian politics. His Twitter feed is a marked departure from the otherwise sunny and positive nature of the Trudeau campaign, and some see Butts' Twitter persona as a true reflection of his personality" (Patriquin 2015, 20). Butts fills the role of the Liberal Party's social media pitbull and an extension of Trudeau in which a unique voice, different from the common cabinet minister, can be shared.

Based on this explanatory case study, we find that Twitter provides opportunities to broadcast publicly a united cabinet – thus heightening the appearance of cabinet solidarity. Twitter offers ministers a chance to articulate cabinet solidarity every day by tweeting their support for government policies and decisions as well as demonstrating social cabinet solidarity by tweeting their support for and highlighting their engagement with other ministers. For example, Bennett regularly demonstrated cabinet solidarity by showing support for her cabinet colleagues with distinct mentions of and links to them in her tweets. Examples of this support include the following tweets, in which Bennett acknowledged cabinet colleagues, including then Minister of Health Jane Philpott, Minister of the Environment and Climate Change Catherine McKenna, Minister of Justice and Attorney General Jody Wilson-Raybould, Minister of International Development and La Francophonie Marie-Claude Bibeau, and Minister for the Status of Women Patty Hajdu:

- We LOVE @janephilpott!!! She gets Health vs. Health Care!!! More emphasis #sdoh #health means less nd4 #healthcare @natnewswatch #cdnpoli (November 7, 2015).
- Ahhhh @cathmckenna we are so proud to work with YOU!!! #cdnpoli (December 8, 2015).
- Exciting! @Puglaas @JustinTrudeau almost here! @mcclaudebibeau @PattyHajdu #cdnpoli #genderparity (March 16, 2016).

For cabinet, the social aspect of social media can reflect collegiality, a perspective previously difficult to attain unless one was a fly on the wall in the parliamentary cafeteria or cabinet retreats. Ministers can conveniently tag another minister to their tweets or post a photo with a minister and share images of team building – an activity regularly missing in the public presentation of politics. Ministers can also tag their tweets with the #lpc (Liberal Party of Canada); with the party hashtag, the tweet's content might be connected by the reader to the party and government and reflect cabinet solidarity.

Although Twitter does not appear to be changing how ministers interact with the public or challenging cabinet solidarity, the platform does present an opportunity for ministers to define their political images not in terms of influence but in terms of personality and presence. As shown in our case study, ministers can highlight their personal connections to their portfolios, their tastes in pop culture, or their personal lives. Because of the small community of political elites on Twitter in Canada, a minister with an active presence can make an amplified impression with a concentrated media audience.

The disruption that social media sites such as Twitter can create was first faced by the Conservative government, led by a prime minister caricatured for message control and strict communication discipline. Surprising to some, a handful of Conservative ministers were able to shape unique political personalities from their presence on Twitter even in the controlled communication environment. How could these ministers get away with what appeared to be off-the-cuff, unfiltered political communication? One theory is that it is difficult to imagine the prime minister or his office disagreeing with the positions taken by ministers on Twitter; frustration might have come in the centre of government only because of staffers' continuous efforts to coordinate government messaging. With this in mind, how might those who followed the Conservative government adopt Twitter? Because Clement and Kenney were independent yet consistently followed Conservative Party ideals with their messages, Canadian federal politics has no precedent for a freelancing social media minister, and no minister has redefined the role and influence of a cabinet minister through her or his approach to social media.

What is the impact of Twitter on the Westminster parliamentary system? Ministers who are politically constrained by cabinet solidarity and communication control by the centre can pragmatically stake out their political images for future cabinet promotions or leadership ambitions. In the short run, ministers' virtual profiles on Twitter reflect their actual profiles in public; ministers draw attention to their portfolios and government policies and act ministerially, within the expected conventions of political discourse, while rarely engaging with so-called internet trolls in bottom-feeder debates or hyperpartisan conflicts with other partisans. In the long run, as ministers' decision-making power and influence remain relatively marginalized by the powerful modern Prime Minister's Office, individual ministers can curate unique and noticeable profiles with successful image management.

Justin Trudeau might have committed to bring government by cabinet back, but the power and influence of the centre have been constants in Westminster systems, only heightened by the modern external pressures of social media and 24/7 news. The changes in communication and political behaviour have followed traditional and safe patterns of supporting the party line while promoting one's personal political brand. The practices are an evolution of traditional approaches to how new platforms are used to follow old political communication norms: the government and the party are supported alongside a modest promotion of a personal political brand. Trends in the use of Twitter by Canadian federal cabinet ministers are not transformative for day-to-day politicking but could be transformative for how ministers bring attention to themselves regardless of the communication regime found in the Prime Minister's Office. However, increased levels of individualization and personalization of political communication could affect its dynamics in the social mediascape. Similar case studies could be performed on other MPs to test the strength of our approach and findings. Notably, we did not consider the possible change in Twitter style of an individual who moved from the government backbenches to the government frontbenches. Additionally, future areas of study of cabinet ministers and Twitter behaviour could include an examination of Twitter use by portfolio and how social interactions among ministers on Twitter reflect cabinet solidarity and government message cohesion.

NOTES

1 The adoption of Twitter in Canadian politics occurred in the context of social media in the form of blogs, which emerged as a central aspect of political communications during the 2006 federal election campaign. By the 2015 federal election campaign, long-form political blogging had been replaced by microblogging on platforms such as Twitter (Raynauld 2015). Twitter was founded in March 2006. As of December 2016, Bennett had approximately 34,000 followers.
2 Government of Canada, "Open and Accountable Government," *Government of Canada,* http://www.pm.gc.ca/eng/news/2015/11/27/open-and-accountable-government#Portfolio_Responsibilities_and_Support.
3 To assess the validity of our empirical study, we completed an intercoder reliability test. A second coder analyzed 20 percent of the sample; there was coder agreement in over 80 percent of the cases, above the standard level of acceptability (following Cronbach's alpha reliability test).
4 In 2019, Gerald Butts resigned in light of the Jody Wilson-Raybould scandal.

REFERENCES

Aucoin, Peter. 2012. "New Political Governance in Westminster Systems: Impartial Public Administration and Management Performance at Risk." *Governance* 25, 2: 177–99.
Aucoin, Peter, and Lori Turnbull. 2003. "The Democratic Deficit: Paul Martin and Parliamentary Reform." *Canadian Public Administration* 46, 4: 427–49.
Ausserhofer, Julien, and Axel Maireder. 2013. "National Politics on Twitter: Structures and Topics of a Networked Public Sphere." *Information, Communication, and Society* 16, 3: 291–314.
Campion-Smith, Bruce. 2008. "How Harper Controls the Spin." *Toronto Star,* May 26. https://www.thestar.com/news/canada/2008/05/26/how_harper_controls_the_spin.html.
Ceron, Andrea. 2017. "Intra-Party Politics in 140 Characters." *Party Politics* 23, 1: 7–17.
Conway, Bethany Anne, Kate Kenski, and Di Wang. 2013. "Twitter Use by Presidential Primary Candidates during the 2012 Campaign." *American Behavioral Scientist* 57, 11: 1596–1610.

Curry, Bill. 2011. "Canada's First Social Media Election Is On, But Will People Vote?" *Globe and Mail*, March 28. https://www.theglobeandmail.com/news/politics/canadas-first-social-media-election-is-on-but-will-people-vote/article574263/.

Dickin, Daniel. 2016. "Organizing the Halls of Power: Federal Parliamentary Staffers and Members of Parliament's Offices." *Canadian Parliamentary Review* 39, 2: 9–16.

Ditchburn, Jennifer. 2014. "Canada's Language Watchdog Probing John Baird's Twitter Account over Lack of French Posts." *National Post*, August 21. https://nationalpost.com/news/politics/canadas-language-watchdog-probing-john-bairds-twitter-account-over-lack-of-french-posts.

Evans, Heather, Victoria Cordova, and Savannah Sipole. 2014. "Twitter Style: An Analysis of How House Candidates Used Twitter in Their 2012 Campaigns." *PS: Political Science and Politics* 47, 2: 454–62.

Frame, Alex, and Gilles Brachotte. 2015. "Le tweet strategique: Use of Twitter as a PR Tool by French Politicians." *Public Relations Review* 41, 2: 278–87.

Francoli, Mary. 2014. "Exploring the Concept of the 'Social Media Campaign.'" In *Transforming Politics and Policy in the Digital Age*, edited by Jonathan Bishop, 133–43. Hershey, PA: IGI Global.

Francoli, Mary, Josh Greenberg, and Christopher Waddell. 2011. "The Campaign in the Digital Media." In *The Canadian Federal Election of 2011*, edited by Jon Pammett and Christopher Dornan, 219–46. Toronto: Dundurn Press.

Giasson, Thierry, Gildas Le Bars, Frédérick Bastien, and Mélanie Verville. 2013. "#Qc2012. L'utilisation de Twitter par les partis politiques." In *Les Québécois aux urnes: Les partis, les médias, et les citoyens en campagne*, edited by Frédérick Bastien, Éric Bélanger, and François Gélineau, 135–48. Montréal: Presses de l'Université de Montréal.

Godbout, Jean-François, and Bjorn Hoyland. 2011. "Legislative Voting in the Canadian Parliament." *Canadian Journal of Political Science* 44, 2: 367–88.

Goldbeck, Jennifer, Justin Grimes, and Anthony Rogers. 2010. "Twitter Use by the U.S. Congress." *Journal of the Association for Information Science and Technology* 61, 8: 1612–21.

Government of Canada. 2011. "Accountable Government: A Guide for Ministers and Ministers of State." *Government of Canada*. http://www.pco-bcp.gc.ca/index.asp?lang=eng&page=information&sub=publications&doc=aggr/2011/ag-gr-eng.htm.

–. 2015. "Open and Accountable Government." *Government of Canada*. http://pm.gc.ca/sites/pm/files/docs/OAG_2015_English.pdf.

Graham, Todd, Marcel Broersma, Karin Hazelhoff, and Guido Van'T Haar. 2013. "Between Broadcasting Political Messages and Interacting with Voters." *Information, Communication, and Society* 16, 5: 692–716.

Graham, Todd, Daniel Jackson, and Marcel Broersma. 2018. "The Personal in the Political on Twitter: Towards a Typology of Politicians' Personalized Tweeting Behaviours." In *Managing Democracy in the Digital Age*, edited by Julia Schwanholz, Todd Graham, and Peter-Tobias Stoll, 137–57. Cham, Switzerland: SpringLink Press.

Gruzd, Anatoliy, and Jeffrey Roy. 2014. "Investigating Political Polarization on Twitter: A Canadian Perspective." *Policy and Internet* 6, 1: 28–45.

Hagar, Doug. 2014. "Campaigning Online: Social Media in the 2010 Niagara Municipal Elections." *Canadian Journal of Urban Research* 23, 1: 74–98.

Hume, Jessica. 2014. "Inquiry a 'Sham.'" *Brockville Recorder and Times,* August 13, A7.

Kirkup, Kristy. 2012. "Ambrose Mum over Controversial Motion." *Sault Star,* September 28, A7.

Leblanc, Daniel. 2015. "Liberals to Offer 'Open Government' Reforms in Bid to Overtake NDP." *Globe and Mail,* June 15. https://www.theglobeandmail.com/news/politics/liberals-to-offer-open-government-reforms-in-bid-to-overtake-ndp/article24971673/.

Leblanc, Daniel, and Laura Stone. 2018. "Clement Forced Out of Caucus after Complaints from Women about Social-Media Interactions." *Globe and Mail,* November 7. https://www.theglobeandmail.com/politics/article-conservative-leader-says-tony-clement-had-terrible-lapse-of-judgement/.

Leblanc, Daniel, Steven Chase, and Gloria Galloway. 2015. "Trudeau Sets Fresh Tone with Cabinet Ready to Tackle Thorny Issues." *Globe and Mail,* November 5. https://www.theglobeandmail.com/news/politics/trudeau-sworn-in-at-rideau-hall/article27096353/.

Maclean's. 2011. "You Can't Govern a Country 140 Characters at a Time." *Maclean's,* February 21, 4–5.

Marland, Alex. 2016. *Brand Command: Canadian Politics and Democracy in the Age of Message Control.* Vancouver: UBC Press.

Patriquin, Martin. 2015. "Trudeau's Brain: How Gerald Butts – Genius Strategist and Often Nastiest Liberal Voice on Twitter – Plans to Make His Best Friend the Next Prime Minister." *Maclean's,* October 5. https://archive.macleans.ca/article/2015/10/5/trudeaus-brain.

Pugliese, David. 2015. "HMCS Mistake Further Cements Jason Kenney's Reputation in DND for Twitter Mess-Ups." *National Post,* April 16. https://nationalpost.com/news/politics/hms-mistake-further-cements-jason-kenneys-reputation-in-dnd-for-twitter-mess-ups.

Radwanski, Adam. 2016. "Gerald Butts: The BFF in the PMO." *Globe and Mail,* September 3. https://www.theglobeandmail.com/news/gerald-butts-the-guardian-of-the-trudeaunarrative/article31692482/.

Raynauld, Vincent. 2015. "The Blog Is Dead! Long Live the (Micro)Blog! Unpacking Dynamics in Political Blogging during #elxn42." In *Canadian Election Analysis 2015: Communication, Strategy, and Democracy,* edited by Alex Marland and Thierry Giasson, 84–85. Vancouver: UBC Press.

Savoie, Donald. 1999. *Governing from the Centre: The Concentration of Power in Canadian Politics.* Toronto: University of Toronto Press.

Small, Tamara A. 2007. "Canadian Cyberparties: Reflections on Internet-Based Campaigning and Party Systems." *Canadian Journal of Political Science* 40, 3: 639–57.

–. 2008. "The Facebook Effect? On-Line Campaigning in the 2008 Canadian and US Elections." *Policy Options* 14, 1: 85–87.

–. 2010. "Canadian Politics in 140 Characters: Party Politics in the Twitterverse." *Canadian Parliamentary Review* 33, 2: 39–45.

–. 2012. "E-ttack, Politics: Negativity, the Internet, and Canadian Political Parties." In *How Canadians Communicate IV: Media and Politics*, edited by David Taras and Christopher Waddell, 169–89. Edmonton: Athabasca University Press.

–. 2014. "The Not-So Social Network: The Use of Twitter by Canada's Party Leaders." In *Political Communication in Canada: Meet the Press and Tweet the Rest*, edited by Alex Marland, Tamara Small, and Thierry Giasson, 92–110. Vancouver: UBC Press.

Small, Tamara A., Harold Jansen, Frédérick Bastien, Thierry Giasson, and Royce Koop. 2014. "Online Political Activity in Canada: The Hype and the Facts." *Canadian Parliamentary Review* 37, 4: 9–16.

Taras, David. 2015. *Digital Mosaic: Media, Power, and Identity in Canada*. Toronto: University of Toronto Press.

Tsalamlal, Yamina. 2014. "The Year MPs Started to Put Social in Social Media." *iPolitics*, December 19. https://ipolitics.ca/2014/12/19/2014-the-year-mps-started-to-put-social-in-social-media/.

Van Dijk, Jan. 2012. *The Network Society Third Edition*. London: Sage.

Wherry, Aaron. 2011. "The MP with Most 'Klout.'" *Maclean's*, March 7. https://www.macleans.ca/society/technology/the-mp-with-the-most-klout/.

White, Graham. 2005. *Cabinets and First Ministers*. Vancouver: UBC Press.

9

Does the Difference Compute?
Data-Driven Campaigning in Canada

FENWICK McKELVEY AND JILL PIEBIAK

Before Cambridge Analytica and AggregateIQ became the centre of a public controversy about privacy and data in politics, most parties would have been happy to highlight their data advantages.[1] The Liberals bragged that their data and digital infrastructure helped them to win the election in 2015. Minister of Innovation, Science, and Economic Development Navdeep Bains remarked on CBC's *The House* that, "if you take a step back when Mr. Trudeau decided to run for the Liberal Party, he really understood the importance of renewing the party and really investing in the party machinery ... So [we were] collecting data, building up the database, building up a ground game" (quoted in Hall 2016). The Liberals continue to invest in data. In 2017, former Liberal digital strategist Tom Pitfield launched Data Sciences, one of Canada's few political data and analytics firms. Liberal Party activity is just one example of the growing trend toward data-driven campaigning in Canada.

Cambridge Analytica, AggregateIQ, as well as countless other firms are part of a growing industry helping political parties to engage in data-driven campaigning. What do they do? Data-driven campaigning is a political logic, as defined by Munroe and Munroe (2018), which considers data resources to be collected and analyzed in campaign decision making. Data-driven campaigning promises to inject some science into campaigns. Unlike much worry about the secret science of political technology, we find its insights as well as its practices subject to constraint and debate in Canada. Our findings show a partial, uneven adoption of this logic. At times, data-driven practices afford a computational management of political work

(Kreiss 2012). This management is partial, limited by institutional constraints, party traditions, and technologies. Calling out these limits, however, does not diminish the significance of the data-driven trend in Canada. The professional sophistication of our participants can be appreciated only by attending to how they find and adapt data-driven practices as well as overcome institutional constraints in the hope of reaching more voters and being more organized.

Better data management has been an important motivation for political technology. Over the past 100 years of electioneering, political data have moved from clipboards and cardfiles to mobile apps and the cloud (Johnson 2016; McKelvey 2018b). Changing data storage techniques have coincided with organizational changes in how parties could coordinate, sort, and contact voters. Unfortunately, there is no proper history of political data in Canada. Parties, presumably as they professionalized by the start of the twentieth century, had to track their membership bases better. Parties began to digitize these records by the 1960s, converting paper records into punch-card databases. Parties gradually digitized these records and began to rely more on statistics and demographics in campaigning (Chartrand 1972; Delacourt 2013; Kreiss 2012; Nimmo 1970; Pool, Abelson, and Popkin 1965). Edwin Black, former president of the Canadian Political Science Association, noted in 1983 that "computers have been used for some time for a variety of political functions: in elections, for polling the electorate, keeping track of mailing lists, recruiting workers, analyzing voting returns, and so on" (676). By the end of the twentieth century, federal parties used electronic databases to track their voters. To many observers, the Conservative Party had a competitive advantage because of its integration of electronic record-keeping early on (Flanagan 2003).

Today all federal parties maintain central databases of voter records. These databases have become part of what we call political engagement platforms (McKelvey and Piebiak 2018). These platforms mediate campaigns and their interactions with voters. Virtual phone banks – popularized by the 2008 Obama campaign – exemplify a stabilized form of citizen-initiated campaigning (Baldwin-Philippi 2015; Gibson 2015). Citizen-initiated campaigns increasingly rely on emerging political engagement platforms that integrate data collection, analysis, and feedback into one unified system (Anderson and Kreiss 2013; Bennett 2015). These platforms still include national databases that connect central offices to local ridings (Munroe and Munroe 2018).

Canadian parties have looked to the private sector for inspiration for what to do with their data. The advent of market research likely changed party record-keeping as political communication shifted from talking to voters to listening to them (Marland 2016, 28–30). Advertising and marketing have had the most tangible influences on data-driven campaigning, part of the important role of political marketing in Canada's history (Delacourt 2013). By the early 1960s, parties depended on market research and advertising. Martin Goldfarb, for instance, advised Prime Minister Pierre Elliott Trudeau about his image among the Canadian electorate through a computer-assisted polling analysis as far back as 1970. Already popular in advertising, computer-assisted direct mail also found its way into party communications. Commenting on the 1972 campaign, Khayyam Paltiel (1974, 348) noted that "one thing is clear, however; the print media such as newspapers are in decline as an election campaign tool, while broadcasting and such devices as computerized 'personal' direct mail are growing in favour." Direct mail merged third-party data, such as magazine subscriber lists, with voter data to begin to "microtarget" voters. Alex Marland (2016, 410) describes microtargeting as "a strategic use of resources, uncovered through market intelligence, designed to focus communications on small segments of the electorate whose profiles indicate a propensity to support the sponsor." Data, comprising a strategic resource, helped parties to profile voters and calculate their propensities.

Growing computational capacity improved market segmentation for microtargeting. Canadians eventually followed advances in market segmentation in the United States as well. For example, the PRIZM system developed by the Claritas Corporation used cluster analysis to identify sixty-two market segments in the United States with names such as Beltway Boomers and Suburban Pioneers (Johnson 2016, 198–99). Beginning in the early 1980s, American campaigns relied on these granular segments. At roughly the same time, Goldfarb launched a comparable system known as "the Goldfarb report," which identified six groups of Canadian voters, such as "day-to-day watchers" and "aggressive" voters.

Data-driven campaigning has undergone its most recent iteration thanks to the use of the internet and social media as sources of "big data" in politics. The first phase of data-driven campaigning (late 1990s to mid-2000s) involved a cautious entry into the internet by established political parties. There was debate in these early days about whether the internet was positive (Poster 2001), problematic (Margolis and Resnick 2000), or marginal (Bimber 1998). Most parties ran websites primarily to communicate information one way (Foot and Schneider 2006; Stromer-Galley 2014). Such reluctance continued even as the internet became a bigger part of Canadians' everyday lives. Aside from the ill-fated NDP Orange Room, Canadian parties preferred to use the internet mostly as a tool to attack opponents or to disseminate information one way in this second phase (Small 2012).

As voters shared more online, parties found better ways to harvest and connect social media and advertising data to electoral records. Social media platforms such as Facebook, Twitter, and Google, keen to attract political customers, have willingly helped parties to access and use data online to target voters (Kreiss and McGregor 2018).

Today data-driven campaigning is marked by growing professionalization and the rise of political consultants. Many of the consulting firms formed after the 2012 Obama campaign – such as NGP VAN, Blue State Digital, and 270 Strategies – actively work in Canada (Kreiss 2016; Kreiss and Jasinski 2016). The same can be said for MoveOn.org as its tactics have become incorporated into a global community of practice (Karpf 2013, 2015). New digital-advocacy groups such as OpenMedia, Shit Harper Did (SHD.com), and Leadnow shared tactics and resources. Formerly upstart conferences such as Personal Democracy Forum and Netroots Nation matured into institutions, and the rise of new conferences such as CampaignTech, organized by the magazine *Campaigns and Elections*, are part of a whole global industry of digital and data consultancy in politics.

CASE STUDY

Our research contributes to an emerging research agenda examining data-driven campaigning in Canada. We specifically wish to understand data-driven campaigning:

- How does it change the work of campaigning, if at all?
- Which technologies are behind it?

- What motivates parties and practitioners to be data driven?
- And, if they are embracing data, how does this alter the current permanent campaign in Canada?

Methods

To answer these questions, we relied on methods of qualitative political communication (Karpf et al. 2015). We triangulated interviews with data-driven campaign practitioners with digital methods in order to study the state of the field in Canada. We surveyed the digital presence of national and provincial parties in Canada and recorded the technologies that they used for their websites, email marketing, and political databases. Building on platform studies methods developed at the Infoscape Center for the Study of Social Media (Elmer, Langlois, and McKelvey 2012), we examined web code and other tags to identify specific political technologies used by parties. We also used the website BuiltWith.com, a tool that analyzes web code to generate a report about its software. For example, we were able to designate a party as a user of the email tool MailChimp if it used a sign-up form linked to a known MailChimp domain such as list-manage.com. We also contacted each party directly to see if it would be willing to disclose which technologies it uses. When it was unclear, we left a question mark. Our review resulted in the first-ever index of political technology used by federal and provincial parties in Canada. Although we know that parties have changed their technologies, the changes have not been dramatic, as indicated in Table 9.1. Aside from the fact that the NDP switched to a new proprietary database, technologies have largely been stable at the federal level or have moved to well-known providers such as NationBuilder, Blue State Digital (BSD), or NGP VAN.

Simultaneously, we interviewed data-driven campaign practitioners in Canada. We collected a list of consultants who use data-driven technologies and surveyed press coverage to develop an initial basket of names. Over the course of 2013 and 2014, we identified and contacted forty-one potential interviewees who worked mostly in large municipalities, provincial politics, or federal ridings. Like many studies of the backrooms of politics (Marland 2016; McLean 2012; Munroe and Munroe 2018; Nielsen 2012), we had difficulty securing interviewees. When we received replies to our initial requests, we often had trouble convincing busy practitioners

TABLE 9.1
Political technology use by federal parties in 2014 and 2017

	Database		Website		Mass mailer	
Party	2014	2017	2014	2017	2014	2017
Greens	?	?	Drupal	Drupal	CiviCRM	CiviCRM
Liberals	NGP VAN	NGP VAN	WordPress	WordPress	NGP VAN	BSD
New Democrats	NDPVote	Populus	Drupal	BSD	CiviCRM	BSD
Conservatives	CIMS	CIMS	WordPress	WordPress	Campaign Monitor	MailChimp
Bloc Québécois	?	?	?	WordPress	?	?

to spend an hour of their time talking to us. Getting access, according to Nielsen (2012, 194), is a crucial task, but "campaign staffers' fear of spies and double-dealers illustrates why it is not always a simple one." In the end, we successfully completed seventeen interviews, listed in Table 9.2. Each interview followed a semi-structured format. Questions sought to understand, in general, the particular work of the interviewee as well as his or her overall impressions of data-driven campaigning in Canada. We also tried to gain a sense of the specific technology used by the interviewee when developing questions in part to ask which features were not used. Many of those interviewed have gone on to be leading voices in their parties, running leadership campaigns and otherwise advancing the craft of data-driven campaigning in Canada.

Findings

Data-driven campaigning, to many of our interviewees, expressed a political desire to use science rather than instinct. This is a sign that data-driven campaigning is guided by a political logic to professionalize campaigns. Participants often cited American success stories as sources of inspiration, from the George W. Bush campaign's microtargeting to the various innovations of the Obama campaign. As Hamish Marshall, the 2019 Conservative Party campaign chair and at the time with the political consulting firm Go Newclear Productions, explained, "the sort of overarching thing connecting all my time in politics is let's try to inject a little bit of math and to see how that works." The results might be only incrementally better than nothing,

TABLE 9.2
List of interviewees (names disclosed with consent)

Number	Interviewee
1	Anonymous, December 12, 2013
2	Anonymous, March 28, 2014
3	Anonymous, Olivia Chow for Mayor campaign, March 20, 2015
4	Anonymous, Groundforce Digital, August 14, 2014
5	Anonymous, NationBuilder, July 7, 2014
6	Brett Chang, cofounder and partner, Adrenaline, July 17, 2014
7	Ethan Clarke, cofounder, Campaign Gears, March 14, 2014
8	Joe Federer, founder, Campaign Central, February 21, 2014
9	Emma Gilchrist, writer/editor of DeSmogBlog, engagement consultant, and former communications director at Dogwood, March 5, 2014
10	Hamish Marshall, chief research officer at Abingdon Research; president and chief operating officer at Go Newclear Productions, March 21, 2014
11	Mike Martens, director of the School of Practical Politics at Manning Centre for Building Democracy, March 5, 2014
12	Graham Mitchell, director of training and leadership, Broadbent Institute, July 18, 2014
13	Brad Oldham, project manager, Popular Change, June 18, 2014
14	Geoff Sharpe, manager, digital, Office of the Premier of Ontario, July 17, 2014
15	Josh Stuart, president, cStreet Campaigns, December 11, 2013
16	Dan Walmsley, chief technology officer, NationBuilder, March 7, 2014
17	Mitch Wexler, principal, Politrain Consulting, March 26, 2014

as Mike Martens, the director of the School of Practical Politics at the Manning Centre for Building Democracy, explained in 2014:

> What we know is that the average campaign doesn't have enough responses to do even testing. So it's anecdotal, but it's better than gut instinct. Let's test those gut instincts to a certain level. It's not scientifically or statistically accurate, but it's better than nothing. I would say that phrase "let's just improve things just a little bit" is the key psychology in adapting new technologies.

This is a good reminder – amid the constant worry about the next disruptive technology (be it artificial intelligence or psychodemographics) –

that politics are human after all. Campaigns are often patched together, ad hoc combinations of experimental tools and people that break down soon after election day (Baldwin-Philippi 2017; Kreiss 2016). Injecting science often involved improved forms of data collection and analysis, better use of email and other forms of voter contact, as well as improved microtargeting.

Data provide a slim but often crucial advantage in today's narrow electoral wins. The effect, in other words, of turning to data is slight but worthwhile. As Emma Gilchrist, the writer/editor of DeSmogBlog, an engagement consultant, and the former communications director at Dogwood, explained, "elections are won in just a handful of ridings and beyond that really just a handful of polling divisions within those ridings ... [So] there is definitely acknowledgment that, if you want to get politicians' attention, you probably want to have a presence in those swing ridings." Interviewees suggested that data allowed campaigners to choose strategically where to spend time and resources. This information often had to be more granular and focused on microtargeting. Mitch Wexler, the principal of Politrain Consulting, developed a political technology called "Track and Field," which he explains "helps [to] focus people on that information so they understand where things stand across the riding, or across the jurisdiction of the campaign, then [ask] where do they need to focus, how do they access the particular information that they need?" In this sense, data-driven campaigning enables better targeting of resources, avoiding voters unlikely to be persuaded.

Email campaigning offers a good example of the realities of data-driven campaigning. Most campaigns need to piece together their infrastructures, connecting databases, email lists, and websites. A successful campaign requires a list of voters along with their email addresses to send campaign messages, drive fundraising efforts, and recruit volunteers. List building occurs through online campaigning, particularly via websites that encourage users to sign up for a party's mailing list. Often these sites disguise themselves, inviting users to register their email accounts to send e-cards or sympathy notes while also sending data to the campaign. Once in the system, voters can be segmented and targeted with different messages. Campaigns write email messages, varying subject line, author, and content hopefully to elicit the voter to visit the website or donate money.

Email messaging requires good copy and constant testing. Campaigns send A/B-test messages, sending two different messages to samples of their lists. Standard analytics tools embedded in the email help to determine the best-performing message. The winning email might then be sent to the rest of the voter list. Alternatively, emails might be more targeted as campaigns try to guide voters to greater participation in the campaigns – what our interviewees called a pyramid of engagement or growth hacking.

Emailing is just one application of data-driven campaigning. We encountered a strong diversity of tools used in Canada in our review of provincial and federal party digital infrastructures. What is striking is the mixture of technologies. Parties appropriated commercial marking tools, adapted open-source products, and developed their own custom software programs. In contrast to the partisan infrastructures developed by the Republicans and Democrats in the United States, Canadian political parties have often used the same off-the-shelf technologies (with the exception of political databases). Both the New Democratic Party and the Conservative Party have custom database systems, whereas the federal Liberal Party ran the Democrats' NGP VAN to power its Liberalist system. However, the Manitoba NDP is a notable exception since it used the same NGP VAN as the federal Liberal Party. Provincial parties show even more diversity, as seen in Table 9.3. All parties have preferred open-source, general-purpose software such as Drupal and WordPress to run their websites. The choice of mailers varied even more. Only MailChimp, a commercial email marketing tool, had repeated adoption.

Each of these technologies brings along certain repertoires of data-driven campaigning. Microtargeting is a key logic operating across campaigns. Websites, databases, and email services collect data passively by logging website traffic or open rates as well as by actively encouraging voters to share the data. These data help to sort and target voters through data analytics. Many off-the-shelf technologies provide what Baldwin-Philippi (2016) describes as analytics made to provide campaigns with platform-specific metrics to evaluate voter interactions. Campaigns often use third-party tools, such as Google Analytics, as other sources of feedback from voters in addition to their own analytics systems. Although we did not gain access to party databases, the Conservative Party database called "CIMS" provided a good example of this computational management.

TABLE 9.3
Political technology use by provincial parties in 2014

Province	Party	Database	Website	Mass mailer
Alberta	Liberals	?	NationBuilder	?
	New Democrats	NDPVote	Expression Engine	Constant Contact
	Progressive Conservatives	?	Dreamweaver	VerticalResponse
	Wild Rose	?	WordPress	?
British Columbia	Conservatives	?	WordPress	?
	Greens	NationBuilder	NationBuilder	NationBuilder
	Liberals	?	n/a	?
	New Democrats	?	Drupal	?
Manitoba	Conservatives	?	Dreamweaver	?
	Liberals	?	WordPress	?
	New Democrats	NGP VAN	Drupal	?
New Brunswick	Conservatives	?	WordPress	?
	Liberals	?	WordPress	?
	New Democrats	SUMAC	Drupal	MailChimp
Newfoundland and Labrador	Conservatives	?	WordPress	MailChimp
	Liberals	NGP VAN	WordPress	MailChimp
	New Democrats	?	WordPress	?
Nova Scotia	Conservatives	?	WordPress	?
	Liberals	NGP VAN	Event Espresso	NGP VAN
	New Democrats	NDP Vote	WordPress	Drupal
Ontario	Conservatives	?	Expression Engine	?
	Liberals	Aristotle	?	Campaigner
	New Democrats	?	WordPress	MailChimp
Prince Edward Island	Conservatives	?	Yoast WordPress	?
	Liberals	?	CMS Made Simple	?
	New Democrats	?	WordPress	?
Quebec	Coalition avenir Québec	Democratik	WordPress	Cakemail
	Liberals	?	CakePHP Framework	Cakemail
	Parti québécois	?	?	?
	Québec solidaire	?	WordPress	?
Saskatchewan	Conservatives	?	?	?
	Liberals	?	Drupal	iContact, Vocus
	New Democrats	?	NationBuilder	NationBuilder
	Saskatchewan Party	?	?	?

Leaked screenshots of the database suggest that CIMS allowed the campaign to rate voters from nonsupporters (-15) to supporters (15). The Liberal Party, according to reports from the 2015 election, had a central analytics team to help local campaigns rank voters on their likelihood primarily of voting and secondarily of voting Liberal. These predictive analytics also assist campaign workers in deciding where to allocate canvassers, what literature to drop off, and how often to contact voters (Munroe and Munroe 2018; Patten 2016).

Money, party, and political logics influence the adoption of these political technologies and their corresponding repertoires of data-driven campaigning. The popularity of ready-made technologies comes down to money. Interviewees explained that their choices of technologies had a lot to do with Canadian politics having less money than American politics. A lack of funds inhibits the development of systems internally and motivates the decision to select a commercially available product. Such a lack also limits importing expensive political technology from the United States or hiring developers to develop it internally. As we discuss elsewhere (McKelvey and Piebiak 2018), data-driven campaigning is ported to Canada, a process of hybridization in which often American developers work with consultants and parties to adapt the tool to the local context.

The lack of funding concentrates data-driven campaigning in parties' central offices, though local campaigns have been sites of technological innovation. Tasked with being hubs, parties have invested in technologies that ease central management. Unlike so much of the press coverage of digital politics in Canada, campaigns often look outside the United States for these solutions. As Marshall explained,

> the idea of centralized literature is foreign [to someone in Washington] ... whereas in the UK ... they came up with a system, an online system, where instead of having graphic designers customizing all these pieces of literature a local campaign could log in, basically upload the pictures that they want, and drop them on standardized literature – with one click of a button add their address, phone number, and website and output printer-ready art. That's something we have tried to do and now have very successfully implemented for various clients in Canada.

Data-driven campaigning thus involves tools to help parties coordinate centrally their different local ridings.

Local ridings can also be sources of innovation and change. Interviewees working in local ridings did discuss the need to adopt the technology used by the central party, but a few campaigns, notably that of former premier of Ontario Kathleen Wynne, broke from party infrastructure to use their own data-driven applications. These innovations were either merged back into the central party or discarded.

Overall, data-driven campaigning involves greater attention to the flows of data, expertise, and technology in hierarchical parties. The diverse list of tools given above illustrates one of the many complications of making data flow. Although these technologies separately collect data, they do not necessarily share data. Interviewees often discussed the challenge of integrating data collected from separate technologies. WordPress, for instance, includes a plug in to add NGP VAN forms easily to websites. Drupal, the other popular website management tool, does not. Interviewees expressed that getting technologies to interconnect is often difficult and complex work. Better data integration is partly why we see growing adoption of integrated political engagement platforms such as NationBuilder in Canada.

As much as it might be attractive to share data and use similar technologies, we do not observe a correlation between federal and provincial technology adoption. Past research has shown the New Democratic Party as the most integrated party, followed by the Liberal Party and then the Conservative Party (Pruysers 2016). A similar pattern would have shown provincial NDP parties using the same technologies as their federal counterpart, less so for the Liberals and Conservatives. Instead, adoption varied greatly. Some provincial parties did adopt technologies used by their federal counterparts, but never a majority, as seen in Tables 9.1 and 9.2. More often a provincial party adopted a different technology. We do not have enough data to make any conclusions about database usage. In our interviews, we saw influence go both ways. The Ontario Conservative Party originally developed CIMS; its federal counterpart later adopted and extended it. The federal Liberal Party, conversely, has led provincial parties to adopt NGP VAN. This suggests that data-driven campaigning was uneven across the same party even though partisanship guided the circulation of data-driven technologies and practices.

TRENDING IN CANADA

Data-driven campaigning is part of the trend toward permanent campaigning (Elmer, Langlois, and McKelvey 2012; Esselment 2014; Giasson, Marland, and Small 2014). The logic of the permanent campaign has led parties to centralize, professionalize, and invest in "formalized election apparatuses (or in the vernacular, party 'machines')" (Elmer, Langlois, and McKelvey 2012, 2). As much as these "machines" might break down and be impermanent (Kreiss 2016), the permanent campaign frames these gaps as failures and adds the logic that parties *should* always be active collecting better data. In this way, the logic of permanent campaigning enforces data-driven campaigning as a political logic. Parties work constantly to update their databases to understand a fragmented and uninterested electorate as well as to find new political supporters. Once voters are in the system, parties keep them engaged and contributing feedback in order to make decisions based on data and not gut instincts.

Data-driven campaigning, based on our findings, orients political activity in three ways: 1) data collection connected to 2) systems of feedback and communication that 3) facilitate greater computational analysis and decision making. In practical terms, these trends have led to the following:

- *Political parties and candidates are developing, populating, and distributing databases.* These systems of data management have been developed by political parties and consultants to store, correlate, and mobilize their data resources. Parties populate their databases by using Elections Canada data and other public records (see Hersh 2015), by generating logs from better tracking of their own activities, by paying political data brokers (Bennett 2013; Kreiss 2012; Kreiss and Howard 2010), and by infusing data from internet advertising and social media profiling (see Turow 2012). This information pools into databases maintained by local ridings as well as by provincial and federal parties.
- *Political parties and candidates are adapting and building systems of communication and feedback between voters and political campaigns.* Feedback varies among media, from metrics of voter support collected

through door knocking to open rates in email messaging. Forms of feedback can be divided between active and passive. Active feedback includes surveys, polls, and donations – overt signals of political support. In addition to these active systems of feedback, websites and email open rates function as what Karpf (2012) described as passive democratic feedback. Voters send considerable passive data when they open a website or an email.

- *Political parties and candidates are appropriating and developing analytical techniques such as cross-tabulation, clustering, performance indexes, email open rates, and predictive analytics.* These techniques developed to identify voter affinities, interpret internal polling results, gauge message effectiveness, and predict voter behaviour (Howard 2006; Malchow 2008). Data-driven campaigns seem to provide them with computational management. Kreiss (2012, 144) defined the concept as "the delegation of managerial, allocative, messaging, and design decisions to the analysis of users' actions made visible in the form of data as they interacted with campaign media." Where he used the term to describe how the 2008 Obama presidential campaign used data to justify campaign spending, we observed passive feedback helping campaigners to make better decisions about messaging as well as voter data helping them to identify priority areas.

Research on the trend toward data-driven campaigns frequently focuses on how these practices change voter privacy as well as the democratic function of elections. Following allegations that automated calling had been used to suppress voting in the 2011 Canadian federal election, the Office of the Privacy Commissioner of Canada published a report on the privacy practices of major political parties (Bennett and Bayley 2012). The report raised concerns about the lack of regulation of parties' data collection practices.

Concerns about unregulated political data and digital campaigning have only been exacerbated by the Cambridge Analytica scandal in 2018, leading to a parliamentary inquiry into its Canadian affiliate, AggregateIQ. Before and during the scandal, the privacy commissioner of Canada called for new regulations for political parties (Therrien 2016). At the heart of these debates and this research is the uncertainty about the role of data in politics. Parties ideally use political engagement platforms to inform citizens about candidates' positions on important issues to help voters make knowledgeable decisions on election day. The literature debates whether data-driven campaigning has helped to create new forms of engagement for voters (Baldwin-Philippi 2015; Karpf 2012; Shirky 2008) or led to a managed citizenship in which campaign interest undermines public interest (Howard 2006; Kozolanka 2014). There are worries in both the academic literature (Bennett 2013; Kreiss and Howard 2010; Tufekci 2014) and the popular literature (King 2015; McGregor 2014) that data will justify an increase in "dataveillance." The line between positive and negative applications of data-driven campaigning is largely normative and suggests that in the wake of public scandals parties would do well to abide by a code to help legitimate these practices. If not, then greater oversight will be necessary.

Throughout these scandals, Canadian political parties continue to operate without any formal regulation of their data practices. They are exempt from the Personal Information, Privacy, and Election Documents Act. They are also largely exempt from the Anti-Spam Act. The law exempts any commercial message "sent by or on behalf of a political party or organization, or a person who is a candidate – as defined in an Act of Parliament or the legislature of a province – for publicly elected office and the message has as its primary purpose soliciting a contribution as defined in subsection 2(1) of the Canada Elections Act" (*Electronic Commerce Protection Regulations*). Instead, most regulation of party conduct comes from the Elections Act, which requires parties to disclose messages with placement fees and to identify the campaign behind the message or from their privacy policies (with which we have no way to measure compliance). In large part, the Elections Act regulates communication between a party or candidate and a voter but not the data collected to inform that relationship.

Privacy regulation does constrain data-driven campaigning in Canada. Compared with the United States, in Canada donation and voter data restrictions diminish the effectiveness of data-driven campaigning, as interviewees explained. Most political software programs require voter information to populate their databases, but data are harder to find in Canada than in the United States. There VoterListsOnline sells data from three cents to twelve cents per record, and NationBuilder offers a free voter file to campaigns. The same data are not as accessible in Canada. The Canada Elections Act only allows registered political parties to access the voter list. Section 111 prohibits the use of "personal information that is recorded in a list of electors for a purpose other than ... to enable registered parties, members or candidates to communicate with electors." This electoral law largely prohibits a third party from accessing voter data in Canada while empowering central political parties. Other demographic information is for sale in Canada, but interviewees mentioned its prohibitive cost. Donation limits – even in provincial elections with higher limits – also diminish the return on investment for finding the right voters. A list of voter data might simply be too costly. These cost/benefit calculations suggest that the political finance reform might be a tool to bring greater accountability to data-driven campaigning. Restoring the per-vote subsidy, for instance, might lessen the incentive for parties to invest the same money in fundraising infrastructure and reduce the pressure to be data driven.

In addition to privacy, we have found other reasons for more scrutiny of the effect of data-driven campaigning on elections. The practice favours incumbents and campaigns invested in perpetual data collection. This raises a set of questions different from the privacy debate related to inequitable access. New campaigns do not receive voter data until the start of the official campaign, a minimum of thirty-six days, and political consultants consider the release to be too late. Elected officials often begin the campaign long before the actual start – an example of permanent campaigning. As Josh Stuart expressed in 2013, "we might only be three weeks out that you might actually have the list of all the eligible voters which is totally, totally crazy." This delayed access favours incumbent campaigns, which retain copies of voter lists from past campaigns or from the central party. As Mike Martins explained, "now the average campaign in Canada, I would say, is getting their data from previous campaigns. The legitimacy of that is highly questionable; just that nobody questions it, nobody challenges it, there are lists just floating around." The shelf life of data encourages more party centralization. It is in every party's interest to keep its data and to develop a party machine to maintain it. Faced with this data disadvantage, new candidates and party outsiders face pressure to enter the permanent campaign as soon as possible. They can either start building their own lists as soon as possible or risk falling further behind in data collection. Such inequity adds another reason to review the privacy laws associated with political data in Canada.

Access to information enables some data collection. According to Eitan Hersh (2015), the importance of the electoral list is just one example of how the state acts as a political information subsidy to parties. In the United States, much of what counts as data-driven campaigning ends up being the aggregation of public data. Not only do parties depend on public data, but also simple data, like voting histories, are often more useful and predictive than much of the complex demographic data sold by third parties in the United States. Although we never determined "the secret sauce" used in predictive analytics or microtargeting (beyond swing ridings), access to information requests to Elections Canada demonstrate a clear demand for public records on campaign donations. For example, someone requested in 2015 "a data extract (e.g., Excel, CSV, Access) of the Contributor's Database that contains the following columns: client ID, name of contributor, political party, contribution given, date received, fiscal year, financial report, class of contributor, monetary, and nonmonetary for the years 2008 to the present" (ATIP Request Number A-2015-00033). Elections Canada (2016) disclosed 40,598 records to that one requester. Perhaps the real secret of data-driven campaigning is more about knowing how to ask for available data than about complex predictive analytics. If data-driven campaigning continues to be a public concern, then formalizing access to these public records, and even improving party access to data maintained by Elections Canada, might help to increase the transparency of political data.

These worries about data-driven campaigning must be contextualized in its uneven adoption. Practitioners shared their struggles for data-driven campaigning to be accepted in everyday politics. Digital strategy, as discussed by our interviewees, is often provided with fewer resources than other parts of the campaign, though this is changing. However, political consultants not only have to sell the idea that these tools can make a difference and are a good investment but confront older approaches and styles of political organizing. Emma Gilchrist, a political organizer, recounted in 2014 that, in environmental movements in Canada,

I don't actually think that the cost of those solutions is the main barrier to curb pursuing. It's more of a culture problem, and there needs to be a serious shift in the way things work. And, even when groups do pursue them, they don't necessarily use them to their full potential, because you know they have a lot of baggage in terms of the way things used to be done.

Other interviewees suggested that there has not been a change in political culture since these technologies have been introduced. Instead, gut reaction or opinion still seems to bear more importance, because people, "especially moderately successful people in politics," Marshall suggested, "have opinions based on their experience, and if they are not numbers people – and most people in politics by nature are not numbers people, they are people – they are less likely to listen."

Marshall also indicated that, even as campaigns begin to acknowledge that investing in this area is "something that is important, and they are willing to spend some money on it ... whether or not that actually affects their opinions or their action[s] is another story entirely." Mitch Wexler echoed this sentiment in terms of on-the-ground campaigning. When it comes down to it, "some people still use good ol' Excel, and, you know, God bless them. They have a tough time, but they have been doing it for so many years, and as long as they can make it work and volunteers are happy then that's all that matters, right?" Reservations about new styles of campaigning, especially the emphasis on data afforded by political software, illustrate the influence of the permanent campaign. The interviewees evaluated technologies in relation to winning campaigns. Although they cited a desire to use new technologies to inform voters better as part of a properly functioning democracy, they ultimately sought the best tools to win on election day.

The final question about data-driven campaigning concerns its impact on democracy. Political data have long concerned scholars and politicians. Edwin Black, in his presidential address to the Canadian Political Science Association in 1983, hoped that "computer simulations and model-testing could, theoretically, lead to innovative policies" (688). However, he worried that what now would be called data-driven campaigning would be put to political ends. "The spread of electronic data-processing could well lead to a takeover of much of our public policy apparatus. It probably will not be the computer specialists themselves who move in. The winners will be those prepared to learn what [electronic data processing] in government is all about and who then go on to bend its promise to achieve their own power goals" (688). It is clear from our interviews that data have a competitive advantage in making political gains if not in advancing democracy. Without regulatory or normative change, we suspect that Black's concerns will be valid for years to come.

NOTE

1 For an updated discussion of some of the data-driven campaigning in light of these controversies, see McKelvey (2018a).

REFERENCES

Anderson, C.W., and Daniel Kreiss. 2013. "Black Boxes as Capacities for and Constraints on Action: Electoral Politics, Journalism, and Devices of Representation." *Qualitative Sociology* 36, 4: 365–82.

Baldwin-Philippi, Jessica. 2015. *Using Technology, Building Democracy: Digital Campaigning and the Construction of Citizenship.* New York: Oxford University Press.

–. 2016. "The Cult(ure) of Analytics in 2014." In *Communication and Midterm Elections: Media, Message, and Mobilization,* edited by J.A. Hencks and D. Schill, 25–42. New York: Palgrave Macmillan.

–. 2017. "The Myths of Data-Driven Campaigning." *Political Communication* 34, 4: 627–33.

Bennett, Colin. 2013. "The Politics of Privacy and the Privacy of Politics: Parties, Elections, and Voter Surveillance in Western Democracies." *First Monday* 18, 8. http://firstmonday.org/ojs/index.php/fm/article/view/4789.

–. 2015. "Trends in Voter Surveillance in Western Societies: Privacy Intrusions and Democratic Implications." *Surveillance and Society* 13, 3–4: 370–84.

Bennett, Colin, and Robin M. Bayley. 2012. "Canadian Federal Political Parties and Personal Privacy Protection: A Comparative Analysis." Office of the Privacy Commissioner of Canada.

Bimber, Bruce. 1998. "The Internet and Political Transformation: Populism, Community, and Accelerated Pluralism." *Polity* 31, 1: 133–60.

Black, Edwin R. 1983. "Politics on a Microchip." *Canadian Journal of Political Science* 16, 4: 675–90.

Canada Elections Act, Statutes of Canada 2000, c. 9. https://laws-lois.justice.gc.ca/eng/acts/e-2.01/.

Chartrand, Robert Lee. 1972. *Computers and Political Campaigning*. New York: Spartan Books.
Delacourt, Susan. 2013. *Shopping for Votes: How Politicians Choose Us and We Choose Them*. Madeira Park, BC: Douglas and McIntyre.
Elections Canada. 2016. "Summaries of Completed Access to Information Requests." http://www.elections.ca/content.aspx?section=abo&dir=atip/summary&document=sum16&lang=e.
Electronic Commerce Protection Regulations, SOR/81000-2-175. http://fightspam.gc.ca/eic/site/030.nsf/eng/00273.html.
Elmer, Greg, Ganaele Langlois, and Fenwick McKelvey. 2012. *The Permanent Campaign: New Media, New Politics*. New York: Peter Lang.
Esselment, Anna Lennox. 2014. "The Governing Party and the Permanent Campaign." In *Political Communication in Canada: Meet the Press and Tweet the Rest*, edited by Thierry Giasson, Alexander J. Marland, and Tamara A. Small, 24–38. Vancouver: UBC Press.
Flanagan, Tom. 2003. "Database Party: The 2002 Leadership Campaign for the Canadian Alliance." *Canadian Parliamentary Review* 26, 1: 8–11.
Foot, Kirsten A., and Steven M. Schneider. 2006. *Web Campaigning*. Cambridge, MA: MIT Press.
Giasson, Thierry, Alexander J. Marland, and Tamara A. Small, eds. 2014. *Political Communication in Canada: Meet the Press and Tweet the Rest*. Vancouver: UBC Press.
Gibson, Rachel K. 2015. "Party Change, Social Media, and the Rise of 'Citizen-Initiated' Campaigning." *Party Politics* 21, 2: 183–97.
Hall, Chris. 2016. "What Lessons Did the Three Main Federal Parties Learn in 2015?" *CBC News*, January 2. http://www.cbc.ca/player/play/2681293066.
Hersh, Eitan D. 2015. *Hacking the Electorate: How Campaigns Perceive Voters*. New York: Cambridge University Press.
Howard, Philip N. 2006. *New Media Campaigns and the Managed Citizen*. New York: Cambridge University Press.
Johnson, Dennis W. 2016. *Democracy for Hire: A History of American Political Consulting*. New York: Oxford University Press.
Karpf, David. 2012. *The MoveOn Effect: The Unexpected Transformation of American Political Advocacy*. New York: Oxford University Press.
–. 2013. "Netroots Goes Global." *The Nation*, October 16. http://www.thenation.com/article/176700/netroots-goes-global.
–. 2015. "Look at the Man behind the Curtain: Computational Management in 'Spontaneous' Citizen Political Campaigning." In *Compromised Data: From Social Media to Big Data*, edited by Ganaele Langlois, Greg Elmer, and Joanna Redden, 61–90. New York: Bloomsbury.
Karpf, David, Daniel Kreiss, Rasmus Kleis Nielsen, and Matthew Powers. 2015. "The Role of Qualitative Methods in Political Communication Research: Past, Present, and Future." *International Journal of Communication* 9: 1888–1906.

King, Robin Levinson. 2015. "How Political Parties Use Your Information and Why They're Not Subject to Corporate Privacy Laws." *Toronto Star*, September 23. https://www.thestar.com/news/canada/2015/09/23/what-canadas-political-parties-know-about-you.html.

Kozolanka, Kirsten, ed. 2014. *Publicity and the Canadian State: Critical Communications Perspectives*. Toronto: University of Toronto Press.

Kreiss, Daniel. 2012. *Taking Our Country Back: The Crafting of Networked Politics from Howard Dean to Barack Obama*. New York: Oxford University Press.

–. 2016. *Prototype Politics: Technology-Intense Campaigning and the Data of Democracy*. New York: Oxford University Press.

Kreiss, Daniel, and Philip N. Howard. 2010. "New Challenges to Political Privacy: Lessons from the First US Presidential Race in the Web 2.0 Era." *International Journal of Communication* 4: 1032–50.

Kreiss, Daniel, and Christopher Jasinski. 2016. "The Tech Industry Meets Presidential Politics: Explaining the Democratic Party's Technological Advantage in Electoral Campaigning, 2004–2012." *Political Communication* 33, 4: 544–62.

Kreiss, Daniel, and Shannon C. McGregor. 2018. "Technology Firms Shape Political Communication: The Work of Microsoft, Facebook, Twitter, and Google with Campaigns during the 2016 U.S. Presidential Cycle." *Political Communication* 35, 2: 155–77.

Malchow, Hal. 2008. *Political Targeting*. 2nd ed. Washington, DC: Predicted Lists, LLC.

Margolis, Michael, and David Resnick. 2000. *Politics as Usual: The Cyberspace "Revolution."* Thousand Oaks, CA: Sage.

Marland, Alex. 2016. *Brand Command: Canadian Politics and Democracy in the Age of Message Control*. Vancouver: UBC Press.

McGregor, Glen. 2014. "The Big Data Election: Political Parties Building Detailed Voter Records." *Ottawa Citizen*, October 18. http://ottawacitizen.com/news/politics/the-big-data-election-political-parties-building-detailed-voter-records.

McKelvey, Fenwick. 2018a. "Protecting Our Information in the Age of Data-Driven Politics." *Policy Options*, July 4. http://policyoptions.irpp.org/magazines/july-2018/protecting-information-age-data-driven-politics/.

–. 2018b. "Hillary 2016." In *Appified: Mundane Software and the Rise of the Apps*, edited by Jeremy Wade Morris and Sarah Murray, 246–56. Ann Arbor: University of Michigan Press.

McKelvey, Fenwick, and Jill Piebiak. 2018. "Porting the Political Campaign: The NationBuilder Platform and the Global Flows of Political Technology." *New Media and Society* 20, 3: 901–18.

McLean, James S. 2012. *Inside the NDP War Room: Competing for Credibility in a Federal Election*. Montreal: McGill-Queen's University Press.

Munroe, Kaija Belfry, and Doug Munroe. 2018. "Constituency Campaigning in the Age of Data." *Canadian Journal of Political Science* 51, 1: 135–54.

Nielsen, Rasmus Kleis. 2012. *Ground Wars: Personalized Communication in Political Campaigns*. Princeton, NJ: Princeton University Press.

Nimmo, Dan D. 1970. *Political Persuaders: The Techniques of Modern Election Campaigns*. Englewood Cliffs, NJ: Prentice-Hall.

Paltiel, Khayyam Z. 1974. "Party and Candidate Expenditures in the Canadian General Election of 1972." *Canadian Journal of Political Science* 7, 2: 341–52, https://doi.org/10.1017/S0008423900038385.

Patten, Steve. 2016. "Data-Driven Microtargeting in the 2015 General Election." In *Canadian Election Analysis 2015: Communication, Strategy, and Democracy*, edited by Alex Marland and Thierry Giasson, 14–15. Vancouver: UBC Press.

Pool, Ithiel de Sola, Robert P. Abelson, and Samuel L. Popkin. 1965. *Candidates, Issues, and Strategies: A Computer Simulation of the 1960 Presidential Election*. Cambridge, MA: MIT Press.

Poster, Mark. 2001. *CyberDemocracy: The Internet and the Public Sphere*. Malden, MA: Blackwell.

Pruysers, Scott. 2016. "Vertical Party Integration: Informal and Human Linkages between Elections in a Canadian Province." *Commonwealth and Comparative Politics* 54, 3: 312–30.

Shirky, Clay. 2008. *Here Comes Everybody: The Power of Organizing without Organizations*. New York: Penguin.

Small, Tamara A. 2012. "E-ttack, Politics: Negativity, the Internet, and Canadian Political Parties." In *How Canadians Communicate IV: Media and Politics*, edited by David Taras and Christopher Robb Waddell, 169–89. Edmonton: Athabasca University Press.

Stromer-Galley, Jennifer. 2014. *Presidential Campaigning in the Internet Age*. New York: Oxford University Press.

Therrien, Daniel. 2016. "Appearance before the Standing Committee on Access to Information, Privacy, and Ethics on Reform of the Privacy Act." *Office of the Privacy Commissioner of Canada*. https://www.priv.gc.ca/parl/2016/parl_20160310_e.asp.

Tufekci, Zeynep. 2014. "Engineering the Public: Big Data, Surveillance, and Computational Politics." *First Monday* 19, 7. http://firstmonday.org/ojs/index.php/fm/article/view/4901.

Turow, Joseph. 2012. *The Daily You: How the Advertising Industry Is Defining Your Identity and Your Worth*. New Haven, CT: Yale University Press.

10

Beyond Market Intelligence
New Dimensions in Public Opinion Research

ANDRÉ TURCOTTE

> How often, or on what system, the Thought Police plugged in on any individual wire was guesswork. It was even conceivable that they watched everybody all the time. But at any rate they could plug in your wire whenever they wanted to. You had to live – did live, from habit that became instinct – in the assumption that every sound you made was overheard, and except in darkness, every movement scrutinized.
>
> – George Orwell, *1984* (3)

> You have zero privacy anyway. Get over it.
>
> – Sun Microsystems CEO Scott McNealy, 1999 (quoted in Schneier 2015, 4)

Ever since its publication, *1984* has been a cautionary tale about the possible future of humankind. One particularly troubling aspect of Orwell's tale is the idea of "being constantly observed" – or under surveillance. The term "surveillance" is derived from the French term *surveiller* or "to watch over."[1] For its part, the US military defines surveillance as "systematic observation" (Schneier 2015, 4), a definition more closely aligned with the feeling of uneasiness associated with this action. An extensive literature has developed over this term. As Hier and Greenberg (2007, 5) noted in *The Surveillance Studies Reader*, contemporary studies on this topic borrow from theorists as varied as Max Weber, Michel Foucault, James Rule, and Anthony Giddens, among others. Moreover, the 9/11 terrorist attacks in New York City led to a wave of scholarly articles looking at the interplay among surveillance, legislative agendas, and technological changes. Scholars such as David Lyon, Kirstie Ball, and Nicola Green from Queen's University Surveillance Studies Centre took an active role in discussing the surveillance repercussions of the post-9/11 era, and scholars now have an active scholarly platform to publish their works with the establishment of the *Surveillance and Society Journal* in 2001.[2] The emergence of big data and subsequent analyses of the implications of big data have further fuelled academic interest in the topic (Ayres 2007; Mayer-Schönberger and Cukier 2013; Schneier 2015). Generally, the term "big data" "refers to things one can do at a large scale that cannot be done at a smaller one, to extract new insights or create new forms of value, in ways that change markets, organizations, the relationship between citizens and governments, and more" (Mayer-Schönberger and Cukier 2013, 6). Evolving toward a world of big data will have diverse impacts. It will allow us to analyze large sets of data instead of having to settle for smaller ones and to replace our focus from seeking causality to embracing the richness of correlation. Here I aim to expand the burgeoning literature on the subject.

Despite the high level of academic interest, there are still several unexplored avenues pertinent to the technological and societal repercussions of big data. One such path is the impact of the surveillance capacities of big data on public opinion research. I explore in this chapter new technological developments and accompanying analytical techniques that make it feasible to understand individual behaviour in real time and surreptitiously. We are in the early stages of these developments and are only beginning to grasp the possibilities associated with these trends.

More than a decade ago, a group of scholars led by Jennifer Lees-Marshment developed a series of tenets that would become the foundations of what is now referred to as *political marketing* (Lees-Marshment 2001; Lilleker and Lees-Marshment 2005; Newman 1999). Out of this process emerged a new way to conceptualize the role of public opinion research in politics. Spurred by the adoption of market research techniques by political practitioners, public opinion research has evolved from a general information-gathering function to strategic marketing and communication applications. As a result, the polling function was described by scholars in political marketing as *market intelligence*.

I make the case here that a new transformation is upon us. New developments in data analytics and digital research are combining to alter substantially yet again public opinion research. Specifically, data management platforms (DMP) are increasingly used in the business world not only to know, but also to track, consumer behaviour at an unprecedented level of granularity. DMPs are relatively new developments, but the pace of change is fast. This technology pushes traditional polling data into a secondary role in the opinion research process and opens up new possibilities in terms of citizen/consumer engagement, activation, and conversion. Political actors are just beginning to grasp the electoral potential of these new technologies (Issenberg 2012), but I argue that it is only a matter of time before political actors embrace these changes. The practical applications of those developments lead me to conclude that market intelligence might soon be better conceptualized and utilized as *market surveillance*, and through this process will emerge a substantially modified approach to public opinion research.

Ever since George Gallup, Elmo Roper, and Archibald Crossley developed a scientific approach to measuring public opinion in the 1930s, the practice of polling has evolved with increasing sophistication. Through his early efforts, Gallup introduced representative sampling as the guiding principle of opinion research. He was also instrumental in entrenching the need to give a voice to citizens as a way to have them play a role in the political process as a whole and in policy making in particular. As he wrote in *The Pulse of Democracy: The Public Opinion Poll and How It Works* (Gallup and Rae 1940, 8): "The kind of public opinion implied in the democratic ideal is tangible and dynamic. It springs from many sources in the day-to-day experience of individuals who constitute the political public, and who formulate these opinions as working guides for their political representatives."

It is now common practice to conceptualize public opinion as "an aggregation of individual opinions" (Glynn et al. 2016, 13). Several more definitions have been developed, such as public opinion as a reflection of majority beliefs (Noelle-Neumann 1984); as a clash of interest groups

(Blumer 1946); or as a reflection of media and elite influence (Lippmann 1922). Nevertheless, the simple characterization of public opinion as the sum of many individual opinions is the most pervasive and can be linked back to Gallup (Gallup and Rae 1940). It serves as a justification for using surveys and polls to measure public opinion.

The next step in the evolution occurred when pollster Lou Harris became part of the presidential campaign for John F. Kennedy in 1960. Whereas Gallup and others had provided advice to politicians prior to the 1960 campaign, Harris "really put polling on the map" (Turcotte 2010, 207). It is generally argued that "the first presidential campaign to rely heavily on polling for strategic insight was the 1960 Kennedy effort" (Medvic 2009, 103). As a result, the role of the public opinion researcher morphed from articulating public opinion to interpreting it. Canada lagged behind the United States in making this transition. The Canadian polling industry was established when Canadian Facts opened its doors in 1933 (Butler 2007, 40), but politicians relied on American advisers until the federal Liberals hired Martin Goldfarb – a Canadian – who became a trusted adviser for Pierre Elliott Trudeau and the federal Liberals. For the most part, though, the influence of public opinion research remained informational rather than strategic. The main research focus was to understand the median voter and convey the general mood of the public. I refer here to this practice of opinion research as the *traditional polling period*.

The move away from traditional polling to market intelligence took several years. Allan Gregg was hired by the federal Progressive Conservatives ahead of the 1979 election, and he was arguably the first Canadian pollster to recognize the strategic potential of public opinion research. He learned that not every voter is to be given equal attention and that a successful campaign needed to identify and consolidate its base of support and understand those relatively few voters who make the difference between winning and losing. The evolution was facilitated by an important technological innovation. Computer-assisted telephone interviewing (CATI) became prevalent in the 1980s and helped to manage the interviewing process. Specifically, it allowed for complicated question sequencing, reduced human errors, and considerably sped up the work of interviewers. CATI's most important component is its data management capability. CATI collects interviewees' responses and builds a database in real time and for immediate analysis. With this technology, it became possible to conduct daily tracking polls. In other words, CATI gave pollsters "the ability to guide campaigns with far more precision" (Medvic 2009, 103). Although this technology pales in sophistication compared with DMPs, it was the first effort to try to measure behaviour in real time as much as possible.

The transition away from traditional public opinion polling and toward market intelligence was accelerated in the aftermath of the 1997 federal election. Shortly after his disappointing showing in that contest, Reform Party leader Preston Manning realized that "uniting the right" was the only way to defeat the ruling Liberals. Market intelligence was better suited to this exercise than traditional polling. The Liberals, and to some extent the federal New Democrats, were able to rely on broad coalitions of voters and continued their traditional polling approach geared to appealing to median voters. By necessity, opinion research conducted as part of "uniting the right" focused on very narrow segments of the electorate – Reformers, flexible Quebec federalists, provincial PC and disgruntled federal PC voters – and supported strategic communication efforts. In 2000, the team of strategists for the Canadian Alliance also relied heavily on the basic tools of market intelligence, such as nationwide campaign tracking polls, focus group testing, and voter tracking programs, to coalesce conservative support. An important turning point occurred after the 2004 federal election, and disappointing results were again the impetus. Although the Conservatives led by Stephen Harper managed to keep the Liberals to a minority government, they were expecting to win the election and consequently were taken aback by the outcome. Tom Flanagan – who managed the Conservative Party national campaign in 2004 – described how the post-2004 election consensus pointed to the need for a more integrated "command and control structure" (2007, 197). As a result, the market intelligence function was incorporated into the party structure, and more emphasis was put on coordinating information from the voter tracking system and public opinion research. This change contributed to three consecutive electoral victories for the Harper Conservatives between 2006 and 2011.

The Conservatives were following the opinion research model developed in several other countries, notably Australia, Great Britain, and the United States. This evolution toward market intelligence is documented in the growing literature on political marketing. Marland, Giasson, and Lees-Marshment (2012, 4) define political marketing as an academic discipline "involving the application of business concepts to the practice and study of politics and government." As such, it looks at various aspects of the practice of politics, such as the political marketplace, the political product, branding, communication, and – most relevant to this analysis – market intelligence. According to the main tenets of this discipline, "market intelligence aims to discover voters' behaviour, needs, wants and priorities" (Lilleker and Lees-Marshment 2005, 10). The key dimension of market intelligence is that it no longer looks at the electorate homogeneously but adopts strategic segmentation techniques that permit for policies and communications to be designed for targeted groups. Another key departure is that market intelligence favours the reliance on a more varied set of instruments to gather information. In contrast to past practice, the accumulation of market intelligence depends on more than surveys and polls and taps into the potential of other formal, as well as informal, means (Kohli and Jaworski 1990, 7). Politicians rely on market intelligence to decide on issue priorities, develop communication strategies, and present themselves as best they can in order to deal with the most important issues facing the segmented electorate. More than previously, the collection and interpretation of market intelligence data are multilayered, ranging from ad hoc and unscientific to highly technical and mathematically sophisticated. In trying to identify differences between traditional polling and market intelligence, it is possible to zero in on eight key components, as presented in Table 10.1. Aside from continued reliance on random sampling as the favoured data collection method, there are several distinctions between the two periods. As noted above, one important difference pertains to the target of analysis. Market intelligence allows for the identification of narrow segments of the electorate that can make a difference between winning and losing an election. For example, "instead of trying to understand the commonalities across more than 23 million eligible voters in the 2006 federal election, the Harper Conservatives identified about 500,000 key voters and designed their election campaign around the needs and wants of those voters" (Turcotte 2012, 85). This approach was largely inspired by how business marketing campaigns are designed with a focus on

TABLE 10.1
Difference between traditional polling and market intelligence

Component	Traditional polling period	Market intelligence
Target of analysis	Median voters	Segmented voters
Influences	Sociology, anthropology, and political science	Marketing, business, and communication
Function	General information gathering	Strategic marketing and communication applications
Methods	Mainly quantitative analysis with occasional qualitative analysis	Mixed methods
Key statistics	Measures of association and correlation	Inferential statistics
Data collection	Random sampling	Random sampling
Research focus	Key trends, issue priorities, and overall impressions	Segmented issue priorities, key messaging, and communication
Role	Pollster as oracle	Pollster as strategist

potential consumers and represents a departure from the more sociological and anthropological parameters that dominated early voting research.

Another set of components relates to which data are collected and how they are used. This set is tied to the evolving role of the pollster within the campaign team. During the traditional polling period, the role of the pollster was to summarize what was typically referred to as "the mood of the nation" when the survey was conducted. This was done mainly through the use of large quantitative surveys and aimed to isolate the key trends and general attitudes of the public. From a statistical perspective, the analysis relied on little more than typical measures of association and correlation with inferential statistics playing a secondary role since large samples meant that statistical significance was almost a given. The transition to market intelligence meant that the pollster took on a more strategic role. His or her analysis focused on narrow tranches of the electorate, which meant that inference could no longer be taken for granted. Instead of isolating general trends, the focus was now on identifying issues that can be leveraged among key segments of the electorate – sometimes described as "wedge issues" – and how the findings can help with the development and execution of campaign communication and marketing imperatives.

Implementing a segmented strategy was facilitated by the emergence of a multichannel media universe. The multiplication of channels and eventually the rise of social media allowed pollsters to deliver narrowly targeted messages to selected audiences.

CASE STUDY

A market intelligence approach to opinion research has become standard around the world (Delacourt 2013; Johnson 2009; Lees-Marshment 2014; Marland et al. 2012). However, recent developments in business, data management, and computer programming are combining to improve the ability of opinion researchers to understand the needs and wants of individual voters. Between 2006 and 2011, the federal Liberals were on the receiving end of market intelligence innovations introduced by the Harper Conservatives. They reversed the situation in 2015. The Liberals hired Dan Arnold as their lead opinion research strategist and followed the example set by Harper and brought their opinion research in-house (Aiello 2015). They were curious about the Obama campaign and its reliance on data analytics – or big data – as a way to get more value out of opinion research (see Turcotte and Vodrey 2017). This was an initial step toward marrying big data and polling. However, as was the case for market intelligence, the business world is innovating at a rapid pace on this front, and political opinion research is playing catch-up. In particular, DMPs allow businesses to know a lot about the behaviour of individuals without having to ask a single question.

Suppose you are an avid runner living in Vancouver. You regularly go online to scan different running magazines, check out race results of different events, consult sites with training programs, or participate in different Facebook groups dedicated to running. You are planning to run your first marathon in a few months, and you are trying to find one event that would be best suited to a novice runner. Weather conditions are an important daily consideration for you, so you visit The Weather Network website regularly and have even downloaded its app on your mobile phone. After a while, you notice that every time you go online, ads for high-performance running apparel appear on your computer screen. More surprisingly, the running gear advertised always seems to match the weather conditions in Vancouver when you are online. Unknown to you, the running apparel company has teamed up with The Weather Network and, through geolocation digital tagging, can offer you running gear in line with your needs at that moment: if it is raining, you are offered rain-resistant gear; if it is unseasonably cold, you are offered thermal pants and running gloves.[3] Then one day you receive an email from the organizers of a local marathon inviting you to sign up for their event. Among the many features of that event is its high completion rate among first-time runners. You sign up ... This is what DMPs are doing for countless companies around the world.

Methods

For this analysis, I examined data management platforms from five different firms. The DMP market is limited, with eight major firms playing lead roles: Adobe, Krux, Neustar, Oracle, Google, KBM Group, Lotame, and Cxense. Several other firms are trying to penetrate the market, such as Taboola, DoubleClick, and Eyereturn. I chose the five separate DMPs based on their relative market positions, differences in their technical applications, and how long they have been operating in the field. Specifically, I chose four companies at the forefront of this emerging data technology: Adobe, Cxense, Oracle, and Lotame. I also selected for analysis a smaller firm, Eyereturn. Adobe is the most established firm and is generally considered to be a market leader. It also offers more data analytics options than others. Oracle is seen as having the best user experience and focuses on data management, whereas Cxense and Lotame are relatively new – yet well-established – entrants in the field. Although Eyereturn is comparatively much smaller than the other four firms, I included it for two specific reasons: it shows what new firms are doing, and it is a Canadian-based firm. These five platforms provide a broad overview of the current field. I focus on them as a case study to provide an overview of the possibilities inherent in this technology.

Each firm was asked to provide details about the following dimensions of its DMP platform in a semi-structured online study:

1. business profile
2. DMP services
3. general functionality of the DMP platform

4   ability to provide audience insights
5   ability to provide content personalization
6   sales-storytelling abilities
7   ad-targeting abilities.

Each firm is structured differently, so different people within the organizations were responsible for providing the information, but typically either senior account executives or directors of technology answered the questions. Follow-up discussions by phone were also conducted for clarifications intermittently between November 2015 and July 2016. A total of fifteen people contributed information to this study. The analysis is exploratory because we are still discovering the potential of this technology. Moreover, some of the information is proprietary, and companies involved are reluctant to provide insights that can affect their competitive advantages. Nevertheless, the case studies reveal enough to allow us to isolate the potential impacts of DMP on opinion research.

Findings

Before going any further, it is important to provide some general definitions of key terms. First, a "data management platform" is a central digital hub that receives and stores audience and/or client data from various online and offline sources: proprietary (first party), second party (data from partners who share their first-party data), and externally acquired (third party). A DMP allows for the creation, analysis, and activation of user segments based on the application of rules and algorithms to those data. Typically, the data stored by a DMP include navigation behaviour (a.k.a. "clickstream" or how users arrive at the site, what they search for, which content they consume, when, how often, on which devices, etc.); registration data (age, gender, postal code, etc.); self-provided or inferred preferences (favourite team, TV shows, hobby, issues, etc.); and shopping behaviour, such as preferred brands, responses to ads, and purchase intentions. One key feature of a DMP is that data storage and computational capacity are almost limitless. Second, DMPs would not have been developed without the invention of the "algorithm." An algorithm is defined as "a procedure for solving a mathematical problem (as of finding the greatest common divisor) in a finite number of steps that frequently involves repetition of an operation or more broadly, a step-by-step procedure for solving a problem or accomplishing some end, especially by a computer."[4] This concept was developed more than sixty years ago by mathematical logicians (Berlinski 2000, xi) and is necessary for completion of the programming required by data management platforms in a finite number of discrete steps. Third, "digital tagging" is the process of inserting a code or an identifier into digital content in order to collect information about visitors and contexts.[5]

The DMP market currently provides a set of standards aimed at delivering on three key metrics: customization, integration, and analytics. Representation from all of the participating firms suggests that every DMP on the market offers a set of components allowing companies to mine their own first-party data to get in-depth understandings of their customers and to make some reliable predictions about usage and consumption patterns. More specifically, every DMP features a data collection function that allows users to collect and store first-party audience/consumer data in one central hub. It also has a data classification function designed to allow for the easy separation of data into organized and actionable groupings as well as a data analysis capacity based on individual behaviour and aimed at predicting consumer intent. The more advanced DMPs – such as Adobe and Oracle and, to a much less efficient extent, Cxense – let companies perform their own digital tag management and thus both actively monitor all of their tags and consolidate disparate consumer data from multiple sources into one internal structure. They also provide for audience segmentation and simple targeting as well as campaign and audience analytics. The latter two features are particularly important for the future of opinion research.

I suggested above that one of the main differences between the traditional polling period and the market intelligence era was an increased reliance on segmentation. DMP takes segmentation to an even more granular level. This technology allows for the development of customer segments from individual profiles based on a wide variety of data points. Instead of relying solely on opinion data, DMP segmentation combines data about interests, demographics, locations, and behavioural and purchasing histories. Furthermore, segments can be discovered by examining actual consumer behaviour. Such advanced segmentation goes beyond simple targeting. It enables businesses to create thousands of highly targeted segments within the DMP and to reach audiences with the right messages at different stages of what the DMP industry describes as "the customer journey." In this sense, this technology is building on the existing trends in opinion research to move away from looking at the median voter and to focus on key segments of the population. DMPs are becoming increasingly proficient at tracking individual behaviour and want to get to a point where users will be able to track individuals consistently and persistently, ultimately to create a "segment of one." In doing so, political parties will be able to understand the needs and wants of individual voters and be increasingly efficient at tailoring campaign messages and issue priorities to those few voters who can make a difference between winning and losing an election.

Campaign and audience analytics comprise another important element of DMP technology. Campaign analytics measure how effectively segmented audiences respond to attempts to communicate with them. Are they accessing the messages sent? Are they effectively led to other sources of information? Are they modifying their behaviour or purchasing a product? Is the campaign managing to convert customers? Audience analytics measures how specific audiences interact with the content of a campaign – usually in real time. Whereas CATI technology enabled the emergence of the market intelligence era by speeding up and streamlining the interview process, and facilitating segmentation analysis, DMPs enable the next era by making analysis instantaneous and focused on individuals. More importantly, this process is seamless with the technology and much less labour-intensive – and thus much cheaper – than traditional polling.

The other application of campaign and audience analytics is the ability to support consumer conversion. A DMP can seamlessly integrate third-party data sources in order to gather intelligence about potential customers. The analysis stemming from third-party data sources is used to develop personalized communication with individual customers targeted for potential conversion. Similarly, the same approach can be used to reconnect with lapsed audiences/customers and to try to reactivate them. A review of specific cases demonstrates the potential of a DMP. It can also shed light on how this technology can be used in a political context and how it can affect opinion research.

In the first example, a Canadian media company teamed up with both Adobe and Cxense to try to understand the media consumption patterns of its audience. The traditional approach would have been to contact Canadians and ask them a battery of questions about how and when they access different media platforms throughout the day. With a DMP, it is possible to follow digitally how individuals access different media platforms. This approach is more reliable since it tracks actual individual behaviour over time rather than asking respondents to recall past behaviour, and it is totally unobtrusive. In broad terms, this exercise leads to a mapping of media habits as follows:

7 a.m.: Wakes up and looks for news headlines typically through Facebook
8 a.m.: Listens to radio in car while driving kids to school
9 a.m.: Catches up on TV shows via on-demand service using a smartphone while on public transit
10 a.m.: Goes for coffee and watches TV while waiting in line
12 p.m.: Has lunch, accesses social media, and shares stories
5 p.m.: Listens to music (podcasts) while on public transit
7 p.m.: Distracted multiscreen experience with kids dictating TV content
9 p.m.: Personal multiscreen experience.

The Canadian media company relies on this map to coordinate communication efforts. It knows that headlines are particularly important early in the morning. It can use the radio to promote upcoming shows in the morning and then push for catch-up video content during the morning commute. Interesting – or "shareable" – stories are most effective at lunch time. It also knows that secondary screens are particularly important during the early evening as parents look for other content while watching TV with their kids. Parents reclaim the TV screen after 9 p.m., and content is modified accordingly.

The second example is from abroad.[6] Next Company – one of Japan's leading real estate classified sites – was looking for ways to increase its sales. It partnered with Cxense to personalize the user experience on its site and to help direct customers to their perfect homes. The DMP began extracting data from regular user interactions on Next's website and developing profiles based on property type, location, budget, and sociodemographic characteristics. This information was used in turn to direct users to future listings as well as suggestions from other buyers with similar profiles. Cxense also incorporated third-party data into its model and targeted casual users of the website with highly tailored information and property recommendations. Moreover, this information was used to advertise products and services of interest to potential homebuyers – such as furniture, home loans, and storage – as well as geotagged services such as local moving or home renovation companies.[7] According to Cxense internal documents, Next has increased its revenue stream since it adopted a DMP. The site is more engaging and has improved its conversion rates for classified listings and advertisements. As one indication that the collaboration was a success, Next has since extended its partnership with Cxense.

TRENDING IN CANADA

Sometime in 2007, reports emerged in the British media that one could find about thirty surveillance cameras "within 200 yards of the London apartment where George Orwell wrote *1984*" (Mayer-Schönberger and Cukier 2012, 160). Surely he would have appreciated the irony and his prescience. It is unclear when the DMP technology will make its way into the political sphere to the same extent now used in the business world. The 2012 Obama campaign made strides, but its approach continued to rely on individual canvassing and cumbersome tracking analyses.[8] The transition from traditional polling to market intelligence took several years, but I suspect that this latest shift will take much less time. Certain is that the technological change will have a definite impact on how we measure and understand political behaviour.

What will be the impact of this new technology on public opinion research? Let us revisit the earlier vignette about the first-time marathon runner from Vancouver and adapt it to politics. Suppose you are a Conservative voter who switched to the Liberals in the 2015 federal election. You define yourself as a fiscal conservative but decided to give a chance to Justin Trudeau, the new leader. Moving ahead a few years, you have grown somewhat disappointed with the Liberal government and its handling of the economy. You start browsing the internet trying to find out which federal parties are offering to return to a more fiscally sound approach to governing. Each time you access the different parties' websites you look up the part of the party platform dealing with the economy in general and fiscal policies in particular. You also browse different news organizations, such as CBC.ca and theglobeandmail.com, for more details. Your research was interrupted for a few days because your car broke down, and instead of looking at party platforms you spent time on autotrader.com. A few days before the election you receive a personal email from the new leader of the Conservative Party inviting you to read how she will return fiscal discipline to governing. And, a few days later, you get another email from your local Conservative association reminding you that advance polls are open followed by a Facebook notification offering you a ride to the polling station. Since you haven't had time to buy a new car, you take the party up on its offer and go vote ... for your local Conservative candidate.

If we re-examine the comparative analysis introduced previously and consider the market surveillance dimension, it is possible to sketch what could be the impact of the emerging technologies on public opinion research and politics (see Table 10.2). We can isolate two specific emerging methodological trends. First, an important departure from previous eras is the abandonment of random sampling as a data collection method. The data storage and computational capacity of a DMP are limitless. Accordingly, the aim is to collect indiscriminately all data from all users. As a result, political actors will have more information about more of their constituents. This will lead to a deeper understanding of individual behaviour and allow for a political system more responsive to the needs of its citizens. Unfortunately, it can also lead to manipulation through increasingly sophisticated and individually targeted communication campaigns. Second, closely related to this development is the rejection of establishing causality as a research objective. As Mayer-Schönberger and Cukier (2013, 7) suggested, "the era of big data challenges the way we live and interact with the world. Most strikingly, society will need to shed some of its obsession for causality in exchange for simple correlations; not knowing why but only what."

Third, the emergence of this market surveillance model will also affect political communication. The focus of any communication will be at a very

TABLE 10.2
Looking ahead at market surveillance

Component	Traditional polling period	Market intelligence	Market surveillance
Target of analysis	Median voters	Segmented voters	Individual voter
Influences	Sociology, anthropology, and political science	Marketing, business, and communication	Information technology, software engineering, and applied math
Function	General information gathering	Strategic marketing and communication applications	Tracking of individual behaviour, message targeting
Methods	Mainly quantitative analysis with occasional qualitative analysis	Mixed methods	Quantitative only
Key statistics	Measures of association and correlation	Inferential statistics	Correlation analysis
Data collection	Random sampling	Random sampling	N = all
Research focus	Key trends, issue priorities, and overall impressions	Segmented issue priorities, key messaging, and communication	Individual preferences, behavioural triggers
Role	Pollster as oracle	Pollster as strategist	Pollster as data scientist?

granular level, effectively the individual voter. The model is influenced by information technologists and software engineers rather than by social scientists, and the objective will be to track individual behaviours and preferences and to develop a strategy to communicate with individuals with highly personalized and effective target messages and behavioural triggers to influence them to behave in predetermined and preferred ways, be it purchasing a product, watching an ad, signing a petition, or voting for a particular candidate.

Fourth, the role of the pollster is still evolving. The business world is currently struggling with this transition, and new roles are being established. Pollsters have evolved from providing information to helping make sense of it. The market surveillance era will bring more changes. For some, "mathematics and statistics, perhaps with a sprinkle of programming and network science, will be as foundational to the modern workplace as numeracy was a century ago and literacy before that" (Mayer-Schönberger and Cukier 2013, 160). One increased role for the pollster could be in the development of digital technology. The skills required will be highly technical with a specialization in software design and digital analytics. It has even been suggested that "algorithmists" will be necessary for impartial and confidential review of data processing, much like accountants and auditors do today (Mayer-Schönberger and Cukier 2013, 180). Another possibility is implementation of the strategy emerging from the data in line with the heads of marketing in digital companies such as Amazon, Netflix, or eBay. These individuals are often described as "data scientists" who combine statistical acumen, software programming, infographics design, and an advanced penchant for storytelling. At this point, the impact of big data remains uncertain. Critics, notably Cathy O'Neil (2016), have raised concerns about big data fostering inequality and being undemocratic. New technological development could lead to extreme personalization, which in turn could negatively affect political discourse. Information silos could easily be created with groups of people who have starkly different understandings of events and issues facing the country. The government's ability to enact national policy mandates and engage in nation building could also be curtailed when confronted with such a fragmented electorate. Whatever the outcome, the new role of the pollster will be a stark departure from what Gallup envisioned.

NOTES

Epigraphs: George Orwell, *1984* (New York: Signet Classic, 1950); Bruce Schneier, *Data and Goliath* (New York: W.W. Norton, 2015), 4.

1 See http://www.merriam-webster.com/dictionary/surveillance.
2 For the Surveillance Studies Centre, see http://www.sscqueens.org.
3 This vignette is based on information provided to me by marketing representatives of Cxense – a DMP provider – on November 15, 2015, in Toronto.
4 See http://www.merriam-webster.com/dictionary/algorithm.
5 See http://digitalmarketing-glossary.com/What-is-Website-tagging-definition.
6 For competitive reasons, companies were reluctant to share examples from the Canadian context.
7 Personal communication with Cxense, November 2015.

8 See www.technologyreview.com/s/509026/how-obamas-team-used-big-data-to-rally-voters/.

REFERENCES

Aiello, Rachel. 2015. "Some Boys Want to Grow Up to Be Prime Minister: I Wanted to Grow Up to Be Allan Gregg." www.hilltimes.com/2015/11/01.

Ayres, Ian. 2007. *SuperCrunchers*. New York: Random House.

Berlinski, David. 2000. *The Advent of the Algorithm*. New York: Harcourt.

Blumer, Herbert. 1946. *Collective Behaviour*. New York: Barnes and Noble.

Butler, Peter. 2007. *Polling and Public Opinion: A Canadian Perspective*. Toronto: University of Toronto Press.

Delacourt, Susan. 2013. *Shopping for Votes: How Politicians Choose Us and We Choose Them*. Madeira Park, BC: Douglas and McIntyre.

Flanagan, Tom. 2007. *Harper's Team: Behind the Scenes in the Conservative Rise to Power*. Montreal: McGill-Queen's University Press.

Gallup, George, and Saul Forbes Rae. 1940. *The Pulse of Democracy: The Public Opinion Poll and How It Works*. New York: Simon and Schuster.

Glynn, Carroll J., Susan Herbst, Mark Lindeman, Garrett J. O'Keefe, and Robert Y. Shapiro. 2016. *Public Opinion*. 3rd ed. Boulder, CO: Westview Press.

Hier, Sean P., and Josh Greenberg, eds. 2007. *The Surveillance Studies Reader*. New York: Open University Press.

Johnson, Dennis W. 2009. *Routledge Handbook of Political Management*. New York: Routledge.

Issenberg, Sasha. 2012. *The Victory Lab*. New York: Random House.

Kohli, Ajay K., and Bernard J. Jaworski. 1990. "Market Orientation: The Construct, Research Propositions, and Managerial Implications." *Journal of Marketing* 54, 2: 1–18.

Lees-Marshment, Jennifer. 2001. *Political Marketing and British Political Parties: The Party's Just Begun*. Manchester: Manchester University Press.

–. 2014. *Political Marketing: Principles and Applications*. London: Routledge.

Lilleker, Darren G., and Jennifer Lees-Marshment, eds. 2005. *Political Marketing: A Comparative Perspective*. Manchester: Manchester University Press.

Lippmann, Walter. 1922. *Public Opinion*. New York: Harcourt, Brace.

Marland, Alex, Thierry Giasson, and Jennifer Lees-Marshment. 2012. *Political Marketing in Canada*. Vancouver: UBC Press.

Mayer-Schönberger, Viktor, and Kenneth Cukier. 2013. *Big Data*. New York: Houghton Mifflin Harcourt.

Medvic, Stephen K. 2009. "Political Management and the Technological Revolution." In *Routledge Handbook of Political Management*, edited by Dennis W. Johnson, 98–112. New York: Routledge.

Newman, Bruce. 1999. *The Mass Marketing of Politics*. Thousand Oaks, CA: Sage.

Noelle-Neumann, Elisabeth. 1984. *The Spiral of Silence: Public Opinion – Our Social Skin*. Chicago: University of Chicago Press.

O'Neil, Cathy. 2016. *Weapons of Math Destruction: How Big Data Increases Inequality and Threatens Democracy.* New York: Penguin Random House.

Orwell, George. 1950. *1984.* New York: Signet Classic.

Schneier, Bruce. 2015. *Data and Goliath: The Hidden Battles to Collect Your Data and Control Your World.* New York: W.W. Norton.

Turcotte, André. 2010. "Polling as Modern Alchemy: Measuring Public Opinion in Canadian Elections." In *Elections,* edited by Heather MacIvor, 199–217. Toronto: Emond Montgomery.

–. 2012. "Market Intelligence in Canadian Politics: The Conservative Resurrection." In *Political Marketing in Canada,* edited by Alex Marland, Thierry Giasson, and Jennifer Lees-Marshment, 76–90. Vancouver: UBC Press.

Turcotte, André, and Simon Vodrey. 2017. "Permanent Polling and Governance." In *Permanent Campaigning,* edited by Alex Marland, Thierry Giasson, and Anna Esselment, 127–44. Vancouver: UBC Press.

PART 3

Engaging, Consulting, and Framing: Trending Practices in Institutions and the Government

11

Covering the Court
How News Media Frame Social Science Evidence and Supreme Court Decisions on Physician-Assisted Dying

ERIN CRANDALL, KATE PUDDISTER,
AND MARK DAKU

For constitutional politics in Canada, the introduction of the Canadian Charter of Rights and Freedoms in 1982 was a watershed moment. Canada went from a system of government operating under parliamentary supremacy to one of constitutional supremacy in which judicial rights review has become a major component of its constitutional order. This transformation is most apparent in the final court of appeal, the Supreme Court of Canada, which went from a body concerned primarily with resolving private disputes between individuals and businesses to one of public law (Manfredi 2001; Songer 2008). This has changed not only Canada's courts but also how Canadians can engage in policy making – as long as the legal argument is framed in the language of the Charter, an issue can be forced onto the agenda, even with the disapproval or uninterest of the political executive. This power of courts to bypass the legislative will of a popularly elected government has led scholars to debate vigorously the democratic legitimacy of rights review in Canada (Hogg, Thornton, and Wright 2007; Kelly 2005; Manfredi 2001; Morton and Knopff 2000).

Because of the political importance of the Supreme Court, the role that news media play in connecting it to the public is essential. Beyond issuing a publicly distributed ruling for each case, courts do not explain their decisions and are relatively inaccessible in comparison to other public officials. In practice, the public relies almost exclusively on the news media for interpretation and dissemination of judicial decisions (Hausegger, Riddell, and Hennigar 2015; Sauvageau, Schneiderman, and Taras 2006; Taras 2017). Moreover, the response to judicial decisions by other political institutions and actors is highly influenced by media coverage of the decisions of the court (Macfarlane 2008; Sauvageau, Schneiderman, and Taras 2006; Taras 2017). This process of mediatization (Strömbäck and Van Aelst 2013) has become increasingly important in a post-Charter era in which the court is often implicated in controversial and partisan debates because of the cases that it decides. Given its generally inaccessible nature, the Supreme Court's control of the message essentially starts and ends with the release of a judicial decision. This is a clear instance of mediated politics in which "journalists are the managers of the political life of judicial decisions" (Peter Russell, quoted in Sauvageau, Schneiderman, and Taras 2006, 8).

News media coverage of the Supreme Court is arguably made more difficult since the court's approach to Charter litigation is dynamic and evolving. In particular, the importance of social science evidence in Charter litigation has been an increasingly noted and important trend (Choudhry 2006; Lawrence 2015; Pal 2014). Its rise in Charter litigation is not just academic but has also been acknowledged by the Supreme Court itself.[1]

In fact, since 2016 the ability to analyze and apply social science evidence has been an explicit criterion used to assess potential Supreme Court judges. The use of social science evidence to inform legal decisions has important implications both for judicial review and for policy making. For example, the introduction of new social science evidence can reopen what once appeared to be settled case law by providing those unable to achieve changes through legislative means with a new tool that can constrain the policy choices of governments. In other words, though social science analysis will not be a new trend for the readers of this book, its impact on the work of the Supreme Court has become increasingly apparent in recent years.

To be sure, not all Charter cases necessarily lend themselves to legal argumentation based on social science evidence (Pal 2014). However, for Section 7 challenges, which deal with the question of whether a law unreasonably violates the "life, liberty and security of the person," it is now common to introduce social science evidence in order to support legal arguments. This is readily evident in several of the Supreme Court's recent decisions, including those dealing with doctor-assisted death (*Carter* 2015), prostitution laws (*Bedford* 2013), safe injection sites for drug users (*PHS Community Services* 2011), and medical marijuana (*Smith* 2015), in which social science evidence was at the crux of the Supreme Court's decision-making process. For example, in *PHS Community Services,* the Supreme Court reviewed social science data regarding the users and surrounding neighbourhood of a supervised safe injection site (Insite) in Vancouver at the centre of the legal dispute. On reviewing the social science evidence, the court found that the failure by the federal minister of health to renew the exception to the Controlled Drugs and Substances Act that allowed Insite to operate threatened the health and welfare of Insite users, who otherwise faced increased risks of disease and overdose. The court's ruling that the government's failure to renew Insite's exception was a violation of Section 7 of the Charter was supported largely by the social science evidence rather than the facts of a single litigant. PHS Community Services supported its argument for continued operation through scientific data and affidavits from medical practitioners that described the nature of drug addiction, the implications for HIV/AIDS, and the effectiveness of supervised injection facilities such as Insite. This evidence also provided an evaluation of the effectiveness of the services offered by Insite. It was the social science evidence in this case, along with compelling legal arguments, which allowed PHS Community Services to force the government to reverse its preferred policy choice.

Although this trend toward social science evidence in Charter litigation is apparent, less clear is whether and how these developments are being communicated. Here we use the "empirical turn" in Charter litigation to analyze news media coverage of the Supreme Court. A unique pair of cases (*Carter* 2015; *Rodriguez* 1993) dealing with the criminalization of doctor-assisted death and decided some twenty years apart facilitate this study.[2] By undertaking a content analysis of English print news media coverage of the court's two decisions on doctor-assisted death, we provide a novel measure of potential changes in the framing of court decisions over time by the news media, thus making both an empirical and a methodological contribution to the study of political communication and Canadian courts. We explore one particular trend in Canadian politics: the use of social science evidence in rights-based judicial decision making and how it is being covered by the media. In doing so, we contribute to an understudied component of Canadian political communication – media coverage of the Supreme Court.

It is difficult to underemphasize the importance of the news media in providing transparency and accountability to decisions of the Supreme Court. However, this relationship has not been the focus of much academic research. Sauvageau, Schneiderman, and Taras (2006) provide the first and only book-length investigation of the relationship between the media and the Supreme Court. In this important work, the authors find that, though the media are essential to disseminating information from the court, news coverage presents several unique difficulties. Most importantly, Supreme Court decisions do not lend themselves to the routine journalistic process. Legal decisions frequently lack compelling visuals and can be very lengthy, abstract, and complex. This makes the subject matter challenging to sensationalize and at times difficult to access for individuals who lack legal expertise. Because of the complexity of judicial decisions and the inaccessibility of the justices, Sauvageau, Schneiderman, and Taras find that news coverage of the court overwhelmingly falls into political framing (the more natural domain for Ottawa journalists). This framing leads to a focus on the strategic aspects of decisions and the winners and losers of cases rather than social-legal implications. In contrast, Miljan (2014), employing a single case study approach, finds that the news coverage of *Saskatchewan v Whatcott*, a free-speech case, relied predominantly on a legal frame. Miljan does not speculate about why news coverage of *Whatcott* relies on legal rather than political framing. Finally, in her review of Supreme Court–media relations, Harada (2017) finds that the court "uncomfortably embraces" the news media by providing limited access in a controlled manner. Also worth noting are the limitations of previous scholarship in regard to temporality. No study has asked whether and to what extent news media coverage of the Supreme Court has changed over time.

The existing literature on the relationship between news media and the courts provides an important foundation for our study. In particular, the rise of social science evidence in Charter cases and the apparent tendency toward politically strategic framing of Supreme Court decisions by news media appear to raise the possibility of a gap between the developing practices of the court and its representation by the media. Here we understand framing as variations of the mode of presentation of a given piece of information by the news media (Entman 1993; Scheufele and Iyengar

2012). How issues are framed helps to define and link them to broader political contexts and can create a dominant understanding that marginalizes other perspectives (Nelson and Oxley 1999; Schnell 2001). Given the rise of social science evidence in the decision making of the Supreme Court, we might anticipate that this change will be reflected in its coverage by news media. However, this would require detailed coverage of the court's reasoning. Otherwise, we might expect coverage to continue to rely on politically strategic framing, which requires less specific knowledge of both the law and social science evidence.

CASE STUDY

An examination of the *Rodriguez* and *Carter* decisions on doctor-assisted death provides the opportunity to address whether this "empirical turn" of the Supreme Court has changed how news media communicate rights-based policy making over time. Accordingly, we ask two main questions: 1) Compared with the *Rodriguez* (1993) case, does news media coverage of the *Carter* (2015) case more frequently use social science- and medical-based framing? 2) Is there a difference between *Rodriguez* and *Carter* in the news media's strategic-based framing of the Supreme Court's decisions? To answer these questions, we present brief descriptions of the cases, including key similarities and differences in the court's decisions, followed by a description of the methodology for the media content analysis and finally our findings.

In 1992, Sue Rodriguez, a woman suffering from amyotrophic lateral sclerosis (ALS), applied for an order to declare Section 241(b) of the Criminal Code invalid so that she could secure a physician-administered death. Rodriguez argued that the criminal prohibition on assisted death violated her right to life, liberty, and security of the person (Section 7), right against cruel and unusual treatment (Section 12), and right to equality (Section 15) under the Charter (paras. 119–21). In a 5-4 decision, the Supreme Court rejected her argument and upheld the prohibition on assisted death. The majority of the court rejected all of her Section 7 claims, finding that "security of the person, by its nature, cannot encompass a right to take action that will end one's life as the security of the person is intrinsically concerned with the well-being of the living person" (para. 14).

Twenty-two years following the strongly divided opinion in the *Rodriguez* case, the Supreme Court was asked in 2015 to rule again on the criminalization of assisted death. The *Carter* case focused on the claims of two individuals, Gloria Taylor and Kay Carter, who (like Rodriguez) faced similar terminal diagnoses. However, unlike in *Rodriguez*, the claimants in *Carter* were successful, with a unanimous Supreme Court striking down the criminal prohibition on assisted death as a violation of Section 7 of the Charter. The *Carter* decision stands in stark contrast to the *Rodriguez* decision. Despite addressing essentially the same legal argument, with similarly sympathetic applicants, the two cases nonetheless reached very different outcomes. This divergence is largely explained by two factors. First, when the court addressed the arguments regarding Section 7 in *Carter*, it did so under a much different understanding of the meaning and implications of Section 7. Indeed, as the court noted, the law concerning overbreadth and gross disproportionality had undergone vast changes since it had decided *Rodriguez* (para. 46). Second, and more central here, the court explained that the social science evidence considered in *Carter* was vastly different from that presented in *Rodriguez*.

At the time of *Rodriguez*, criminal prohibitions on aiding or assisting in the termination of life were the norm internationally (Bloodworth 2014; *Rodriguez* 1993, paras. 48–52). In *Rodriguez*, the Supreme Court's analysis and discussion of social science evidence were limited. The court briefly considered the legislative history of the criminalization of assisted suicide in Canada and the legality of assisted suicide in foreign jurisdictions, noting that a complete prohibition was the norm in Western countries. By the time of *Carter*, a number of jurisdictions comparable to Canada – including Belgium, the Netherlands, and the states of Oregon and Washington – permitted and regulated physician-assisted death. In *Carter*, the trial judge was presented with a great deal of social science evidence from Canada and other jurisdictions on end-of-life practices, regulatory regimes that permit physician-assisted death, and medical ethics. Compared with *Rodriguez*, not only was the amount of social science evidence examined by the court in *Carter* more considerable, but also the weight placed on this evidence by the court was more substantial. This change in the available facts required fresh analysis and loosened the restrictions placed by established precedent (*stare decisis*), allowing the court to revisit an issue that had already been decided (para. 47).

The outcome in *Carter* demonstrates the important trend of social science evidence in Charter litigation, which can provide opportunities for litigants to influence the courts and to re-examine established precedents. Adherence to *stare decisis* is a defining feature of the Canadian common law legal system. Once the Supreme Court has decided a legal issue, its decision will stand. Put differently, after a decision by the court, similar cases with similarly situated litigants will be treated similarly by all courts going forward. The case study of *Rodriguez* and *Carter* demonstrates that the inclusion of social science evidence can disrupt this practice, allowing courts to re-examine seemingly established legal issues. If the Supreme Court was unwilling to consider new social science evidence, it is unlikely that it would have heard *Carter* and reversed its position on assisted death. Yet this case study demonstrates that the greater acceptance of social science evidence by the court provides a novel opportunity for individuals and groups to challenge legal issues previously decided by the court.

Methods

The similarities between these two Supreme Court cases facilitate this research study by minimizing potentially influencing factors. This allows us to focus more easily on our variable of interest – how news media frame the court's decisions on doctor-assisted death. Newspaper articles were collected from the Dow Jones Factiva database for two time periods, the six months prior to and after each of the Supreme Court's doctor-assisted death decisions (for *Rodriguez*, March 30, 1993, to March 30, 1994; for *Carter*, August 6, 2014, to August 6, 2015). The data set features all articles that included the designated search terms.[3] The newspapers used in this study are the *Globe and Mail*, *National Post*, *Toronto Star*, *Montreal Gazette*, and *Winnipeg Free Press*. The search resulted in 323 articles for the first time period and 466 for the second time period, for a total of 789 articles. Although our selection of newspapers is relatively small, it does include both national and local news coverage, allowing us to make tentative observations about differences in coverage, including in Quebec, where the provincial government was unique in its legislative activity on the issue during the *Carter* period. The *Globe and Mail* and *National Post* are Canada's two major national newspapers. The *Toronto Star*, though an Ontario-based paper, is generally treated as a national newspaper as well. The *Winnipeg Free Press* is the most widely circulated and considered the newspaper of record for Manitoba, and the *Montreal Gazette* is considered the English newspaper of record for Quebec.

We performed a dictionary-based analysis of these articles using Lexicoder 3.0, a java package developed for automated content analysis (Daku, Soroka, and Young 2015). Although dictionary-based analyses have trouble accurately capturing nuance, humour, and context, over a large enough data set, characteristics of the corpus emerge that can be difficult to observe with close readings. This approach is also clear, straightforward, and replicable since the counts do not depend on the interpretation of a particular researcher. Limitations aside, the automated coding of topics proves to be promising vis-à-vis the reliability of human coders (Albaugh et al. 2013), and it can provide insights at a macro-level (Lawlor 2015; Soroka, Stecula, and Wlezien 2015).

This approach relies on custom dictionaries built specifically to capture particular frames in the text. For this study, we used five dictionaries: legal, strategic, legislative, social science, and medical. Although legal, strategic, and legislative dictionaries have been used to study media coverage of the courts and other political actors in previous studies (Giasson 2012; Johnson and Socker 2012), the medical and social science dictionaries were unique to this study and customized for the topic of doctor-assisted death. The legal and strategic dictionaries were built using keywords compiled from previous researchers (Giasson 2012; Johnson and Socker 2012), and they were supplemented by examining a random sample totalling 5 percent of the stories from the two time periods in order to identify words and phrases for all five dictionaries. The *Rodriguez* and *Carter* decisions and facta submitted by litigants were also reviewed to identify additional words and phrases for the medical and social science dictionaries. The legal dictionary contains phrases such as *reasonable limits* and *minimal impairment* and is designed to capture framing related to coverage of the law. The strategic frame dictionary contains words such as *dogma* and *ideology* and is designed to capture the sometimes dramatic and calculated nature of politics, whereas the legislative dictionary, which contains words and phrases such as *legislate* and *first reading*, is designed to capture framing related to the legislative process. Finally, the social science dictionary contains phrases and words such as *expert evidence* and *statistics*, whereas the medical frame dictionary includes phrases such as *terminally ill* and *informed consent*, and they are designed to capture the technical framing of the issue of doctor-assisted death.[4]

Recall our research questions set out earlier, which asked whether the content of framing varied between media coverage of the two Supreme Court cases. Because of the increased prominence of social science evidence in the court's recent decision making, we would expect an increase in the frequency of frames using social science–based words from *Rodriguez* to *Carter* if this change was indeed picked up in media coverage. Given that the topic in question, doctor-assisted death, is likely to use medically based language in discussions about research and policy, we might also anticipate a corresponding increase in medical-based frames.

Findings

Figure 11.1 illustrates the mean number of frames by decision. For both cases, frames featuring medical-based words were by far the most prominent. The mean frequency of medical frames does increase from *Rodriguez* to *Carter*; however, this increase is statistically insignificant and tempered by the fact that the mean number of legal, strategic, social science, and legislative frames also increased from *Rodriguez* to *Carter*. Arguably most notable about Figure 11.1 is what we do not observe: a substantial increase in the mean number of social science–based frames (see also Table 11.1). This, considered alongside coverage of medical-based frames, suggests that there was little change in how the media covered these Supreme Court decisions and the topic of doctor-assisted death over time.

Differences between the media's coverage of the Supreme Court's decisions can be further unpacked by comparing the coverage before and after the decisions, which permits us to consider how the court might have affected media coverage of doctor-assisted death. This breakdown is presented in Figure 11.2 and shows some interesting differences both within and between the two cases. In *Rodriguez*, there is little change in the mean number of mentions for any of the dictionaries when comparing before and after the court's decision, and none reaches statistical significance (see

FIGURE 11.1
Overall media coverage of doctor-assisted death

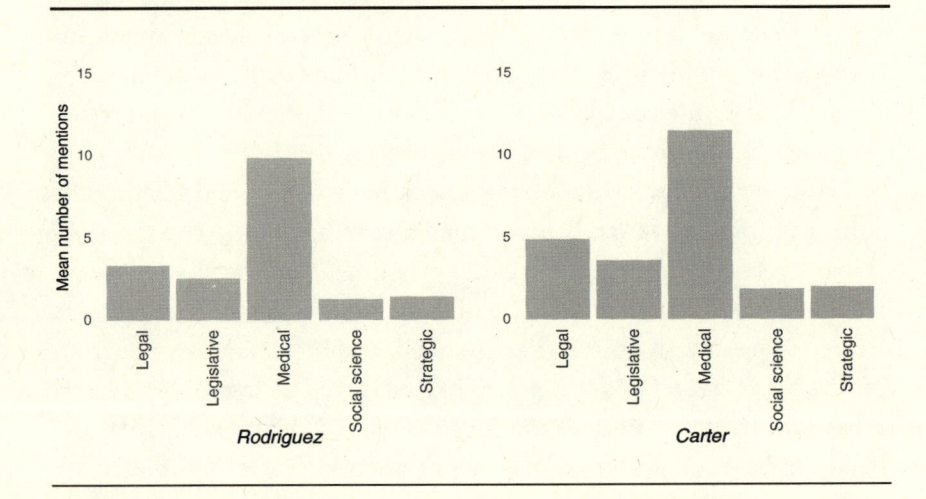

TABLE 11.1
Summary statistics by case

	Rodriguez	Carter	Two-tailed t-test
Legal	3.37 (.31)	4.88 (.32)	0.00***
Strategic	1.43 (.11)	1.95 (.14)	0.00***
Legislative	2.55 (.21)	3.58 (.26)	0.00***
Social science	1.26 (.11)	1.82 (.14)	0.00***
Medical	9.96 (.65)	11.48 (.65)	0.11

Notes: * significant at 10 percent; ** significant at 5 percent; *** significant at 1 percent; standard error in parentheses.

Table 11.2). This absence of observable change is arguably not surprising given that the court's decision to uphold the ban on doctor-assisted death meant that the legislative status quo would remain in place.

Coverage of the *Carter* decision yields two frames whose changes reach statistical significance: legislative and strategic. The increase in the mean number of legislative-based frames (from 2.85 to 4.11) is again arguably not surprising given that the Supreme Court's decision to strike down the prohibition on doctor-assisted death meant that a legislative response would be expected from Parliament. The decrease in the mean number of strategic frames by about 0.5 mentions might first appear a bit more

FIGURE 11.2
Media coverage of doctor-assisted death, before and after Supreme Court decisions

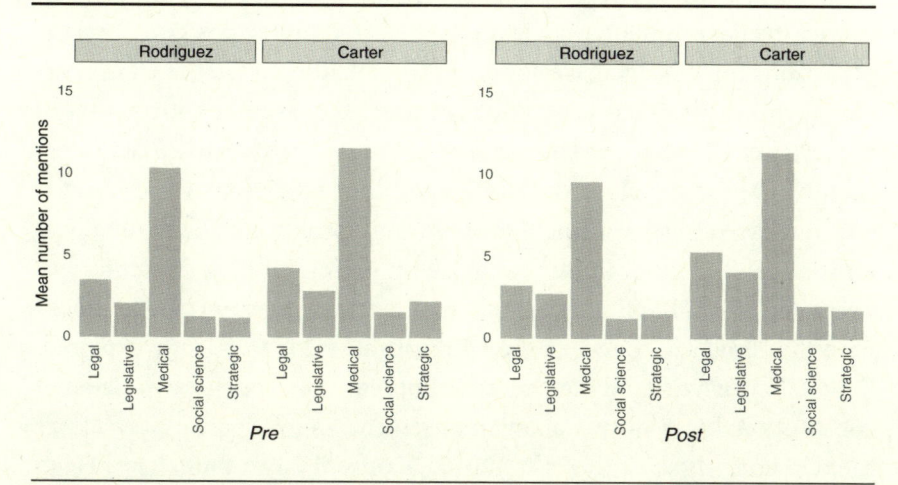

Note: "Pre" is media coverage six months prior to decision, and "Post" is media coverage six months after decision.

TABLE 11.2
Summary statistics by status of case

		Before decision	After decision	Two-tailed t-test
Rodriguez	Legal	3.60	3.27	0.63
	Strategic	1.20	1.53	0.17
	Legislative	2.12	2.77	0.15
	Social science	1.30	1.24	0.80
	Medical	10.55	9.68	0.54
Carter	Legal	4.27	5.32	0.11
	Strategic	2.22	1.75	0.10*
	Legislative	2.85	4.11	0.02**
	Social science	1.58	2.00	0.13
	Medical	11.59	11.39	0.88

Notes: * significant at 10 percent; ** significant at 5 percent; *** significant at 1 percent.

puzzling. Recall that the strategic dictionary is intended to capture the jockeying and competition of politics in action. Although popular support for doctor-assisted death has increased significantly since the original *Rodriguez* decision, it nonetheless remains a politically divisive topic. We might anticipate, then, that this divisiveness would be reflected in an increase in the use of strategic-based framing after *Carter* as the decision moved the government away from its preferred policy position. Two explanations for this decrease appear to be plausible. First, the Conservative government opted to essentially ignore the issue in anticipation of the October 2015 federal election. The Supreme Court provided a twelve-month suspension of its declaration of unconstitutionality in *Carter*, which allowed the government to opt for low-profile public consultations on the issue. Second, in the literature on policy-making dynamics between the government and the Supreme Court the question of who should have the "final say" between the two institutions is frequently explored. Researchers have found that, once the Supreme Court issues a decision of constitutional invalidity, Canadian governments overwhelmingly accept the decision whole cloth (Baker 2010; Manfredi 2007; though see Hogg and Bushell 1997). Although both branches of the government have a legitimate role to play in constitutional interpretation, this drop in strategic framing might also reflect a general unwillingness by governments to engage politically on an issue after the Supreme Court has rendered its decision on it.

Finally, though there is a small increase of about 0.4 mentions in the mean number of social science frames, it falls just outside the range of statistical significance. Like our findings in Figure 11.1, there is little indication that the importance placed on social science evidence by the Supreme Court in its decision was reflected in coverage by media.

The media studies literature suggests that there are differences between national and local news coverage of public policy issues (Lawlor 2015). Do we see this with Canadian news coverage of doctor-assisted death? Interestingly, the breakdown of media coverage by newspapers in Figure 11.3 shows that the two national newspapers largely drove the increase in legal frames seen during the *Carter* period. The most striking difference in media coverage during that period, however, is between the two regional newspapers. Coverage by the *Montreal Gazette* saw nearly double the mean number of medical-based frames compared with coverage by the *Winnipeg Free Press*. This difference in coverage is likely accounted for, at least in part, by the distinctive legislative realities experienced in the two provinces, and it is consistent with earlier research on media coverage of the Supreme Court, which found that coverage in Quebec differs from that in the rest of Canada (Sauvageau, Schneiderman, and Taras 2006). Beginning in 2014, Quebec was the first jurisdiction in Canada with legislated medical assistance in dying (predating *Carter*). This policy was created by Bill 52, a law based on recommendations from the Dying with Dignity Committee, established under Liberal premier Jean Charest, later introduced by the Parti Québécois government, and finally enacted into law by the Liberal Party under Premier Philippe Couillard (CBC 2014). In contrast to Quebec, Manitoba, like the rest of Canada, faced a policy vacuum. Thus, though we do see differences in this sample of national and regional media coverage, the differences between the two regional newspapers mean that it is difficult to draw any generalized observations.

TRENDING IN CANADA

An important trend in Charter litigation is the use of social science evidence in legal challenges. As the case of doctor-assisted death demonstrates, the introduction of social science evidence can be the difference in some instances between a win or a loss before the Supreme Court. Unpacking the full implications of this development will likely be a major focus of research on constitutional politics moving forward, and indeed not all of them might be positive (Daly 2016; Lawrence 2015).

The *Rodriguez* and *Carter* cases illustrate one of the most important political consequences of the use of social science evidence in Charter litigation: the ability to reopen what appears to be settled case law. In practice, this means that the Supreme Court has demonstrated its continued willingness to be an active player in policy making and rights debates in Canada. A reliance on social science evidence also has important consequences for applicants in constitutional cases. It places a significant empirical burden on would-be applicants, who must develop a detailed record in order to make a compelling facts-based argument. This greater reliance on social science evidence, in turn, brings up concerns about access to justice. Because of the costs associated with building the needed social science evidence, less well-resourced public interest applicants face a clear disadvantage compared with their well-funded counterparts. For example,

FIGURE 11.3
Media coverage by newspapers

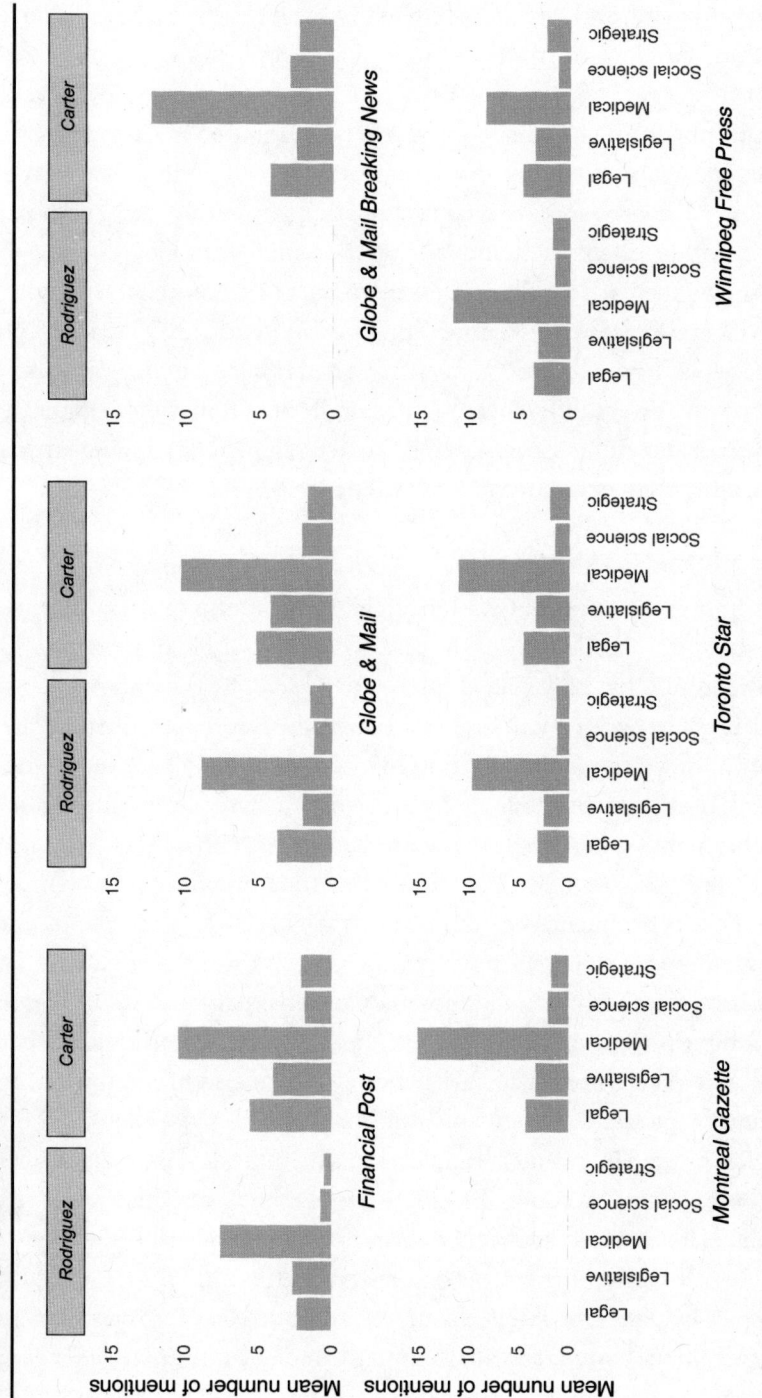

in the recent Supreme Court case on prostitution laws, the evidentiary record consisted of over 25,000 pages in some eighty-eight volumes (*Bedford* 2013, para. 15). There also remain difficult questions about the limits of social science evidence. The complicated nature of policy making means that social science research can never be absolutely certain, and judges – who are not necessarily trained social scientists – can misunderstand or misinterpret key data. The 1990 case of *R v Askov*, in which the Supreme Court misapplied social science evidence regarding trial delays that resulted in thousands of cases being stayed or withdrawn in a one-year period, serves as a case in point (Baar 1997).

In a volume that grapples with the question of how digital technologies have changed political practices in Canada, this chapter stands apart. This is not surprising. For an institution such as the Supreme Court of Canada, in which considerations of judicial independence and impartiality and the strict rules associated with the judicial process will always limit its interactions with the public and other political elites, digital technologies are less likely to have transformative roles in the ways seen in other chapters. However, digital technologies have not left Canada's judicial branch untouched. Like other Canadian political elites, the Supreme Court now has a Twitter account, though it is used more as a message board for traditional one-way communication than as a mode for interactive engagement with the public. That said, even though the court is not an active player on social media, other legal actors have more substantively engaged with this mode of communication. For example, during the unprecedented conflict in 2014 between the Conservative government of Prime Minister Stephen Harper and Chief Justice Beverley McLachlin (Ivison 2014), legal academics, more so than elected representatives or members of the media, were quick to take to Twitter to comment on this event in real time. Notably, these comments were overwhelmingly in support of the chief justice (Crandall 2018). How the work of the Supreme Court is framed on social media and who is doing this framing are questions primed for additional study.

We have illustrated here how a different type of trend, the use of social science evidence, can affect the opportunities for citizens to use the judicial branch as a tool for policy change and, in turn, how this trend might not be clearly communicated to the public. Because of the significant consequences of the Supreme Court's decision making, it is important that the public be aware of its work. If changes in how the court operates are not reflected in media coverage, then citizens' opportunities to understand developments, such as the use of social science evidence, are limited. Ultimately, citizens might be less well equipped to understand the role that the Supreme Court plays in policy making and governance. By analyzing the same legal issue (doctor-assisted death), considered in two separate Supreme Court cases spaced some twenty years apart, we were able to consider whether news media coverage of the court has changed over time and, in particular, if the trend toward social science evidence in Charter cases, of which doctor-assisted death is a part, is reflected in media coverage. The answer appears to be that there has been little change. Although the court has undergone significant changes in its approach to Charter litigation, our results suggest that these changes are not reflected in Canadian print news media. The finding that the importance of social science evidence in major rights-review cases is not necessarily being picked up by the media is significant insofar as the media serve as an intermediary between the Supreme Court and the public. Moreover, this is almost certainly compounded by the fact that the court's decisions receive relatively little coverage by national news media (Miljan 2014; Sauvageau, Schneiderman, and Taras 2006). In other words, changes to how the Supreme Court approaches Charter litigation do not appear to be a trend being communicated to the public.

Our study also makes a methodological contribution to the study of political communication and Canadian courts. Although a developed body of research has looked at how Charter jurisprudence has developed over time and its consequences for Canadian governance and policy making, far fewer studies have focused on how these Supreme Court decisions are communicated by the media, and none has considered which changes, if any, have occurred over time. The use of automated content analysis makes this kind of longitudinal media analysis more practicable and can allow us to identify trends that might otherwise go undetected. Moving forward, findings from our study suggest that closer attention should be paid to possible differences in national versus local media. The limitations of our analysis also prompt questions for future study. Although we do not find substantive differences in framing between *Rodriguez* and *Carter*, this type of automated approach cannot address some of the nuances of media coverage. In particular, it would be useful to undertake a manual analysis to consider to what extent, if at all, the media make explicit reference to social science evidence in their coverage of doctor-assisted death, which could further build on this area of study. The same type of analysis could be extended to social media in order to understand better how coverage of the Supreme Court differs between communication formats.

NOTES

1 It is useful to clarify the two different types of facts considered in constitutional litigation – adjudicative facts and legislative facts. As set out by the court in *Danson v Ontario (Attorney General)*, [1990] 2 SCR. 1086, adjudicative facts are related to the particular context of the immediate parties involved in the case. They are specific and must be proved by admissible evidence. In contrast, legislative facts establish the purpose and background of legislation, including its social, economic, and cultural contexts (para. 53). Such legislative facts can include social science evidence, in which case they are often referred to as social facts or social science–based facts. Whereas in the 1995 case *RJR-MacDonald Inc. v Canada (Attorney General)*, [1995] 3 SCR. 199 the court suggested that legislative facts were owed less deference than adjudicative facts, by 2013 this hierarchy had been explicitly dissolved. Writing for a unanimous court in *Canada (Attorney General) v Bedford*, [2013] 3 SCR. 1101, a case dealing with the constitutionality of Canadian prostitution laws, Chief Justice Beverley McLachlin explained that the use of social science evidence and expert witnesses in Charter litigation had evolved significantly in the years since *RJR-MacDonald* and that "the distinction between adjudicative and legislative facts can no longer justify gradations of deference" (para. 53).
2 We use the terms "doctor-assisted death/suicide" and "physician-assisted death/suicide" interchangeably here. Although there are subtle differences between these terms, both are used within the literature and commentary on this issue (see Nicol and Tiedemann 2016).
3 The full search terms were "doctor-assisted suicide" OR "doctor-assisted death" OR "doctor-assisted dying" OR "physician-assisted suicide" OR "physician-assisted death" OR "physician-assisted dying" OR "medically assisted dying" OR "medically assisted death" OR "medically assisted suicide" OR "assisted death" OR "assisted dying" OR "euthanasia."
4 The full dictionaries, data set, and code are publicly accessible at the git repository https://github.com/mdaku/scc-social-science/.

CASES AND LEGISLATION

Canada (Attorney General) v Bedford, [2013] 3 SCR 1101.
Canada (Attorney General) v PHS Community Services Society, [2011] 3 SCR 134.
Canadian Charter of Rights and Freedoms, Part I of the *Constitution Act, 1982*, being Schedule B to the *Canada Act, 1982* (UK), 1982, c. 11.

Carter v Canada (Attorney General), [2015] 1 SCR 331.
Carter v Canada (Attorney General), [2016] SCC 4.
Criminal Code of Canada, RSC, 1985, c. C-46.
Danson v Ontario (Attorney General), [1990] 2 SCR 1086.
R v Askov, [1990] 2 SCR 1199.
R v Smith, [2015] 2 SCR 602.
RJR-MacDonald v Canada (Attorney General), [1995] 3 SCR 199.
Rodriguez v British Columbia (Attorney General), [1993] 3 SCR 519.
Saskatchewan (Human Rights Commission) v Whatcott, [2013] 1 SCR 467.

REFERENCES

Albaugh, Quinn, Julie Sevenans, Stuart Soroka, and Peter John Loewen. 2013. "The Automated Coding of Policy Agendas: A Dictionary-Based Approach." Paper presented at the 6th Annual Comparative Agendas Conference, Antwerp, Belgium.

Baar, Carl. 1997. "Court Delay Data as Social Science Evidence: The Supreme Court of Canada and 'Trial within a Reasonable Time.'" *Justice System Journal* 19, 2: 123–44.

Baker, Dennis René. 2010. *Not Quite Supreme: The Courts and Coordinate Constitutional Interpretation.* Montreal: McGill-Queen's University Press.

Bloodworth, Michelle. 2014. "A Fact Is a Fact Is a Fact: *Stare Decisis* and the Distinction between Adjudicative and Social Facts in *Bedford* and *Carter*." *National Journal of Constitutional Law* 32: 193–211.

CBC. 2014. "Quebec Passes Bill Allowing the Right to Choose Death." *CBC News*, June 5. http://www.cbc.ca/news/canada/montreal/quebec-passes-landmark-end-of-life-care-bill-1.2665834.

Choudhry, Sujit. 2006. "So What Is the Real Legacy of *Oakes*? Two Decades of Proportionality Analysis under the Canadian Charter's Section 1." *Supreme Court Law Review* 35, 2: 501–35.

Crandall, Erin. 2018. "Supreme Court Judges: Traditional Elite Roles in a Digital Age." In *Political Elites in Canada: Power and Influence in Instantaneous Times*, edited by Alex Marland, Thierry Giasson, and Andrea Lawlor, 128–48. Vancouver: UBC Press.

Daku, Mark, Stuart Soroka, and Lori Young. 2015. *Lexicoder (Version 3.0)*. www.lexicoder.com.

Daly, Paul. 2016. "An Age of Facts? *R v Smith*, 2015 SCC 34." *Administrative Law Matters*, May 13. http://www.administrativelawmatters.com/blog/2015/06/23/an-age-of-facts-r-v-smith-2015-scc-34/.

Entman, Robert M. 1993. "Framing: Toward Clarification of a Fractured Paradigm." *Journal of Communication* 43, 4: 51–58.

Giasson, Thierry. 2012. "As (Not) Seen on TV: News Coverage of Political Marketing in Canadian Federal Elections." In *Political Marketing in Canada*, edited by Alex Marland, Thierry Giasson, and Jennifer Lees-Marshment, 175–92. Vancouver: UBC Press.

Harada, Susan. 2017. "The 'Uncomfortable Embrace': The Supreme Court and the Media in Canada." In *Justices and Journalists: The Global Perspective*, edited by Richard Davis and David Taras, 81–100. New York: Cambridge University Press.

Hausegger, Lori, Troy Q. Riddell, and Matthew A. Hennigar. 2015. *Canadian Courts: Law, Politics, and Process*. Toronto: Oxford University Press.

Hogg, Peter W., and Allison A. Bushell. 1997. "The Charter Dialogue between Courts and Legislatures (or Perhaps the Charter of Rights Isn't Such a Bad Thing after All)." *Osgoode Hall Law Journal* 35: 75–124.

Hogg, Peter M., Allison A. Bushell Thornton, and Wade K. Wright. 2007. "Charter Dialogue Revisited: Or, Much Ado about Metaphors." *Osgoode Hall Law Journal* 45, 1: 1–65.

Ivison, John. 2014. "Tories Incensed with Supreme Court as Some Allege Chief Justice Lobbied against Marc Nadon Appointment." *National Post*, May 1. http://nationalpost.com/news/politics/tories-incensed-with-supreme-court-as-some-allege-chief-justice-lobbied-against-marc-nadon-appointment.

Johnson, Tyler, and Erica Socker. 2012. "Actions, Factions, and Interactions: Newsworthy Influences on Supreme Court Coverage." *Social Science Quarterly* 93, 2: 434–63.

Kelly, James B. 2005. *Governing with the Charter: Legislative and Judicial Activism and Framers' Intent*. Vancouver: UBC Press.

Lawlor, Andrea. 2015. "Local and National Accounts of Immigration Framing in a Cross-National Perspective." *Journal of Ethnic and Migration Studies* 41, 6: 918–41.

Lawrence, Sonia. 2015. "Expert-Tease: Advocacy, Ideology, and Experience in *Bedford* and Bill C-36." *Canadian Journal of Law and Society/Revue canadienne droit et société* 30, 1: 5–7.

Macfarlane, Emmett. 2008. "Terms of Entitlement: Is There a Distinctly Canadian 'Rights Talk'?" *Canadian Journal of Political Science* 41, 2: 303–28.

Manfredi, Christopher P. 2001. *Judicial Power and the Charter: Canada and the Paradox of Liberal Constitutionalism*. Don Mills, ON: Oxford University Press.

–. 2007. "The Day the Dialogue Died: A Comment on *Sauvé v Canada*." *Osgoode Hall Law Journal* 45, 1: 107–23.

Miljan, Lydia Anita. 2014. "Supreme Court Coverage in Canada: A Case Study of Media Coverage of the *Whatcott* Decision." *Oñati Socio-Legal Series* 4, 4: 709–24.

Morton, Frederick L., and Rainer Knopff. 2000. *The Charter Revolution and the Court Party*. Peterborough, ON: Broadview Press.

Nelson, Thomas E., and Zoe M. Oxley. 1999. "Issue Framing Effects on Belief Importance and Opinion." *Journal of Politics* 61, 4: 1040–67.

Nicol, Julia, and Marlisa Tiedemann. 2016. "Bill C-14: An Act to Amend the Criminal Code and to Make Related Amendments to Other Acts (Medical Assistance in Dying)." *Library of Parliament: Legislative Summary*, No. 42-1-C14-E, 1–16.

Pal, Michael. 2014. "Democratic Rights and Social Science Evidence." *National Journal of Constitutional Law/Revue nationale de droit constitutionnel* 32, 2: 151–71.

Sauvageau, Florian, David Schneiderman, and David Taras. 2006. *The Last Word: Media Coverage of the Supreme Court of Canada*. Vancouver: UBC Press.

Scheufele, Dietram A., and Shanto Iyengar. 2012. "The State of Framing Research: A Call for New Directions." In *The Oxford Handbook of Political Communication*, edited by K. Kenskie and K.H. Jamieson, 1–26. New York: Oxford University Press.

Schnell, Frauke. 2001. "Assessing the Democratic Debate: How the News Media Frame Elite Policy Discourse." *Political Communication* 18, 2: 183–213.

Songer, Donald R. 2008. *The Transformation of the Supreme Court of Canada: An Empirical Examination*. Toronto: University of Toronto Press.

Soroka, Stuart N., Dominik A. Stecula, and Christopher Wlezien. 2015. "It's (Change in) the (Future) Economy, Stupid: Economic Indicators, the Media, and Public Opinion." *American Journal of Political Science* 59, 2: 457–74.

Strömbäck, Jesper, and Peter Van Aelst. 2013. "Why Political Parties Adapt to the Media: Exploring the Fourth Dimension of Mediatization." *International Communication Gazette* 75, 4: 341–58.

Taras, David. 2017. "Introduction: Judges and Journalists and the Spaces in Between." In *Justices and Journalists: The Global Perspective*, edited by Richard Davis and David Taras, 1–13. New York: Cambridge University Press.

12

The Notion of Social Acceptability
Lay Citizens as a New Political Force

STÉPHANIE YATES WITH MYRIAM ARBOUR

In an era characterized by an ambient cynicism toward public institutions and that acknowledges the value of "lay knowledge" (Callon, Lascoumes, and Barthe 2001) in political discussions, the traditional managerial – or top-down – approach has faced increased criticism (Fung 2006). Confronted by better-educated and better-informed citizens who wish to contribute to societal debates and to participate directly in decision-making processes, government authorities must now rethink their traditional modus operandi when developing projects that raise societal concerns. Indeed, because of citizens' will to become involved in decision making or at least informed about the rationales behind government decisions, authorities can no longer operate behind closed doors and simply rely on their own legitimacy as citizens' representatives to justify their choices. Representative democracy is no longer enough and must give way to some forms of participatory democracy. In this context, in order to gain social acceptability for their projects, public authorities are increasingly pressured to rely on new modes of governance derived from participatory approaches (Falise 2003; Fung and Wright 2003). With these new modes, lay citizens are invited to share their visions for a given project in an early phase of its development, allowing for a process of "co-construction" (Akrich 2013). This clearly marks a reconfiguration of the relationship between those who govern and those who are governed. In a context in which social acceptability is progressively becoming the norm, this trend appears to be here to stay.

Relatively new in the Canadian sociopolitical landscape, the notion of social acceptability emerged at the turn of the twenty-first century in an environment marked by tensions between classic economic growth supporters and civil society actors worried about the social and environmental externalities of this growth. In Canada, governments have witnessed the failure of several projects harshly contested by citizens. The project to move the Casino of Montreal presented by Loto-Québec and the Cirque du Soleil in 2005 is often referred to as a remarkable example of government authorities who failed to grasp how views have evolved in this regard. Badly prepared and presented without prior consultations with local communities, the project provoked a general outcry, which eventually led to its rejection (for more details, see Yates and Arbour 2013).

Following this failed project, government authorities have come to acknowledge that social actors' approval of large-scale projects – or their "social acceptability" – is an essential requirement for their success, similar to the needs for financial soundness and environmental certification. The unfolding of recent government initiatives further substantiates this trend. Among them, it is worth mentioning the launch of the Chantier sur l'acceptabilité sociale by the Quebec government and the recent release of a "green book" on this question (Gouvernement du Québec 2016) as well as the social acceptability process developed by the City of Montreal (Savard 2013).

Despite these developments, the meaning, purpose, and application of social acceptability remain unclear and lack consensus. First, the notion applies to different types of projects or objects likely to raise issues regarding acceptability. It can concern not only infrastructure or municipal development projects but also products, services, technologies, heavy industrial processes, social behaviours, educational strategies, and regulatory or political measures (Batellier 2015, 18–19). Second, some actors, especially those preoccupied with the acceptance of their projects, have taken over the notion and reduced it to a process that mainly aims at suppressing conflicts. Unsurprisingly, this tactic has raised suspicion among affected populations (see, among others, Massé 2013).

If definitions of social acceptability vary (see, e.g., Fortin, Fournis, and Beaudry 2013; Gendron 2014; Gouvernement du Québec 2016), the notions of shared values, collective judgment, process, and conditions stand out as common denominators. As such, social acceptability can be seen as a collective judgment of a project first and foremost based on citizens' values regarding its economic, environmental, or social aspects. The notion of social acceptability is close to the concept of "social licence to operate" but distinct from it since it implies a process that can evolve over time. By focusing on the idea of obtaining a "licence," the latter notion is more static and tends to evacuate contextual elements and collaborative dialogue to emphasize the result: obtaining a permit to forge ahead with a project (Owen and Kemp 2013). From a social acceptability perspective, when some values come into conflict with others, participatory mechanisms must allow promoters and stakeholders to communicate about the project in a transparent manner that also takes into account the emotive aspects of the initiative (Baba and Mailhot 2016). Such a process should allow for projects to adapt to the values and expectations of stakeholders and, in some instances, facilitate the negotiation of certain conditions before their approval.

If this openness to citizen participation is profoundly changing government authorities' practices, this paradigm shift is generating unanswered questions and complex challenges. Among them figure participants' representativeness, the quality of participation, the role of government authorities, and the legitimacy of participatory processes as perceived by concerned populations (see Table 12.1).

The representativeness of participants and the representativeness of different stances or points of view emerging from consultation processes are often questioned. First, since recruiting participants from more marginalized segments of the population often poses a challenge, inclusiveness remains a complex issue. How can we make sure that every citizen who has a legitimate stake in the process has a say and is fairly represented around the table? Second, how can we ensure that the opinions voiced are not unduly influenced by power dynamics that might prevail between different types of participants (e.g., "ordinary citizens" versus experts or interest group representatives)? Indeed, some observers have questioned the very notion of ordinary citizens in a context in which the multiplication of consultation processes has seen some of them emerge as "participation experts," embodying a "new elite" of participants (Bherer 2005). Given that citizens who engage in public consultations are not so ordinary,

TABLE 12.1
Questions and challenges associated with participatory processes

Questions	Challenges
Participants' representativeness	Reach for inclusiveness Avoid traditional power dynamics between participants
Quality of participation	Find the right balance between inclusiveness and the quality of deliberation Find the right conditions to provide environments that facilitate genuine exchange and dialogue, with meaningful and durable results
Role of government authorities	Conciliate the roles of promoter, mediator, and arbitrator
Legitimacy of participatory processes	Demonstrate that there is room for citizens' points of view in the decision-making process Justify the real benefit of participation for projects viewed as unproblematic

to what extent can the results of these consultations actually reflect the will of the majority?

The question of inclusiveness sometimes conflicts with the ideal of deliberation since a vast array of participants can alter the quality of the dialogue around the table. From a normative perspective, participatory processes should favour authentic exchanges among participants and the emergence of a "collective intelligence" involving opportunities for co-creation (Durand 2012). How many participants should we aim for in order to generate these types of exchanges? The right balance between inclusiveness and quality of deliberation is not always easy to achieve. Moreover, the actual efficiency of different mechanisms of participation is still debated. Although some best practices are slowly emerging, innovative approaches – such as online participatory platforms, the use of social media, or open labs – are still being developed and seem to be promising. Which conditions must be met to provide offline and online environments that facilitate genuine exchange and dialogue, with meaningful and durable results? What are the consequences of these new modes of engagement on citizens' inclusiveness in these participatory processes?

Government authorities' expected roles and responsibilities in participatory processes are numerous and sometimes contradictory, especially in the context of public projects. In these cases, authorities are seen as promoters – public projects being presented as their own initiatives – and citizens expect them to exert leadership in discussions on these projects. It is also expected that they will play a mediating role, allowing for better dialogue among stakeholders so that they can better understand each other's expectations. Finally, they are expected to play the traditional role of arbitrator, deciding to go further or not with a given project and determining its precise shape. In these circumstances, in which government authorities act first as promoters and then as mediators, it can be difficult to determine when it is time to intervene as arbitrators, bringing the discussion on a given project to a close and thus fixing the limits or the frontiers of participation.

Finally, the legitimacy of the decision to implement a participatory process in order to discuss a given project cannot be taken for granted. The process itself might be criticized if it seems that the fundamental decisions on the project in question have already been made or if there is an impression that the results of the consultation will not be considered in the final decision-making process. Finally, government authorities must sometimes justify their decisions to organize participatory processes in order to discuss projects not considered to be problematic. After all, citizens have limited time to become involved and expect their government to manage their financial resources wisely. Therefore, the true benefit of participatory processes must sometimes be emphasized.

CASE STUDY

We study how social acceptability can be operationalized in order to reach its full potential as a tool for democracy through the case of Vision 2035, a major public consultation project focused on an urban planning concept for the francophone municipality of Saint-Bruno-de-Montarville (south of Montreal). The approach put forward for the discussion of Vision 2035 is a notable example of openness to social actors and the acknowledgment of their role in designing projects that raise social and environmental issues.

Methods

Our analysis relies on field observations coupled with an examination of diverse institutional documents and online materials. It also includes the consideration of five semi-directed interviews with citizens and stakeholders who actively participated in the consultation process.[1] A case study approach in this context is appropriate since it allows for the examination of a contemporary phenomenon intimately linked to its context (Yin 2009, 15) and then attempts to theorize from it.

The Vision 2035 initiative emerged when the city of Saint-Bruno-de-Montarville had to propose a new urban planning concept to manage its developments better. Several issues had to be tackled, including the preservation and development of a durable environment, with a social and generational mix, and the transformation of existing neighbourhoods. To present a planning concept that would rally the population – and hence be socially acceptable – the municipality organized large-scale public consultations aimed at collecting citizens' views on these issues. The Institut du Nouveau Monde (INM), a nonprofit organization specializing in citizen participation, and Vivre en Ville, another nonprofit organization specializing in the development of sustainable communities, were brought in to help the city organize the consultations, launched in February 2015. The approach put forward was as inclusive as possible, with the deployment of several consultation mechanisms targeting interest groups, families, internet users, youth, and the elderly. The objective of the consultations was to encourage citizens to think about how they envisioned their city in twenty years. They were invited to share their thoughts through an online survey, written comments, or an online consultation platform. They were also called to participate in a Citizen Day dedicated to discussions on the future of the municipality (for more details on the process, see INM 2015).

We focus on the Citizen Day and the online deliberative platform to assess their innovative aspects and to examine how the different challenges presented above were met through these processes. The Citizen Day was held in a high school on March 28, 2015. One member of our research team attended the activity, following the principles of field observation. The presence of the researcher was announced at the beginning of the day, and participants had the chance to express their discomfort with this presence (nobody did). Following the typology of Gold (1958), the researcher was a "complete observer": throughout the day, she sat among participants, observed what occurred, and took field notes with the help of an observation grid (plenary discussions were recorded for future reference).

She did not actively participate in the discussions. Of the six workshops held simultaneously in the afternoon, she observed one of them, which tackled the future of the downtown area. Thus, the observations that follow apply specifically to this workshop and cannot be generalized to the five others.

Findings

The morning of the Citizen Day was dedicated to a short movie on the renewal of urban practices and principles regarding the concept of sustainable neighbourhoods (known as *écoquartier* in French). It was followed by discussions and activities for families (e.g., photo booth, drawing, citizen minigolf). During the afternoon, participants were invited to join one of six workshops dedicated to different areas of the city. The day ended with a plenary session in which participants were asked to share discussions from the workshops and organizers made final comments. One hundred sixty-five people took part in the activity.

The online platform was available from February 18 to April 3, 2015. We systematically compiled comments and reactions shared on it throughout the consultation. Forty-two people subscribed to the platform (including one member from our research team), and 63 percent of them actively participated by posting 252 comments. The most active person made thirty-eight contributions (the mean contribution per participant was 6.6).

Our analysis shows that the different mechanisms put forward reached diverse groups of citizens. Participants' age at the Citizen Day was high, with a large number of elderly people, though there were also many families with young children. We also noted that most people who spoke after morning presentations were men, whereas men and women participated in a more even manner during the afternoon workshop that we observed. Interestingly, it seems that the online platform and the written process reached different people: we identified only two participants on the online platform who also submitted a paper or brief as part of the consultations (though it is difficult to determine if some participants on the platform were also associated with an interest group who filed a written comment). Hence, it seems that the different participative mechanisms complemented each other well in order to reach different segments of the population.

That said, all of the respondents whom we met expressed their surprise and concern regarding the low rate of participation in the different mechanisms used for this consultation. Consequently, they questioned the representativeness of the exercise. According to INM, the participation rate – which hovered between 1 percent and 2 percent for the whole process – was nevertheless decent compared with other participatory processes undertaken in Quebec. Yet one respondent summarized her reflections on this matter by claiming that "we really think this (rate) was in the abstract" (respondent 5).[2] Another respondent was more pragmatic, acknowledging that, "if we take only the numbers, it is few indeed" but that participation takes time: "Voicing an opinion demands effort. Even though the means is easy – everyone can play on his phone keyboard – it requires an effort. You have to make the effort to think and to voice your opinion" (respondent 1).

If participants' representativeness was questioned, both our observations and the interviews showed that the quality of participation during the Citizen Day was particularly high: participants seemed to be at ease to express their views and listened and reacted to others' interventions. If the comment and question period held after morning presentations followed a traditional feedback communication approach, in which citizens could react to the content presented earlier, afternoon workshops gave room for a more dialogical communication. The fact that groups were smaller seemed to facilitate participation from some citizens – especially children and younger adults – and to encourage genuine exchanges. From the perspectives of several of the interviewees, there was a certain level of interinfluence among participants.

The moderators, part of INM personnel, encouraged and helped this dialogue. Throughout the day, they played an important role, notably in rephrasing or interpreting some of the interventions. Doing so allowed for a broader understanding of comments. Participants with visions different from those of the presentations were encouraged to speak out. Furthermore, moderators helped participants to refocus the discussions on the main question of the consultation. The facilitators ended the day with a summary of the talks. All respondents agreed that this summary reflected accurately the views expressed during the day. In the end, as

TABLE 12.2
Degree of exchange between participants on the online platform

Number of initial contributions that generated no reaction	52
Number of initial contributions that generated one reaction from another participant	17
Number of initial contributions that generated two reactions from other participants	10
Number of initial contributions that generated more than two reactions from other participants	8
Number of initial contributions that generated exchanges between at least two individuals	11

observed and as confirmed by our interviews, the Citizen Day was viewed as a positive experience. One of the respondents even summarized the event by stressing that "people were enchanted by the unrolling of the activities" (respondent 2).

The findings are more nuanced when it comes to the online platform, which generated some degree of interaction among participants, as shown in Table 12.2. Of the ninety-eight initial contributions, 47 percent generated reactions from other participants (including exchanges), whereas 11 percent of the initial contributions generated real exchanges. With these exchanges, the initial contributor responded to a reaction following her own contribution and then received an answer from the person who had reacted initially. These exchanges can be qualified as bidirectional or even multidirectional in the several instances in which many persons took part in the exchanges and answered each other. This can be associated with a dynamic close to the dialogic model of communication (Kent and Taylor 2002). The platform moderator, part of INM personnel, regularly intervened by asking questions and providing online references relevant to the discussion. A public servant from the municipality played a similar role, providing answers to factual questions and proposing online references.

Impressions of this exercise varied among our respondents. One argued that "we start from our tastes, our ideas ... The process was managed, which was good, and information and links were sent" (respondent 2). She also appreciated the fact that the platform provided a space for free expression in which she could intervene without the fear of being judged: "It was not an experts' thing, we could also dream." Another respondent agreed, insisting on the creative potential of the platform thanks to the interactions that it allowed (respondent 3).

The same respondent was more critical, however, about the lack of interaction among participants, which limited the real advance of people's comments: "Often it only remains ideas" (respondent 3). She also noted that "the space was not used to really contribute to the process," with the platform's characteristics limiting "the possibility of a real debate on ideas." According to her, experts such as the nonprofit Vivre en Ville could have contributed to discussions in order to share their specific knowledge and explain some of the constraints of a given idea. Although the municipal public servant active on the platform played this role partially, a more systematic approach could have allowed for deeper and more informative discussions. It could also have helped to focus the discussions on paramount and large projects. Indeed, as noticed by a respondent, a large portion of contributions was about urban agriculture, an interesting concept but not fundamental to the future development of the municipality.

Nevertheless, one respondent was surprised by the quality of contributions. In this regard, our field observation of the Citizen Day coupled with content analyses of written documents submitted and of comments on the online platform showed rich and diverse viewpoints. Moreover, topics of concern differed from one consultation mechanism to another: the fact that the Citizen Day was launched with two presentations on specific themes, bearing a certain vision of development, could provide a partial explanation. Indeed, according to this vision, densification, the improvement of public transportation, and citizens' appropriation of unoccupied spaces were presented as imperative. These ideas likely oriented in part the exchanges that followed during the day. Moreover, the influence of some leaders within each workshop might have limited the scope of discussion. Papers, briefs, and other written comments presented to the municipality and those put forward on the online platform were formulated in a more flexible environment, which might have left more room for creativity. For instance, some exchanges compiled from the online platform focused on the burying of electrical wires, the construction of minihomes, the development of wi-fi zones throughout the city, or the launch of a community television station. To our knowledge, these ideas were not discussed during the Citizen Day. The diverse views expressed through the different mechanisms could also be explained by the fact that these forums reached different target groups, reinforcing the thesis of their complementarity.

If the process seemed to have generated new ideas, the perception of the real benefits of the consultations was mixed. Government authorities officially remained distant from the whole consultation process, the mediating role having been confided to INM. Nevertheless, some observed that many Citizen Day participants were close to the municipal political party currently holding power. As highlighted by a respondent, "it was not organized ... except that politicians in place talked about it ... It is obvious that they mix with people who support them" (respondent 2). In this context and as underlined by one respondent, opinions put forth during the day were similar to those championed by the mayor's team: "At the end of the day, we are not surprised to realize that what emerged from all this goes hand in hand with what elected representatives think" (respondent 3). In fact, for one respondent, the main objective of the consultation was to corroborate the vision developed by the municipality (respondent 2). This is exactly what was suggested by a journalist from a local newspaper who presented the consultation exercise as a way to "reinforce the municipality in its policies" (Khalkhal 2015).

Others were more critical, questioning the utility of such a consultation when the die was already cast, given the sizable financial resources that it required. One respondent voiced her fear that "it won't give anything concrete ... Elected representatives will retain things and ideas they agree with but will put aside what cannot fit with their development plan" (respondent 5). An article published one month prior to the consultation process seemed to confirm these suspicions, quoting the mayor describing his vision for one of the municipal sectors that remained to be developed (the Sabourin area). The mayor argued for a residential project corresponding to a sustainable neighbourhood (écoquartier) supported by alternative means of transportation (Champagne 2015). Yet, during the consultation, no consensus emerged on the need to develop a real estate project for this sector. Indeed, as highlighted in a summary of the participatory process published by INM in May 2015, the idea to develop the Sabourin area was among the few that did not reach a consensus, along with the question of densification. Again this questions the necessity of holding a consultation when fundamental decisions have already been made.

According to INM, most other ideas associated with the future development of the municipality were welcomed quasi-unanimously, such as the need to encourage appropriation of and access to downtown, to develop convenient collective transportation, or to protect agricultural land. The "vision statement" of the municipality was elaborated based on this summary of the whole exercise and submitted to its eight consultative committees. This allowed them to assess whether the statement adequately reflected the outcome of the consultations. The vision statement was then adopted by the municipal council and made public in October 2015.

In the end, the consultation process aimed at developing a vision based on a collective exercise, consistent with the idea of social acceptability. That said, the vision statement remains a general orientation document that does not include concrete propositions for specific projects. It is thus simple to reach a consensus on the broad principles at the core of the vision, such as "integrated natural environment," "economic and working environments that are attractive and sustainable," or "community, cultural and leisure activities that are dynamic and adapted" (Saint-Bruno-de-Montarville 2015, 6). It is when government authorities will promote concrete projects within this vision, and will eventually embody their arbitrator role and make decisions regarding these projects, that tensions will likely occur, testing the dynamic aspect of social acceptability.

TRENDING IN CANADA

Our objective in this study was to reflect on the notion of social acceptability, a concept becoming the norm in the discussion of projects raising societal issues, and to illustrate how it can be operationalized in the discussion of a concrete project. The Vision 2035 initiative offered a suitable case study, notably because of the innovative participatory approach that it put forward. Although the initiative was deployed in the specific context of Quebec – where, among other things, reaction and sensitivity to projects' economic, environmental, and social impacts might be different from those elsewhere (Léger, Nantel, and Duhamel 2016) – we think that the case still provides major insights that can be generalized to other jurisdictions. It helps us to understand better how the social acceptability trend has unfolded and how it will likely evolve in the coming decades.

Our analysis shows that elected officials are now more open to receiving citizens' input on visions or projects, such as the one studied here. This openness to participatory processes has constituted a strong trend over the past fifteen years, with private businesses following suit (Yates 2015). Best practices are beginning to emerge as diverse principles of participatory processes are adopted not just in Canada but also around the world (e.g., Baiocchi 2003; Röcke and Sintomer 2005). The participatory process organized within the framework of Saint-Bruno-de-Montarville's Vision 2035 can be considered as an archetype of these best practices, respecting state-of-the-art rules in this emerging domain.

Participatory processes illustrate a clear change in elected representatives' conception of democracy, in which participatory components replace mostly elite, unidirectional, and persuasive decision-making approaches previously the norm. This participatory turn can be seen as the evolution of a small breach in the elitist model that began in the 1970s, when a few participatory mechanisms were adopted, notably in Quebec, with the more systematic use of public audiences in parliamentary commissions (Deschênes 1981) and the creation of the Public Hearings on the Environment Office (Bureau d'audiences publiques sur l'environnement) in 1978. But the main incentive for government authorities to move toward this era of participation was admittedly the number of projects abandoned over the past fifteen years because of the fierce contestations that they provoked (see, e.g., Yates, Hudon, and Poirier 2013).

Acknowledging the legitimacy of the participation of citizens in the discussion of projects affecting their lives is one thing; understanding the concrete implications of the choices underlying participatory processes is another. In this regard, our case provides insights into questions and challenges still pending when it comes to social acceptability. These lessons could be useful in the development of future participatory approaches so that they can truly become new opportunities for citizens to engage in the political process, providing an alternative to traditional repertoires of contestation.

Our case stresses the fact that participation requires time and engagement. Indeed, citizens who wish to add their voices to the discussion must make the effort to know the ins and outs of the project. The time invested in consultations must also be taken into account, whether a whole Saturday dedicated to a Citizen Day or a few hours to write a paper or contribute to an online platform. Consequently, it would be naive to expect that a majority of the population will actively participate in a consultation process. Hence, the logic of quantitative representativeness must arguably be put aside, and a qualitative appreciation of citizens' inputs should be favoured.

The case also demonstrates that citizens' input can be of great value. Their contributions to the discussions on the vision of their city were rich. They have materialized in numerous propositions that might not have been envisioned by the city in the first place. Hence, the case illustrates that citizen contributions can be associated with "lay knowledge" in opposition to "expert knowledge." The former consists of pragmatic knowledge stemming from concrete experience of a given territory. For instance, citizens will indicate that a given road junction is particularly dangerous or that a parking lot not used at its full capacity represents a good opportunity to replace it with something more attractive to citizens.

That said, the case shows that it would be a mistake to oppose expert knowledge and lay knowledge and favour one over the other, for they can complement each other in useful ways. Lay knowledge can be brought in to supplement expert consideration, thus providing nuance and perspective. Openness to this knowledge is paramount, but expertise remains an essential input to foster discussion or "activate" the lay knowledge.

The case further highlights that a participatory process must rely on an array of mechanisms in order to reach diverse segments of the population and that the setting associated with these different mechanisms allows for the emergence of complementary ideas. A more formal setting in which participation is preceded by presentation of specific content – as was the case during the Citizen Day – will likely generate informed and focused discussions. In that sense, it is a good way to make sure that citizens tackle inescapable subjects. In return, a more flexible setting – such as the one associated with the online platform – can generate discussions on innovative ideas. Even if these ideas sometimes appear to be less relevant or more difficult to implement, they can become sources of inspiration for a more pragmatic vision then developed by the municipality. Since the influence of some leaders is subtler online, a more flexible setting might also encourage participation by people who might otherwise remain passive observers.

The role of moderators appears to be crucial for the successful realization of participatory forums such as the Citizen Day. As long as moderators are seen as neutral, they can encourage constructive dialogues, such as by reframing the debate or following up with participants on a given issue. To a certain extent, this role can also be played online, where moderators can contribute to the quality of exchanges, notably by providing relevant information or references, as observed in our case.

The case finally confirms that the legitimacy of participatory processes cannot be taken for granted since the real benefits of these processes are not always obvious for concerned populations. Indeed, the literature reveals that several justifications can support participatory initiatives (McComas 2010). According to a *substantive* point of view, participation is a good way to improve projects by having access to lay knowledge. From this perspective, participation exceeds the immediate issue at stake since it is also deemed to be a good way to increase social capital, individuals' political efficiency, and more broadly communities' capacities to become mobilized in order to control their destinies. From a *normative* point of view, participation is based on a profound belief that in a democracy, individuals have the right to express their voices on issues about which they are concerned. Finally, in a purely *instrumental* manner, communities' engagement can be encouraged since it will increase the likelihood that decisions will be accepted and that citizens will have confidence in public authorities. In our case, the impression, partly fed by the media, that the mayor held consultations mainly to confirm his vision, rather than to co-develop a shared vision with citizens, mainly associated the process with these instrumental considerations. This impeded its legitimacy.

Regardless of their genuine motivations, government authorities must ultimately decide what to do with a given project and thus embody their role as arbitrators. Although this dimension was not specifically highlighted in our case, since the adoption of a vision precedes those difficult arbitrations between concrete projects, the conciliation of this role with the roles of promoter and mediator remains an important challenge when reflecting on social acceptability. When is the appropriate moment to bring the discussions on a project to a close and move to the next step? An interesting avenue could be to promote the government's accountability to citizens, especially those who participate in consultation processes. In that sense, we can think that the closure of a debate will be judged opportune or not based on the rhetorical justifications of the decision. A more systematic explanation of the logic behind government authorities' decisions on a project would allow the authorities to demonstrate how and to what extent they have taken into account the views brought forward in the participatory process. This could be useful even if the decision leans in a direction different from the one advocated by the majority during consultations, making more transparent the different types of rationalizations that support a decision. In the end, this would help to build the legitimacy of authorities' decisions.

Openness to participation in the discussion of projects that raise acceptability issues seems to be here for good; moving forward, citizens can expect to be consulted on projects that raise concerns and societal issues. The fact that the government of Quebec released a "green book" on this question in February 2016, part of a broader discussion on social acceptability, further illustrates this point. It indicates the gradual institutionalization of the notion and its reach beyond the municipal level. The federal government seems to be ready to follow suit, with the announcement of an initiative aimed at revising the environmental assessment process for large-scale projects, notably focusing on openness, transparency, and inclusiveness (Government of Canada 2016).

This trend changes how government authorities make decisions and justify them to the population. It also modifies profoundly lay citizens' relationships with these public decisions. In a context in which they will increasingly have occasions to voice their concerns and credibly believe that they will be heard, it will be more difficult to justify the single use of repertoires of contestation. To maintain their legitimacy, opponents of a given project will have to show that they first voiced their concerns within these new spaces of participation before turning to contestation. Case studies that examine the rhetoric deployed by such opponents and its impact on their legitimacy would be welcomed to further our understanding of these dynamics. Hence, it remains to be seen if these new spaces of participation will foster the resolution of conflicts and promote harmony in the discussion of projects that raise societal concerns. In the end, we can hope, they will lead to the development of projects with better economic, social, and environmental impacts and thus ultimately favour the public good.

NOTES

1 This fieldwork was conducted for a research project entitled Social Acceptability of Large-Scale Projects: Identification of Good Practices and Proposition of a Dialogical Model supported by the Fonds de recherche du Québec – Société et culture, under the direction of Stéphanie Yates.
2 Because the five interviews were conducted in French, these excerpts have been translated.

REFERENCES

Akrich, Madeleine. 2013. "Co-Construction." In *Dictionnaire critique et interdisciplinaire de la participation*, edited by I. Casillo et al. Paris: GIS Démocratie et Participation. http://www.dicopart.fr/fr/dico/co-construction.

Baba, Sofiane, and Chantale Mailhot. 2016. "De la controverse à l'acceptabilité sociale: Le rôle constructif du conflit." *VertigO: La revue électronique en sciences de l'environnement* 16, 1. https://id.erudit.org/iderudit/1037566ar.

Baiocchi, Gianpaolo. 2003. "Emergent Public Spheres: Talking Politics in Participatory Governance." *American Sociological Review* 68, 1: 52–74.

Batellier, Pierre. 2015. "Acceptabilité sociale: Cartographie d'une notion et de ses usages." Cahier de recherche. Montréal: Les Publications du Centr'ERE.

Bherer, Laurence. 2005. "Les promesses ambiguës de la démocratie participative." *Éthique publique* 7, 1: 82–90.

Callon, Michel, Pierre Lascoumes, and Yannick Barthe. 2001. *Agir dans un monde incertain: Essai sur la démocratie technique*. Paris: Seuil.

Champagne, Stéphanie. 2015. "Vie de quartier: Saint-Bruno le huppé." *La Presse*, January 31. http://plus.lapresse.ca/screens/60c503e5-a638-49ab-9712-48ae48b740a8__7C___0.html.

Deschênes, Gaston. 1981. "Notes sur l'évolution historique des commissions parlementaires (1867–1980)." *Bulletin de l'Assemblée nationale* 11, 2: 1–27.

Durand, Caroline. 2012. "L'art de faire émerger l'intelligence collective comme processus de changement émergent." In *Théorie U. Changement émergent et innovation*, edited by I. Mahy and P. Carle, 163–95. Québec: Presses de l'Université du Québec.

Falise, Michel. 2003. *La démocratie participative: Promesses et ambiguïtés*. Paris: Éditions de l'Aube.

Fortin, Marie-Josée, Yann Fournis, and Raymond Beaudry. 2013. "Acceptabilité sociale, énergies, et territoires: De quelques exigences fortes pour l'action publique – Paper Submitted to the Commission sur les enjeux énergétiques." Rimouski: Groupe de recherche interdisciplinaire sur le développement régional, de l'est du Québec, Centre de recherche sur le développement territorial, Université du Québec à Rimouski.

Fung, Archon. 2006. "Varieties of Participation in Complex Governance." *Public Administration Review* 66, 1: 66–75.

Fung, Archon, and Erik Olin Wright. 2003. *Deepening Democracy: Institutional Innovations in Empowered Participatory Governance*. London: Verso.

Gendron, Corinne. 2014. "Penser l'acceptabilité sociale: Au-delà des intérêts, les valeurs." *Revue internationale de communication sociale et publique* 11: 117–29.

Gold, Raymond L. 1958. "Roles in Sociological Field Observation." *Social Forces* 36: 217–23.

Gouvernement du Québec. 2016. "Orientations du Ministère de l'énergie et des ressources naturelles en matière d'acceptabilité sociale." *Gouvernement du Québec*. www.mern.gouv.qc.ca/territoire/acceptabilite.jsp.

Government of Canada. 2016. "Government Launches Review of Environmental and Regulatory Processes to Restore Public Trust." *Government of Canada*, June 20. http://news.gc.ca/web/article-en.do?nid=1088199.

Institut du Nouveau Monde (INM). 2015. "Rapport de consultation. Vision stratégique 2035. Imaginons Saint-Bruno-de-Montarville." *Institut du Nouveau Monde*. https://www.stbruno.ca/sites/default/files/pdf/VS2035_Rapport-de-consultation_22mai2015_INM.pdf.

Kent, Michael L., and Maureen Taylor. 2002. "Toward a Dialogic Theory of Public Relations." *Public Relations Review* 28, 1: 21–37.

Khalkhal, Frédérick. 2015. "Résultat d'une consultation publique à Saint-Bruno. Énoncé de Vision stratégique 2035." *Les versants*, October 16. http://www.versants.com/resultat-dune-consultation-publique-a-saint-bruno/.

Léger, Jean-Marc, Jacques Nantel, and Pierre Duhamel. 2016. *Le code Québec: Les sept différences qui font de nous un peuple unique au monde*. Montréal: Les Éditions de l'Homme.

Massé, Bruno. 2013. "L'acceptabilité sociale, ou l'art de se faire avoir?" *Huffington Post*, September 24. http://quebec.huffingtonpost.ca/Bruno%20Mass%C3%A9/acceptabilite-sociale-concept_b_3972876.html.

McComas, Katherine A. 2010. "Community Engagement and Risk Management." In *The SAGE Handbook of Public Relations, 2nd Edition*, edited by R.L. Heath, 461–76. Thousand Oaks, CA: Sage.

Owen, John R., and Deanna Kemp. 2013. "Social Licence and Mining: A Critical Perspective." *Resources Policy* 38, 1: 29–35.

Röcke, Anja, and Yves Sintomer. 2005. "Les jurys citoyens berlinois et le tirage au sort: Un nouveau modèle de démocratie participative?" In *Gestion de proximité et démocratie participative: Une perspective comparative*, edited by M.H. Bacqué, H. Rey, and Y. Sintomer, 139–60. Paris: La Découverte.

Saint-Bruno-de-Montarville. 2015. "Énoncé de Vision stratégique 2035. Imaginons une collectivité viable." *Saint-Bruno-de-Montarville.* http://www.stbruno.ca/vision-strategique-2035_enonce-de-vision-version-integrale.

Savard, Jean. 2013. "De l'immobilisme à l'appropriation citoyenne: Regard sur le processus d'acceptabilité sociale à Montréal." In *Communication et grands projets,* edited by V. Lehmann and B. Motulsky, 45–80. Québec: Presses de l'Université du Québec.

Yates, Stéphanie. 2015. "Relations publiques et gouvernance participative: Une vision partagée du 'vivre ensemble'?" *Communiquer – Revue internationale de communication sociale et publique* 15: 98–112.

Yates, Stéphanie, and Myriam Arbour. 2013. "La place des processus de consultation institutionnalisés dans l'acceptabilité sociale des grands projets: Étude de deux cas québécois." Paper presented at the annual conference of the Société québécoise de science politique, Montreal, May.

Yates, Stéphanie, Raymond Hudon, and Christian Poirier. 2013. "Communication et légitimité: Une analyse comparative des cas du Mont Orford et de Rabaska au Québec." In *Communication et grands projets,* edited by V. Lehmann and B. Motulsky, 97–112. Québec: Presses de l'Université du Québec.

Yin, Robert K. 2009. *Case Study Research: Design and Methods.* 4th ed. Thousand Oaks, CA: Sage.

Conclusion
Unpacking Trending Practices in Canadian Politics

MIREILLE LALANCETTE, ERIN CRANDALL, AND VINCENT RAYNAULD

THE OLD, THE NEW, AND THE TRANSFORMATIVE

This volume began by discussing transformations occurring in the public sphere. By unpacking these different trending practices, this book offers a way to make sense of some of the transformations occurring in the fields of political behaviour and communication. We have conceptualized trends as emerging areas of scholarly research and practice at the intersection of political science, communication, sociology, political management, and journalism, and these trends are likely to gain prominence and, to some degree, influence different aspects of Canadian politics in the coming decades. Thinking about communication and politics in terms of trends can help us to understand and meet the demands of the present while also planning for the future.

Several questions guided the contributors to this volume in their analyses of the trends:

1 What is the nature of changes in media practice and political communication?
2 How are these changes transforming political engagement and political action repertoires?
3 To what extent do these trends transform the relationships between political actors and institutions and democracy in general?
4 What are the consequences for the practice and study of Canadian politics?

Unsurprisingly, the contributors yielded diverse answers to these questions. However, by looking at their chapters collectively, we can discern the trends and the transformations that they are helping to bring about. Here we take a step back and use the findings in the chapters to consider these changes as well as their implications. The goal is to unpack these trends and examine how they are likely to affect how we think about, perceive, and understand political science and communication and how research is done in these fields.

In relation to the first question, it can be argued that trends are about the adoption of new patterns of behaviour in the public sphere and/or transformations of political communication practices. Several chapters focus on the uses of social media by citizens, activists, politicians, and governments. Others attend to how technological developments related to big data are contributing to the remodelling of different areas of political activity, including surveys and campaigns. Democratic and policy-making processes are also affected by trending practices. Social acceptability consultation and social science evidence in the courts are changing how the public can engage in and influence decision making.

OUT WITH THE OLD, IN WITH THE NEW?

Several elements should be considered when unpacking transformations in political science and communication. First, the trends studied in this volume manifested themselves in a variety of ways, but all are related in one way or another to the introduction of new technologies and/or the adoption of new practices. According to some of the contributors, Web 1.0 and Web 2.0 media channels are integral components of trending phenomena in political communication and behaviour. In fact, they can be viewed as nearly unavoidable in today's politics. As we have seen, the ways in which and the extents to which they are used by a large number of formal and informal political players are affecting social movements, transforming grassroots organizations, shaping citizens' understandings of and relationships with politics, and affecting how political parties communicate and interact with the public. They are also raising questions about the place of corporations in politics as well as renewing how political institutions connect with constituents. In the case of social media, we are witnessing a transformation of political communication practices. As noted by Andrew Chadwick, "at stake is whether we are living through a time of fundamental change in the nature of political life as a result of the disrupting influence of digital communication" (2013, 3).

How should we conceptualize this disrupting influence? First, these practices are part of an axis of internet-based and internet-supported actions (Van Laer and Van Aelst 2010). This distinction is central to digital media's shaping effects on traditional, or more conventional, action repertoires, such as petitions, street demonstrations, strikes, or other forms of protest. Van Laer and Van Aelst's typology emphasizes the internet's *creative function* and how it can expand the "action toolkit" (1148). Their focus is on social movements, whereas the interest in this volume is much broader, including civil society members, politicians, political parties, and political institutions. This expansion of the action toolkit is captured well by Thomas Poell in Chapter 6. He documents how protesters used smartphones to document what was happening – especially regarding police work – during the 2010 G20 summit in Toronto. They then turned to Twitter, Facebook, Flickr, and YouTube to voice their discontent and to offer a counterdiscourse to the coverage of events by elite media organizations. Blogs and nonmainstream media news sites also provided accounts of the protests. Poell illustrates how, for a moment, these practices of communication blurred the boundaries among local, national, and global settings. These new tools are broadening the public sphere, no longer situated only in a national framework. In this context, protesters' and civil society members' practices and discourses must be understood in terms of what Poell calls "a transnational public sphere."

Since deliberations can take place in multiple settings and on multiple platforms, questions are raised not only about *where* social media protest takes place but also about *what* content is being communicated during social media protests. In his analysis, Poell breaks down a complex and multilayered ecosystem that is simultaneously local, national, and transnational. Through the use of various social media platforms with distinct functional capabilities, in many ways civil society members are adopting and, to some degree, reproducing communication practices similar to those of mainstream media. In other words, their activities in the social mediascape are informed by traditional means of acquiring and consuming information. Social media–based debates during events such as the Toronto G20 summit or the Quebec student strike, or during environmental protests such as those about pipelines from Alberta, took place in this hybrid media system fashioned by "the interactions among older and newer media logic – where logics are defined as technologies, genres, norms, behaviours and organizational forms – in the reflexively connected fields of media and politics" (Chadwick 2013, 3).

This hybridity is well documented in Chapters 2 and 3, which analyze how social media activity is intertwined with political events and mainstream media coverage, illustrating how mainstream media still play a pivotal role in the public sphere. This significant responsibility is also raised in Chapter 11, which considers news coverage of the Supreme Court and its use of social science evidence in Charter litigation. This trend is important but has not been picked up by media in their coverage. Since the use of social science evidence can affect the court's decision-making process, this relative silence raises questions about whether civil society is aware of this change. Considering the hybridity of media and digital practices, the trend is unlikely to be picked up by social media users, activists, and "citizen journalists."

Even with the emergence of an "ambient political engagement repertoire," discussed in Chapter 2, media coverage is still central in public conceptions of the world and has significant power in framing how civil society members, political actors, and corporations perceive and take on legal, social, and political questions. Borrowing journalistic-like practices says a lot about the enduring power of professional broadcasting organizations. As Chadwick argues, the power of political and media elites might have been disturbed by the emergence of digital media, more relational and based on cooperation and asymmetrical relationships, but their power remains significant:

> Grassroots activism fueled by newer media logic must be set in the context of the broad and continuing power of the political and media elites who have carved out reserved domains that enable them to control what are still the main vehicles for politics in a liberal democracy; organized parties, candidates' campaigns, and, of course, the extremely powerful, and increasingly renewed, mass medium of television. (2013, 208)

As demonstrated by contributors to this volume, these digital tools are not replacing other means of communication. They are intertwined in various ways.

Social media sometimes allow for the emergence of internet-based practices that otherwise would not have taken this form or this level of prominence. In some cases, the practices look new, but they are borrowing from existing repertoires. For example, political internet memes can often look like signs and posters used during public protests. Their catchiness has a slogan-like facet. Public opinion research is undergoing major transformations. As documented in Chapter 10, traditional telephone surveys can be seen as out of date compared with the promises of market intelligence. As discussed in Chapter 9, data-driven campaigning can change political practices for all political parties. In an era of permanent campaigning (Marland, Giasson, and Esselment 2017), big data collection and analysis comprise an important trend.

TRENDING: TRANSFORMATIONS OF POLITICAL ENGAGEMENT AND DEMOCRATIC PRACTICES

Two of our questions require particular attention. How are these trends transforming political engagement and political action repertoires? And to what extent do these trends transform the relationships among political actors and institutions and democracy in general? First, because the changes documented in this volume are diverse and complex, their implications bring up different issues. Second, depending on a researcher's perspective on a trend, his or her answers to these questions vary greatly. Some authors adopt a pessimistic tone, whereas others are more optimistic about the potential of these trends to bring positive outcomes. Put together, several chapters in this volume allow us to consider how trends are affecting relationships with politics, renewing political engagement and political action repertoires. More importantly, they examine how these trends might be indirectly changing different facets of democracy in Canada.

When studying civil society practices, it is possible to see how the growth in user-generated digital media channels (e.g., Instagram, Snapchat, YouTube) has made possible communication, mobilization, and organization in ways not conceivable during the broadcast era of politics. These tools *facilitate* and *support* both online and offline action. They are transforming political action repertoires in various ways as new modes of action emerge. For instance, public criticism is simpler and faster through social media. The use of political internet memes, scrutinized in Chapter 5, is a good example of this trend. According to Adams Mills (2012, 162–69), four key factors for a successful viral campaign are spreadability, propagativity, integration, and nexus. All of these factors are at play when it comes to digital political memes. Their dissemination is achieved through social media tools such as Twitter, Facebook, Instagram, and websites dedicated to this phenomenon. Their viral potential resides in social media's highly networked structure, which facilitates the spreadability of content. In a matter of a few clicks, a message can be received by hundreds, thousands, even millions of people depending on the message's entertainment, engagement, and likeable value. Memes possess these characteristics. With a single image and a few words, they can tackle a topic with humour and wit, creating an emotional reaction and a connection with the audience. Moreover, the nexus factor is attained since these viral movements and moments do not necessarily stay in the social media space. They are frequently picked up by mainstream media, which offer a second breath to a movement and, by extension, enhance its virality.

The rise of social media as tools for communication, mobilization, and organization is simplifying political action. It is also giving a voice to new actors and, by extension, empowering them politically. Platforms such as Twitter, Facebook, and blogs that integrate videos are used by citizens and environmental groups to spread information, as discussed in Chapter 1. Activists selected, shared, and commented on news media content from various legacy media organizations. They acted as citizen journalists within their communities. Information sharing was also a key activity on Twitter during the Toronto G20 summit and the Quebec student strike, as illustrated in Chapter 6 as well as in Chapter 2. These journalistic-inspired practices on social media are making visible and framing protest and activist phenomena.

The picture is not all bright. Some chapters raise questions about the sustainability of these movements. As seen in the cases of the Quebec student strike and the G20 protests, the relevant hashtag eventually stops trending, public interest dissolves, and mainstream media organizations lose interest in the events. This is hardly surprising given that social media often foster connections between users for short periods of time. As noted by Thomas Poell and José Van Dijck (2015), social media platforms are designed by commercial interests to fulfill various objectives not necessarily aligned with needs related to political participation, including that of community formation. In this context, "the challenge[s] for activists [or politicians and institutions] is to profit from the affordances of social platforms while simultaneously gaining public attention for the fundamental issues at stake in contemporary protests, and to continue building communities around these issues" (535).

A need to reconceptualize political participation and engagement is alluded to in many of the chapters. The "how" and the "who" are two important aspects. Foremost, for the "how" aspect, the trend of online participation underlines the need to redefine political participation and engagement. For some, stand-alone online participation is sufficient. This is one of the findings in Chapter 1, whose authors determine that some supporters of environmental causes are active only online and see no need to be active offline. That was left to activist organizations. This can be seen as a form of "identity politics," which "broadly describes social movements that no longer require collective action reflexive of the interest of a social group – they revolve more around personal identity and sense-making of cultural information" (Papacharissi 2010, 40). This development in activism practices is often presented as a type of personalization of engagement. It suggests that "the individuals' own narratives rather than collective identity frames become important in activist mobilization and communication processes" (Poell and Van Dijck 2015, 532). In *The Logic of Connective Action: Digital Media and the Personalization of Contentious Politics*, Bennett and Segerberg (2013) offer a thorough analysis of this trend. They show that connective action gets traction with easy-to-personalize ideas such as "we are the 99 percent." Here the framework is outside traditional structures such as unions. The networks created, which have less hierarchical structures, are more flexible than conventional activist organizations.

This raises many questions. How can individual and collective action function together? How can we identify and study these fractured and more polarized publics? How should we think of and produce communication strategies that appeal to these individualized collectives? The case of meme creation is interesting in this respect. As argued by Paolo Gerbaudo (2015), memes are a tool to identify with protest movements. Meme creation in Canada can be viewed as a form of identity politics, such as when citizens created political internet memes to express their disapproval of Stephen Harper's Conservative government. Their discourse mirrored themes discussed in the public sphere. Memes can offer a sense of togetherness for their creators and audiences. Nevertheless, when looking at political meme creators through a more traditional lens of political participation, these activities can be easily linked, at first glance, to slacktivism. However, as shown in Chapter 5, meme creators demonstrated an impressively deep political knowledge and offered an informed look at ongoing political events surrounding Prime Minister Harper. This is just one form of low-threshold, internet-supported engagement. These findings suggest that it is a trend worthy of continued attention and study.

Meme creation is part of the expansion of political protest action repertoires that have minimal costs and risks. These repertoires can help to lower the barriers of engagement but raise questions about how their creators can or will connect to higher-threshold activities such as demonstrations or protest marches. In the context of trending practices, offline mobilization is still a challenge for all organizations and causes. Similar to the hybridity of media practices, e-participation is unlikely to overtake conventional political involvement, but it can supplement more conventional forms of engagement. This trend is not a radical transformation but a change layering onto and expanding political action repertoires.

In the case of the G20 protest in Toronto discussed in Chapter 6, activists contributed to the shaping of the political debate through Twitter. By reporting on-the-ground police violence during the summit, social media users made it publicly visible. By highlighting the illegitimate use of state power, they politicized the issue and helped to shape debates on state practices. However, activist work is not only about protests and debates. Some activist work is about publicizing issues, and social media represent good tools for doing so. However, they often foster more spectacular practices (e.g., "Twitter shaming") and an immediacy of response that could be at the expense of the message itself. From a broader perspective, it can be argued that civil society members are caught in the logic of digital media. This raises questions about the influence of these media channels on politicking practices. That said, a trend of interest not addressed in this volume is the growing traction of fake news – also known as "viral deception" – and its effect on different facets of the political process in different national contexts.[1] Fake news – defined as "news articles that are intentionally and verifiably false, and could mislead readers" – is credited with having played a role in shaping online political agendas and, by extension, public attitudes during electoral campaigns in several national contexts, including the United States and France (Allcott and Gentzkow 2017, 4; see also Tandoc, Lim, and Ling 2018). This should be studied in the years to come.

As interactions between older and newer media intensify, framing and controlling the debates are also issues raised by the uses of social media for political action. By exploring all posts with the phrase "Energy East" on Facebook, Twitter, Tumblr, and other digital media platforms, Patrick McCurdy and Jacob Groshek unpacked in Chapter 3 the advocacy dynamic of the environmental debate on tar/oil sands and pipeline construction. They highlighted that the phrase "tar sands" was often used negatively to frame the actions of Energy East. The #cdnpoli hashtag was frequently used, which helped to place the issue within matters related to Canadian politics. In a similar way, politicians also promote their messages on various political platforms, as illustrated in Chapters 7 and 8. Social media have been used to broadcast political messages to maximize visibility.

Several chapters discussed active citizens' practices of engagement. They documented the many ways in which civil society members are engaged. But what about the people who remain disconnected? On the "how" of participation, Chapter 4 filled an important gap in the academic literature by discussing Canadian youths' political engagement. To date, research on social media has been focused, for the most part, on political elites. By taking an interest in disengaged youth, Shelley Boulianne demonstrated the existence of a reinforcement/virtuous circle and mobilization/transformation process among younger adults. Some activities, such as sharing information and signing a petition, serve as predictors of a mobilization/transformation process.

As is the case for meme creation, these activities require relatively low effort and do not require offline engagement. Does this suggest that a revised vision of citizenship is in order? In light of these new practices, citizenship could be defined as "a representation of socio-political identity, which pertains specifically to how individuals relate to the administration of public affairs" (Papacharissi 2010, 84). It is not difficult to see how new practices of political engagement can implicate and possibly complicate a renewed understanding of citizenship. In particular, differences between those who use digital media for politicking and those who are not internet or digital media savvy can bring about a "democratic divide" (Norris 2001). This raises questions about how publics can be reached if in some cases social media actors are already preaching to the converted. This echo-chamber dynamic could be balanced by the engagement of "new" actors in these trending political engagement repertoires.

TRENDING: POLITICAL ELITES AND INSTITUTIONAL PRACTICES

With civil society members becoming increasingly active online, it is not surprising to see politicians and political parties turning to social media platforms not only to stay up to date on this trending factor but also to communicate, to mobilize voters and volunteers, and to raise money. In the case of political insiders in Canada, social media provide a way to bypass traditional media and other institutional filters in order to deliver messages directly to the public. The promises of social media have been framed as participatory democracy with the "broadest opinion formation," but the most recent evidence points to a more legalistic view of democracy, with these media tools maintaining and, in some cases, strengthening more traditional political processes (Van Dijk 2012, 106–8).

It appears that early optimism about social media transforming relations between politicians and citizens by bringing more two-way communication has receded. Research shows that politicians often use these platforms in more offline-inspired broadcast ways, such as sharing information with mass audiences (Graham, Jackson, and Broersma 2016; Vergeer, Hermans, and Sams 2013). Alongside Twitter (Giasson et al. 2013; Small 2014), a tool becoming increasingly important for Canadian politicians' campaigns is Instagram. Justin Trudeau and his team use it to cultivate both his and the Liberal Party's brands. The leaders of the other parties seem to be following the trend and have a heavier presence on this platform. Instagram was also abundantly used during the 2016 US presidential campaign. Internationally, many authors have looked at Facebook as a campaign tool, such as during the 2008 US presidential campaign (Bronstein 2013; Nielsen and Vaccari 2013). As Nigel Jackson and Darren Lilleker (2009) put it, parties have more of a "Web 1.5" style of communication during campaigns even when they use "Web 2.0" tools. Arguably, when it comes to the adoption of social media platforms, politicians and political parties are innovating at a slow pace.

Good news could be ahead. As demonstrated in Chapter 7, political parties are slowly modifying their uses of social media. They were more engaged in the 2012 Quebec campaign than in previous elections on Facebook. Nevertheless, these parties were more likely to post partisan content on Facebook than to discuss policy issues. Smaller parties, such as Québec solidaire and Option nationale, were more likely to stay "on message" when campaigning on these platforms. These parties often have difficulties getting the attention of mainstream media, and social media provide them with a different set of opportunities. First, they enable them to reach voters directly in relatively inexpensive ways. Second, they allow them to gain traditional media attention. These tools played an important role during the 2015 federal election in Canada when Green Party leader Elizabeth May tweeted during a televised leadership debate to which she had not been invited. This trend could gain traction in the next decade. As seen in the 2016 US election cycle, Donald Trump efficiently used social media to gain visibility in mainstream media and, in some cases, shape their election coverage through often incendiary statements and personal attacks against opponents of all political persuasions (Wells et al. 2016).

Research also shows that the stakes are different when it comes to incumbents and officeholders, as reflected in their discourses during elections (Borah 2014). When having to defend past actions and unpopular decisions, politicians and parties often frame their messages in positive ways. Consequently, they are more likely to use social media in ways different from opposing parties and aspiring candidates. Because the use of social media in campaigning is relatively new, research on their potentially transformative effects remains limited. To date, scholars have generally focused on party leaders, who have the most impact on the electoral process. That said, understanding how social media are potentially transforming the political lives and practices of other actors remains important. Chapter 8 of this volume takes a look at the impact of cabinet solidarity on the uses of social media by federal ministers in Canada. The case study unpacks some of the key dimensions of this trending practice. By focusing on Carolyn Bennett's tweeting before and after her elevation to cabinet, the authors compare her use of this social media platform and highlight differences in the behaviour of a backbencher on the one hand and a cabinet minister on the other. As an opposition party backbencher, Bennett was more aggressive and pleading in her tweets, whereas as a cabinet minister she has tailored her tweeting to respect principles of cabinet solidarity. In this regard, digital media use has not changed how Canadian politics is done, for Bennett adapted her tweeting style to the demands of her new position. The cabinet conventions of Canada's tightly controlled style of Westminster government remain in place.

Political parties are also adopting data-driven campaigning in order to win elections. This comes with challenges for party organizers, as noted in Chapter 9. The authors show that campaigning practices in Canada are less structured than those in the United States. Political parties are using a range of instruments to tackle data-driven campaign challenges, including building voter databases, building systems of active (e.g., surveys, polls, fundraising) and passive (e.g., websites, email opening rates) feedback, and developing analytical techniques to predict voter behaviour. Email lists and messages are carefully crafted to reach and appeal to small audiences. Not surprisingly, money as well as parties and political logic affect the adoption of data-collecting tools. Because parties cannot afford to develop their own software, commercial products that come with lower price points are most frequently selected. This trend could gain even more traction if parties can overcome the financial barriers related to technology acquisition and staff professionalization in order to leverage the potential of data-driven campaign tools.

Practices of mass data collection are also raising questions about voter information privacy. Some of these issues are addressed indirectly in Chapter 10. New technological developments and analytical techniques now offer the possibility to monitor individual behaviour in real time. What are the rights of citizens and groups under these conditions of constant surveillance? Market intelligence and surveillance are undoubtedly transforming the work of public opinion researchers, who have to develop new skills and tools in order to understand and deal with massive volumes of data. It is also reconfiguring how citizens are perceived. They are now individuals who can be tracked through research based on their behaviour. If the business world is fertilizing politics, then where is this likely to lead us? If surveys give a voice to citizens, then have citizens become voiceless if their online behaviours are scrutinized surreptitiously? Data-driven campaigning and market intelligence trends are likely to change the role of political strategists and the approaches to politicking. If they have the means to analyze and process data, then this could lead to better micro-targeting techniques. It could allow parties with adequate financial resources to gain a considerable campaign advantage over others. Moreover, political communication strategies can be adapted to give preference to highly personalized and targeted messages.

TRENDING: ENGAGING CITIZENS IN GOVERNMENT DECISIONS

Following trends in digital media adoption, government institutions are turning to the internet in order to inform, interact with, and mobilize citizens. These initiatives also highlight challenges posed by the reconfiguration of democratic practices. How can all segments of the population be reached? How can these processes be inclusive? These questions are considered in the analysis of social acceptability in Chapter 12. These consultations allow managers and leaders to act as negotiators mandated to adapt projects to the values and expectations of citizen stakeholders. The chapter shows that a diversity of voices and groups of citizens can be engaged by making different consultation mechanisms available (e.g., online platforms, roundtables, workshops). The presence of professional moderators during a Citizen Day produced high-quality participation, appreciated by elected officials open to receiving citizen feedback on the project under review. This type of engagement can transform contemporary democratic practices, which could take a more participatory approach. Adopting such practices can help to prevent protests, which can lead to projects being abandoned. Admittedly, however, it is a labour-intensive approach, taking both time and money, which can create its own delays and hurdles.

This openness to citizens' participation could profoundly change government practices. In other words, this is the appearance of a potential paradigm shift. In the case of these consultations, we might be witnessing an important reshaping of the relationship between members of civil society and political institutions. Giving a primary and more active role to citizens, or "lay citizens" in the case in Chapter 12, moves the perspective away from representative democracy in which citizens are involved through more conventional channels of civic engagement such as voting. The representative function of elected officials might be challenged if more citizens are involved in the decision-making process.

TRENDING: CORPORATE TACTICS

Corporations are no strangers to the trending tactics that have been taken up by members of civil society. If digital media are used as venues for political action by citizens, they can also be used by corporations. If they can serve as channels to promote accommodation and openness in the case of social acceptability consultations, they can equally be adopted to serve more questionable practices. An interesting ethical question is brought to light in Chapter 3, which reveals that TransCanada has engaged in astroturfing-like practices. In this case, the uses of social media, coupled with the creation of "grassroots websites" and email blasts, were designed to mirror those of civil society but to serve the corporation's interests. The different chapters suggest that connective activity starts not only from the grassroots but also from the top, where organizations with more money and, by extension, more political communication power are leveraging these tools to serve their interests. This raises questions about the regulation of digital media practices, including the importance of monitoring corporations' tactics by mapping and understanding the corporate repertoire of digital astroturfing.

Astroturfing looks like an understudied and emerging field of investigation. To our knowledge, only one book has been dedicated to the subject and was published in French (Boulay 2015). Since astroturfing can be used as a "tool for promoting and reinforcing ideological positions" (Reader

2005, 45), it can influence citizens' understanding of issues. By usurping citizen identity, this phenomenon has potentially detrimental effects on democracy. It could affect the credibility of messages and modify the power relations in favour of corporations and wealthy political groups (Boulay 2015). Media education and critique could comprise a way to circumvent these disruptive repercussions for the political system.

Another important aspect of trends needs to be addressed: the corporatization of public debates and democratic practices. Most digital media platforms studied by the contributors to this volume are owned by corporations whose goal is not necessarily to foster public participation and animate political communication practices. As Poell and van Dijck (2015, 528) argue,

> through technological features, such as "retweeting," "liking," "following," and "friending," as well as algorithmic selection mechanisms, which privilege particular types of content, social platforms shape how users can interact with each other through these platforms. These forms of technological shaping do not necessarily correspond with user interests, let alone with activist interests, but are first and foremost informed by the business models of social media corporations.

Social media are aimed at targeting advertisements and services – often in the realm of politics – to specific segments of the population (Kruikemeier, Sezgin, and Boerman 2016). As noted in Chapter 6, with the rise of social media, activists and grassroots movements are less dependent on mainstream/legacy media to communicate their messages and reach large audiences. This newly gained autonomy does not mean that they are completely free, however. The power is now in the hands of a different category of media players: social media corporations. It will be interesting to see how their for-profit character affects mobilization and engagement in the coming years. The vitality of the public sphere also lies in the hands of alternative media, as illustrated in Chapter 6. It is crucial that they keep their place in the media ecosystem. Mainstream media corporations are also adapting themselves to a complex media environment of dissolving and dispersed audiences and acute financial pressures. This environment places them in a position where the for-profit reality of their business models becomes central to their decision making. Furthermore, the activities of citizens, activists, protesters, politicians, political parties, and institutions in the social mediascape are generating large volumes of data that overrun the reporting capacity of mass media. In this context, it is possible to question the readiness and ability of legacy media organizations to deal with this wealth of data as newsrooms and reporting practices are also undergoing transformations (Felle 2016; Solop and Wonders 2016). Also, as mentioned, how are the dynamics of fake news as well as online bots, propaganda, and viral deceit affecting this dynamic (McKelvey and Dubois 2017)?

TRENDING: RESEARCH CHALLENGES

With all of this in mind, we are faced with the following question: What are the consequences of trends for the study of Canadian politics? The challenges of studying trends are undoubtedly vast since researchers must try to stay up to date on the different transformations that they are studying. Multiple methodological approaches will be needed in order to grasp the complexities of phenomena and to analyze the different data that they bring to research projects. The contributors to this volume turned to a wide range of sampling and analysis methodologies to answer the questions raised by the trends studied. For example, a big data approach was used in both Chapter 3 and Chapter 7 to grasp the communication practices of tar/oil sands debaters and those of the Quebec political parties during the 2012 provincial election, respectively. Quantitative and more qualitative interpretive methods were also used by many authors to offer portraits of the different social media practices of citizens, political parties, and politicians. Surveys were useful in Chapter 4 for understanding the different activities of potentially politically disengaged youth, whereas interviews were useful in Chapters 9 and 10 to understand practices of data collection by parties and new survey methods of companies. Interviews were also used in Chapter 12 to grasp the complexities of processes of social acceptability. The authors also turned to field observation as well as analysis of institutional documents and other online materials to complete their case study. Software is often put to great use in order to grasp the complexity of the abundant volume of material. Automated textual analysis was used in Chapter 7 to identify the topics and the tones of the large quantity of messages studied. Specific programs such as Lexicoder helped the authors to identify sentiments in the Facebook posts. This software was also useful in Chapter 11 for understanding how mainstream media organizations covered the practices of the Supreme Court. The diversity of research practices highlights the need to adopt different theoretical and methodological approaches for the study of trends.

We are convinced that if the researchers of this volume (and researchers in general) were given more time and money they would want to do more with their data in order to document, analyze, and better understand how trends are transforming our lives – including day-to-day activities such as texting, going to work, shopping, teaching, consuming media, protesting, and voting – and ultimately shaping how we see the world. Some might argue that some of the case studies explored here are "old" in the world of trends. However, the authors all displayed how their case studies raise new questions that will continue to build on this trending research.

To understand these trends, more comparative research is needed; to facilitate this type of research, tools need to be developed, systematized, and shared. In particular, the growing trend of digital media brings with it an increasing number of videos and images that will require analysis. Images and videos also have a higher "virality" component, as illustrated in Chapters 5 and 7. These challenges will vary by platform. Whereas the content of Facebook, Instagram, or Twitter is "easily" archived, videos in other Web 2.0 tools, such as Snapchat, disappear after a certain amount of time. Academics need to develop new theoretical and methodological approaches to analyzing these new practices of political communication. As social media platforms become more popular and diversified, researchers will find themselves collecting, archiving, and analyzing ever-growing volumes of data. The software ASPIRA, created by the Groupe de recherche en communication politique, is one example of a research tool capable of tackling these challenges of big data collection. However, the challenge of keeping up to date with private companies' different algorithms and features remains.

The trend of online political activism and participation also raises the "who" question. In some cases, it is difficult when studying online platforms to know who "really" is the source of the message. This was the case for the political internet memes considered in this volume. Here the implications of anonymity are not as important as those of silence. As illustrated in Chapter 3, only a small fraction of Canadians were engaged in the online debate about the Energy East Pipeline, yet a huge number stood to be affected by the project. Many Canadians are still not on social media platforms, and only a minority is politically active on these platforms. Yet digital media are transforming political practice and behaviour in many ways. This is why it is crucial to unpack their dynamics and shed light on their social, cultural, political, and institutional implications. The emergence of new platforms on which citizens can debate and participate in the democratic process will continue to be an important research focus moving forward. Facebook is now an integral part of the daily lives of many citizens, and research shows that segments of the population are getting their information exclusively from this platform. As for the Twittersphere, it is where people turn when they want to express themselves about trending topics, and these topics are often political. Hashtags offer the chance to link individual conversations, helping to create a more collective discussion. Social media uses have also been studied in Canada and elsewhere (Boulianne 2015; Theocharis and Quintelier 2016; Vissers and Stolle 2014) in order to see their effects on citizen engagement and political practice. Some of the results tend to reinforce existing patterns of interest. Members of civil society already concerned and engaged show the most interest in online engagement practices. Mobilization could then be easier for this group.

CONCLUSION: TRENDS AND THE STATE OF CANADIAN DEMOCRACY

In the Introduction, we discussed the potential for trends to reconfigure, sometimes in a minor way and other times in a profound fashion, the dynamics of democratic life in Canada. Trends can alter how political science and political communication are thought about, researched, and understood. This volume has scrutinized trends in Canadian politics and highlighted what lies ahead in terms of political behaviour and communication. As indicated throughout this volume, political communication and behaviour in Canada have seen important changes in the past several years. These transformations are visible at various levels of governance – local, provincial, and federal – and can be linked to technological developments as well as to the adoption of new political practices. Two main categories of actors – political elites and members of civil society – are challenged by these trends, which have reshaping effects for the contemporary mass media environment, political empowerment, and conceptions of the public sphere.

Finally, it is not technologies themselves or new practices that are transforming democratic practices but the ways in which they are picked up, used, and sustained by civil society members, elites, and institutions. As Zizi Papacharissi (2010) underlines in *A Private Sphere: Democracy in a Digital Age,* democracy has a complicated relationship with technology. She adds that democracy is often treated as a static concept, but when we accept that democracy is a "negotiable abstraction" it becomes an "evolving and fluid" concept allowing us to consider "the public or media (dis-)engagement with the democratic system" (11). Following this line of thought, this volume offers a positive but realistic look at these trends and how they are transforming democratic life in Canada. Rather than adopting a kind of naive optimism about trends, we have pointed out several limitations. As the different chapters illustrate, the trends sometimes change political life for the better, sometimes challenge the status quo, and sometimes encourage/inspire/stimulate political parties, governments, public servants, courts, citizens, interest groups, and corporations to adapt their practices. Since these trends are changing politics in various ways, a theoretically interdisciplinary and multimethodological account is needed in order to unpack and shed light not only on the trends themselves but also on their different outcomes for Canadian political and civic life. By their nature, trends are not static, and this book is intended to start a conversation that should be useful for students, practitioners, and researchers who want to know more about the political world in which they live and work.

NOTE

1 For viral deception, see http://www.cnn.com/videos/tv/2017/03/05/new-name-for-fake-news-viral-deception.cnn.

REFERENCES

Allcott, Hunt, and Matthew Gentzkow. 2017. "Social Media and Fake News in the 2016 Election." *National Bureau of Economic Research.* https://www.aeaweb.org/full_issue.php?doi=10.1257/jep.31.2#page=213.

Bennett, W. Lance, and Alexandra Segerberg. 2013. *The Logic of Connective Action: Digital Media and the Personalization of Contentious Politics.* New York: Cambridge University Press.

Borah, Porismita. 2014. "Facebook Use in the 2012 Presidential Campaign: Obama vs. Romney." In *Social Media in Politics: Case Studies on the Political Power of Social Media,* edited by Bogdan Pătruț and Monica Pătruț, 201–11. New York: Springer International.

Boulay, Sophie. 2015. *Usurpation de l'identité citoyenne dans l'espace public: Astroturfing, communication, et démocratie.* Québec: Presses de l'Université du Québec.

Boulianne, Shelley. 2015. "Social Media Use and Participation: A Meta-Analysis of Current Research." *Information, Communication, and Society* 18, 5: 524–38.

Bronstein, Jenny. 2013. "Like Me! Analyzing the 2012 Presidential Candidates' Facebook Pages." *Online Information Review* 37, 2: 173–92.

Chadwick, Andrew. 2013. *The Hybrid Media System: Politics and Power.* Oxford: Oxford University Press.

Felle, Tom. 2016. "Digital Watchdogs? Data Reporting and the News Media's Traditional 'Fourth Estate' Function." *Journalism* 17, 1: 85–96.

Gerbaudo, Paolo. 2015. "Protest Avatars as Memetic Signifiers: Political Profile Pictures and the Construction of Collective Identity on Social Media in the 2011 Protest Wave." *Information, Communication, and Society* 18, 8: 916–29.

Giasson, Thierry, Gildas Le Bars, Frédérick Bastien, and Mélanie Verville. 2013. "#Qc2012: L'utilisation de Twitter par les partis politiques." In *Les Québécois aux urnes: Les partis, les médias, et les citoyens et campagne,* edited by F. Bastien, É. Bélanger, and F. Gélineau, 135–48. Montréal: Les Presses de l'Université de Montréal.

Graham, Todd, Dan Jackson, and Marcel Broersma. 2016. "New Platform, Old Habits? Candidates' Use of Twitter during the 2010 British and Dutch General Election Campaigns." *New Media and Society* 18, 5: 765–83.

Jackson, Nigel, and Darren Lilleker. 2009. "Building and Architecture of Participation? Political Parties and Web 2.0 in Britain." *Journal of Information Technology and Politics* 6, 3–4: 232–50.

Kruikemeier, Sanne, Minem Sezgin, and Sophie C. Boerman. 2016. "Political Microtargeting: Relationship between Personalized Advertising on Facebook and Voters' Responses." *Cyberpsychology, Behavior, and Social Networking* 19, 6: 367–72.

Marland, Alex, Thierry Giasson, and Anna Esselment, eds. 2017. *Permanent Campaigning in Canada.* Vancouver: UBC Press.

McKelvey, Fenwick, and Elizabeth Dubois. 2017. "Computational Propaganda in Canada: The Use of Political Bots." *The Computational Propaganda Research Project.* http://comprop.oii.ox.ac.uk/wp-content/uploads/sites/89/2017/06/Comprop-Canada.pdf.

Mills, Adams J. 2012. "Virality in Social Media: The SPIN Framework." *Journal of Public Affairs* 12, 2: 162–69.

Nielsen, Rasmus Kleis, and Cristian Vaccari. 2013. "Do People 'Like' Politicians on Facebook? Not Really. Large-Scale Direct Candidate-to-Voter Online Communication as an Outlier Phenomenon." *International Journal of Communication* 7, 1: 2333–56.

Norris, Pippa. 2001. *Digital Divide: Civic Engagement, Information Poverty, and the Internet Worldwide.* Cambridge, UK: Cambridge University Press.

Papacharissi, Zizi A. 2010. *A Private Sphere: Democracy in a Digital Age.* Cambridge, UK: Polity.

Poell, Thomas, and José van Dijck. 2015. "Social Media and Activist Communication." In *The Routledge Companion to Alternative and Community Media,* edited by Chris Atton, 527–37. London: Routledge.

Reader, Bill. 2005. "Who's Really Writing Those 'Canned' Letters to the Editor?" *Newspaper Research Journal* 26, 2–3: 43–56.

Small, Tamara. 2014. "The Not-So Social Network: The Use of Twitter by Canada's Party Leaders." In *Political Communication in Canada: Meet the Press and Tweet the Rest,* edited by Alex Marland, Thierry Giasson, and Tamara Small, 92–110. Vancouver: UBC Press.

Solop, Frederic I., and Nancy A. Wonders. 2016. "Data Journalism versus Traditional Journalism in Election Reporting: An Analysis of Competing Narratives in the 2012 Presidential Election." *Electronic News* 10, 4: 203–23.

Tandoc, Edson C., Jr., Zheng Wei Lim, and Richard Ling. 2018. "Defining 'Fake News': A Typology of Scholarly Definitions." *Digital Journalism* 6, 2: 137–53.

Theocharis, Yannis, and Ellen Quintelier. 2016. "Stimulating Citizenship or Expanding Entertainment? The Effect of Facebook on Adolescent Participation." *New Media and Society* 18, 5: 817–36.

Van Dijk, Jan. 2012. *The Network Society Third Edition.* London: Sage.

Van Laer, Jeroen, and Peter Van Aelst. 2010. "Internet and Social Movement Action Repertoires: Opportunities and Limitations." *Information, Communication, and Society* 13, 8: 1146–71.

Vergeer, Maurice, Liesbeth Hermans, and Steven Sams. 2013. "Online Social Networks and Micro-Blogging in Political Campaigning: The Exploration of a New Campaign Tool and a New Campaign Style." *Party Politics* 19, 3: 477–501.

Vissers, Sara, and Dietlind Stolle. 2014. "Spill-Over Effects between Facebook and On/Offline Political Participation? Evidence from a Two-Wave Panel Study." *Journal of Information Technology and Politics* 11, 3: 259–75.

Wells, Chris, et al. 2016. "How Trump Drove Coverage to the Nomination: Hybrid Media Campaigning." *Political Communication* 33, 4: 669–76.

Contributors

MYRIAM ARBOUR has worked on the factors contributing to social acceptability and on public participation initiatives. Under the supervision of Stéphanie Yates, she was responsible for the fieldwork for the research project Social Acceptability of Large-Scale Projects: Identification of Good Practices and Proposition of a Dialogical Model, supported by the Fonds de recherche du Québec – Société et culture. She is also the co-author of several contributions in relation to this project.

SHELLEY BOULIANNE is an associate professor of sociology at MacEwan University. She completed her PhD in sociology at the University of Wisconsin–Madison. Her research focuses on media use and civic and political engagement as well as survey research methodology. She conducts research on media use and public opinion, as well as civic and political engagement, using meta-analysis techniques, experiments, and surveys.

ERIN CRANDALL is an assistant professor in the Department of Politics at Acadia University. She researches Canadian politics, courts, and constitutional law. Her work has appeared in the *Canadian Journal of Political Science, Canadian Journal of Women and the Law,* and *Canadian Public Administration,* among others.

MARK DAKU is an assistant professor of political science at Texas Christian University. He researches data science, the politics of health, and African politics. His work has appeared in *Communication Research, Social*

Science and Medicine, and *Journal of Comparative Policy Research*, among others.

YANNICK DUFRESNE is an assistant professor of political science at Université Laval and Leadership Chair in the Teaching of Digital Social Sciences. He specializes in the study of public opinion, political communication, and elections. His research has been published in various journals, such as *Political Analysis, British Journal of Political Science, International Journal of Forecasting,* and *Journal of Elections, Public Opinion, and Parties*.

THIERRY GIASSON is a professor of political science at Université Laval in Quebec City. He is the director of the Groupe de recherche en communication politique and a member of the Centre for the Study of Democratic Citizenship. His research focuses on political journalism, online politics, and the effects of political communication and marketing practices on electoral campaigns and political participation. He is a co-editor of the series Communication, Strategy, and Politics at UBC Press. His work has been published in the *Canadian Journal of Political Science, Canadian Journal of Communication,* and *Journal of Public Affairs*.

JACOB GROSHEK is an associate professor of emerging media studies at Boston University. Topically, his areas of expertise are online and mobile media technologies since their use can relate to sociopolitical and behavioural health change at the macro (i.e., national) and micro (i.e., individual) levels. His work includes analyses of media content and user influence in social media.

MIREILLE LALANCETTE is a professor of political communication at Université du Québec à Trois-Rivières. She has published on the construction of the mediatized image of politicians, gender, and representation and on the use and impact of social media by citizens, grassroots organizations, and political actors in Canadian and international research publications in French and English. She is the primary investigator on the SSHRC project called "Uses of Social Media during Contested Projects Raising Social Acceptability Issues." Researcher for the Groupe de recherche en communication politique, she is also the author of *ABC de l'argumentation pour les professionnels de la santé ou toute autre personne qui souhaite convaincre* (with Marie-Josée Drolet and Marie-Ève Caty) and the editor (with Pierre Leroux and François Hourmant) of *Selfies and Stars: Politique et culture de la célébrité en France et en Amérique du Nord.*

GUILLAUME LATZKO-TOTH is an associate professor of communication and digital media at Laval University (Quebec City), where he is also the associate dean for research creation and graduate studies in the Faculty of Humanities. He is a founding member and co-director of the Laboratory for Communication and the Digital and a member of the Interuniversity Center for Research on Science and Technology. His research and publications address users' contributions to the development of digital media; the role of artifacts in digitally supported communities; and methodological and ethical issues related to research in digital contexts.

PATRICK MCCURDY is a professor in the Department of Communication at the University of Ottawa. His research draws from environmental communication, media theory, and social movement studies to examine media as a site and source of social struggle and contestation. His current research examines the mediated debate on Canada's oil/tar sands with an interest in the evolution of advertising for and campaigning on Alberta's oil/tar sands from 1970 to the present. His work has been published in several academic journals, and he is the co-author of *Protest Camps* (2013) and the co-editor of three books: *Protest Camps in International Context: Spaces, Infrastructures, and Media of Resistance* (2017), *Beyond WikiLeaks: Implications for the Future of Communications, Journalism, and Society* (2013), and *Mediation and Protest Movements* (2013).

FENWICK MCKELVEY is an associate professor in information and communication technology policy in the Department of Communication Studies at Concordia University. He studies digital politics and policy. He is the author of *Internet Daemons: Digital Communications Possessed* (2018) and a co-author, with Greg Elmer and Ganaële Langlois, of *The Permanent Campaign: New Media, New Politics* (2012).

FLORENCE MILLERAND is a professor in the Department of Social and Public Communication at Université du Québec à Montréal. She holds the Research Chair on Digital Technology Uses and Changes in Communication. She is also a co-director of the Laboratory for Communication and the Digital and a member of the Interuniversity Center for Research on Science and Technology. Her research focuses on the study of social changes associated with the rise of digital media and technologies.

JILL PIEBIAK has many years of experience in political and issue-based digital campaigning in Canada and the United States. In 2015, she led the online campaign #NoTaxOnTampons to end the unfair tax practice of imposing GST on menstrual hygiene products. In less than a year, 85,000 online signatures led to the removal of GST. She also served as the deputy director of digital for BC NDP's successful 2017 provincial election campaign. Currently, she is the digital strategist for a Canadian federal public sector union bringing online tools and techniques to the labour movement. She has a master's degree in media studies from Concordia University.

MAXIME PRONOVOST serves as the coordinator for MICRO, a franco-Ontarian community radio organization. His areas of research interest and publication while completing his master's degree at Université du Québec à Trois-Rivières included internet memes and transformations in citizen political engagement. He is also interested in Canadian political actors, grassroots organizations, and social media.

KATE PUDDISTER is an assistant professor in the Department of Political Science at the University of Guelph. She researches law and politics, Canadian politics, and criminal justice policy. Her work has appeared in *Publius: The Journal of Federalism, Canadian Journal of Law and Society,* and *Canadian Public Administration.*

VINCENT RAYNAULD is an assistant professor in the Department of Communication Studies at Emerson College (Boston) and an affiliate professor in the Département de lettres et communication sociale at Université du Québec à Trois-Rivières. He is also serving as a research associate in the Groupe de recherche en communication politique in Canada. His areas of research interest and publication include political communication, social media, research methods, e-politics, and journalism. His interdisciplinary work has appeared in English- and French-language peer-reviewed publications, including *Information, Communication, and Society, Journal of Information Technology and Politics, Politique et sociétés, French Politics,* and *American Behavioral Scientist.*

TAMARA A. SMALL is an associate professor in the Department of Political Science at the University of Guelph. Her research interest is digital politics: the use and impact of digital technologies by Canadian political actors. She is a co-author of *Fighting for Votes: Parties, the Media, and Voters in an Ontario Election* (UBC Press) and a co-editor of *Political Communication in Canada: Meet the Press, Tweet the Rest* (UBC Press) and *Mind the Gaps: Canadian Perspectives on Gender and Politics* (Fernwood). She is the primary investigator on the SSHRC project called "Digital Campaigning in Canada: A Comparative Study." She held the Fulbright Visiting Research Chair at Vanderbilt University in 2018.

MICKAEL TEMPORÃO is a PhD candidate in the Department of Political Science at the Université Laval and a Mitacs Accelerate Fellow. His research focus is on the measurement of public opinion using digital traces. His research has been published in various academic journals, such as *Political Analysis, International Journal of Forecasting,* and *Nations and Nationalism.*

GHADA TOUIR is a part-time professor in the Department of Communication Studies and the School of Community and Public Affairs at Concordia University in Montreal. She is an affiliated researcher with the Centre de recherche en éducation et formation relatives à l'environnement et à l'écocitoyenneté. Her research examines civic engagement and citizen participation in environmental issues and social media.

SOFIA TOURIGNY-KONÉ has pursued her doctoral studies in communication at the Université du Québec à Trois-Rivières. Her research interests include social media, feminism, and activism. Her work led her to turn her attention to women's rights and advocacy projects. She has published in *Revue approaches inductives* and *French Politics.*

ANDRÉ TURCOTTE is an associate professor in Carleton University's School of Journalism and Communication as well as in the Riddell Graduate Program in Political Management. His areas of research focus on political marketing, public opinion research, and electoral behaviour. Over the years, he has also provided public opinion research advice to politicians at all levels of government in Canada as well as to many of Canada's leading private sector firms and government organizations.

STÉPHANIE YATES is a professor in the Département de communication sociale et publique at the Université du Québec à Montréal. Her work focuses on lobbying and, more precisely, on interest groups' and citizens' roles in the governance of states and businesses. From this perspective, she studies public relations and mediatization strategies put forward by public and private actors in controversies that raise social acceptability issues. She also studies public participation initiatives that aim to foster a dialogue between stakeholders. Using an interdisciplinary approach, she has published several articles and chapters in communication, political science, environmental, and management publications. She is also the editor of *Introduction aux relations publiques: Fondements, enjeux, et pratiques* (2018).

Index

Note: "(f)" following a number indicates a figure; "(t)" following a number indicates a table

1984 (Orwell), 216, 229

action/activism: ambient digital political engagement and, 57; collective vs connective, 26; connective, 26, 282; connective leadership in, 58–59; continuing power of political/media elites vs grassroots, 279; by corporations, 289–91; digital platforms, 33; expansion of repertoires, 283; expansion of toolkit, 278; hybridization of repertoires, 8; internet, 112, 121; nature of activists in social media campaigning, 78; online advocacy groups/movements and, 36; political memes and, 120–21, 122–23; social media and, 10, 33, 281; social media and grassroots, 78–79; technological change and redefinition of repertoires, 12–13; transnational, 130; youth and, 9, 11, 12. *See also* protests; slacktivism

activist communication: and accountability for state violence, 141–42; alternative vs social media in, 140; and boundaries among local/national/transnational, 136; changing topology of, 127–28; content/"what" of, 140–41; distribution modes, 136; division of labour within, 136; geographic location/"where" of, 134–36, 140–41; mainstream vs social media in, 140; and public sphere, 140–41; social media, 136, 138–39, 140–42; solidarity/togetherness in, 138–39; spectacle/violence in, 138

Adobe, 224, 226, 228
AggregateIQ, 194, 207
Ambrose, Rona, 174
Anti-Spam Act, 208
Arab Spring uprisings, 4, 153
Arbour, Myriam, 14
Arnold, Dan, 223
Askov, R v, 251
ASPIRA, 152, 154, 292
astroturfing, 71, 80, 289–90
automated textual analysis, 154–55, 291–92

backbench MPs: and cabinet solidarity, 171, 177; and social media, 186; and Twitter, 171, 175, 177–86, 287
Bains, Navdeep, 194
Baird, John, 174

Baldwin-Philippi, Jessica, 202
Bastedo, Heather, *Canadian Democracy from the Ground Up: Perceptions and Performance*, 7
Becker, Howard S., 39n2
Bedford, Canada (Attorney General) v, 238, 253n1
Bennett, Carolyn: attack tweets, 178, 179, 183; audience for tweets, 185; broadcasting vs conversing in tweets, 186-87; broadcasting tweets, 178, 179; as cabinet minister vs backbencher, 177-86, 287; government program tweets, 187; history as politician, 175-76; impact of cabinet solidarity on approach, 185-86, 187-88; as opposition MP, 179; personal tweets, 178, 179, 183-85; portfolio tweets, 178, 180-81, 182-83, 186-87; pride in team, 184-85; social tweets, 178, 179, 182-83, 186; tweeting practices, 11; volume of Twitter use, 176-77, 179, 180
Bennett, W. Lance, 37, 38, 107, 109; *The Logic of Connective Action*, 282
BHIVE, 76
Biden, Joe, 108
big data: collecting/archiving/analyzing ever-growing volumes, 292; and data-driven campaigning, 196-97; in debates over tar/oil sands, 291; defined, 217; impact of, 217, 232; marriage with polling, 223; Obama campaign and, 223; political parties and, 291; and public opinion research, 217; in Quebec 2012 election, 291; and surveillance, 217
Bimber, Bruce, 10
bitumen, 66, 67, 69
Black, Edwin, 195, 211-12
Bode, Leticia, 76
Borah, Porismita, 152
Borra, Erik, 65
Boulay, Sophie, 289
Boulianne, Shelley, 11, 284
Bric à bacs, 30(t), 35
BuiltWith.com, 198
Bureau-Blouin, Léo, 166n3

Bush, George W., campaign microtargeting, 199
Butts, Gerald, 187

cabinet government, 175, 189
cabinet ministers: and cabinet solidarity, 170, 171, 187-88; image management, 189; political objectives, 186; and social media, 176, 186; and Twitter, 170-71, 173, 175, 177-86, 189, 287
cabinet solidarity: about, 170; backbench MPs and, 177; cabinet control, 287; cabinet ministers and, 170, 171, 187-88; of cabinet ministers vs backbench MPs, 171; and message control, 172; open public dialogue vs, 175; pride in teamwork and, 185, 187-88; social media and, 11, 173, 185-86, 287; Twitter and, 170-71, 173, 180-81, 183, 187-88, 189
Callison, Candis, 45
Cambridge Analytica, 194, 207
CampaignTech, 197
Canada Action, 75
Canada (Attorney General) v Bedford, 238, 253n1
Canada (Attorney General) v PHS Community Services Society, 238, 239
Canadian Alliance, and market intelligence, 220
Canadian Association of Petroleum Producers (CAPP), 67
Canadian Democracy from the Ground Up: Perceptions and Performance (Gidengil/Bastedo), 7
Canadian Facts, 219
candidates. *See* political candidates
CAQ. *See* Coalition avenir Québec (CAQ)
Carter, Kay, 242
Carter v Canada (Attorney General), 238, 239, 242-43, 244, 246-48, 252
Casino of Montreal, 258
Castells, Manuel, 129
Castleden, Heather, 66
CBC Television, *Royal Canadian Air Farce*, 119

CEFRIO (Centre facilitant la recherche et l'innovation dans les organisations), 47
centralization of government, 116, 172, 189
Chadwick, Andrew, 65, 79, 88, 278, 279
Chantier sur l'acceptabilité sociale, 258
Charest, Jean, 48, 153, 249
Charter of Rights and Freedoms: and governance, 252; impact of, 237; and media coverage of Supreme Court, 238; and mediatization, 238; and policy making, 237, 252; Section 7, 238–39, 241, 242; and social science evidence, 238–39, 243, 249, 252, 279; and Supreme Court, 237, 252
CIMS, 202, 204, 205
citizen consultations/participation: array of mechanisms, 270–71; Citizen Day, 262–65, 270, 288; citizen informants/reporters, 32; contestation vs, 269, 272–73; and democracy, 269, 288–89; diversity of population groups reached, 263; efficiency of mechanisms of, 260; elected officials' openness to, 269; elitist model vs, 269; emergence of best practices in, 269; experts in, 266; gender in, 263; government authorities as arbitrators, 271–72; and government authorities' decision making, 272–73; government authorities' roles/responsibilities in, 260–61; inclusiveness vs quality of deliberation in, 260; on infrastructure projects, 14; instrumental point of view, 271; interaction among participants, 266; as lay vs expert knowledge, 270, 271; leaders' influence in, 266–67; legitimacy of, 271; legitimacy of decision to implement, 261; mechanisms, 263, 266, 288; moderators, 264–65, 271, 288; normative point of view, 271; online platform, 263, 265–66, 270; online surveys, 262; power dynamics and, 259; and protest prevention, 288–89; quality of, 264, 266, 288; questions/challenges regarding, 259, 260(f); rate of, 264; representativeness in, 259–60, 270; and social acceptability, 268, 272, 288; substantive point of view, 271; time/engagement requirement, 270; value of, 267–68, 269, 270; in Vision 2035, 262
Citoyen du monde J.D., 30(t)
Les citoyens au courant, 30(t), 35
civil society: citizen participation and, 289; digital media channels and, 280–81; revised definition of citizenship, 285; social media and communication practices of, 25; social media and political activity by, 10; social science evidence and, 279; trends and, 5, 13–14, 294
Clark, Lynn Schofield, 48, 108–9, 112, 114
Clement, Tony, 173–74, 187, 189
clicktivism, 166
climate change: Energy East and, 69; oil sands and, 67
Clinton, Hillary, xii
cluster analysis, 196
Coalition avenir Québec (CAQ): in 2012 election, 156–61; and 2012 student protests, 153; Facebook use, 156–61
Coderre, Denis, 71
connective action, 26, 282
connective leadership, 58–59
Conservative Party: and CIMS, 202, 204, 205; custom database system, 202; as most integrated party, 205
Conservative Party (federal): and 2004 election, 220; and 2006 election, 221–22; cabinet ministers' Twitter use, 173–74; and censorship, 116; electronic record-keeping, 195; and Energy East project, 64; and gender parity, 117; identification of key voters, 221–22; and market intelligence, 220, 223; memes regarding, 110–11, 114, 121 (*see also* memes); message control, 188–89; muzzling cabinet ministers, 173; opinion research model, 220–21; and physician-assisted

death, 248; relations with China, 118; and Twitter, 188–89. *See also* Harper, Stephen
Conservative Party (Ontario), and CIMS, 205
Controlled Drugs and Substances Act, 239
corporations: campaigning, 80; media, 140, 279, 290; trends and tactics by, 289–91
Couillard, Philippe, 249
Couldry, Nick, 131
Coule pas chez nous, 25, 31
Crandall, Erin, 14
Crimson Hexagon, 69, 70, 75, 76, 78
Crossley, Archibald, 218
Cukier, Kenneth, 230
Cxense, 224, 226, 228–29

Dahl, Robert A., 15
The Daily Show, 122
Daku, Mark, 14
Dans ma cour, 30(t)
Danson v Ontario (Attorney General), 253n1
data analytics: Obama campaign and, 223; and polling, 14
data collection: access to information and, 210; costs and, 287; interviews regarding, 291; permanent campaigning and, 206; political parties and, 210, 287; and voter information privacy, 287–88
data management platforms (DMP): algorithm and, 225–26; and audience media consumption patterns, 228; audience segmentation, 226–27; campaign/audience analytics, 226, 227; consumer conversion, 227; and correlations vs causality, 217, 230; data analysis function, 226; data classification, 226; data collection, 226, 230; data storage, 225, 230; definition, 225; digital tagging, 226; direction of homebuyers, 228–29; and individual behaviour, 223–24, 227, 230, 231; numbers of firms, 224; and political behaviour, 229; and public opinion research, 218, 229–30; standards, 226; targeting, 226; uses of, 218
Data Sciences, 194
data storage: changing techniques, 195; DMP and, 225, 230
data-driven campaigning, 14–15; about, 194–95; accountability in, 209; advertising/marketing and, 196; and changing political practices, 280; and data collection/management, 206; and data flow, 205; and democracy, 211–12; diversity of tools used in, 202; and election wins, 201; and email campaigning, 201–2; funding, 204; hybridization in, 204; inequity in, 209–10; internet and, 196–97; interviews with practitioners, 198–99; and microtargeting, 288; microtargeting in, 202, 204; mixture of technologies in, 202; in parties' central vs local offices, 204–5; and permanent campaigning, 206, 209–10, 211, 280; as political logic, 194; political parties and, 280; privacy regulation and, 208–9; and professionalization of campaigns, 199; put to political ends, 211–12; and resource targeting, 201; and science vs instinct, 199–201; technological revolution and, xiii; in UK, 204; unevenness across parties, 205–6, 210–11; and voter privacy, 207–9; and voters' lists, 201; and winning elections, 287
Dawkins, Richard, *The Selfish Gene*, 106
Dean, Jodi, 131, 138
democracy: astroturfing and, 290; centralization of government power and, 172; citizen consultations and, 288–89; citizen participation and, 269; citizens' attitudes toward, 15; corporatization of practices within, 290; data-driven campaigning and, 211–12; deliberative process, 151; as evolving/fluid vs static, 294; participatory vs representative, 257; political participation and representation

in, 87; representative, 257, 289; and social acceptability, 257; social media and, 172, 285; technological revolution and, xi, xiv; technology and, 294; trends and, 15–16
Desjardins, Marlene, 166n3
Dewberry, David R., 107–8, 118
Dijck, José van, 6, 65, 290
Dow Jones Factiva, 243
Drupal, 202, 205
Dufour, Pascale, 44
Dufresne, Yannick, 11
Dutil, Patrick, xiv
Dying with Dignity Committee, 249

Earl, Jennifer, 134
ecocitizenship: citizen informants/reporters in, 32; defined, 25, 27; Energy East and, 69; and Facebook, 29; forms of, 26–27, 29; gender and, 13, 36–37; gender and mobilization around, 34–35; groups, 31, 32–34; increase in bottom-up participation/collective action, 27–28; initiatives, 25; and mobilization, 33; moderators, 32; platform technical characteristics/constraints and, 31; preference for online vs offline engagement, 34; purpose, 29, 31; Quebec online engagement in, 13; sharing practical information in, 33; social interactions in, 32–33; and social media, 25; Twitter and, 79; types of activities/engagement, 26–27, 32–34; volume of online activity, 31
Edelman (company), 71
Egyptian revolution, 135, 139
election campaigns: citizen-initiated, 195–96; data-driven (*see* data-driven campaigning); DMP and analytics, 226, 227; fake news in, 284; as less structured in Canada vs US, 287; pollster's role in, 222–23; public records of donations to, 210; social media and, 102; social media in, 286–87. *See also* data-driven campaigning

election candidates. *See* political candidates
elections: data, and winning of, 201; donation limits in, 209; market intelligence and winning vs losing, 221–22. *See also* United States; *and headings beginning* federal election
Elections Act, 208, 209
Energy East Pipeline, xi; about, 63–64, 68–69; astroturf campaign for, 71, 80, 289–90; crisis, 31; economics and, 63–64; as export pipeline, 69; hybridity of media used in protests, 279; international interest in, 77; numbers involved in debate regarding, 293; online activities around, 33–34; as political issue, 73; proponents vs critics' views on, 66; protests over, 13; as "tar sands" pipeline, 69
Energy East Pipeline on social media, 13, 69–78; corporate campaigning, 80; and environmental debate, 284; geographic location of activity, 79; nature of debate, 64; Twitter, 70, 73–76, 79; urban vs rural interest, 77–78, 79
engagement. *See* political engagement/participation
Ensemble contre les sables bitumineux (Together against Oil Sands), 30(t), 31, 34
environmental issues/activism. *See* ecocitizenship
Epstein, Ben, 76
European Commission, EU Fuel Quality Directive, 77
Eyereturn, 224

Facebook: in 2008 US presidential campaign, 286; about, 293; advertising, 149; Application Programming Interface, 154; automated content analysis, 160–62; automated textual analysis, 154–55; and civic participation, 90–91; Danish politician/citizen communication on, 165–66; differences across Western democracies in, 166; discrepancies in political party Facebook use, 163; and environmental citizen-based groups, 29; and environmental public policy issues, 27; "like" button, 162; media components, 160–62; numbers of friends on, 97(t), 100(t); numbers of members per group, 31; numbers of users, 149; and parties reaching specific voters, 165; partisan topics vs policy issues in, 157; and political communication, 163; political parties and, 149, 162–63, 286; in Quebec, 149; in Quebec 2012 election, 11, 152–66, 286; Quebec political parties and, 11, 152–66; small opposition vs large traditional parties in, 163–64; social program issues, 157; statistics on pages, 31; targeting in, 164–65; tone of messages in, 159–60; in US, 149–50, 158; US political parties and, 150; in US presidential election campaigns (2012), 152; user comments, 155–56, 159–60; user sociodemographics, 149; visual components, 164; youth accounts, 94–95

federal election (2006): blog use, 10; market intelligence and, 221–22; social media in, 172

federal election (2015): Liberals in, 194; social media in, 286; youth and, 87

federal election (1997), market intelligence in, 219

federal election (2004), market intelligence in, 220

federal election (2011), automated calling in, 207

Financial Post, 250(f)

Flanagan, Tom, 220

Fraser, Graham, 174

Fraser, Nancy, 128–29, 129–30

Free Trade Agreement with Central America and the Dominican Republic (CAFTA), 27

G20 summit protest communications: blogosphere in, 137; blogs/alternative news sites reporting, 135; content/ "what" of, 133, 136–38; contribution to democratic discourse, 130; event-oriented focus, 137; expansion of toolkit, 278; geographic location/ "where" of, 133; information sharing, 134, 281; lack of debate/conversation, 136–37; loss of original issues/ activities, 138; newspapers' use of social media, 136; police/security forces and, 134–35, 141–42, 278, 283; social media, 12, 45, 65, 134–35, 278, 279; solidarity/togetherness in, 138–39; Twitter use during, 283

G20 summit protests: about, 127; data collection, 132; and dissolution of interest/sustainability of movements, 281–82; end of, 139; freedom to document, 134–35

Gallup, George, 218, 219, 232; *The Pulse of Democracy: The Public Opinion Poll and How it Works*, 218

Gauja, Anika, 7

gender: Conservative government and, 117; and environmental issues, 13, 34–35, 36–37; in participation in Citizen Day consultation, 263; and social media, 37; Trudeau cabinet and, 120

Gerbaudo, Paolo, 109, 113, 283

Giasson, Thierry, 11, 157, 159, 221

Gidengil, Elisabeth, *Canadian Democracy from the Ground Up: Perceptions and Performance*, 7

Gilchrist, Emma, 201, 210–11

Global Climate March, Ottawa, 2015, 33

Globe and Mail, 243, 244, 250(f)

Gold, Raymond L., 262

Goldfarb, Martin, 196, 219

Google Analytics, 202

Google Real-Time Scraper, 132

governance: Charter and, 252; memes, 112, 113, 114–18, 114(t), 120; social acceptability and, 14

Graeff, Erhardt, 122–23

Greenberg, Josh, *The Surveillance Studies Reader*, 216–17

Greenpeace Canada, 71, 73, 75, 80

Greens (Quebec). *See* Parti vert du Québec

Gregg, Allan, 219
Groshek, Jacob, 13, 79, 284
Groupe de recherche en communication politique, 292
Gruzd, Anatoliy, 66

Habermas, Jürgen, 79, 129, 130; *Strukturwandel der Öffentlichkeit (Structural Transformation of the Public Sphere)*, 128
Hagen, Loni, 7
Harada, Susan, 240
Harper, Stephen: centralization of government, 116; and EU Fuel Quality Directive, 77; and McLachlin, 251; and media, 116; muzzling of cabinet, 173; and scientific community, 117; and Twitter, 174, 251; Twitter use, 173. *See also* Conservative Party (federal)
Harper memes, 13, 283; about, 110–11; creator knowledgeability in, 120; and dissent, 118, 121; governance, 112, 113, 114–18, 114(t); images used, 112–13, 114(t), 120; keywords, 111; personality, 112, 113, 114, 116, 118–19; policy, 115, 117–18, 121; relations with China, 118; rhetorical contents, 113, 114(t); society, 115; stock characters used in, 112, 117, 120; trolling and, 111–12; Pierre Elliott Trudeau in, 114(f), 116
Harperland (Martin), 115–16
Harris, Lou, 219
Hawking, Stephen, 117
Hermida, Alfred, 45, 47–48
Hersh, Eitan, 210
Hestres, Luis E., 66
Hier, Sean P., *The Surveillance Studies Reader*, 216–17
Hooghe, Marc, 15
Howard, Philip N., 48, 53, 57
Hudema, Mike, 73, 75
Huntington, Heidi E., 109
Hussain, Muzammil M., 48, 53, 57

identity politics, 282, 283
Idle No More, 4, 45
images/video: in Harper memes, 112–13, 114(t), 120; in social media campaigns, 150; virality of, 292
inequalities: in political participation, 89–90, 92; related to protests, 86; in use of social media, 78; among youth in political participation, 86
Infoscape Center for the Study of Social Media, 198
Instagram, 285–86
Institut du Nouveau Monde (INM), 262, 264, 267, 268
internet: activism, 112, 121; and citizen engagement, 35; creative function, 278; and data-driven campaigning, 196–97; expansion of action toolkit, 278; global information networks, 129; and real vs virtual action, 65; trolls/trolling, 111–12, 189
Invisible Children, *Kony 2012*, 109–10
Ion, Jacques, 36

Jackson, Nigel, 164, 286
Jean, Brian, 75–76
Jennings, Kent M., 9
Jordan, Gerard, 45

Karpf, David, 207
Kavada, Anastasia, 139
Kennedy, John F., 219
Kenney, Jason, 174, 187, 189
Keystone XL Pipeline, 64, 66, 68, 77
Khazraee, Emad, 46
Kinder Morgan, 68
Kligler-Vilenchik, Neta, 109–10, 121
Klout, 70, 76, 173
Kony 2012, 109–10
Kreiss, Daniel, 207

Lalancette, Mireille, 11, 12, 13
Lalanne, Michelle, 37
Lapeyre, Nathalie, 37
Lariscy, Ruthann Weaver, 151, 159
Latzko-Toth, Guillaume, 13
Laurier, Wilfrid, xiv
Lees-Marshment, Jennifer, 217, 221
legacy media. *See* mainstream media
Lewis, J.P., 11

Lexicoder, 154, 244, 292
Liberal Party (federal): in 2015 election, 194; and big data, 223; central analytics team, 204; data/digital infrastructure, 194; and Instagram, 285–86; and market intelligence, 223; as most integrated party, 205; and NGP VAN, 202, 205; "Personal and Partisan Use of Social Media by Ministers and Parliamentary Secretaries," 176; polling approach, 220; and social media, 176; and Trans Mountain Pipeline, 68; "uniting the right" and, 220
Liberal Party (Quebec). *See* Parti libéral du Québec (PLQ)
Lilleker, Darren, 164, 286
Logic of Connective Action: Digital Media and the Personalization of Contentious Politics, The (Bennett; Segerberg), 282
Losey, James, 46
Lotame, 224

MacKenzie, David, xiv
Maclean's: on Harper government and Twitter, 174
MailChimp, 198, 202
mainstream media: corporations, 290–91; data generation overrunning reporting capacity of, 291; local/national/transnational categories in, 136; political parties and, 286; in public sphere, 279; in Quebec student strike of 2012, 54–55, 56; and social media, 136, 141, 278–79, 286; social media and control of, 174
Manheim, Joseph, xii
Manning, Preston, 220
Maple Spring, xi, 153
market intelligence: about, 218; Conservatives and, 220, 223; evolution of polling to, 219–23, 229; Liberals and, 223; as market surveillance, 218; and microtargeting, 288; and political marketing, 221; politicians' uses of, 221; pollster's role in, 222–23; and public opinion research, 218, 223, 288; and segmentation, 221; telephone surveys vs, 280; and wedge issues, 222–23
market segmentation. *See* segmentation
Marland, Alex, 196, 221
Marres, Noortje, 130–31
Marshall, Hamish, 199, 204, 211
Martin, Lawrence, *Harperland*, 115–16
Martin, Paul, 175
Martens, Mike, 200, 209
mass media. *See* mainstream media
May, Elizabeth, 177, 286
Mayer-Schönberger, Viktor, 230
McCurdy, Patrick, 13, 69, 284
McKelvey, Fenwick, 14–15
McKibben, Bill, 63
McLachlin, Beverley, 251, 253n1
media: audience consumption patterns, 228; centrality of coverage, 279–80; and counterdiscourses, 128–29; coverage of physician-assisted death, 245–49; coverage of social science evidence, 245–49, 252, 253; coverage of Supreme Court, 245–49, 250(f), 251–52, 253; fake news, 284; Harper and, 116; hybridity, 278–79; national vs local, 252; and public sphere, 128; (re)shaping political communication, 128; and social science evidence, 239; symbolic contests on, 64–65
media corporations: power of, 279; social media and, 140, 279
members of Parliament (MPs): and social media, 170. *See also* backbench MPs; cabinet ministers
memes: about, xii–xiii, 106–7; and activism, 122–23; argumentative significance, 107–8; creator knowledgeability about politics, 120, 123; defined, 106; discursive purposes, 107; editorial cartoons compared to, 121–22; examples of, 106, 108; functions, 107; governance, 112; humour in, 108, 122; and identity politics, 283; intertextuality, 108; knowledgeability of creators, 283; macro-images, 110, 111; and offline engagement, 285; personality, 112; and political action,

120–21; and political participation, 283; politics vs personality, 120; and politics-democratic practices relationship, 120; and protest movements, 109; and public sphere, 283; and redefinition of grammar of digital activism, 13; sharing, 121; signs/posters compared to, 280; and slacktivism, 122–23; stock characters, 112, 117, 120; studies/research on, 108–9, 111, 123; timeliness, 120; virality of, xii, 107, 121, 281. *See also* Harper memes
Mercer, Rick, xii, 71
message control: cabinet solidarity and, 172; Conservative government and, 188–89; social media and, 172
microtargeting: in data-driven campaigning, 202, 204, 288; increasing use of messages, 150; market intelligence and, 288; market segmentation for, 196
Miljan, Lydia Anita, 240
Millerand, Florence, 13
Mills, Adams, 281
Milner, Ryan M., 108, 116
mixed-methods analysis, 66–67, 80
mobile communication devices, 3, 8
mobilization: digital platforms and, 33; ecocitizen groups and, 33; and numbers of group memberships on social media, 99; online vs offline, 283; and petition signing, 98; prior interest/engagement and, 92; during Quebec student strike of 2012, 53, 55–56; reinforcement vs, 89, 90, 94–95, 101; social media and, 33, 78, 79–80, 89, 92, 94–95, 98, 101, 102, 293; technological revolution and, xi; of youth, 92–94, 98, 99, 100(t), 101, 102, 284
Monterde, Arnau, 8
Montreal, City of, social acceptability process, 258
Montreal Gazette, 243, 244, 248–49, 250(f)
MoveOn.org, 197
Munroe, Doug, 194
Munroe, Kaija Belfry, 194

Nadeau-Dubois, Gabriel, 166*n*3
NAFTA, xi
National Energy Board (NEB), 68, 71
National Post, 243, 244
NationBuilder, 198, 205, 209
Netroots Nation, 197
New Delhi gang rape (2012), 137
New Democratic Party: custom database system, 202; as most integrated party, 205; Orange Room, 197; polling approach, 220
New Democratic Party (Manitoba), and NGP VAN, 202
news media: citizen informants/reporters watching/sharing, 32; coverage of social science evidence, 241; framing of oil sands, 66; national vs local, 248–49; social media activist communication vs, 140; Supreme Court coverage, 237–38, 239–41, 243–44
Next Company, 228–29
NGP VAN, 198, 202, 205
Nielsen, Rasmus Kleis, 199
Niemi, Richard H., 9
Noah, Trevor, xii
Noelle-Neumann, Elizabeth, xiii
Norris, Pippa, 89, 92
Northern Gateway Pipelines, 45, 68
Notley, Rachel, 71

Obama, Barack: 2008 campaign, 195, 207; 2012 campaign, 152, 197, 229; and big data, 223; campaign innovations, 199; elections, 4; and Facebook, 152; and Keystone XL Pipeline, 68
Occupy Wall Street movement, 4, 108, 116, 130, 139
Office of the Privacy Commissioner of Canada, 207
oil/tar sands: about, 67; big data in debates over, 291; campaigners' targeting of pipelines, 67–68; and climate change, 67; cost of projects, 64; and Energy East project, 63; European campaigns, 77; news media framing, 66; Twitter and, 45, 73

Oliviera, Maria de Fatima, 139
O'Loughlin, Ben, 88
O'Neil, Cathy, 232
online advocacy groups: leaders, 38; organizationally enabled networks, 26, 37; and political behaviour, 35; self-organizing network model, 26, 37; as social experimentation laboratories, 38
online engagement: and citizens–representatives/political institutions relationship, 38; commitment, vs offline, 34, 36; engagement with associations vs, 37; individual action framework, 37–38; offline vs, 36; and sense of agency/capacity for action, 38; time constraints vs offline, 34; types of activities, 36
Option nationale (ON): in 2012 election, 156–61; and 2012 student protests, 153; Facebook use, 156–61, 163–64, 286; partisan posts, 157; pursuit of political vs communication goals, 157; topics/content of posts, 157
Oracle, 224, 226
Orwell, George, *1984*, 216, 229
Oser, Jenny, 15

Paltiel, Khayyam, 196
Papacharissi, Zizi, 138–39; *A Private Sphere*, 294
Parti libéral du Québec (PLQ): in 2012 election, 154, 156–61, 157; and Bill 52, 249; Charest as leader, 153; Facebook use, 156–61; images used by, 161; mentions of Quebec issues, 158; tone of messages, 159
Parti québécois (PQ): in 2012 election, 154, 156–61; and 2012 student protests, 153; and Bill 52, 249; Facebook use, 156–61; images used by, 161; mentions of Quebec issues, 158; and separatism, 158, 164; visual media use, 164
Parti vert du Québec (Greens): in 2012 election, 156–61; Facebook use, 156–61, 164; partisan posts, 157; topics/contents of posts, 157

Parties to the United Nations Framework Convention on Climate Change (UNFCCC), 27
permanent campaigning: and data collection/analysis, 206, 280; data-driven campaigning and, 206, 209–10, 211, 280; message control in, 172; trends and, 5
Personal Democracy Forum, 197
Personal Information, Privacy, and Election Documents Act, 208
petition signing: social media and, 98, 99, 101–2; youth and, 101, 102, 284
Pew Research Center, 95
PHS Community Services Society, Canada (Attorney General) v, 238, 239
physician-assisted death, 14, 241–43, 244, 245–49
Piebiak, Jill, 14–15
Pipe-Up Against Enbridge, 25
Pitfield, Tom, 194
Poell, Thomas, 6, 12, 45, 65, 278, 282, 290
Poirier, Claude, 56
policy/policies: announcements on Twitter, 174; Charter and, 237, 252; Harper memes and, 115, 117–18, 121; political memes and, 120; social media and, 78; social science evidence and, 238, 251–52; Supreme Court and, 249
political action. *See* action/activism
political behaviour: changes in, 189, 293–94; communication technologies and change in, 8; digital media channels and, 8; DMP and, 229; online groups and, 35; political interest and, 91; supporting party line vs personal branding and, 189; transformations in, 276; trends and, 8–9; Web 1.0/2.0 media channels and, 277–78
political candidates: following on social media, 102; incumbents/officeholders vs, in use of social media, 286–87; liking/friending/linking to, 95; social media connections with, 88–89, 98

political communication: changes in, 189, 293–94; communication technologies and change in, 8; digital media channels and, 8; dynamic/flexible publicness and, 142; Facebook political campaigns and, 163; globalization and, 129; market surveillance and, 230–31; media (re)shaping, 128; social media protest activity and, 131–32; social media and transformation of, 277–78; supporting party line vs personal branding and, 189; topology of, 131–32; transformations in, 276; trends and, 4–5, 8–9; Twitter and, 174; Web 1.0/2.0 media channels and, 277–78
political consultants, 197, 198
political elites/insiders: grassroots protests vs, 11; grassroots vs, 11–12; segmented society and, xi; and social media, xii, xiii–xiv, 79–80, 87, 285; social media and power of, 279; trends and, 5, 294; and Twitter, 175; youth and different paths of political activity vs, 9
political engagement/participation: ambient, 46, 48, 55, 57, 58, 279–80; and citizenship, 285; clarification of notion of engagement, 39n2; commitment compared to engagement, 39n2; community formation in, 282; and democratic representation, 87; Facebook and, 90–91; inequalities in, 86, 89–90, 92; memes and, 283; micro- vs macrolevel generational transition in, 9; mobile communication devices and, 8; need for redefinition of, 282; online vs offline, 282, 283; personalization of, 282; platforms, 195–96; political interest and, 91; reinforcement vs mobilization, and, 89; reinforcement/normalization hypothesis, 88; social media and, 3, 35, 87, 88, 89, 90, 92–93, 282, 293; social media and politically uninterested, 88–89; technological innovations and offline, 12–13; technological revolution and, xi; Twitter and grassroots, 50; of youth, 86, 94, 99, 101, 284
political interest: and political behaviour, 91; and political participation, 91; and posting opinions on social media, 98–99; prior, and connecting to political candidates/parties on social media, 98; prior, and mobilization, 92; social media and, 86–87; social media and uninterested, 88–89; and use of social media, 96, 98–99, 101; by youth, 94
political marketing: about, x–xi; and data-driven campaigning, 196; defined, 221; and market intelligence, 221; message control in, 172; and public opinion research role in politics, 217–18
political memes. *See* memes
political parties: adaptation/building systems of communication/feedback, 206–7; and analytical techniques, 207; and big data, 291; connection on social media, 98; and correlation between federal-provincial technology adoption, 205–6; data collection, 207–8, 210, 287; and data integration, 205; data management, 195, 196, 206; data storage, 195; data-driven campaigning, 202, 203(t), 210–11, 280, 287; discipline, and backbench MPs, 177; discipline, and changes in behaviour/communication, 189; donation limits to, 209; and Facebook, 11, 149, 162–63, 286; financial limits on, 150; index of political technology, 198; interactivity with voters, 151, 165; and mainstream media, 286; membership databases, 195; per-vote subsidy, 209; political marketing, 196; in Quebec 2012 election, 11; and role of data in politics, 207–8; social media and, 27, 88–89, 95, 102, 149, 150, 151, 160–61, 165, 285, 286; Twitter and, 188; and voter data, 196; and voter privacy, 207; websites, 197

political parties (Quebec): and Facebook, 152–66; and social media, 150–51
political parties (US), and Facebook, 150
politicians. *See* political elites/insiders
polling: data analytics and, 14; digital research and, 14; evolution of, 218–19; market intelligence vs, 221–23; marriage of big data with, 223; move to market intelligence, 219–20; role of pollsters, 222–23, 231–32; transition to market intelligence, 229
Postill, John, 8
Pour une moratoire sur le gaz de schiste/For a Moratorium against Shale Gas, 31
Prime Minister's Office, 116, 172, 189
Private Sphere: Democracy in a Digital Age, A (Papacharissi), 294
Privy Council Office, 172
PRIZM system, 196
projects: abandonment/failure of, 258, 269; co-construction of, 257; contestation over, 258, 269; environmental assessment for, 272; government authorities' roles/responsibilities in, 260–61; lay citizen vision sharing regarding, 257; social acceptability and success of, 258; societal concerns around, 257
Pronovost, Maxime, 13
protests: accountability for state violence, 141–42; activists as information brokers, 135; avatars, 109; citizen consultations vs, 288–89; digital technologies and, 39; in Egypt, 135, 139; Energy East Pipeline, 13; event-oriented focus in communication, 138; geography/"where" of communication, 135–36; grassroots-driven phenomena, 11–12; Harper memes and, 115, 118, 121; hashtag activism, 46–47; inequality related to, 86; mediated publicness and issues transcending, 141; memes and, 109; offline-inspired modes of, 46; police/security forces and, 134–35; Quebec student strike of 2012 as grassroots-driven, 44, 45; reporting by blogs/alternative news sites, 135; six-phase cycle of grassroots, 57; social media and, 39, 45–46, 58, 96, 98, 101; social media and grassroots-driven, 44, 45; spectacle/violence in, 138; sustainability of, 281–82; traditional mobilization phenomena vs, 11–12; transnational activity, 130; in Tunisia, 135, 137, 139; youth involvement in, 93–94
public debate(s): corporatization of, 290; in G20 protest, 283; hybridity of media in, 279; lack of, 136–37; and public sphere, 79, 140; quality of, 64, 79
public opinion research: big data and, 217; Conservatives and, 220–21; DMP and, 229–30; evolution of, 217–18; interpretation vs articulation role in, 219; market intelligence and, 218, 223, 288; and needs/wants of individual voters, 223; political marketing, and role in politics, 217–18; public opinion definitions, 218–19; surveillance and, 288; traditional polling period of, 218, 219; transformation of, 280
public sphere(s): alternative media and, 290; contentious social media communication and, 132; ecocitizenship and, 27; internet action tools and, 278; mainstream media in, 279; media and, 128; memes and, 283; multiplicity of, 128–29; pluralist conception of, 128–29; public debate and, 140; social media and, 64, 80, 131, 140–41, 142; theory, 128–29, 130, 138, 140–41, 142; trajectories of publicness vs, 140–41; transformations in, 276; transnational, 129–30, 132, 278; trends and changes in, 5; Twitter as, 79; web vs, 131
Puddister, Kate, 14
Pulse of Democracy: The Public Opinion Poll and How it Works, The (Gallup), 218

Quebec: Bill 78, 55; Chantier sur l'acceptabilité sociale, 258; Facebook in, 149; "green book" on social acceptability, 258, 272; petition protesting oil/hydrocarbon projects in, 33; Public Hearings on the Environment Office (Bureau d'audiences publiques sur l'environnement), 269; Quiet Revolution, 49; separation, 164–65; tuition fee increase, 48–49

Quebec 2012 election: big data in, 291; context of, 153–54; Facebook in, 152–66, 286; issues in, 157–58; political corruption and, 153–54, 158, 159; political parties in, 11; social media in, 150–51; student strike and, 158, 159; student strike of 2012 and, 153

Québec solidaire (QS): in 2012 election, 156–61; and 2012 student protests, 153; Facebook use, 156–61, 286; partisan posts, 157; pursuit of political vs communication goals, 157; social media use, 157; topics/content of posts, 157

Quebec student strike of 2012, 4; and 2012 Quebec election, 153, 158, 159; about, 44–45; and ambient digital political engagement hypothesis, 58; attacks on political opponents/critics, 53, 54–55, 56; content analysis, 50–52; and dissolution of interest/sustainability of movements, 281–82; effects, 44; as grassroots-driven protest, 44, 45; history, 49–50; information circulation during, 52, 53–54, 55, 281; key dates/phases, 50–52, 57; legacy media coverage, 54–55, 56; mobilization during, 53, 55–56; opinion-sharing during, 52, 53–54, 57; self-expressive tweets during, 56; social media in, 45, 50, 153, 279; Twitter in, 12, 50–59, 58; youth involvement in, 93–94

Queen's University Surveillance Studies Centre, 217

Quintelier, Ellen, 90, 91, 92, 93, 94, 95, 96, 99, 101

R v Askov, 251
R v Smith, 238
Rainie, Lee, 95
Ramsay, Gordon, 118
Rathgeber, Brent, 116
Raynauld, Vincent, 11, 12
Redford, Alison, 70–71
The Rick Mercer Report, 122
RJR-MacDonald Inc. v Canada (Attorney General), 253n1
Rodriguez, Sue, 241
Rodriguez v British Columbia (Attorney General), 239, 242–43, 245–46, 247, 252
Rogers, Richard, 130–31
Romney, Mitt, 152, 165
Roper, Elmo, 218
Royal Canadian Air Farce, 119

Saint-Bruno-de-Montarville, 261, 262, 269
Salas, M., 27
Sampert, Shannon, 121
Saskatchewan v Whatcott, 240
Sauvageau, Florian, 240
Savoie, Louis-Philippe, 44
Schattschneider, Elmer E., xiii
Schneiderman, David, 240
Sci, Susan A., 107–8, 118
Segerberg, Alexandra, 37, 38, 107, 109; *The Logic of Connective Action: Digital Media and the Personalization of Contentious Politics,* 282
segmentation: about, xi, 14; DMP and, 226–27; hyperfragmentation and, 16; market intelligence and, 221; for microtargeting, 196; of society, xi–xii; of voters, 201–2
Selfish Gene, The (Dawkins), 106
Shifman, Limor, 107, 113
Singh Pandey, Jyoti, 137
slacktivism, 27, 34, 35–36, 110, 122–23, 166, 283
Sloam, James, 7
Small, Tamara, 13
Smith, R v, 238
social acceptability: about, 258–59; citizen participation/consultations

and, 268, 272, 288; emergence of, 258; and governance, 14; interviews, 291; participatory democracy and, 257; Quebec "green book" and, 272; and success of projects, 258; Vision 2035 initiative and, 268–69

Social Acceptability of Large-Scale Projects, 273n1

social media: and action/activism, 10, 33, 45–46, 78, 281, 293; alternative media and, 65, 141, 142; and ambient digital political engagement, 58; and ambient journalism, 47–48; audience width/size, 33; backbench MPs vs cabinet ministers and, 186; blogs/alternative news sites, 135; cabinet ministers and, 176, 186; and cabinet solidarity, 11, 173, 185–86, 287; and central power/influence, 189; and citizen engagement, 35, 293; and citizen journalism, 281; and civil society communication practices, 25; and collegiality, 188; commercial nature of, 131, 139; and connective action, 26; and control of traditional media, 174; conventional vs transformative adoption of, 171; corporations, 290; correlation of online discussions with offline events, 80; and data-driven campaigning, 196–97; and democracy, 142, 151, 285; dependence of effects on uses of, 87–88; and digital ambient political engagement, 46; ecocitizenship and, 25; in election campaigns/elections, 78–79, 102, 150, 151, 160–61, 165, 172, 286–87; Energy East Pipeline and (*see* Energy East Pipeline on social media); frequency of use, 76–77, 95, 97(t), 98, 99, 100(t); in G20 summit, 12, 45, 65, 278; generation of political interest/participation in uninterested, 88–89; geographic location of activity, 78–79; and government central power/influence, 189; as hybrid media system, 65, 80; importance in political mediascape, 10–11; and individual action, 37–38; inequalities in use of, 78; influentiality of users, 76; Liberal government and, 176; and mainstream/mass media, 136, 141, 278–79, 286; and material realities, 65; and media power, 140, 279; and message control, 172; and mobilization, 33, 78, 79–80, 89, 90, 92, 101, 102, 293; and MPs, 170; narrowly targeted messages to selected audiences, 223; numbers of friends on, 95, 96, 97(t), 98, 99, 100(t); numbers of group memberships, 99, 101; numbers of members, 293; and participatory democracy, 172, 285; "Personal and Partisan Use of Social Media by Ministers and Parliamentary Secretaries," 176; and petition signing, 98, 99, 101–2; as platforms of natural collectivity, 131; and policy, 78; and political candidates, 95, 96, 97(t), 98, 100(t), 102, 286–87; and political elites/insiders, xii, xiii–xiv, 79–80, 87, 88, 98, 285–86, 286–87; and political engagement/participation, 3, 35, 78, 86–87, 88, 89, 90, 92–93, 99, 282, 293; political vs communication goals in use of, 157; and political parties, 27, 88–89, 95, 96, 97(t), 98, 100(t), 102, 149, 150, 151, 160–61, 285, 286; populist approach to, 79; posting political thoughts/comments on, 95, 97(t), 98–99, 100(t), 102; and power structures, 78, 290; prevalence of, 3; prior engagement/interest, and use of, 96, 98–99, 101; and protests, 39, 44, 45–46, 57, 58, 96, 98, 101, 131–32, 134–38, 278–79; public figures speaking out on, 71; and public sphere(s), 64, 80, 131–32, 135–36, 142; publicization of issues, 283–84; quality of discourse on, 79; in Quebec 2012 election, 150–51, 152–66; Quebec political parties and, 150–51; in Quebec student strike of 2012, 45, 50, 153; "real" political events and activity on, 71–72; and reinforcement vs mobilization, 89,

90–91, 94–95; short-lived connections in, 282; and slacktivism, 35–36, 122; and social interaction, 35–36; and social movement/interest group expansion of membership bases, 102; and speed of public criticism, 281; as transformative, 79, 87, 89–90, 92, 98, 99, 101, 102, 277–78; and "trending," 6; urban vs rural usage, 77–78; users' comments in, 151–52; uses of, 87–88; and virality, 6, 281; and virtuous circle theory, 90, 92, 94–95, 101; and voters/voting, 87, 88, 102, 151, 165; women and, 37; youth and, 11, 87, 101–2. *See also* Facebook; Instagram; Twitter

social science evidence: and access to justice, 249, 251; Charter and, 238–39, 243, 249, 252, 279; and civil society, 279; limits of, 251; media coverage of, 239, 245–49, 252, 253; news media coverage of, 241; and policy, 238, 251–52; reliance on, 249, 251; and *stare decisis*, 243; Supreme Court and, 14, 238–39, 241, 242–43, 245–49, 251, 279

Statistical Package for the Social Sciences (SPSS), 96

Stolle, Dietlind, 90, 91, 92, 93–95, 96, 99

Strukturwandel der Öffentlichkeit (Structural Transformation of the Public Sphere) (Habermas), 128

Stuart, Josh, 209

Supreme Court of Canada: Charter and, 252; and Charter litigation, 238; digital technologies and, 251; effect of Charter of Rights and Freedoms on, 237; media coverage, 245–49, 250(f), 251–52, 253; news media coverage, 237–38, 239–41, 243–44; and physician-assisted death, 14; and policy making, 249; and rights debates, 249; and social science evidence, 14, 238–39, 241, 242–43, 245–49, 251, 279; Twitter account, 251

surveillance, 216–17, 229, 230–32, 288

Surveillance and Society Journal, 217

Surveillance Studies Reader, The (Hier, Greenberg), 216–17

Sweetser, Kaye D., 151, 159

Tapscott, Donald, xii

tar sands. *See* oil/tar sands

Taras, David, 240

Tay, Geniesa, 121

Taylor, Gloria, 242

telephone surveys: computer-assisted telephone interviewing (CATI), 219–20, 227; market intelligence vs, 280

Temporão, Mickael, 11

Theocharis, Yannis, 90, 91, 92, 93, 94, 95, 96, 99, 101

Thorson, Kjerstin, 109–10, 121

Todd, Brad, ix, xiii

Toronto Community Mobilization Network (TCMN), 132

Toronto Star, 243, 244, 250(f)

Touir, Ghada, 13

Tourigny-Koné, Sofia, 12

"Track and Field," 201

traditional media. *See* mainstream media

Trans Mountain Pipeline, 68

TransCanada: astroturfing, 289–90; and Energy East, 13, 31, 63, 69, 71, 75, 77; and Keystone XL, 64; pipeline, 34; on Twitter, 73, 76–77

trends: and bottom-up perspective on political action, 9; in Canadian political/social spheres, 4; and changes in public sphere, 5; and civil society, 5; and civil society-media institution relationship, 13–14; defined, 6, 277; and democracy, 15–16; at global level, 4; limitations of, 294; in marketing, 6; and permanent campaigning, 5; and political behaviour, 8–9; and political communication, 4–5, 8–9; political elites/insiders and, 5; research in, 6–7; social media and, 6; and transformation of everyday life, 292; transformative effects, 4

Trimble, Linda, 121

Trudeau, Justin: 2015 election of, 4; and Bennett's tweets, 182; on cabinet

government, 175; and Energy East Pipeline, 71; and government by cabinet, 189; and Instagram, 285–86; and marketing, xiii–xiv; memes regarding, 120, 123; and open/transparent government, 175; social media, and brand, xii; and Trans Mountain Pipeline, 68
Trudeau, Pierre Elliott, 114(f), 116, 172, 196, 219
Trump, Donald: "Crooked Hillary" meme, xii; election of, 4; and Keystone XL, 64, 68; and marketing, xiii–xiv; shifting subject, xii; social media, and brand, xii; uses of social media, 286
Tunisian uprising, 135, 137, 139
Turcotte, André, 14
Turow, Joseph, xi
Twitter: in 2012 Quebec student strike, 12, 50–59; about, 293; as alternative to formal political/media elites' discourse, 57–58; attack tweets, 178, 179, 183; blogs and adoption of, 190n1; broadcasting tweets, 178, 179; cabinet ministers and, 170–71, 173, 189; cabinet ministers vs backbench MPs and, 171, 175, 177–86, 287; cabinet solidarity and, 170–71, 173, 180–81, 183, 187–88, 189; Canadian use of, 47; Conservative cabinet ministers on, 173–74; Conservative government and, 188–89; and crowdsourcing, 45; effecting of change, 78; on Egyptian revolution, 139; Energy East Pipeline and, 64, 70, 73–76; and environmental consultation/issues, 45, 66, 79; in G20 summit, 283; geographic location of posts, 77–78; #ggi tweets, 50–56, 57, 58; in grassroots political engagement, 50; Harper government and, 174; Harper-McLachlin conflict on, 251; hashtag activism, 46–47, 122; hashtag-based sampling, 50; hashtags, 73, 293; in Idle No More movement, 45; and impression management, 175; lack of debate on, 137; lack of statistics on pages, 31; May and, 177, 286; New Delhi gang rape on, 137; and oil/tar sands, 45, 66–67, 73; percentage of users per population, 79; personal tweets, 178, 179, 183–85; policies on, 189; policy announcements on, 174; and political communications, 174; political elites/insiders and, 175; political parties and, 188; portfolio tweets, 178, 180–81, 182–83, 186–87, 189; as public sphere, 79; Quebec activity, 47; as site of political engagement, 65; social tweets, 178, 179, 182–83, 186; students and, 47; studies regarding, 47–48; Supreme Court and, 251; TransCanada on, 73; transformative use of, 189; during Tunisian uprising, 137, 139; Tweet Archivist, 50; and Westminster parliamentary system, 189. *See also* Bennett, Carolyn

United States: data-driven campaigning in, 210; Facebook in 2008 presidential election campaign, 286; Facebook in 2012 presidential election campaign, 152; Facebook political campaigns in, 149–50, 158; Instagram in 2016 presidential election campaign, 286; political parties, 150 (*see also* Democratic Party; Republican Party); social media in 2016 presidential election campaign, 286; voter data privacy regulation in, 208–9
Université Laval, 49–50
Université du Québec à Montréal, 49–50

Vaccari, Cristian, 88
Van Aelst, Peter, 7, 65, 121, 278
Van Dijck, José, 282
Van Laer, Jeroen, 65, 121, 278
Verville, Mélanie, 150
virality, xii, 6, 121, 162, 164, 281, 292
virtuous circle theory, 90–91, 92, 94–95, 96, 98, 101, 102, 284
Vision 2035, 261, 262, 268–69; Citizen Day, 262–65, 266–67, 270, 288; online survey, 262, 265–66

Vissers, Sara, 90, 91, 92, 93–95, 96, 99
Vivre en Ville, 262, 266
VoterListsOnline, 208–9
voters: lists, 201; microtargeting of, 196; privacy, 207–9, 287–88; public opinion research and, 219; restrictions on data regarding, 208–9; segmentation of, 201–2; social media and connections with political candidates, 89; social media and political parties' interactivity with, 151, 165; social media and voting behaviour, 87, 88, 102

Wall, Brad, 63, 75
Way, Laura, 121
websites: as issue networks vs public debate, 130–31; political party, 197
Westminster parliamentary system: cabinet control, 287; central power/influence in, 189; impact of Twitter on, 189
Wexler, Mitch, 201, 211
Whatcott, Saskatchewan v, 240
White, Brittany, 45, 66, 79
White, Graham, 170
Williams, Anthony D., xii
Winnipeg Free Press, 243, 244, 248–49, 250(f)
Woodworth, Stephen, 174
WordPress, 69, 202, 205

Wynne, Kathleen, 205

Yahoo Inlink Scraper, 133
Yates, Stéphanie, 14
youth: attitude toward politics, 8–9; and bottom-up perspective on political/civic action, 9; civic participation, 94; contact with public official, 94; Facebook accounts, 94–95; frequency of social media use, 95, 97(t), 100(t); group memberships, 94; involvement in protests, 93–94; liking/friending/linking to political candidates/parties, 95; and memes, 108–9; and mobilization, 92–94, 98, 99, 100(t), 101, 102, 284; numbers of friends on social media, 95; participatory inequality among, 86; petition signing, 102, 284; political activity/engagement/participation, 8–9, 11, 12, 87, 99, 101, 284; political interest, 94; posting political thoughts/comments on social media, 95, 97(t), 100(t); prior engagement/interest, and social media use, 96, 98–99, 101; reinforcement/virtuous circle process among, 96; and social media, 11, 87, 101–2; surveys, 291

Zéro déchet/Zero Waste, 25
Zito, Salena, ix, xiii